« RACIAL BLACKNESS AND INDIAN OCEAN SLAVERY »

Racial Blackness and Indian Ocean Slavery

Iran's Cinematic Archive

PARISA VAZIRI

University of Minnesota Press
Minneapolis
London

The University of Minnesota Press gratefully acknowledges the financial assistance provided for the publication of this book by the Hull Memorial Publication Fund of Cornell University.

A different version of chapter 2 was previously published as "Pneumatics of Blackness: Nāsir Taqvāʾī's Bād-i Jin and Modernity's Anthropological Drive," in *Persian Literature and Modernity: Production and Reception,* ed. Hamid Rezaei Yazdi and Arshavez Mozafari, 213–42 (New York: Routledge, 2018); copyright Parisa Vaziri; reproduced with permission of the Licensor through PLSclear. A different version of chapter 3 was previously published as "Arbʾain and Bakhshū's Lament: African Slavery in the Persian Gulf and the Violence of Cultural Form," *Antropologia* 7, no. 1 (2019): 189–21.

Copyright 2023 by the Regents of the University of Minnesota

All rights reserved. No part of this publication may be reproduced, stored in a retrieval system, or transmitted, in any form or by any means, electronic, mechanical, photocopying, recording, or otherwise, without the prior written permission of the publisher.

Published by the University of Minnesota Press
111 Third Avenue South, Suite 290
Minneapolis, MN 55401-2520
http://www.upress.umn.edu

ISBN 978-1-5179-1474-5 (hc)
ISBN 978-1-5179-1475-2 (pb)

Library of Congress record available at https://lccn.loc.gov/2023033982.

The University of Minnesota is an equal-opportunity educator and employer.

Contents

Note on Transliteration	vii
Preface and Acknowledgments	ix
Introduction. Indian Ocean Slavery, Cinema, and the Perversion of Context	1
1 Blackface and the Immemorial: *Fīlmfārsī's* Navel	31
2 *Zār* and the Anxieties of the Iranian New Wave	73
3 Irano-Afro-Iran: The Racial Aesthetic	119
4 The Black Maternal and the Interruptive Imagination: *Bashu*	161
Conclusion. The Collective for Black Iranians: On Digital Anamnesia	209
Notes	233
Bibliography	297
Index	345

Note on Transliteration

In this book, I follow a Persian transliteration scheme based on the American Library Association–Library of Congress romanization system, with slight variations. The names of Iranian filmmakers with international recognition are represented as they are found in English language sources. Persian generic terms, theoretical concepts, and ideas are indicated with italics. For my capitalization practices regarding the terms *black* and *blackness,* please see the introduction.

Preface and Acknowledgments

The seeds of this book grew out of my PhD dissertation at the University of California, Irvine. I was working on the very last stage of revisions when protests erupted throughout Iran in September 2022. The death of a twenty-two-year-old woman, Mahsa Amini, compounded by ongoing violence against women in the Islamic Republic of Iran, prompted a wave of protests throughout Iranian cities, and was led largely by women, under the slogan *Zan, zindigī, azādī* (Women, life, freedom). This movement, feminist at its core, transformed me in unexpected ways and, coinciding with final book edits, demanded renewed attention to the articulation of gender in my presentation of contents.

The gendered body is a peculiar site of violence. In 1936, the first Pahlavi monarch, Reza Shah, banned the veil, abolishing a cultural practice that has been immemorially widespread in Islamicate regions, if not enforced by law. Though not everyone lamented its loss, eliminating hijab was one example of various modes of forced sociocultural modernization that would eventually lead to widespread regime dissatisfaction. Over forty years and a revolution later, the Islamic Republic would reverse this mandate, making the veil obligatory for women. Since then, the hijab has been a marker of the Islamic Republic's reactionary political experiment, just as its abolition served once as the marker of the state's prideful modernization campaign. While the injunctions to veil and unveil are too easily collapsed as identical and are in fact informed by structurally disparate ideological projects, they both show how the female gendered body is marked, seemingly perennially, as a site of ideological power. The female's prohibited exhibition after the Revolution has rendered this body, ironically, vulnerable to unconscionable forms of violence.

This book is about the history (or rather, nonhistory) of African enslavement in the western Indian Ocean. Indian Ocean slavery's

« X »   Preface and Acknowledgments

resistance to facticity, I argue in forthcoming pages, challenges historiographical dating. Resistance to facticity undermines dominant assumptions about the *adequacy* of locating the emergence of racial blackness in time. My engagement with cinematic texts as the method through which I arrive at such claims has necessitated attention to femaleness as it appears in twentieth-century Iranian cinema. But due to the intersecting strains that compose each argument's chapter, engagement with gender sometimes fades into the kaleidoscope of other thought-patterns. In my chapter synopses at the end of the introduction, gender is barely mentioned. In taking this rather idiosyncratic approach to a preface, I hope to draw attention to, and thereby save from oblivion, a through-thread in this book that is alive but embedded, and whose submergence awaits patient readers, or future authors.

The performance of twentieth-century Iranian nationalism takes the female body as its stage, and the imaginary, but also literal, stage is one perennial space where cinema tethers the phantasmatic female. Symbol of the nation's honor, in prerevolutionary Iranian cinema the female body is denuded, maimed, raped, murdered, reified as paradigmatic consumer, and paradigmatically consumed by the camera's devouring gaze. In chapter 1, I focalize the proximity between the *raqās,* female dancer, and the *siyāh,* literally the "black," or ambiguously male protagonist of the Persian improvisatory tradition of *siyāh bāzī.* Spatial proximity with the *siyāh* shows the centrality of gender and sexuality to the racial mise en abyme that is Iranian cinematic "black play." Reified, partitioned binaries are guarded by an ungendered blackness that is historically tied to a literal and metaphysical castration, eunuchism.

If *filmfārsī* hypersexualizes the female, politicized Iranian cinema ravages her in an alternative way. The face of the nation, the cinematic female crystallizes pathologies of Western modernity on her body, in her cosmeticized features, exposed limbs, her loosened mores, her strengthening death drive (chapter 2). Like the *zār* practitioners whose ritual practices modernism sublates into experimental art, the gendered body generates language for the articulation of social grievance against Pahlavi modernization. Meanwhile, the grievances that accrue from this sublation dissolve inside the process of their aestheticization into cinema. Toward the end of the book, in the chapter on Bahram Beyzai's *Bashu, the Little Stranger,* blackness

Preface and Acknowledgments « xi »

and gender are rethought together as the resistance to facticity that I theorize throughout the book as an impossibility of proper context.

This book is indebted to many souls, present and past, better and lesser known, in this realm and in many other realms. I am foremost thankful to my first scene of intellectual maturation, the department of Comparative Literature at UC Irvine. I am forever grateful to have met there my dissertation advisor and friend, Rei Terada, who supported my project before it existed, and who taught me how to recognize, value, and nurture its idiosyncrasies. Her imprint continues to grow, transform, shapeshift into new transmissions. I am also thankful for the support of my dissertation committee: Nasrin Rahimieh, Nahum Dimitri Chandler, Tiffany Willoughby-Herard, and Adriana Campos Johnson. They each contributed in invaluable ways to the development of ideas that would eventually take the form of this book. I benefited from the camaraderie and intellectual engagement of various cohorts in the Comparative Literature Department and Culture and Theory Program at UC Irvine, and thank each of the graduate students I met along my journey through the enigmatic maze of the PhD program. I would also like to thank Fred Moten and R. A. Judy for their generosity and feedback on the first draft of this book. I am grateful to my current colleagues in the Comparative Literature and Near Eastern Studies Departments at Cornell University. Their ongoing encouragement has supported me through the process of publishing this book. Many of the revisions here benefited from interactions I had with the brilliant undergraduate and graduate students I have had the honor to teach at Cornell. I would also like to thank the friends in Ithaca who have sustained me these past few years through the course of revising this book, especially Natasha Raheja, Begüm Adalet, and Seema Golestaneh.

I am incredibly grateful to my partner, Reza Golestani. Without him, this book would not have been possible. I am thankful for his limitless support, and will not forget the endless nights that were weathered alone while I was working across the country. I am thankful for all the ways he challenges me, intellectually and otherwise. I am grateful to my parents, Ariana Barkeshli and Faramarz Vaziri, who instilled and fostered my intellectual curiosity from an early age. I am honored to be their daughter.

Finally, I am thankful to the land. Over the past few years I have come to see the incredible magic and might of this enchanted place. I do not take my right to exist here for granted. We cannot undo the violences of history. In recognizing the original ties of the Gayogohó:nǫ' (Cayuga) people to my current home, I can only honor their respect for the land, continue every day to remember to see what is here. This remembrance and recognition of what is already really here, will be an underlying core, I hope, of the feminist revolution to come.

« INTRODUCTION »

Indian Ocean Slavery, Cinema, and the Perversion of Context

> Historical objectivity regarding facts, the quiet
> assurance of established history, is no more than a
> luxury of those who can enjoy truth without conflict.
> —Marc Nichanian, *The Historiographic Perversion*

This book explores Iranian cinema as a media archive for the legacies of African enslavement and racial blackness in the western Indian Ocean. Although Indian Ocean slavery spanned millennia, scholarship on it is notoriously sparse and undertheorized in relation to the far more robust and theoretically sophisticated field of study on transatlantic slavery, where the relationship between enslavement and racial blackness has been developed and articulated most compellingly, particularly in the field of black studies.[1] The sense of absolute rupture and discontinuity introduced by meditations on the Middle Passage has long interrupted the triumphalism of transatlantic history, demanding consistently renewed attention from scholars of diverse fields. By contrast, our knowledge of slavery in the Indian Ocean (a sprawling region covering the vast oceanic space between Africa and Asia) is confined primarily to minor, regional historicisms. Thus, despite the long-standing significance of slavery in their geographical areas of focus, Indian Ocean slavery is not a subject particularly well explored by scholars of Middle Eastern studies. I engage twentieth-century Iranian cinema to reassess the legacy of Indian Ocean slavery in Iran, while posing questions about the legitimacy of archival norms to the history of African enslavement and to the history of racial blackness more generally. By virtue of its formal capacities, cinema

« 1 »

« 2 » Introduction

demands that we reexamine the assumptions underlying traditional methodological approaches to the past.

Iran might be situated, in spite of its irrefutable idiosyncrasies, as a case study for broader inquiries about the legacies of African enslavement in the Indian Ocean. Cultural, geographical, and historical specificity, I contend, is a problem, not a self-evident truth awaiting exposure by the responsible scholar adequately equipped with the proper linguistic, analytical, and disciplinary tools. Despite the unavoidable specificity of modern place-names inflected by the legacies of (racial) nationalism, my focus on blackness as a figure of disruption and decontextualization displaces at the outset both the insularity of the nation-state and the inevitable habits of thought that naturalize its frame. As I will argue throughout this book, in its global resonance, blackness destabilizes context specificity. And it is precisely an *anxiety about context* that produces one particular mode of racialization exemplified by blackness.

Like other historians of the Middle East (henceforth, Southwest Asia), South Asia, and North Africa more generally, historians of Iran, with few exceptions, have traditionally ignored the region's history of slavery.[2] The message communicated by this general elision is clear: Indian Ocean slavery did not really exist, or, its legacies are unworthy of remark. But from the East African and Red Sea coasts to Persian Gulf ports of Muscat, Sur, Būshihr, Kīsh, Hurmuz, and others, dhow and caravan networks supplied Iran and other Southwest Asian territories with enslaved African labor from antiquity through the early twentieth century. This slavery was domestic, sexual,[3] military,[4] bureaucratic, agricultural,[5] disjointed, differentiated, and largely undocumented, especially prior to modernity.

But what do these facts mean? And how does the very demand for facticity betray an injustice that historiography neutralizes? Only relatively recently has the subject of slavery in Southwest Asia become a specialized and highly marginal topic of academic interest. It is therefore unsurprising that scholars of visual culture have also only rarely acknowledged the subject of African enslavement in the Indian Ocean and its possible influences on diverse visual media. Yet, in my readings of generically disparate Iranian films from the 1950s to the 1980s, figures of blackness agitate assumptions about the simple absence of Indian Ocean slavery's racial legacy, while suggesting cinema as an exemplary medium through which to probe in just what this disruption consists.

By *figures of blackness,* I not only mean representations of black people (already a fraught formulation in the context of Southwest Asia—a point to which I will repeatedly return). But rather, I also mean references to practices whose association with people of African descent is the subject of ongoing debate, such as the Persian improvisatory tradition of *siyāh bāzī,* or "black play," which I discuss in chapter 1. I mean too, an interrogation of the models of syncretism and hybridity that inhere in contemporary signifiers like "Afro-Iran," a theme I deal with at length in chapter 3. Finally, by *figures of blackness* I also mean reference to forms of cosmological inhabitation like the ubiquitous Indian Ocean spirit healing ritual *zār,* which is the focus of chapter 2, and more obliquely, chapter 4. *Zār,* considered a relic of Indian Ocean slavery because of its association with African descendent communities, describes an assemblage of beliefs and rituals centered on spirit winds that afflict the self with physical and psychic pain. Methodologically, the trancelike practice of *zār* infects this study, even where it recedes thematically into the background. For *zār's* organization is at odds with the discursive norms required for authoritative claims to truth. Refracted through the cinematic medium, figures of blackness complicate traditional assumptions about the nature of historical fact, while confounding, because they both presuppose and exceed, commonplace articulations of the racial.

Archival Paucity and the Destitution of Facts

Because it often situates itself, sometimes begrudgingly, as a foil of transatlantic slavery, a chain of recurring, interlocked tropes generally characterizes scholarship on Indian Ocean slavery. These include the "good-treatment" thesis—the infamous colonial-era inheritance that asserts that, in contrast to Atlantic slavery, Indian Ocean slavery was largely mild, even harmless, from the point of view of masters' treatment of slaves. These recurring tropes also include Indian Ocean slavery's domestic rather than agricultural character; its nonproductive rather than capitalist foundations; its nonracial, or "transracial," and assimilative nature; and finally, Indian Ocean slavery's absence rather than commemorative importance in collective historical memory.[6] Despite its undeniable heterogeneity, the above tropes can be identified, in one iteration or another, in most Indian Ocean slavery scholarship, regardless of regional specificity.[7] (These tropes can also be identified in scholarship on trans-Saharan slavery, which shares many points of contact, and which is why practices associated with trans-Saharan slavery will sometimes inflect my analyses.) Yet questions of treatment, taxonomy, production, and assimilation neither account for nor resolve the recurring violence of an *original deracination*—an irrevocable natal alienation. The slave is a figure for the absolute loss of context.

Indian Ocean slavery is compulsively comparative and depends upon transatlantic slavery for its cohesion and coherence, as well as its distinguished context specificity. Indian Ocean slavery stakes its difference and particularity upon generalized, generic slavery, whose definition transatlantic slavery dominates. At the limit of a drive to distinction and comparison thus lingers a question about the unity and possibility of a history of slavery, for nothing ensures it.[8] Often wondering whether the word *slavery* is even an appropriate translation of their object, scholars admit "there is no consensus as to the meaning of slavery" in the Indian Ocean.[9] Without its foil, Indian Ocean slavery's history is at risk.[10] Without its context specificity, so is its purity.

Another singularly unifying theme that threads through Indian Ocean slavery scholarship is the lament about lack of archival materials. One frequently encounters variations on the following theme: the "Atlantic dominates both the evidence for and the literature of the middle passage"; yet, there is "no equivalent for the Indian Ocean trade to the kind of maritime and commercial record-keeping for the Atlantic trade that has allowed sophisticated computer analysis."[11] Instead, "motley archiving practices" scatter history.[12] And quantitative estimation of Indian Ocean slavery is frequently deemed "impossible" due to the "limited nature of extant records."[13] Given the longevity of the history of slave trading from East Africa to Southwest Asia, which, by some accounts dates back thousands of years, lack of archival sources, especially for antiquity and the premodern era, is understandable. (Indeed, most historical studies of Indian Ocean slavery are grounded firmly in the modern period, where archival materials are most accessible, because they exist.)[14] In addition, the absence of specialized units of transport specific to the slave trade render quantitative data unreliable.[15] Thus, one of the most frequently cited numerical estimates, which places African enslavement in the Indian Ocean on the same quantitative scale

Introduction « 5 »

as transatlantic slavery, albeit over a much longer period, is equally often referred to as suspect.[16] Movement in the Indian Ocean was unstructured, rather than regulated, antithetical to the facticity of quantity.

Lack of archival sources for slavery is compounded by the fact that, like the historiography of slavery in other regions, Indian Ocean slavery rests upon material evidence that is not itself produced from the position of the enslaved, but by bureaucratic or otherwise formalized modes of correspondence. The overreliance on evidentiary proof for the truth of the past endangers history's fidelity to its intrinsic theoretical openness. The document, potentially, often, reifies the past into autocratic truth. But although the authority of the archive may be lamented or critiqued by its historian guardians, the archive is "never finally arguable." The historiographic project is entangled with institutionalized structures of power that make the archive, its fetishism, and its forms of subjectivation possible, but also invisible.[17]

Familiar obstacles, like the absence of the archive and the ideological manipulation of the archive, have led scholars of the Indian Ocean to propose creative historiographical methods. While this book might be considered a partial response to that call, I posit Iranian cinema as a media archive of Indian Ocean slavery counterintuitively. This is because one overarching argument of *Racial Blackness and Indian Ocean Slavery* moves against the presumption that mining archives for content can simply result in the production of truth. Instead, my terminological invocation of the archive draws upon the term's more elastic connotations, its abstract expression of reference to conditions of possibility, rather than the more literal sense of a storage of knowledge or, even more capaciously, as a center of interpretation.[18] Though it has become a hegemonic norm, the "document/object-centered" regime of the archive is one possibility among others, "not the ultimate form of ... being-with history."[19]

Rather than lament the fragmentation of Indian Ocean slavery's archives, and rather than assume the archive as a natural right—which suggests, first and foremost, that archival practices are themselves natural—I operationalize the archive's poverty and carry archival absence to its own logical limits. More originally, I show how the facts of Indian Ocean slavery present a certain indeterminacy, an absence that is intrinsic to the very structure of its facticity.[20] Fact's indeterminacy troubles the historiographic project of rigorously situating, stabilizing, and *contextualizing* Indian Ocean slavery. Against the extractive mode of content mining and content production, I turn to cinema as an inspiration for thought. Cinema does not communicate information about slavery, if by *communication* one simply understands the transmission of facts. Rather, cinema reflects a primordial conjunction, an immemorial *and* that undermines the very autonomy of slavery's facts prior to, and in the course of, their transmission. Cinema deranges context, emerges from the technological ruins of context's ever-dissolving coherence.

There is no secure, conquerable fund of information to plunder. Instead, blackness in Iranian cinema urges us to question the very process by which historical facts are constructed in the first place. Transmission, a condition of possibility for the very facticity or factuality of fact, opens fact to its own erosion, perversion, and displacement—to falsity, forgetting, and decontextualization. An inevitable, ineradicable falsity inheres at the heart of (historical) truth. On the one hand, fact's self-erosion is constitutive, rather than accidental; fact affects itself from within. And thus, cinema helps us to recognize something immemorial, and immemorially disavowed, about facticity. On the other hand, as a modern technological medium, cinema also demands a certain reckoning with the complex specificity of its own historical inception: a modernity whose defining feature is displacement, decontextualization, and conjunction.

If, as I will argue, slavery allows for a certain thematization of violence and displacement in modernist Iranian cinema, this is because slavery is itself context perversion of the most radical kind. Abstractions condemn "the enslaved to the living historical hell of decontextualization," protest historians of slavery.[21] But isn't the historian's anxiety about stabilizing and policing slavery's contexts merely a pale reflection of the *vertiginous loss* of context that slavery originarily is? The cinematic orphaning of the image bodes a soft natal alienation for which the violence proper to enslavement is the unthinkable limit. It is no coincidence that slavery's historical truth is imperiled by the very distortion of experience that slavery fundamentally is, prior to its emergence as a desirable object of knowledge. And if the nature of historical fact is to conceal, by presuming the conditions of possibility for consensus about its existence, slavery destroys every pretension to consensus, every assumption of self-evidence, every claim to fact. In a sense, slavery cannot be a fact. For slavery is the very destruction of facts.[22]

Cinematic Form and Conjunction

Although internationally recognized, Iranian cinema is primarily known for its arthouse repertoire, and thus, generally confined to circuits of elite exchange. Both prerevolutionary New Wave and post-revolutionary arthouse films were, and continue to be, regular contenders at international film festivals. By contrast, *filmfārsī*, a mode of commercial filmmaking that describes popular prerevolutionary films of the 1950s to 1970s is largely unfamiliar to most audiences and film scholars outside of Iran. In scholarship and critical opinion, *filmfārsī* is the detritus of Iranian cinema, abased and embarrassed by the prestigious, globally acclaimed, but statistically marginal Iranian New Wave and postrevolutionary art cinema. Prerevolutionary cinema absorbs modernity's violent diremptions and reflects them thematically. Characterized by core plot themes that often revolve around familiar conflicts enmeshed within the opposition between tradition and modernity, *filmfārsī* is replete with escapist melodrama, clichés, hyperemotional romance, and gendered violence.

Filmfārsī offers ambivalent responses toward accelerated modernization by internalizing acceleration at the level of its form. Frequent, usually erratically placed scenes, digressions into musical interlude, and inexplicable ellipses are just some of the critically maligned, discordant, and sensationalized stylistic means by which this absorption plays out. Domestic popular film tunnels through to collective desire and fantasy, an estranged zone that gives us "those darker images—crushed, trampled, slackened, or dense—of all that swarms in the lower depths of the mind."[23] Despite its unfamiliarity to most film scholars, prerevolutionary commercial cinema was far more popular than Iranian arthouse films have ever been domestically, undermining the confident distinction between high and low, value and nullity. *Filmfārsī* fabulizes, seduces, distracts, fictionalizes life, reveals life as fiction, and is the ground against which alternative, modernist, or New Wave cinema arises to demand mature, politicized engagements with reality. And yet, thwarted by a blackness that destabilizes confidence in perception, such dignified political prescriptions are set adrift, devolving into anxiety about the very possibility of a univocal reality to be grasped.

The films discussed in this book include both art cinema (New Wave, alternative, or modernist cinema—terms I invoke interchangeably), as well as experimental documentary and commercial films (*filmfārsī*, under which I sometimes appear to indiscriminately subsume difficult-to-categorize prerevolutionary titles; I invoke *filmfārsī* as an *idea,* not as a rigid taxonomic form).[24] Particularly because they are lesser known, in certain cases frankly obscure, my readings of Iranian films demand some engagement with specific sociohistorical contexts and genre distinctions. Nevertheless, my approach to Iranian cinema is primarily motivated by cinematic form as a mode of thinking. This is in line with contemporary film and media theory that treats cinema as a philosophical reflection upon experience and consciousness, rather than, or in addition to, being a ready-made aesthetic form in history available to endlessly debatable taxonomy.[25] In other words, while I recognize that, like other national cinemas, Iranian cinema is traditionally approached as a geographically and culturally bound instantiation of a historical medium, my readings of specific films are foremost preoccupied by the ways in which cinematic form demasks the self-assurance of context specificity. Decontextualization and conjunction are the very basis of the cinematographic image, its "tragic phenomenology."[26]

Because films are complex, world-making objects that expose the fragility of distinction between the real and imaginal, cinematic analysis demands methodological innovation, flexibility, and anarchical modes of address. I therefore move fluidly between meditations on context and form, allowing the formal capacities of the object of analysis to work retroactively on the imposition and overdetermination of meaning characteristic of context. Indeed, I argue that cinema is constitutively oriented toward a certain extenuation of context, or rather, toward a certain infinitization of contexts. This includes contexts and ways of seeing that would cast doubt upon the humanist valorization, and projection of autonomy, of aesthetic form itself. In turn, I take the inevitable proliferation of context that cinema generates as a model for inquiry into the inherent destitution of autonomous, context-bound historical fact.

Cinema does not communicate fact. And nor does it posit equivalences. Cinema produces conjunctions: "Racial blackness" *and.* The paratactic operator aggregates. *And* "doesn't just upset all relations, it upsets being."[27] Against proclamation: provocation, conjunction. The term *racial blackness* in the title of this book may appear as a surprise and anomaly, even an anachronistic affront to scholars and historians who are familiar with Indian Ocean historiography. I ask the alarmed to pause and patient the *and.* The weightlessness of this small, here italicized word, the third word of this book's title, only appears to bear a comfortable self-evidence. For both the copula and its negation are impossible absolutes. *And* is spacing itself. Space is a kind of and.

Whether one considers mise-en-scène as its quintessence, découpage (cutting, editing, montage), or its particular intimacy with the economic processes underlying globalization, cinematic functions are propositional, cultivating proximities through disjunction, violating contexts. Cinema's formal potentialities are modes of punctuation.[28] Among its best elaborated theorizations in the twentieth century, both mise-en-scène and montage have come to stand, alternately, for the essence of cinema as a form of intelligence. It is well known that for the most radical filmmakers of the early twentieth century, montage was considered a revolutionary discovery, a process whose theorization carried out into the 1950s and 1960s during the various global waves of new cinema. By contrast, in published periodicals and interviews, Iranian filmmakers and critics derogated prerevolutionary commercial cinema precisely for the ubiquity of its promiscuous sampling of montage; the haphazard, confusing, unfinished feel of its editing; its seemingly chaotic discontinuities and conjunctions; its sense of authorlessness (*fāqid-i kārgardān*, as the famous critic Amīr Hūshang Kāvūsī characterized them); its context nihilism.[29] In response, alternative Iranian cinema reveals a proclivity for the long take evocative of neorealism, and is why the New Wave's stylistic inheritances have been described as amphibolic.[30] The slowness of the long take rebels against commercialized aimlessness, against the blustering cuts of puerile montage—as if political dissatisfaction might be modulated through cinematic techniques that stabilize perception and sharpen attention, orienting the viewer properly toward what is real.

Despite the emphasis on its allegorical dimensions in film criticism and scholarship, the Iranian New Wave is thoroughly saturated by a drive for realism. Realism, in turn, expresses an attraction to fact.[31] But the well-worn opposition between the singular, self-enclosed image and the abstract result of "copulative hieroglyphics," montage, belies cinema.[32] For in its most generalized sense, cinema *is* always already montage—decontextualized instants, combined, permutated, "nothing but cutting and splicing," the mutilation of history before the lens.[33] It is no wonder that cinema has been interpreted as the exemplary technological embodiment of modernity. For modernity itself is conjunctive, compressive, shrinking space, speeding up time. Thus, writes Bernard Stiegler, a "process of global unification has taken place through cinema."[34] Cinema ceaselessly coordinates the global with the extremely local.[35] As theorists of film have speculated since the early years of its invention, cinema expresses a reflexive relationship to the technological universe it represents, the art form best capable of mediating between the human sensorium and the industrial shock of increasingly urbanized, mechanized life, serving a "cognitive and pedagogical" as well as "remedial and therapeutic" function.[36] This is because conjunction is also coercive, injurious, annihilative, demanding compliance and adaptation through unsolicited encounters.[37] Modernity introduces conjunction on a generalized, indefinitely exponentializing scale, as if contradicting its own drive for facticity, its own increasingly confused commitments to a technoscientific real. To be fact is to be able to sterilely repeat as same, to manufacture an orthographic certitude. Film, audiovisual recording, is itself the eventual achievement of a rigor of reference that begins with bare signs. But there lies the inevitable gap between frames, the blink at the heart of visual continuity, just as there is the space, the *and,* in which fact must self-repeat to authenticate its own actuality. Conjunction is the inevitable deviation, the unbearable perversion at the heart of repetition. In the tension between *filmfārsī* and the New Wave, between the low and the high, between false consciousness and political righteousness, montage is more than denigrated style—the sign of an organic resistance at the heart of (technoscientific) evolution.[38]

Alternative cinema (*sīnamā-yi dīgar*) is a more capacious, and perhaps more appropriate, name for the movement internationally recognized as the Iranian New Wave and that lives somewhere between second and third cinema.[39] Among filmmakers and critics, prerevolutionary alternative cinema, dating from roughly 1969 to 1979, was primarily recognized for its oppositional stance toward modernity and accelerated modernization. Political fractiousness connects alternative Iranian cinema of the 1970s with other global anticinematic movements: not only various global New Wave movements in Europe and Asia but also the third cinema movement in Latin America, for example. (Indeed, each "'new wave' is itself a symptom" of the global.)[40] Alternative cinema in Iran thus reflected major political currents and upheavals in Iranian society that were in turn informed by disparate global trends, such as the spurious accession to power of Muhammad Reza Pahlavi Shah, Reza Pahlavi's son, which consolidated Pahlavi dynastic authoritarianism; the decisive 1953 coup d'état, which ousted Prime Minister Mosaddeq from power and—according to optimistic versions of this narrative—diverted Iran's path to democracy; the ensuing campaigns toward forced modernization, including the controversial land reforms that characterized the White Revolution of the 1960s; more generally, the reviled phantom of the imperial West (particularly, the United States and Great Britain) as a malicious force of destruction and interference; the ascendency of Marxist thought in the third world and the gravitation of intellectuals and artists to communist factions; thus, the violent repression of leftist politics; the rise of politicized Islam globally; and the general surge of anticolonialism and revolutionary independence movements across the Global South.

Like its global counterparts, Iranian alternative cinema is one articulation of the ideological and stylistic project of international modernism, inclining toward abstraction and reflexivity, abandoning traditional narrative structure and psychologism in favor of politicized meditations on form, perception, and temporality. Without intending to resolve the various antinomies of the term, I understand cinematic modernism as an internally differentiated, aesthetic response to modernity that is inflected by concurrent and contiguous intellectual trends and philosophical milieux. In brief, Iranian cinema is both a technological manifestation *of* modernity, and a repository for reflections *on* modernity. This reserve is split along modal or genre lines. On the one hand, despite its aesthetic flaws, prerevolutionary commercial cinema reflected the cryptic, aggressive requirements for assimilation demanded by Western modernity, including the assimilation of the impersonal cinematic apparatus itself, smatterings of "scattered scenes" glued together with the "special tape of cinema."[41] In the twentieth century, cinema slowly depletes the intimacy of traditional storytelling forms like *naqqālī* or *pardahdārī* (literally, "screen-holding") that revolved around a master orator (*naqqāl*) delivering performances of Persian epic to live audiences in intimate settings like coffeehouses.[42] Traditional modes of cultural, and historical, transmission are oral, aural, bodily, literally chest-to-chest (*sīnah bih sīnah*). Cinema absorbs the energies of poetry.[43] In destroying the sense of locality, familiarity, and embeddedness embodied by more familiar models of cultural transmission, the anonymous technological apparatus of cinema obliterates the self-assurance of context altogether, fragmenting time and space,

« 12 »   Introduction

conjoining time and space, rarely according to coherent, intelligible logics. Indeed, the "blinking return from another world" that characterizes exit from the traditional cinematic experience makes non-cinematic reality appear "random, structureless, chaotic."[44] *Fīlmfārsī*'s alleged flaws coalesce into style spatiotemporal disruptions happening elsewhere. Its vexing, anarchic divagations only intensify the sense of total attention-surrender and dispersion that cinema requires. For cinema captures, renders attention involuntary, in its "raw state emits something of the atmosphere of trance."[45]

On the other hand, in the primarily leftist critical output that constitutes Persian aesthetic modernism and inflects Iran's alternative cinema movement, modernity is articulated as a force of destruction and loss. These themes are carried over and borrowed from Iranian intellectual history, but also represent a broader anticolonial stance characteristic of the global 1960s.[46] In cinema, loss is articulated through expressions of anxiety. Closed-form strategies show political constriction and suffocation (*dawrān-i ikhtināq*, referring to the political atmosphere of the 1950s): tight, paralytic spaces, dim lighting, gravid and dejected characters (Ibrāhīm Gulistān's *Brick and Mirror*; Nāṣir Taqvā'ī's *Tranquility in the Presence of Others*; Bahrām Farmānārā's *Prince Ehtejab*; Muhammad Riżā Aslānī's *Chess of the Wind*; Abbas Kiarostami's *The Report*). At other times, New Wave articulations of loss summon open spaces and ruined landscapes. Inasmuch as the land is ground and grounding, filmed landscape suggests an investment in realism as an antidote to *fīlmfārsī* levity, instability, and vacillation. In this sense, cinematic landscape dismantles the distinction between open and closed, sobering the viewer into confrontation with political truth. As a signature of realism, landscape invites, even if it cannot guarantee, the spectator's meditation on underlying causal complexes that merely frivolous, manipulative entertainment is thought to mask. Thus, cinematic modernism is famously premised, among other things, upon active spectator vigilance, upon salvation from the soporific doom of mental and spiritual passivity.

In Iranian documentary cinema of the 1950s and 1960s that precedes the feature films associated with the New Wave, ruined landscapes communicate the history of oil extraction and British economic imperialism, which to a large extent constitute "*the* founding resource of the Iranian film industry."[47] The anticolonial undertone of experimental and alternative cinema preoccupies itself with a critique of modernity that is modulated, admixed. Cinematic anticolonialism is tinged by a specter of slavery whose geographical and historical location is incorrigibly lost, dissolved by an inner lyricism. The significance of oil in Iran's modern history, as well as in the broader political and economic histories of Southwest Asia, is well known. Iran was the first country in the Persian Gulf where it was discovered; in the 1920s, petroleum became, and remains to this day, the country's largest industry. Oil is simultaneously the fount of Iran's rapid economic progress and its accelerating cultural modernization in the twentieth century, and ultimately the source of the profound political dissatisfaction that culminated in the 1979 Revolution.[48]

The "oil film" is sometimes treated as a subgenre of Iranian documentary film. The midcentury oil city films that antecede the consolidation of formal documentary film programs sought to reconcile a technologically changing landscape imposed by foreign private interests through the deliberate cinematic aestheticization of southwestern cities.[49] Yet, in a sense, all Iranian cinema is oil cinema, to the extent that oil financially powers the film industry through the twentieth century, across private and state sector lines.[50] But if the lyrical documentary filmmaking subtending the New Wave is economically and aesthetically grounded in the pyrotechnics of the south, it is not only because the southern landscape is potent with oil-bearing fields. For embedded in the image of oil is the apparition of the slave. The history of slaving dispersed enslaved Africans across various Southwest Asian contexts. But because they were often sold in ports on the Persian Gulf, communities of their descendants today remain largely associated with the coast.[51] Thus, if the south is a figure for oil, it is also a crystalline figure for slavery. (But Indian Ocean slavery is itself a coruscating figure for the unthinkable, for what continues to remain unthought.) As a repository for expressions of relation to modernity, Iranian cinema reveals something about Iran's relation, or more precisely, nonrelation, dissolved relation, to the history of African enslavement, and in turn of the legacy of slavery in the western Indian Ocean more broadly.

Globally, oil replaced slavery in the twentieth century as the source of the world's surplus capital.[52] As contemporary work on Indian Ocean slavery has suggested, the nearly exclusive association of the Persian Gulf and Southwest Asia with oil has tended to overshadow the region's much longer histories of economic activity, namely, date cultivation and pearling. Although a common stereotype freezes Indian Ocean slavery in the paradigms of archaic domestic slavery, an agriculture-based export economy thrived in the Persian Gulf during the nineteenth century, fueled largely by, and in turn stimulating, global consumerism. In *The World and Africa*, W. E. B. Du Bois drew a lucid connection between Atlantic, Indian Ocean, and trans-Saharan slavery, showing how the "Arab trade in ivory," was financed with "the slave cotton kingdom" of American plantations.[53] Du Bois suggested that wealth generated by transatlantic slavery fueled the expansion of African enslavement in Central and Eastern Africa, anticipating more recent studies that explore the integration of the Persian Gulf within global commodity circuits.[54] In turn, global demands for goods and luxury items associated with the rise of bourgeois consumerism powered the demand for enslaved African labor in the date plantation and pearling economies of the Persian Gulf. Thus, in contrast to traditional portraits of Indian Ocean slavery (unproductive, noncapitalist), contemporary scholarship demonstrates the neglected economic intimacies between modernity and Indian Ocean slavery. *At the same time,* the archaic, immemorial dimension of Indian Ocean slavery revives older, more opaque conjunctions with the global. This includes the fragmented and fallible history that connects sugar cane cultivation in Southwest Asia to the development of sugar cane in the Mediterranean, and later in the Americas, for example.[55] Indeed, Khūzistān (literally, "land of sugar," according to etymological lore) in southwest Iran was one of the most important provinces for the cultivation of sugar in antiquity.

The spate of comparative scholarship on slavery and the intrusion of cliometrics that characterized the study of Atlantic slavery in the late 1950s and 1960s clarified the (now-established) centrality of sugar to the development of slavery in the modern period.[56] Sugar, dates, pearls, the commodity history underwritten by slavery that pre-dates the Persian Gulf's current and ubiquitous association with petroleum articulates a speculative pattern of relation that connects the Indian Ocean and Atlantic slave trades. But, while agitating against the common tendency to imagine these as two entirely separate histories, the resonances between transatlantic and Indian Ocean slavery also resist the absolutism of causal chains. Indian Ocean slavery pre-dates Atlantic slavery, but the latter builds the foundations for the realization of the former, circuitously. Cinematic blackness, and the invasion and return of a certain blankness, antagonizes the very distinctions that are the result of evidentiary claims to periodization, and other modes of epistemic conquer. The document-based archive is "a regime of coordinated thresholds."[57] But cinema is a regime of the recurring absence at the heart of cause.

Zār

The rediscovery of an internal absence is elliptically transmitted in the black healing ritual *zār,* a potent theme in midcentury Persian aesthetic production. The rise of oil and the abolition and disappearance of slavery both invigorate a new phase in modernity and call for the enigmatic return of the black slave as a healing resource. The "wounds of slavery" cure still other wounds.[58] Blackness is not merely associated with the "sin of unbelief," as some scholars of slavery in Southwest Asia and North Africa have argued, but with the ground of another, prehistorical sphere of belief.[59] In Iranian films of the 1960s that center on the south, black people are simultaneously called upon to heal, articulated as the fetishized locus of a primitive world that struggles to survive destruction, obscured from the anticolonial horizon of critique, and denied the values attached to indigeneity, even when, contradictorily, they are imagined as autochthonous to the land.

In experimental coastal films, the southern landscape holds the purportedly regressive spirit rituals practiced primarily by African slave descendants: *zār.* The practice of *zār* in contemporary Southwest Asia and North Africa is thought to constitute a fraught relic of Indian Ocean and trans-Saharan slavery spread with the movement of enslaved Africans eastward and northward. Thus, today *zār* can be found in most modern-day countries in Southwest Asia and the Persian Gulf, North Africa, parts of South Asia, and East Africa. Organized by ailment, movement, rhythm, secrecy, and above all a loss of consciousness, by definition *zār* is at odds with the model of documentation required for qualification as historical evidence, therefore of the order of knowledge required for definitive fact-claims. Lived out in a realm beyond empirical observation, there is no *true* trace of *zār,* only the scribbled, synthesized notes of the external, ethnographic gaze, or the degraded, poorly preserved audiovisual traces of a recording machine. The Iranian ethnographic films about *zār* from the late 1960s that I examine in chapter 2 attempt to both capture *and* repress *zār's* historical relation to African captivity. And in both disclosing and concealing, these films also present the challenging historicity of Indian Ocean slavery. From one audiovisual recording of *zār* to another, the facts of slavery evaporate into sinuous abstractions. In its recession from the demands of intelligibility, *zār* suggests the possibility of experiences that refuse transcription into the symbolic and that evade the materiality of testimony.

In his 1958 ethnography, Taghi Modaressi complained of the inscrutability of the incantations' lyrics in *zār*, for it was "very hard to distinguish the words."[60] Scattered sounds, strung-together consonants, "gibberish," ethnographers complain, replace intelligible words.[61] Even "the leaders of the ceremony do not understand these languages: only the sounds of the words of the songs have been transmitted from one generation to the next."[62] In *zār*'s parallel black healing rituals in North Africa, like Tunisian *stambeli* or Afro-Maghrebi *dīwān*, musicians sometimes choose to mumble the words, preferring "nasal, understated delivery" that abandons Arabic music's ideals of enunciation and comprehension. The word transcends the referent, holds spiritual energy. To mumble is to protect the lyrics' power from theft.[63]

Thus, on the one hand, the ritual resists comprehension, transcription, and transmission. On the other hand, more troublingly, the cinematic recordings that chronicle *zār* show how, far from a guaranteed access to the past, transcription itself merely confirms the constitutive impossibility of a truth to Indian Ocean slavery that would remain continuous, grounded, pure, based in eternally guaranteed facts. A necessary, technological pause in the image's flowing forth accosts the purity of certitude. Cinematic *zār* requires us to reflect on the unspoken consensus that ties truth to fact, fact to testimony and evidence, and that relegates the untranscribable, and by extension, the *incapacity for facticity* to what is not real, to what is not true, and to what can only be mumbled, guarded by evasion and forgetfulness, by an opacity that protects. Cinema guides us toward a dehiscence at the heart of slavery that is not captured by familiar notions of historical break, discontinuity, or rupture.

Anthropologists understand *zār* as a trace of Indian Ocean slavery that tracks a diffusion from Africa to Southwest Asia, a "multifunctional medium" that "shifts, hides, and changes."[64] But *zār* is not a trace. *Zār* is a disorientation. A trace is a relic of something that has once been present. But it is precisely the security of having-once-been that cinematic *zār* undermines. In the face of documentary

Introduction

« 17 »

techniques intended to capture presence, an imperceptible break intervenes, cuts the object's integrity, lines it with absence. *Zār* is experienced as *"passione,* as a cosmological encounter."[65] It suggests a model of history in which the past exists not simply as a voluntarily retrievable residual substance of human memory and imagination, nor as material inscription. The object of *zār* disappoints the camera's confidence, just as the historical memory incubated by *zār* defies mastery, individual and collective. Unlike the regnant, if unspoken, model of historiography, in which facts lie sepulchered in archive-tombs, waiting to be decoded and revivified by reasonable agent-historians, *zār* suggests an absolute void at the heart of intentionality. A therapeutic, rather than nihilistic void. For at the height of the *zār* ceremony, consciousness falters, self-presence dissolves, the subject of language recedes. Trance is a self-mutilating exaltation, healing, emptying, dynamogenic, unrepeatable. And because it is also a phenomenon whose dissemination is linked to the historical practice of African slavery in the Indian Ocean, *zār*'s particular iteration of historicity—the being-of-history—emerges *from* slavery and not the other way around. That is, a neutral, ontologically prior concept of history and method of history writing is insufficient to interpret *zār.* Instead, *zār* articulates another sense of the being of history.

Scholarship on *zār* spirals anxiously around the desire for origins, as if chasing air, sketching recursive lines through deep etymology that wind through links between East Africa to Persia but with insecurity about the orientation of that connection. *Zār* thus generates a profusion of conflicting, apocryphal stories of origin.[66] For example, one etymological claim suggests *zār* as an onomatopoeic expression for suffering in Persian.[67] Thus, Leo Frobenius attributed to a myth of early Persian influence in East Africa the origins of both the *zār* rituals he witnessed in Omdurman and bori in Hausaland. Other theories argue for an Arabic origin. *Zār,* some scholars insist, is a contraction of *zahar* ("he visited") that seeped at some point into Amharic, and was then reloaned back into Arabic.[68] While some East African spiritual traditions do attribute belief in *zār* to Arabic origins,[69] other accounts invert the direction of this etymological transference, asserting *zār*'s Ethiopian origins. Thus, another often cited etymology identifies *zār* as a Kushitic loan word into Amharic, meaning "sky god."[70] The medieval Persian philosopher al-Ghazzali referred to *zār* as a Persian expression meaning "coming nigh to destruction." But, in coinciding phonetically with the Arabic contraction of *zahar,* he notes, the word *zār* is a site of imaginative interpretation.[71] According to al-Ghazzali's anecdote, language is most ecstatic where its possible referents multiply, converge, evanesce.

Zār elicits a kind of linguistic dispossession that reflects the syncope at its height, a profusion of uncertainty that flouts the drive for its origin. Ethnographic accounts of *zār* sometimes begin with an invitation to speak. The *zār* adept elicits spirit-speech, luring the wind through the voice of its body-medium. The afflicted person delivers, confusing languages, or speaking in an admixture of unknown languages—for example, Swahili, Arabic, Hindi, Urdu, Persian, Malayam, Marathi—or radically shifting timbre and tonality. This speaking in tongues is a speaking without speaking, a "singular experience of not knowing what one says," a lawless voice.[72] Language takes place, a meaningful acoustic transmission, but with neither the guarantees of intentionality nor comprehension. A void thus lies at the heart of *zār*'s most crucial linguistic interaction, for only the identification of the wind allows its appeasement. And this absence recurs in all of *zār*'s knowable facets—its origin and its phenomenology (trance), its etymology and its historical causality—and is reflected in the failures of its cinematic recording. Slavery is itself the "end of traceable beginnings."[73] But as *zār*'s etymological haze adumbrates, *zār* is an inadequate vestige of Indian Ocean slavery inasmuch as Indian Ocean slavery is itself a deficient residue of *zār*.[74] For the consensus about *zār*'s diffusion through slavery, its spread from Africa to Southwest Asia, accounts neither for the persisting myths that identify its linguistic origins in Persian and Arabic nor for the fact that *zār* must precede its own diffusion, must be prior to Indian Ocean slavery. *Zār* is immemorial, beyond historical time, the transmission of a most original discontinuity, an emptiness, a spacing, an *and* at the heart of the observable.

Action, will, knowledge, even experience—these concepts subtend normative models of the self-continuous, liberal subject. If I am interested in our reception of *zār* through the act of recording, it is because the convergence of *zār* and cinema crystallizes a particular mode of historicity that eludes the horizon of the subject.[75] For this mode of historicity is felt as surrender, absence that is not mere negativity, loss that is not merely melancholic.[76] Like the cutting and splicing that underlies the foundational cinematic mechanism, *zār* gathers together absences. This absence is absolute, complete, incurable. For it is itself the cure. Ritual time creates a "virtual time," a descent, a "concentration of force," a "density and expansion."[77] *Zār* is a time warp.[78] Film does not merely absorb *zār*'s ritualistic atmosphere, but transforms it. Cinema is a future kinesthesia, a future world, a future thinking, but one premised upon access to the unlived past, access to what is unlivable. To record is to defer, to transmit the unlivable.

Anticolonial Horizon

The failure of *zār*'s capture bodes a resistance exceeding refusal. Modernist, ethnographic 1960s cinema, riposte to modernity, nevertheless seeks to seize it. Politicized image making is a path toward regaining proper orientation in the wake of modernity's radical disorientations. And black healing ritual is a particularly potent phenomenon for the articulation of anticolonial grievance. One need only recall Frantz Fanon's famous remarks in *The Wretched of the Earth* on the naturally induced choreography of spirit possession as lens for therapeutic interpretation. Fanon's ethnographies of North African possession rituals informed his clinical translations of what he understood to be the psychopathological symptoms of colonization: "muscular stiffness," "paroxysmal tachycardia," "idiopathic tremors," "hypersomnia," "stomach ulcers," and numerous anxiety disorders, phobias, and psychoses.[79] Fanon goes so far as to remark on the indispensability of possession to any study of the colonial world. In the passages in question Fanon may not think specifically of *zār* but possibly an analogous kind of spirit ritual practiced in North Africa, where he was stationed as a psychiatrist and observed ritual ceremonies: "The colonized's affectivity is kept on edge like a running sore flinching from a caustic agent. . . . The psyche retracts, is obliterated, and finds an outlet in muscular spasms" (56). And, "Any study of the colonial world therefore must include an understanding of the phenomena of dance and possession" (19).

As in Southwest Asia, slavery was an antique inheritance in North Africa—a history virtually dissolved by Fanon's otherwise compelling insights into the colonized psyche.[80] Fanon's dissipation of the distinction between native/colonized and enslaved symptomizes a more ubiquitous dissolution. If Indian Ocean slavery cannot be thought independently of transatlantic slavery, nor can it really be thought independently of the histories of colonialism and imperialism in the

Indian Ocean. These historical threads are most visibly knotted in the antislavery and abolitionist campaigns that justified nineteenth-century British imperial intervention in the Indian Ocean (and which make its archives possible), but also in the fifteenth-century imperial adventures in the Indian Ocean that presage and inaugurate the "discovery" of the Americas and attendant histories of indigenous genocide.[81] Yet, the indistinction between the colonized and the enslaved cannot merely be attributed to an ignorance or mishandling of context. It is unlikely that Fanon had any awareness of the long history of African enslavement in Algeria.[82] (*Lack of information,* I argue in chapter 2, is not a sufficient ground through which to understand the corrosion of slavery's legacy.) There are "problems in the formulation of the relation of power from which slavery arises, and there are problems in the formulation of the relation of this relation of power to other relations of power."[83]

The indistinction between the colonized and the enslaved survives, on the one hand, as the legacy of postcolonialism's all-encompassing figure of the "colonized," as if the critique of colonialism must restrain a paralyzing inquiry into the history of the colonized-as-enslaver, and the slave as other-than, or more-than colonized. On the other hand, the indistinction between colonized and enslaved *also* exists as the intrinsic generalizability of black spirit ritual, its total availability, its total exposure to a loss of reference. "Everyone is equal in *zār.*"[84] Although *zār* adepts reside primarily in poor black neighborhoods, the winds "affect everyone."[85] According to a common belief in Ethiopia, everyone "has a *zār.*"[86] "All winds are contagious."[87] Historical amnesia regarding Indian Ocean slavery cannot merely be attributable to familiar models of forgetting and repression. For there is something in the history of slavery, *zār* seems to convey, that deflects facticity itself, is irreducible to historiographic psychologism.

Global modernity, materially synonymous with the rise of capitalism and Western hegemony, and epistemologically synonymous with the ascendance of facticity, has become irrevocably associated with transatlantic slavery. Yet there is little in the bodies of cultural production oppositional to this hegemony (partially articulated within the fields of postcolonial theory and black studies) to suggest consciousness of any relation between Indian Ocean slavery and modernity, nor, by extension, of Indian Ocean slavery and transatlantic slavery. This is not merely a question of parochialism, as the frequently malignant charge against North American black studies goes. Relatedly, nor is the disconnect merely attributable to the so-called politics of location. (As if location were isomorphous with itself. The "West" is not a "bounded geographical domain," but a "universalizing temporal schema" through which the "East" seeks to articulate, to historicize itself, to crystallize its own facticity.)[88] The same ignorance of Indian Ocean slavery recurs in the anticolonial cultural production generated in precisely the regional contexts and historical periods where one might expect such consciousness to surface. A set of now quasi-canonical texts attests to the anticolonial ethos of the Iranian 1960s, such as Jalāl al-i Ahmad's infamous *Westoxification* (*Gharbzadegi*), sometimes generously cited as a precursor to Edward Said's 1978 *Orientalism,* as well as the political writings and speech transcriptions of Alī Shari'atī, whose works are today considered pivotal to the series of events leading up to the watershed 1979 Revolution.[89] Nowhere does Indian Ocean slavery rise to the horizon of redress.

Despite their growing "familiarity" with histories of slavery and racism elsewhere, and despite increasing solidarity with racial liberation movements around the globe, public and intellectual engagement with Indian Ocean slavery "remained obscure and inchoate," even at the height of anticolonialism.[90] Similarly, just as the politicized attempt to record *zār* is met with a representational mise en abyme, so too does anxiety in the Iranian New Wave indicate a kind of ontological disorientation that exceeds the contingencies of history. Is this at all surprising? What kind of judgment does it impel? As cinematic *zār* suggests, Indian Ocean slavery persists as the very *dissolution of horizon.*

Blackness and Racial Anachronism

The New Wave rebellion against *filmfārsī* entails stylistic revisions intended to renew relation to truth: deliberate, measured editing, extended shot durations that sober against intoxicating whirls of haphazardly strung-together images. The long take is a cinematic technique for exact capture. But film itself is the evolved form of an ongoing technological drive for the real, whose essence, as early theorists of cinema remarked, is calculation, precision.[91] What this media technology shares in common with the concept of race, to which blackness is tethered as if immemorially, is a drive for fixity and

« 22 »   Introduction

organization that is exemplary of modernity more generally.[92] Many of the films I deal with in this book overlap with the post-1953 period in Iranian intellectual history, whose racial context is partly defined by the inheritances of early twentieth-century Iranian nationalism. The Aryan or Indo-European thesis, associated with nineteenth-century comparative philology, is rooted in identifications of linguistic resemblances between Greek, Latin, Persian, and Sanskrit that were rapidly transformed into grounds for justifying racial affiliation between Europeans, Persians, and Indians.[93] Assimilated and rearticulated into late nineteenth-century discourse, Aryanism describes one of the strongest currents of Iranian nationalism and continues to earnestly animate modern debates about Persian racial standing.[94] Aryanism informed Iran's self-conception as white, immemorially connected to Europe, and thus distinct from its Arab, Semitic, Muslim neighbors, a supposed "accident of geography," displaced from its original, authentic context—displaced from origin itself.[95]

Due to its association, however debated, with modern science, and therefore, with universality and objectivity, the concept of race is treated as the epitome of historically variable forms of thinking difference. The nonracial is shaped by a hyperpoliced understanding of race (and its various declensions: racism, racial, racialization). In scholarship, race management is charged.[96] A systematic articulation of taxonomic differences that could be affixed to unchangeable qualities, like blood and hereditary descent, is unidentifiable in Indian Ocean societies. Thus the legacy of Indian Ocean world slavery is generally characterized as nonracial, because it is opposed to a history of racial slavery against which its differences are easy to define. And yet, this very distinction between racial and nonracial slavery continues to be articulated *through* blackness. Inasmuch as transatlantic slavery gets metonymized by the enslaved African destined for racial blackness, Indian Ocean slavery stakes its unity on a certain distance, which is also to say, relation to this figure. Indian Ocean slavery and racial blackness are incommensurable, it would appear. But what is this *and* that enables the coherence of simple inconsonance?

One manages or rejects racial blackness, that is, a factified blackness, by instead turning to taxonomy in the historiographic mode. The historian Īraj Afshār Sīstānī distinguished between a black population who lived in southwestern Iran before the Elamites (2600–330 B.C.), and a subsequent slave group from Zanzibar with which native black people (*siyāh pūstān*) in Iran had intermingled.[97] In a documentary on Būshihr,[98] *durzādīhs* (literally, "pearl-born") distinguish themselves from black Iranians who are slave descendants. Similarly, Africans who have been living in India since "millennia" are considered distinct from "those who make up the Indo-African population" in recent memory.[99] In Tunisia, *wārgliyya,* indigenous blacks from the southern Tunisian oases, are distinguished from the rest of the black population, "descendants of displaced sub-Saharans, the vast majority of whom were slaves."[100] In the western Sahel and southwest Morocco, the Haratin are aboriginal black populations distinguished from black people of slave descent, but further differentiations split differences between generations of slave descendent communities. The *shwāshin,* "ancient" groups of freed black slaves, are distinguished from those that arrived after the seventeenth century, primarily from western and central Sudan.[101]

There is no need to contest the value of the internal differentiation of blackness—an established theme in especially Black British cultural studies in the 1980s and 1990s, which famously decried the representative "ventriloquism" of a single univocal category, urging the need for distinctions that would attend to geographical specificity but also language, gender, sexuality, and class.[102] What is now popularly called *intersectionality* offers fuller vision into the range of oppressions that accrue to black embodiment when it is most robustly qualified.[103] On a very different but parallel register, minute historical distinctions may laudably restore dignity and impart sense and coherence to historical violences that are otherwise incomprehensible. However, in appearing or attempting to undo the processes of homogenization of which racial blackness is the outcome, the resources that are made available *to* blackness through these same processes also disappear.[104] Frequently, if subtly and imperceptibly, distinction is mobilized to deny, moralize, and control relationality. Indian Ocean exceptionalism clouds the relation and being-in-common between black diasporas around the globe, strains prospects not only of global black relationality but of global relationality *to* blackness. Inasmuch as its authority derives from the hegemony of facticity, historiographic taxonomy cannot avoid the violence of reification constitutive of racialization.

More, historiographic taxonomy cannot locate the racialization of blackness in time. Easy terminological disambiguations are not *simply* available. If racialization encompasses processes of homogenizing and metonymizing into color, as contemporary theorists of race propose, then the heterogeneous geographical terms used to describe Africans from different parts of the continent (*Habāshī, Zangī*), were already accomplishing this work as early as the medieval era, distortive of any real sense of heterogeneity, absorptions of ancient, Ptolemaic residues (see chapter 3).[105] Antique judgments about the torrid zone, the classical theory that rendered Africa uninhabitable, argues Sylvia Wynter, live on a continuum both with the invention of race in modernity and with the distinction between reason and unreason that defines our most enduring and incorrigible inheritance: humanism itself, the intelligence of self-transcendence, facticity, history-as-science, the capacity to master context.[106] Even once reasonable and responsible scholars have historicized and safely secured race to its rightful, supposedly immovable epistemological context, how does one account for a blackness that lags before and after, like the cinematic interval, both exceeding and escaping the frame, irreducible to its own name?[107]

The supposed "single social category" of blackness decried in the 1980s was itself the historical amalgamation of global political movements in the 1960s, and has therefore always been inherently heterogeneous, inherently universal, inherently *decontextualized* and dispersed, despite the contemporary aspersions of those who repudiate both the alleged parochialism of racial blackness and the presence of racial blackness where it is supposedly out of place, outside its correct, local, insular context.[108] It should not go without saying that the very possibility that people exist all around the world who might be unified by political, spiritual, and familiar modes of knowing that are mediated by blackness—however internally differentiated—bodes a potential for global insurrection that those whose position is threatened by this truth necessarily wish to reduce and disappear, however logically sound or sophisticated their strategies.

One of the primary motivations for insistence on differentiation is the disambiguation of blackness with abjection that appears to arise through the fraught associations of Africanness, blackness, and slavery, as if these associations were inevitable. But those who flout racial blackness have already fated the overdetermination of its meaning. What would it mean to *not* assume that racial blackness is known, or fully knowable? What would it mean to recognize something other than the abjection that the enslaver, and the nonslave, systematically project onto the slave, the free subject's scapegoat?[109] If slavery is ubiquitous and endemic to human society, as so many scholars of slavery have compellingly argued, then to refuse the world shaped by the master-slave relation is also to align oneself against mastery. This includes the mastery and policing of context, as well as the systematic denigration of and self-distancing from the slave that defines modern, civic subjectivity and is reproduced in the global desire for and overvaluation of whiteness, and the concomitant self-distancing from and devaluation of blackness. Abjection is borne of a relation to submission that contradicts the modern (academic, and popular) desiderata of the sovereign, liberal subject, the subject-as-agent, the able subject, the subject-as-master, the subject-as-real, the subject-as-fact. The capacity to manage context is racialized.

Chapter Outline

Anxiety about context shapes contemporary debates on the Persian improvisatory tradition of *siyāh bāzī*, or "black play." In chapter 1 I explore films from the decade prior to the onset of the Iranian New Wave, in prerevolutionary film and in the popular commercial cinema known domestically and disparagingly as *filmfārsī*. Chapter 1 explores the transformation of *siyāh bāzī*, the indigenous theatrical tradition of Persian black play, into a thematic staple of Pahlavi-era commercial film. Though it was disseminated across cinema and television screens after its assimilation to celluloid, film scholars have rarely paid sustained or critical attention to the translation of improvisatory *siyāh bāzī* to screen.[110] In *siyāh bāzī*, the *siyāh*, literally the "black," is the protagonist minstrel in blackface who pesters, sweet talks, mimes, and rebels against authority characters. He often banters with an *arbāb* (master), and speaks in mutilated, malapropic Persian that appears to capture the fantasy of blackened speech. Despite the *siyāh*'s obvious resonance with the glyph of the black slave, and despite *siyāh bāzī*'s undeniable resemblance to more globally familiar, racialized forms of blackface minstrelsy, an intractable discourse denying *siyāh bāzī*'s translation as blackface, as well as its historical relation to slavery, continues to suppress analogies.

In chapter 1 I show that *siyāh bāzī*'s translation to the screen exposes the tradition to its own internal instability. Fragmented by the discontinuities of prerevolutionary film's capricious editing styles, placed against omphalic symbolism, and embedded as a prop within voluble, heterosexual narrative intrigues, the *siyāh* is absolutely atomized. If *fīlmfārsī* returns *siyāh bāzī* to its allusive relation to African enslavement, it also returns *siyāh bāzī* to racial enigma, masking, and myth. Above all, cinema dehistoricizes *siyāh bāzī* to the extent that it *dis*embeds it, proliferates its possible contexts to infinity. Contemporary Persian discourse, both academic and popular, takes refuge in a certain notion of (cultural, historical) context to disavow the *siyāh*'s slave genealogy. But slavery is itself the most radical derangement of context. The cinematic *siyāh* erupts out of this unreliable enclosure that context is, explodes its pretensions to safety and sovereignty.

Slavery writhes context, and *zār* is the enigmatic trace of this contortion. In chapter 2, experimental filmmaking reveals that at cinema's core, as at the heart of *zār,* lies a recurring absence that challenges facticity. *Zār*'s defining feature—a lapse of consciousness, a descent into absence—merges with cinema's blinking internal discontinuity and destabilizes the safe model of fact that would underly expectations for a historical memory of Indian Ocean slavery. Winding loops thwart *zār*'s etymology, as warbled incantations ward off reason's gaze. This protection is *zār*'s resistance to the objectification of knowledge. The 1960s fascination with *zār* manifest in Iranian ethnographic filmmaking of the period shows *zār* to be an intransigent object of perception. Anxiety and madness are two ubiquitous tropes that characterize the Iranian New Wave and its coevolution with ethnographic desire. In exploring the bond between experimental documentary filmmaking and the emergence of alternative cinema in the late 1960s and 1970s, I show how *zār* infuses Iranian cinematic modernism with an anxiety whose opaque referent exceeds its own historical context.

In the space between its own repetition, fact erodes. Thus, space, like context, is the object of extreme modes of policing. In chapter 3 I show how the space that intervenes between hyphenated identity incubates contradictions. "Afro-Iran" and "Afro-Iranian" are terms applied to a range of contemporary objects and ideas that purport to exhibit blackness in Iran. They are also implicitly opposed to static notions of "Iran" and "Iranian" that are therefore assumed to be pure, devoid of mixture, nonblack—in short, essential. From Mahdi Ehsai's 2016 photography collection *Afro-Iran* to Kamran Haydari's 2014 film *Dingomaro* about an Afro-Iranian musician, to Behnaz

Mirzai's 2013 ethnographic documentary *Afro-Iranian Lives*, to the black response to the racial exoticism inherent in these aesthetic objects, "Afro-Iran" has gained traction over the past few decades as an obvious term describing a purportedly self-evident state of affairs. Through a reading of an experimental documentary from the early 1970s that chronicles a Shi'i mourning ritual (Nāṣir Taqvā'ī's *Arba'īn*), I show that invocations of hybridity, syncretism, and mixedness hopelessly reproduce the very system of values (namely, identity, essence, purity) that they seek to overturn. The tautological force of the syncretic is a confused locus of anxiety that proliferates various fictions of origin. Taqvā'ī's documentary chronicles the syncretic character of Shi'i mourning rituals as they are practiced in the southwest of Iran, Būshihr, where the presence of African descendent communities has infused the tradition of Muharram with a distinction that is colored, above all, by animated rhythm. In attending to *Arba'īn*'s forms of sonic montage, I argue that (cinematic) rhythm articulates a form of conjunction that crystallizes the tautologies of hybridity.

In chapter 4, I read Bahram Beyzai's *Bashu, the Little Stranger* as an allegory for the weak facticity of Indian Ocean slavery. Cinema's *and*, its interval, is a space of possibility and violence. Conjunction orphans the image, but also destroys the illusion of its self-integrity. It is perhaps unsurprising that the child protagonist pervades postrevolutionary Iranian cinema, as in cinemas from the Global South more generally. *Bashu* is famous for its depiction of phenotypical racism against a child from the south of Iran, but Bashu's blackness is a question of considerable ambiguity. (Film commentators have rarely settled on a consensual description.) Bashu practices a theatrical version of *zār* to heal his prosthetic mother when she falls ill; he is treated as potentially enslavable labor by the extended family that adopts him; Bashu's dark color is a perpetual object of derision for town dwellers; the reappearance of his spectral biological family—and especially his mother—suggests East African origins. *Bashu* is saturated with an ideology of cultural nationalism in which language mediates antagonisms generated by ethnoracial difference. But Bashu's blackness, the film ultimately suggests, is the site of an absolute resistance to the assimilation of context. Blackness, I argue throughout the book, is irreducible to its facts. This resistance—to assimilation and incorporation—exceeds the categories that have been and continue to be invented, in order to comprehend, contain, and manage its sense.

Most of the films discussed in the foregoing chapters would not have survived without the advent of digital media. Prerevolutionary films were sacrificed to nonexistent storage techniques, as well as the more intentional pyrotechnic destructions of the 1979 Revolution, which, in addition to wiping out nearly half of the country's movie houses, destroyed innumerable archival prints. The revolution's resultant diasporic communities radically dispersed Iranian cinema globally through an underground, largely anonymous culture of film collection, distribution, digitization, and illicit streaming.[111] Modernity's *ands*, as we know, continue to proliferate at even higher speeds and scales in the internet age. Digital platforms thus make possible the survival and ongoing transmission of the traces of blackness in Iranian cinema that I examine throughout this book. These same platforms enable responses to representational annihilation, creating unprecedented opportunities for global black conjunction around the world, as recent scholarship on black digital counterpublics optimistically suggests.

In the conclusion I turn to a recent group known as the Collective for Black Iranians. The Collective for Black Iranians (Ja'mi'at-i Īrāniyān-i siyāh pūst) emerged amidst the tumultuous Black Lives Matter protests of summer 2020 as I was completing the first draft of this book, quickly garnering a wide social media following. Through engagement with the Collective's digital aesthetics, I suggest that Indian Ocean historiography's authority is already being challenged, in ways that may be compared to the revisionist challenge to transatlantic historiography by a generation of antiracist postwar historians of the 1950s and 1960s.[112] Traditionally, historians of Indian Ocean slavery have denied any political exigency to the study of slavery in the Indian Ocean context.[113] But black digital communities across Southwest Asia and North Africa generate contrasting narratives, protesting in particular the unexamined state of antiblackness in the region that derives, in part, from entangled legacies of slavery across the Indian Ocean, trans-Saharan *and* Atlantic worlds. In contrast to traditional scholarship on Indian Ocean slavery, which posits a history without a racial legacy, the Collective for Black Iranians and their digital counterparts attempt to defy the stranglehold of historiography's perversion—its dissociation of fact from experience, its silent withdrawal of access to the means for contesting consensus. In my readings of the Collective's artwork I show how representation in digital art is belied by an internal repetition, a looping that destabilizes appearance, and that opens up even the crispest and clearest of images, the sharpest of facts, to an erosion that is intimate, self-constituting, a general and generative dissolution that is both prior and internal to fact.

« 1 »

Blackface and the Immemorial

Fīlmfārsī's Navel

A fanged zoomorphic puppet hangs from an invisible ceiling beam in the initial moments of Farukh Ghafārī's *Shab-i Qūzī,* or *Night of the Hunchback.* Various perspectives of the puppet's hunched body alternate with images of a lit paper moon sign. A low-angle shot of the puppet allows the viewer to gaze into his glassy eyes, which blink mechanically, devilishly, at the camera as the figure spins slightly on its axis. He wears a horned helmet and holds a stick capped with the head of a horned animal. A leftward pan reveals the title of the play displayed in Persian, "'The Demon's Revenge,' with the participation of the well-known actor, Asghar Qūzī." The puppet blinks twice, before the frame reveals his entire body: animal torso, hooved feet. A force winds the helmet from Qūzī's laughing head.

"The Demon's Revenge," the play within the film (or, the very brief sequence from a play adapted from a mysterious compilation of textual fragments) inaugurates the 1964 critically acclaimed, commercial failure *Night of the Hunchback.*[1] The film derives from a story embedded in the famous Indo-Perso-Arabic collection of mythology and folktale, *Hizār va Yak Shab,* (*The One Thousand and One Nights,* also known as *The Arabian Nights*). This important, if forgettable, detail germinates a promise about *Night of the Hunchback*'s exemplarity for the study of cultural transmission and the double bind of its analysis. Lodged within a dense meshwork of spurious texts, the film reproduces in a new form the disquieting mise en abyme from which it emerges. *Mise en abyme* is the immanent reflection that alters what it reflects and is altered by its own reflecting. On a theater stage, a hysterical woman with rope-bound feet hits her head in refusal to marry the demon, Qūzī, the puppet come to life. She enjoins Qūzī's threatening laughter with her own demonic wails. Curtains fall upon the miniscule sequence, veils that interrupt, cover, but simultaneously denude the performance, heralding metalepsis, reduplication, repetition. Qūzī and the female actress return to the makeup room, where the third and fourth members of their *dastah,* or acting troupe, prepare themselves for a second performance that evening at a party in a middle-class Tehran home, this time, in blackface.

In the makeup room backstage one of the actors blackens his face with grease as Qūzī now kneels with a thick marker in front of the fourth actor's stomach and begins drawing eyes below the nipples. A close medium shot focalizes this transposition of stomach to face, a displacement of another scene of crossing, from bare to blackface. As the credits roll through santour tones, darkness descends on the belly-painted-face, which appears stark in the next shot, dolled up in a curly black wig. Belly rolls and hips gyrate a crooked mouth whose painted red lips envelop the navel, a "figure of the unfathomable."[2] The navel is chiasmic—a doubled source of finitude and infinitude, of natality and death, the mark of an ancient accident.[3] In *Night of the Hunchback,* the dysmorphic navel-face moves, its motions cosmetic. A curious metastasis ensues: a traditionally feminine form of exotic, mystical, but also thoroughly commodified movement—belly dancing—is here performed by a recognizably male body, as the locus of recognition disintegrates from face to navel, and again from navel to face, oscillating flesh between form and formlessness, and conjuring, like the navel itself, the inside of the skin, the flesh that one never sees, the "foundation of things," as well as the originary inherence of an outside at the heart of the inside.[4] The cosmopsychological symbolism of the body's perspectival vanishing point, the navel, catalyzes a transformation that a subtle drift in mise-en-scène establishes.

Warm, moody light engulfs the dancing belly and shadowy domestic details emerge: a vase of flowers, a ewer, a cloth hanging over a mantel, the outline of a jeweled turban. With the brightening light the site of action transforms the setting from theater house to living room. This alchemical shift from the public to the domestic drives the navel's dense symbolism of the impenetrability of the trivial and will echo through the subsequent unfolding of actions in relation to the film as a whole. A compositional fragment in revolt of its ancestral source, filmic *siyāh bāzī* (black play), unveils a curious entanglement of unlikely, fused signifiers: blackness, slavery, sexuality,

Blackface and the Immemorial «33»

and gender; fantasy, myth, historicity, and cinema.[5] In this chapter I take the example of the prerevolutionary Iranian commercial film, subsumed under the shorthand *fīlmfārsī* (1950s–1970s), to explore the imagination of blackness in Southwest Asian (Middle Eastern) cultural production and concurrently to explore the *resistance* of the imagination of blackness to (historical) analysis.

Like the meaningless scar that is the trace of a vital force connecting being to another origin, the figure of the navel in Ghafārī's cinematic work captures the difficulty of the perception, interpretation, and narrativization of what it also gives one to think. In psychoanalytic theory and the tradition of philosophy that inherits and reinterprets it, the navel is the site not only of an insoluble resistance to sense but of a structure of "resistance that exceeds resistance itself."[6] That is, the navel is a figure for the knotted relation of forces that gives rise to analysis and that simultaneously constrains analysis. Ghafārī's navels (and there are multiple) thus prompt us to approach afresh the obscure dramatic improvisatory tradition of *siyāh bāzī*, or Persian black play, against and through which it appears in mid-twentieth-century Iranian cinema. In Iranian films, black play approaches a hermeneutic limit that arrests automatic seeing. Meanwhile, *siyāh bāzī* also transcends the expectations implicit in historical realism, generating provocations about the corpuscular, immemorial relation between blackness and cultural transmission at the global scale. The *immemorial* as I invoke it throughout this book addresses not only what has been empirically forgotten, what has been unarchived, uncanonized, and unthought in history—and especially, what has been unthought in the historical itinerary of racial blackness. The immemorial, like the navel that gestures to a time before birth, to a nonorigin embedded within the origin, marks a site upon the flesh of that which is both unrememberable and simultaneously unforgettable. The immemorial exposes a double bind, the unanalyzable resistance to analysis, the unhistoricizable stricture that riddles all history.

After developing *Night of the Hunchback*'s relation to its parent-text, *The Thousand and One Nights*, I turn to Ghafārī's controversial and highly redacted film, *Rivalry in the City*, or *Riqābat dar Shahr* (1964), drawing references to representations and evocations of blackness in Iranian films released during the same period: Sāmū'il Khāchikiyān's box-office hit *The Midnight Terror* (*Faryād-i Nīm-i Shab*, 1961) and Riżā Karīmī's peculiar slapstick comedy *Forced Vacation* (*Murakhaṣī-'i Ijbārī*, 1965). Long dispraised in film scholarship

Figure 1. Scenes from Farukh Ghafārī's *Night of the Hunchback* (1964). Top: Still from opening credits. Bottom: The dancing belly intervenes between the dancer and the *siyāh*.

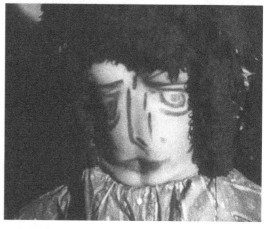

as untoward, inconsequential, and unworthy of scholarly attention, prerevolutionary commercial cinema reactivates in nuanced ways obsolescent ancient Near Eastern archetypes, religio-mystical symbols and medieval courtly practices that amalgamate historically potent, collective imaginative universes. Thus, its sometimes moniker, *sīnamā-yi rawyāpardāzī* (literally, "dream-weaving cinema"). At the same time, in appearing chronologically promixate or subsequent to the era of classic Hollywood film, *fīlmfārsī*'s gestures are unavoidably hybrid, thoroughly disembedded, cannot point toward an authentic origin, nor to meanings that would not already be dispersed, globalized, and no-longer-specific, the outcome of world-formative transformations, conjunctions woven with the unknowable.

Siyāh Bāzī: Black Play

As the domestic scene at the beginning of *Night of the Hunchback* hints, *siyāh bāzī* entails comedic improvisatory performance featuring a male character disguised in black makeup, sarcastically kowtowing to another male in a position of power through muddled Persian speech. Based loosely on "The Hunchback" story cycle in *The One Thousand and One Nights,* Ghafārī's film chronicles a night in the drama surrounding a hunchback's corpse, ludically killed by force-feeding in the first ten minutes of the film, as he is in the first sentences of the *Nights*' "Hunchback" story cycle.[7] During their shared meal in the woods where the troupe has wandered after their in-house *siyāh bāzī* performance, the female dancer playfully stuffs Qūzī's mouth with a piece of bread and chicken, on which he chokes to death. (Qūzī's name means "hunchback" in Persian.) Panicked about being blamed for Qūzī's death, the dancer and the *siyāh,* or blackface protagonist, furtively drop the corpse off at the home of a neighbor, played by the filmmaker Ghafārī himself. The ensuing plot details the neighbors' attempts to rid themselves of Qūzī's corpse, as, following the course of *The One Thousand and One Nights* version, it is shuffled off from one neighbor to another. The corpse shuffling, Ghafārī's main interest in the "Hunchback" cycle, which he thought poignantly reflected his country's sociopolitical atmosphere in the 1950s and impressively eluded censors, remained central in his film version despite various omissions and adaptations.[8]

In a film so bedazzled by animated, ludicrous action, the *siyāh bāzī* scene withdraws from plot significance, adding mere comic frivolity, a trifle best captured by what the filmmaker Ibrāhīm Gulistān dismissively calls the nonsense of a dancing belly-face.[9] In an almost literal way, the synchronic belly personification and face blackening form the impenetrable navel of the film. The unserious, "middle" quality of *Night of the Hunchback,* an excommunication from high culture it inherits from its *Arabian Nights* urtext, details a precarity of cultural prestige that derails and confuses but does not extinguish its artifactual significance.[10] Low cultural prestige exacerbates chaos between narrative elements. Unlike the New Wave art film, which is the focus of chapter 2, *filmfārsī,* proximate with the Hindi film and pre-1960s Egyptian melodrama, often eschews cogent, normative forms of character-focused storytelling in favor of frequent divagations, a genre deprived of centers.[11] Shortly after he

« 36 » Blackface and the Immemorial

saw Ghafārī's *South of the City,* the famous film critic Amīr Hūshang Kāvūsī (known for coining the aspersed term *filmfārsī*) complained that the film patched together a panoply of fragments rather than offering a unified vision, deriding Ghafārī's incapacity to maintain filmic continuity.[12] *Night of the Hunchback* is not usually categorized as part of the *filmfārsī* mode. Difficult to place, it is sometimes incorporated into the New Wave canon or seen as a parody.[13] Nevertheless, it shares these digressive, narratively vexed features with *filmfārsī,* in addition to an apsychological emphasis on action over character development that resonates with the formal structure of *Arabian Nights.* It thus delivers a unique type of causality based on digression, extended predication, gaps, and retroaction.[14]

Night of Hunchback's siyāh bāzī takes place following the navel choreography described at the start of this chapter, and introduces a new dance sequence, suggesting a curious sexual transaction that the blackface protagonist's purposeful gender confusion elicits. Upon the conclusion of the belly dance, brightened light reveals the jeweled turban sitting atop the head of an *arbāb* (master), who, reposed on the carpet with a pipe hanging from the corner of his mouth, watches the dancing navel, a human doll. As the music dies, the actor in blackface launches himself awkwardly into the spotlight, throwing his velvet cap in the air. With a barely scrutable accent and screeching solecisms he asks whether his master has enjoyed the music: "Please allow this house-born slave [*ghulām-i khānahzād*] to entertain you. Musicians, play!" he cries, as the unmoved master sips smoke from his hookah. The "house-born slave" in blackface pours liquid from the ewer on the mantel into a cup small enough to be a shot glass and places it on his forehead as he shimmies, bending backward low enough so that the master can grab it. Downing the glass, the *arbāb* hits the *siyāh's* back with the tip of his hose. As the *siyāh* walks away, the master throws a shoe at him. The *siyāh* arches and shrieks in pain cartoonishly.

Like, but less so than most of the pre-1979 Iranian films discussed in this book, *Night of the Hunchback's* surviving copies bear the degradations of time and revolution. Celluloid, the film's self-cannibalizing material substrate and condition of archivability, incurs a gradual deterioration accelerated by typically improper storage techniques, obligatory frugality, and censorship, and is why most photosynthetic Iranian films now preserved in digitized form and uploaded to popular sharing platforms appear slightly washed by a

Blackface and the Immemorial

Figure 2. The *siyāh* dances for his "master" at a house performance of *siyāh bāzī*. Still from Ghafārī's *Night of the Hunchback* (1964).

purplish cast. Like memory itself, film submits to erosion, but also repetition and renewal. A sense of agedness endows *Night of the Hunchback* with a maturity belied by its ludicrous narrative. The music track replays this oscillation between sobriety and knavishness with its defamiliarizing juxtapositions: Ray Charles and Claude Bolling wafting through traditional Persian melodies.[15] The sartorial details of this brief *siyāh bāzī* scene evoke the timeless quality of the *Arabian Nights*. Like many of the *Nights*' tales, Ghafārī's original script was set in eighth-century Baghdad under the reign of the Abbasid caliph Harun al-Rashid.[16]

Fīlmfārsī "pop-ness," expressed through characters' European fashion and music tastes, betrays an impure temporality that complements the archaic orchestrations of *siyāh bāzī*: sultans, gleeful black servants, harem dancers, and *mutrib* (musicians and minstrels) cavort in a tenseless past that could equally belong to the nineteenth century as it could the sixteenth or third, thus staging the staticness of historical time embodied by cinema's sense of prerecorded nowness.[17] (In a film from Parvīz Sayād's famous *Samad* film series, Samad imagines himself in a dream where a beautiful Persian woman commands her two black slaves, conflating his late twentieth-century present with the fantasy of an unnamed, earlier dynastic period.) Prerevolutionary Iranian film recharges the fantasy of an atemporal Iran whose nationalist image it contributes to forging and reifying. *Siyāh bāzī*, too, undergirds this fantasy, a relic revived under Reza Shah Pahlavi purportedly in an effort to supplant the more popular Islamic theater of Ta'zīyah in favor of pre-Islamic, and therefore authentically, timelessly Persian practice.

The various and contradictory attempted exorcisms of Islamic signification under the Pahlavi dynasty's nationalist projects attempted to racialize Iran as Indo-European, white, immemorially connected to Europe.[18] Part of the nationalist project thus entailed the preservation and popularization of indigenous cultural performance traditions disconnected from Islamic history.[19] *Siyāh bāzī* was considered one such authentically Persian tradition. In the twentieth century technological distribution and dissemination of *siyāh bāzī* on film, black play thus whitens Iran. Anthropological readings of *siyāh bāzī* theater point out that its comedy succeeds primarily as an effect of a stark power differential between the *siyāh* and his audience. It is in particular because the blackface protagonist belongs to the lowest possible echelon of being that audiences find his insolence toward authority figures appealing and politically provocative, a social outcast "with whom they can identify, but who will not be identified with them."[20] (*Fīlmfārsī* scenes of giggling children delighting in *siyāh bāzī* performances drive this point home: the most vulnerable members of society, children seem to be the ones most affected by this buffoonery.)[21] One commentator calls the *siyāh*'s blackness a kind of "mask" that justifies his wild antics, according to the unequivocally antiblack logic that "a person who is black is beyond society."[22]

Siyāh bāzī thus binds class, in the most general and familiar senses of this term, as well as cultural and linguistic unity, and effectively does so under the guise of innocent laughter. The *siyāh*'s subtle grammatical distortions, phonetic substitutions, mispronunciations, and idiomatic disfigurations require a deeply intimate knowledge of the Persian language in order to provoke humor. By the same token, this fundamentally cohesive quality of the performance suggests that *siyāh bāzī*'s audience excludes black people from the arrangement of its humor—or more accurately, excludes consciousness of a perspective that might be called black. Or rather, such a perspective is included only to the extent that it is called upon to integrate that which represses it. Within the economy of *siyāh bāzī*, blackness constitutes Persian community through farce. But *siyāh bāzī*, as film shows, is itself difficult to segregate from other blackface minstrelsy contexts, moving "Persian" to a realm broader than the national, linguistic, cultural, or racial, extending to the global.[23]

In short, filmic *siyāh bāzī* is synonymous with national-racial subject formation and is historically specific, even while simultaneously conjoining disparate contexts: Iranian nationalism with a broader project of global whiteness, Aryanism. And yet, at the same time, *siyāh bāzī* en abyme—that is, atomized, distributed, embedded in cinema as a spectacle within a spectacle—creates a splitting of which it is itself both the cause and effect. Cinematic *siyāh bāzī* is both historical and fundamentally unhistoricizable. Or rather, cinematic *siyāh bāzī* shows how historical context, historical specificity, is always already riddled by a perspective that is both immanent to, and irrevocably *beyond,* the scene. This is what the integration of *siyāh bāzī* performance into cinema raises to the order of reflection. The spectator confronted with spectatorship is made to reflect upon what precisely *siyāh bāzī* spectacularizes. Holding up a reflection of the whole back to itself, filmic *siyāh bāzī* transforms, doubles, but also suggests that the spectacle is never, and will never be, simply what it is. To record is to disembed, to expose to a future context. Cinema is the technological realization of a radicalized decontextualization that is both historical and originary.

A dramatic practice with an arcane history whose description and ambiguous genealogy dovetails in unexpected and inexplicable ways with the equally mysterious histories of Italian commedia dell'arte and Anglo-European blackface minstrelsy, *siyāh bāzī* queers time in *fīlmfārsī,* appearing in both traditional and assimilated guises. That is, it appears both as typically Iranian *siyāh bāzī* scenarios and as filmic blackface performances, actors acting in black makeup with no explicit reference to the Persian *siyāh bāzī* tradition. Filmic *siyāh bāzī* thereby resists any mode of inquiry guided by quaint notions of influence, origin, and genealogy. The cinematic examples explored in the last part of this chapter show how the gendered difference between Persian black *play* (*siyāh bāzī*) and "generic" black*face* bars a normative mode of analysis that would attempt to feverishly manage the distinction between cultural particularity and global universality. Specificity, rendered cinematic, is always already nonspecific, dispersed.

More, *siyāh bāzī* cannot be stabilized along a chronological timeline. For the very tradition of masking whence blackface itself emerges in human history belongs to the ahistorical realm of the ancestral, to myth. Blackface is always already ahistorical in this sense, immemorial. Certainly, this does not mean blackface practices cannot be historicized.[24] This only means that there is no guarantee that the truth of blackface belongs to history. (Nor that history does not bear something of the ahistorical at its heart.) But if *siyāh bāzī*'s truth will

« 40 »   Blackface and the Immemorial

not be captured by the modern discourse genre we know as historiography, there is equally no guarantee that *siyāh bāzī* has a truth outside of the force field of relations from which its analysis must derive. This is the navel's reminder.

Commentators claim that, before becoming an unremarkable trope of lowbrow prerevolutionary cinema, circumambulating troupes performed *siyāh bāzī* throughout Iranian countrysides, urban centers, and in aristocratic courts since at least the Safavid sixteenth century, inaugurating its documentation (not origin). It was performed for weddings and circumcision ceremonies on raised wooden platforms planking backyard garden pools, whence its sometimes synonym *rūḥawẓī* or *takht-i hawẓī*, literally, performances "on the plank."[25] Commentators, whether rightly or wrongly, trace *siyāh bāzī*'s origins as far back as the Sumerian (4500–1900 BCE), Achaemenid (550–330 BCE), Sassanian (224–651 CE), Safavid (1502–1736 CE), and Qajar (1789–1925 CE) periods.[26] *Siyāh bāzī* is vaguely, spuriously, associable with a genealogy of black play forms that could be connected to Turkish, Arab, Indian, pan-Asian, Italian, and other European traditions that overlap religious ritual and social satire of the elite with *shādī āvar,* "joy making." For example, as Kathy Foley shows, "set character theater" in Iran, based upon a simple class dichotomy supplemented by ethnic ridicule, resonates with similar forms in China and India. It also resembles the ancient itinerant street theater that commedia dell'arte scholars identify as precursor to the more formal theatrical tradition, and to which commentators often compare *siyāh bāzī*.[27]

In combining blackface with his obsequious, disfigured speech, the *siyāh* conjures the projected image of the enslaved African. *Siyāh bāzī* therefore unambiguously evokes the history of African slavery in Iran—and, as I will discuss later, more specifically, eunuchism. Moreover, the very cartoon, cliché manner through which *siyāh bāzī* appears is racialized to the extent that the process of simplification constitutive of the cartoon and of the cliché is also constitutive of processes of racialization.[28] Nevertheless, the most common narrative about *siyāh bāzī* avoids the history of slavery, and of racial blackness entirely—indeed refutes them. In the twentieth century, a revered linguist and mythologist drew a correlation between the face blackening of Hājī Fīrūz (the stock blackface character of the Persian New Year, a genre of *siyāh bāzī*) and the ancient Mesopotamian practice of women blackening their faces in mourning at an annual festival—Dumuzi, from the myth of a shepherd who becomes king through marriage with the goddess Inanna.[29] Mihrdād Bahār's enormously, inexplicably popular speculations about *siyāh bāzī*'s origins in Sumerian ritual have been thoroughly assimilated into popular consciousness and continue to be routinely taken up by *siyāh bāzī*'s defenders (see the conclusion). Mythological narratives about *siyāh bāzī*'s origins also invoke Zoroastrian traditions of fire tending and worship as precursor for the *siyāh*'s blackened visage. In addition to their insistence on vague, ancient roots, proponents of *siyāh bāzī*'s racial innocence insist upon the singularity of the *siyāh*'s politically transgressive and beloved, rather than racist and caricatural, status: "Contrasting with his dark and sombre face is a luminous heart, and the common people identify with him. He is the voice of the oppressed and expresses their deepest emotion, their discontent with life, and their fears and hopes for the future."[30] Through the proclamation of exceptionalism, defenders of the *siyāh bāzī* tradition ignore the global ubiquity of such political iterations of blackface. Through proclamations of context contamination, defenders of the *siyāh bāzī* tradition also moralize cultural specificity, ironically melding together various ahistorical explanations to cement *siyāh bāzī*'s supposedly more rigorous, because context-specific, indigenous history. Myth, disguised as science (history), isolates and protects *siyāh bāzī*'s true meaning from the violent effects of foreign context contamination.

By contrast, recent historiographic scholarship insists upon *siyāh bāzī*'s unequivocal relation to slavery, as well as its highly recent emergence.[31] *Siyāh bāzī* is deeply entangled with the libidinal economy of slavery, connecting the fungibility of the slave body to the dynamic of identification that imbues *siyāh bāzī* with its cohesive power. For the very possibility of substitution, of placing one's "oppressed" self in the position of the *siyāh,* is bound up with the economy of slavery that subordinates singularity for the generic, subject for object commodity, and life for death.[32] And yet, despite the clarity with which the *siyāh* seems to reactivate the image of the African slave, despite recent scholarship that insists upon this reactivation through sound acts of historicization, and despite the evidenceless basis upon which its most popular, nonracial narratives are rehearsed, we have no way to adequately account for the victory of the *siyāh*'s mythologization. What makes "some narratives rather than others powerful enough to pass as accepted history?"[33] Is this victory of the *siyāh*'s birth in myth finally analyzable, itself historicizable? The force of the mythologization of the *siyāh* in the most popular narratives that enmesh him suggest that the time of *siyāh bāzī* is not the time of history. In the broken speech of *siyāh bāzī*, sense leaks from *siyāh bāzī*.

Elsewhere I synthesize with greater detail the unsatisfying information available about *siyāh bāzī*'s history and connect the tradition to the emergence of global public spheres.[34] Here, I suggest that film experience and the cinematic apparatus underlying it overwrite the ontological privilege accorded to expectation for such a history. Or rather, that the cinematic mise en abyme through which *siyāh bāzī* appears itself reveals something aporetic about any history that would claim to conquer its truth. It is not only that *siyāh bāzī*, and improvisatory performance more generally, in their origination in myth and ritual elide the model of archival documentation demanded by historiographical norms. Historiography is a modern, hegemonic form of thought-inquiry that effaces its own historicity, dissimulates the contingency of its methods as natural conditions for the production of truth. Even the controversial but influential scholarship that disavows *siyāh bāzī*'s antiblackness and historical relation to slavery in favor of its supposed link to the archaic cements the tradition's religio-mythic, rather than historical, origin and therefore destabilizes its own claim to authority. Its ahistorical character cannot be the only reason why narrative fails to deliver *siyāh bāzī*'s truth. For all history is structurally ahistorical, informed by the assumption of a pure temporal mode— presence—that itself never changes. Instead, the necessarily recorded status of filmic *siyāh bāzī* orients the tradition toward a time to come and places it within the belated temporal structure that would fulfill, or reorder, its meaning elsewhere. Cinema disembeds *siyāh bāzī*. *Fīlmfārsī*'s frenzied montage in particular marks a certain impropriety of perspective that is violently ungrounding, stylistically symptomatic of a broader metaphysical upheaval. Hence, *fīlmfārsī* is the object of avant-garde anxiety, of critical derision. But the very ontology of audiovisual recording reveals something that is irreducible to manic aesthetics. Film draws our attention to something that is more than merely cinematic.

Like commedia dell'arte's folkloric images and underworld stock characters, whence the best known of the *zanni* (servant characters) derives, the *siyāh* is a starting point without a point, a nonorigin that descends into indecipherable translation, or, in the "sacred origin of

Blackface and the Immemorial   « 43 »

risus (laughter)."[35] Creating an almost farcical labyrinth of flows and tautological loops of influence, scholars of American blackface minstrelsy, like commentators on *siyāh bāzī*, sometimes identify commedia dell'arte's Harlequin in black mask as the American blackface minstrel's prototype. Meanwhile, scholars of commedia dell'arte in turn hint at Harlequin's potential Near Eastern origins in Iranian, Arab, and Turkish improvisatory traditions.[36] Evoking primordial rituals of masking, the *siyāh* emerges from an event marking a rupture in the cosmos, or collapse in world order, crossing boundaries and liberating energies that his ongoing technological evolution allows him to absorb and reproject, an originarily transmedial, anachronistic force.

Night of the Hunchback's *siyāh bāzī* reflects the Pahlavi-era authoritarian dissolution and censorship of *siyāh bāzī*'s purportedly inherent politicism as the practice was transposed from site-specific but ambulatory performance to cinematic form. From itinerant courtyard theater (*rūḥawẓī*) to its migration into theater halls (*tamāshawkhānah*) as precurtain skits and entr'actes (*pīshpardah*) under the Qajars, *siyāh bāzī* is originally self-dislocating, originally self-disembedding, self-decontextualizing.[37] Otherwise known as a tradition voicing and mediating the political unconscious through at times sophisticated, and furtive, oratory flourishes, *fīlmfārsī* vaporizes *siyāh bāzī*'s politicism to distill *siyāh bāzī*'s essence as racial caricature—its most enduring legacy and primordial shape.[38] But by reembedding the improvisatory form within more elaborate, time-structured plot narratives, *fīlmfārsī* also imbues *siyāh bāzī* with new potential for reflexivity. The compulsion to laugh that defines comedy suggests unbearable forms of intersubjectivity produced through a supposedly natural capacity to "get" the joke.[39] It is precisely this naturalized dynamic burying the violence of a collective pronoun (we) that the looming navel in Ghafārī's cinematic *siyāh bāzī* excavates, calls into question, and places en abyme.

Diegetic theatrical references in film pose, at the very least, questions about spectatorial relations. A "theatrical impulse" saturates the very melodramatic mode of *fīlmfārsī*.[40] As a theatergram, or modular, plastic theatrical seme movable and alterable across traditions, in the twentieth century the *siyāh* now interpenetrates the multiplicity of formal aspects and rhythms composing the larger narrative text of *fīlmfārsī,* fusing with and affecting new elements.[41] Unlike theater, whose ontological integrity depends upon a spectator and a sense of presence, cinema absolves this fundamental dialectic in favor of a heightened relation with its own formal possibilities.[42] But this interpenetration of narrative elements in turn strengthens and elucidates the significance of the primordial spectator-*siyāh* relation, and the way that an ambiguous but *familiar* blackness, embodied and invented by the *siyāh* figure, normalizes, reproduces, and guards an unplumbable sense of we-ness. The "contemptable Black," suggests Cedric Robinson of the American blackface minstrel, is "at one and the same time the most natural of beings and the most intensely manufactured subject."[43] Until very recently, in cinema around the world, there was "no other place" for black performers to "recur in, except just the role within which we have already met them"; the black character is the prototypical "type."[44] We "know him, we all know him, our fathers and our fathers' fathers knew him," writes one commentator of the most famous *siyāh* figure of all, Hājī Fīrūz.[45]

Original Slave, Woman

"So you didn't like it?" the *siyāh* in *Night of the Hunchback* asks, as he returns the shoe to the master. "Kiss it," replies the master, alluding to his foot. And the *siyāh* complies. Unscathed, the *siyāh* rises, promising a more palatable dancer. The music recommences. The dancer, familiar as the demon's enslaved wife from the skit opening the film, capers onto the living room floor wearing a white veil draped over two long, dangling black braids and a headdress, and loose striped pants under her skirt and vest. Clapping, the *arbāb* expresses his satisfaction and joins the actors in dancing, as the frame eventually widens to include the partygoers who applaud to conclude, then join the spectacle within a spectacle, this mise en abyme of racial disguise.

In this genre or commercial mode of Iranian film from the mid-twentieth century, the *siyāh* and female dancer (*raqāṣ*) often share a stage. A primordial element in improvisatory theater up until the twentieth century, the role of the dancer was played in traditionally gender-segregated spaces by prepubescent boys (*bachah-raqāṣ*).[46] Reza Shah Pahlavi's mandatory unveiling in 1936 not only marks a shift in this practice, exchanging the male child for adult female dancers, but sets off a regnant tradition of installing hypersexualized female dancers into film, not only adopting but exaggerating Hollywood's divorce of Oriental female solo dance from its spiritual roots. A tradition with its alleged source in ancient Semitic goddess

Figure 3. The dancer performs in Ghafārī's *Night of the Hunchback* (1964).

cults, "the sight of a woman dancing alone ... stirs strange feelings and triggers incomprehensible anxieties," a suggested, if romantic, underlying cause for the domestication and global commoditization of belly dance.[47] If minstrelsy reifies and perverts black performance,[48] popular belly dance reifies and consumes the hypnotic and disconcerting spectacle of autoaffective female dance, attempting to capture, to domesticate the navel.

As a folk practice considered unseemly to Pahlavi-cultivated bourgeois taste, *siyāh bāzī* appears in prerevolutionary commercial film less frequently than the ubiquitous and class-transcendent dancing female body. There, she extends a range of public spaces from the traditional dingy *qahvih-khānah* (coffee house) setting in the ghettoized South of Tehran, to the more sophisticated, Europeanized *kābārah* (cabarets) of North Tehran.[49] Masūd Kīmīyā'ī's action-packed 1975 *Beehive* (*Kandū*) famously thematizes the socioeconomic marking of Tehran's coffeehouses. Dancing female bodies framed by cabaret-like café settings featured in even early twentieth-century Iranian films, such as 'Abdulhusayn Sipāntā and Ardishīr Īrānī's 1932 *The Lor Girl* (*Dukhtar-i Lur*), the first Iranian sound film, in which Gulnār (Rūḥangīz Sāmīnizhād), the narrative's love interest, worked as a singing dancer at a caravanserai after being kidnapped by a group of bandits. Hypodiegetic dance segments abound in *fīlmfārsī*, inflected by orientalist interpretations of Eastern dance, while the café setting forms a cathected, iconic spectator-spectacle motif. Harkening back to cinema's roots in vaudeville, burlesque, and minstrelsy, the omnipresent cabaret trope bears Iranian cinema's ongoing relation to the camera's infancy as a stationary machine awaiting "interesting movement."[50] Though present in early cinema,

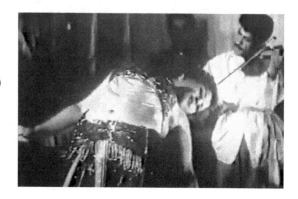

Figure 4. Belly dancer performing on a café stage in Ghafārī's *Rivalry in the City* (1960/1964) discussed below.

the cabaret trope gathered striking force in the 1960s, reflecting and perhaps contributing to the physical proliferation of Tehran cabarets, coffee shops, and music halls, coextending the international popularity of American jazz and the expansion of an eroticized homosocial public sphere.[51] The ubiquitous *fīlmfārsī* dancer also connects the appearance of the unveiled female body to the racial nationalist project, an attempt to mark Iran's proximity to Western civilizational progress; in Islamicate societies, "dressing up for modernity has been fashioned through undressing women."[52] But if the naked female body means to whiten Iran by sacrificing culturally regressive modesty codes to a purportedly liberated modernity, the *fīlmfārsī* belly dancer, the denuded female belly-in-motion, also bodes a certain danger. For despite its equivocal symbolism as a site of natality, pleasure, and comfort, "the place where the body was last joined to its maternal origins,"[53] the navel is also the origin of invasion, corruption, and death.

In *Night of the Hunchback* the dancer moves in a style reminiscent of Persian *raqṣ-i sharqī* (Eastern dance), emphasizing hand movements and manipulation of lips and eyebrows over the brisk pelvic movements or abdomen rolls more characteristic of North African styles; thus her performance, embedded as it is in a *siyāh bāzī* sequence, is not quite representative of the sexualized style of dance in *fīlmfārsī*'s cabaret scenes.[54] In an interview, Ghafārī claims there is "absolutely" no dancing and singing in the film, which suggests that the dancer's movements unfold upon an order that diverges from the ostentatious *fīlmfārsī* genre.[55] It also reaffirms the difficult generic placement of the film, its departure from, rather than easy assimilation into, *fīlmfārsī*. Theatrical spectacles are alchemical, rather

Blackface and the Immemorial   « 47 »

than simply representational, condensing "fragments of reality first diluted and disseminated elsewhere."[56] The juxtaposition of racialized gesticulation in *siyāh bāzī* and sexualized female dance in *Night of the Hunchback*'s living room scene sounds a resonance that echoes beyond the short sequence, beyond the film as a whole, just as the "progenitive force" of blackface minstrelsy has always reverberated beyond the proscenium.[57] In citing blackness as androgynous, asexual, neither male nor female, and juxtaposed *against* a hyperbolically feminized, sexualized form of dance, the film's *siyāh bāzī* disorganizes gender coding, as it simultaneously thwarts easy racial intentionality. For in infecting the supposedly whitening female dancer through propinquity, *siyāh bāzī* instead blackens the female and seems to suggest that embedded within this racial mise en abyme, yet simultaneously enveloping and interrupting it, lies sexuality, that primordial model of human organization that is also the basis of life.

In *Night of the Hunchback,* the *siyāh* and dancer share the theatrical stage's substitute in domestic space: the stage of a living room floor. The *siyāh,* failing to sufficiently regale his master with his acrobatic shimmies, twirls, and backbends, inducts the female dancer—formerly, from the audience perspective, slave—to administer amusement. Proximate, but not quite fungible, this sibylline intimacy between the blackface protagonist and female slave aggregates, impelling but overwhelming decryption, positing a mire from which none of these familiar terms would be able to emerge disambiguated. The doubled iconography of the dancing belly and black-painted face creates racialized tension for "the sexual destiny of Being" cited by the navel-womb in motion.[58] The diegetic spatial proximity between *filmfārsī*'s *siyāh* and *raqāṣ* suggests a contiguity that, while perhaps impenetrable to the defunct field of film semiotics, nevertheless compels focus.[59] The *siyāh*'s chameleonic presence prompts questions about how to interpret the unnameable form of socialization, cohesion, and gender dimorphism that a certain projection of blackness sutures, even while it itself remains merely residual, unthought—like the navel, resisting analysis, driving analysis.

The *siyāh* glides between the worlds of the domestic and the public and produces their difference, just as, according to enthusiastic commentators, he enframes and charges community through voicing its unconscious. The *siyāh*'s liminality, boundary crossing, and contiguity to the female dancer in *filmfārsī* activate two historical correlates in Southwestern Asia: the imagined suitability of black slaves as vestibular guardians of gender difference, that is, eunuchism, and relatedly, the conceptual force of slavery in shaping articulations of licit sexuality and marriage. Slavery constitutes a ubiquitous trope for constructions of proper marital relations between men and women in early Islamic jurisprudence. The same term *milk* (dominion) operates, with varying semantic ranges, in the property relation inscribed in the master-slave dynamic, as in the husband–wife, king–subject and God–subject relationships, each shaped by the historical contexts of enslavement.[60] Only the presence of *milk*, ownership, thus hierarchical relation, renders sexuality licit. The ubiquity of references to slavery in legal texts suggests a prevalence whose quantification is otherwise impossible to excavate from traditional documentary evidence. More importantly, this pervasiveness suggests a conceptual power: "Slaves are useful to think with."[61]

Qūzī enslaves the actress on a theater stage, before she appears as a private dancer in a living room parlor. Her adjacency to the *siyāh bāzī* moment conveys a curious relationship between black slavery and the female body whose nearly mythological status is sharpened by the 1964 scene's connection to *The One Thousand and One Nights*. The extended predication constitutive of the *Nights* unfolds upon a phantasmic plane the film medium (and its twenty-first-century conversion into stored data) etherealizes and diffuses. *Night of the Hunchback* reflects the entropic texture of its fraught urtext, that "monument of untidiness."[62] *One Thousand and One Nights'* intractable history continues to haunt scholars with its elusory boundaries; its unknown origins famously begin in translation— purportedly from Persian to Arabic sometime in the eighth century (and peppered with Indian and Greek folkloric spores), before being reanimated by the French antiquarian Antoine Galland in the eighteenth century after his chance encounter with a three-volume Syrian manuscript dated from the mid-fifteenth century. *One Thousand and One Nights'* near pulp status centuries later flattens its convoluted history and weakens the text's call to produce new readings, even though an immense body of scholarship continues to engulf it, expanding and condensing its borders through tortuous textual criticism. So voluminous and brimming with contestation is the question of the compilation's content and authenticity that it is easy to forget that, at its core, *One Thousand and One Nights* is founded upon a simple but powerful taboo on an untranslatable sexual act. Dissolved from the abridged popular memory of *The Arabian Nights*

Blackface and the Immemorial « 49 »

is the narrative context surrounding Shahrazad's marital entrapment in King Shahriyar's grip. Prior to their marriage, Shahriyar, the "Sassanian king" of India and China, watches his wife from over a fence making love to Mas'ūd, her black slave, propelling a structural mise en abyme.[63] The *Arabian Nights'* frame story, one of the most famous narratives in world literature, and its one unchanging feature as well as the basis upon which it is popularly recognized, involves this unforgiveable transgression, raised to infinity.

Nights commentators see adulterous "liaison with a black slave" as the "worst blow" a woman can impart in a patriarchal society that devalues both black people and slaves, and in which male honor, and thereby sociality itself, depends on the protracted manipulation and management of female sexuality.[64] Antiblackness in the *Nights* is treated as a mere appendage to its misogyny and similarly lacks the orientation of clear chronology.[65] A papyrus folio containing the earliest known fragment of the *Nights* dates the frame story back to at least the ninth century, although the roots of the *Nights* in South Asian storytelling suggest a much longer, undatable history that is compounded by a series of conversions and translations.[66] When, centuries later in *filmfārsī*, the female body ciphers the nation, male honor will play a similar role: to guard sexuality, and thereby protect the nation, blackness must be neutered, neutralized, invented through its deanimation.

Feminist scholars categorize the *Nights* as part of the "wiles of women" (*makr-i zanān,* in Persian; *kayd al-nisa'* in Arabic), a capacious genre "centered on the theme of woman's insatiable heterosexuality and guile," and which is far from extinct, as the domestic success of *filmfārsī* in the twentieth century demonstrates.[67] It continues to spool through contemporary cultural production. (The chief architect of Reza Shah's modernized education system in the early twentieth century would champion the tales in *Hizār va yak Shab,* the modern Persian translation of *One Thousand and One Nights,* claiming they contained important, millennia-old moral lessons from the ancient East with continued social relevance.[68]) While now canonical feminist readers of this narrative genre consistently omit blackness as a problem for thought, *filmfārsī* curiously amplifies it, disguising, masking, repurposing the mythical sexual intercourse that gives birth to the omphalic place of the film-dream.

Persistent genital anxiety resurfaces in *filmfārsī* via *siyāh bāzī*'s contiguity to sexually exploitative female dance and involvement in melodramatic prerevolutionary narratives. The *ghulām-i khānahzād,* the cartoonish house-born slave and the caricatural female dancer he inducts onto the living room floor hyperbolize one another, through a sexual contiguity that is neutered, neutralized, compensatory. The prologue of the *Nights,* Shahrazad's emergence as deft storyteller, that aspect of the frame story burned into popular memory, depends upon an initial criminal sexual transaction, the "primordial misdeed" that vitiates the paradisiacal garden—a naturalist trope in Persian medieval poetry through which lovers' unification reflects the perfection of Eden.[69] But opposed to the carnal, ape-like Mas'ud, the impertinent black slave who despoils the sanctity of the garden by thrusting himself down from a tree onto his adulterous queen seductress in the *Nights* frame tale, the *siyāh* in black play exchanges bestial virility for asinine jest. Audiences love him for his shamelessness (*bī-ḥayāyī*), remarks a *siyāh bāzī* actor about the dying theater tradition.[70] But the *siyāh*'s shamelessness is tempered by a metaphysical castration. In a sequel to the 2004 documentary *The Joymakers,* a contemporary *siyāh bāzī* troupe who has traveled to Paris refuses to emend their script to create sexual tension between the *siyāh* and a married female character at a French theater director's request. To depict the *siyāh* as lascivious would damage his reputation before the audience, the troupe leader protests.[71] Although *siyāh bāzī* performances often incorporate the *siyāh*'s subtle flirtations and sweet talking (*shīrīn sukhanī*), scenarios rarely feature the *siyāh* as an object or subject of romance.[72] Rather, he is the frequent go-between, as the plethora of *siyāh bāzī* stock scenarios suggests. (In *Siyāh-i rāstgū* [*The Truthful Black*], or *Hājī du zaneh,* [*The Man with Two Wives*], the *siyāh* accidentally discloses his new master's polygamous lifestyle to the *hājī*'s two wives who live in separate homes. While in *Naṣīb va qismat,* or *Fate and Destiny,* the *siyāh* helps his master's daughter unite with her suitor, spoiling her father's schemes to prevent the relationship.) The *siyāh* is a farcical rather than dramatic character, an object or accessory. His inclusion automatically converts any serious drama or tragic narrative into comedy.[73] In blackface minstrelsy, the "persistent disfiguring of Black humanity," depends upon "the reduction to servile, pathetic, caricatured appendices to *real* (white) life."[74] Transitioning between the worlds of the animate and inanimate, the *siyāh* is also a puppet in *khaymah bāzī,* or puppet play, a tradition evoked by *Night of the Hunchback*'s opening scene of a demonic puppet swinging on a string. For Henri Bergson, comedy illustrates the victory of automatism, of the inanimate, over living vital force, "inert matter dumped down upon living energy."[75] In the twentieth century, consumerism's marketing of the arts saves blackface minstrelsy from impending demise. Blackface migrates to the "expansive flickering reach of celluloid," but also to designs of children's toys, postcards, modular paraphernalia.[76] In *siyāh bāzī,* excessive animation (cartoon, caricatural blackness) becomes indistinguishable from deanimation, from inanimateness. What the *siyāh* and the *Nights'* black slave have in common is an uncanny untimeliness that sets black being adrift.

Rivalry in the City (Riqābat dar Shahr), Farukh Ghafārī's less successful rerelease of his mythologized censored film from 1959 (*South of the City*), recharges *siyāh bāzī* with a more pointed historical valence, while simultaneously revoking the certitude of referentiality. *Rivalry's siyāh bāzī* scene invokes simultaneously the metaphysical and empirical castration connected to the history of enslavement, strengthening *siyāh bāzī's* relation to eunuchism. That is, the scene affirms the sense that *siyāh bāzī* may be, after all, a parody of black eunuch slaves.[77] On a café stage, a theatrical spectacle within a film, two noblemen sit around a table with their guard, musicians playing behind them. One man leans over to the other and stiffly introduces the *siyāh,* a "slave from Basra." Historically, Basra in modern-day Iraq was one of the most important gateways for the slave routes from East Africa to the Persian Gulf. Basra was a major commercial hub, especially after the sixteenth century, and a dominant port in the caravan routes from the Gulf to Iran's interior during the nineteenth and twentieth centuries.[78] The *siyāh* wears a knee-length white robe over clashing multicolored garments: a shirt of circular animal-like prints and loose pants with blocked patchwork of irregular cloth sizes, evoking the dress of the wild man or fool of medieval iconography, as well as the *zanni* or Harlequin, and their mythical prototype, an African slave.[79]

When asked his name, the *siyāh* causes an uproar with his reply: "My name is Leila," he answers, mutilating the syllable order for malapropic effect (*imsh-i bandah,* instead of *ism-i bandah*—my name is). One of the noblemen complains, "Leila is not a man's name." "Well, sir, I'm not a man. They named me Leila," the *siyāh* shrugs, with the same keening, effeminate voice typical of the *siyāh* protagonist. "Hamīnjūrī," he mumbles, meaning "Just like that. They named me." "What is your father's name?," the official continues.

"My father's name is Zahra," the *siyāh* replies. "Zahra? But Zahra is a woman's name." The café audience laughs harder, as the *siyāh* circumvents the question, repeating the response: "They changed our names, just like that," he mumbles, gesturing indifference or ignorance toward the obvious cause of his renaming and suggesting a dance to entertain and distract his interlocutors. He twirls languidly, then more briskly, lifting up his long coat to reveal his hyperbolically swollen bottom as he turns, while his eyes roll back in his head.

The antics douse the profound gravity of the situation that the actors in the scene elicit with their confusion, incredulous that a male can be named Leila (a typically feminine name). "Hamīnjūrī," the *siyāh*'s self-effacing colloquial response, in addition to meaning "Just like that," indicates the irrelevance of the question. It can mean "My name doesn't matter" (my identity doesn't matter), as well as "They [my masters, traders] named me, just like that," giving no thought to the name's propriety. Renaming ritualized slaves' natal alienation and violently ruptured ipseity, transforming human being into owned thing. Names like Mas'ūd (the Queen's slave in *Arabian Nights*) extend from the Arabic root *sa'd* (happiness; felicity), referencing the ancient Near Eastern tradition of naming things as their opposites.[80] *Sa'd* suggests the antinomy of a happy slave, the epistemic impossibility of a joy that is affected for another, as well as a rupture with context that is so total, it can only be captured, as in *fīlmfārsī* typology, by the barren imagination of extremes. That Leila is a female name suggests an even more insidious conversion. Leila could be a eunuch, a possibility the *siyāh*'s typically shrill voice endorses. But the fact that his "father" is named Zahra, also a female name, suggests a cloudier story. His blackface seems to excommunicate the *siyāh* from any intelligible gender code, from being itself. And yet, as his placements in prerevolutionary melodramas suggest, the *siyāh* nevertheless certifies, *affirms,* the very dimorphism from which he is excluded. In logic, the principle of a series, in its exemplarity, withdraws from the meaning it confers.

Traditionally the position of harem guard is synonymous with that of the eunuch, or castrated male in demand for supervising the female harems of rulers and nobility.[81] This model of eunuchism dates back to the mid-Assyrian period (fourteenth to tenth century BCE) and was maintained throughout the entire early history of Persian dynastic rule.[82] Long before its punitive Western association with accusation and fear of black on white rape, castration prepared

Figure 5. Scenes from Ghafārī's *Rivalry in the City.* Top and middle: The *siyāh* performs for a tripled audience. Bottom: Fakhrī Khurvash watching the *siyāh bāzī* performance from behind a curtain.

« 54 »   Blackface and the Immemorial

some captured male slaves in Indian Ocean societies for the guardianship of female sexuality.[83] Famously, for Hortense J. Spillers, the violence of black enslavement absolves gender distinction. The Middle Passage suspends African persons in the "oceanic," an "analogy for undifferentiated identity," where captives were "*nowhere* at all," "thrown in the midst of a figurative darkness that 'exposed' their destinies to unknown course."[84] Like the ungendering transatlantic nowhere of the oceanic poignantly described by Spillers, slaves in Southwest Asia were often marched long distances and castrated in isolated areas both far from where they were captured and far from the Mediterranean, North African, and West Asian slave markets where they would be eventually sold.[85] Slaves were castrated in remote border areas, villages, and islands (Aswan, Asyut, Girga, Tahta, Zawiyat al-Dayr, Abu Tig, Washlu, Hadya, Socotra), with a high mortality rate reflected in their comparatively exorbitant market prices.[86] Eunuchs' high prices reflected not only the inherent and common risk of hemorrhaging to death but the prestigious value of sexual ownership. Against the traditional tendency to represent Indian Ocean domestic slavery as benign, mastery-as-prestige educes its utter perversion.

The importance of gendered spatial bifurcation in Islamicate societies generated a strangely robust demand for eunuchs. Commonly stationed in vestibule-like architectural spaces, the eunuch embodies a paradox: despite his charge with guarding social and sexual order, he is in his very "[person] the embodiment of social and sexual ambiguity."[87] Uprooted from his lifeworld and unable to build new kin ties, the eunuch was the ideal servant—one reason eunuchs were largely employed in positions so close to power in the Byzantine and Ottoman Empires. Scholars of eunuchism interpret this proximity to power as a form of social mobility, going so far as to call eunuchism a "privilege."[88] Such readings ensue naturally from taking account of sociohistorical contexts in which degraded dependency relations and little prospects of socioeconomic transformation were the rule. Exorcizing context, *fīlmfārsī siyāh bāzī de*historizes the eunuch figure as it reassembles the fragments comprising his mythical truth, reinventing him in his originary, sacrificial perversion. The sterile eunuch "[locks] and [unlocks] doors,"[89] guards sexual difference, and thereby, the sexual copulation that prefigures the philosophical copula of all being (the *I am*). So too, the *siyāh* generates life through the death that is his mask.

Elaborate, violent descriptions of castration accentuate already exoticized accounts of Eastern harems in Orientalist writings.[90] To reproduce such descriptions is inevitably to participate in this heritage. Nevertheless, the peculiar correspondence between methods of castration and skin color warrants pause for some contemporary historians of eunuchism. For while Circassian, Turkish, and Slavic slaves were partially castrated (lost only their testicles, and called *spadones*) African slaves commonly had the entirety of their sexual organs amputated, "shaved," made "level with the abdomen."[91] The Christianization of Slavs and Islamicization of Turks in the eleventh century, two peoples with long histories of enslavement in Western Asia, positioned Africans to become an increasingly significant source of eunuchs in later centuries, in the Ottoman Empire as well as under the Qajar dynasty. Castrated so that he might develop no attachments and therefore remain loyal only to his master, the eunuch contorts the relation between sexuality and slavery. If the female body is theoretically enslaveable because vulnerable to parturition, thus of psychological attachment to the master who rapes her and to the economization of her womb, the eunuch is enslaveable because his body is incapable of reproduction and thus presumably of generating kinship; both are objects of reproductive manipulation.[92] Like the genitally obliterated eunuch entrusted with guarding the most integral and enduring forms of social dimorphism (male and female, the sacred and the profane, interior and exterior), the *siyāh* inhabits a vestibular position in *fīlmfārsī*, between male and female, private (*andarūnī*) and public (*bīrūnī*), terrestrial and divine, animate and inanimate. Castration, which is on the order of "lacerations, woundings, fissures, tears, scars, openings, ruptures, lesions, rending, punctures" creates the distance between culture and "cultural *vestibularity*."[93]

Rivalry in the City's *siyāh bāzī* scene cuts to images of the audience laughing or smiling fixedly at Leila, positioning him as a spectacle of hypnotic enjoyment and affirming cinema as the site of *siyāh bāzī*'s formal accession to a new level of reflexivity and recursion. For the diegetic incorporation of the theater audience doubles, triples the spectatorial relation. It also magnifies the *anachronism* inherent in the twisted temporality of *siyāh bāzī* comedy. The film audience watches the theater audience who watches the noblemen-actors enjoy the staged spectacle of *siyāh bāzī*. (Meanwhile, embedded in this watching-having-watched is a nonpresent future watcher; the true meaning of the recorded spectacle is threatening

«56» Blackface and the Immemorial

inasmuch as it never fully arrives.) The *siyāh*, who appears male, professes a female name and incites pandemonium. Never formally central to a *siyāh bāzī* narrative, rarely mentioned in script synopses, the *siyāh* is peripheral and yet strangely pivotal. In his well-known book on theater in Iran, the filmmaker Bahram Beyzai calls him the *mihvar* (axis, pivot), the wellspring of audience entertainment. As in *Night of the Hunchback,* the *siyāh bāzī* scene's brevity in *South of the City* reflects its apparent irrelevance to the overall narrative; a ludic breath between two tired love plots. Instead, the overarching narrative orbits around the main character Efat's honor and chastity, her slow demise and eventual salvation in remarriage and domesticity. And yet, the *siyāh bāzī* scene is also central to Efat's peripety in that it facilitates an inscrutable plot movement that shapes her future as a licit (sexual) being. *Siyāh bāzī* binds with the melodramatic mode of prerevolutionary film to excavate the moral occult from which they both emerge, a form of pantomime whose first impulse is dramatization, a push *"through* manners to deeper sources of being."[94] One could go so far as to suggest *filmfārsī* flourishes from the seed of *siyāh bāzī,* to fulfill in technologically evolved form its original mythological function and destiny.

Improvising from a repository of hyperbole, disguise, cliché, and fiery emotionalism, *filmfārsī* narratives push as their primary intrigues polar oscillations between extreme states of being, virtue and evil, persecution and reward. Mimicking a schematism of declivous female biography popular and typical of *filmfārsī* plots, in *Rivalry in the City* the young widow Efat (Fakhrī Khurvash) accepts the socially degraded position of a café waitress in the economically trodden area of South Tehran after her husband dies. She attracts two frequent customers: Asghar, a thuggish mafia head, and Farhad, an aspiring gentleman—two ambiguously oppositional but idealized forms of traditional masculinity given new visibility in *filmfārsī* and attesting to the power of melodrama to reassemble remnants of cultural myth in the service of nationalist aspiration. *Javānmardī* (literally, young manliness) and *lūtīgarī* (gentlemanliness) are prehistorical masculine ideals desacralized, revived, and vaunted by *filmfārsī* but that might be said to date back to the mythical eras chronicled in medieval Persian epic literature. Firdawsi's eleventh-century *Shahnamah,* or *Book of Kings,* is famously replete with ancient ideals of masculinity embodied in stories of the *javānmard, pahlavān,* and *ayyār.*[95] In a scene from *Rivalry in the City,* the thuggish (*jāhil*) Asghar ominously enters a teahouse where gentlemanly (*lūtī*) Farhad listens to a *naqqāl,* a traditional storyteller, who recites a fifteenth-century poem as the camera scans a large-scale painting of Fereydun on horseback, a mythic king from Iranian prehistory, recognized in the *Shahnameh* for his courage in defeating the evil Zahhak. Coffeehouse recitations of Shi'i and pre-Islamic parables in the Persian tradition of storytelling called *naqqālī* combined and layered multiple temporalities and tragic historical events, contributing to the formation of a "warrior masculinity" among marginalized men.[96] This social formation was accelerated by *fīlmfārsī's* popularization of *lūtīgarī. Fīlmfārsī* elevates domesticity into the ground for the unfolding of "violent tensions in Iranian national life."[97] It also transforms the female body into the symbol of the nation that male heroes must protect from moral devolution, prostitution, and dishonor.

Majīd Muhsinī's *The Chivalrous Rogue (Lāt-i Javānmard),* released in 1958, is thought to have initiated the *lūtī,* or tough-guy film, a quasi subgenre of *fīlmfārsī.* In this earlier film, the cinema star Fakhrī Khurvash plays a role almost identical to her role as Efat in *South of the City,* an abject single woman who attempts suicide by jumping in front of a car in the first minutes of the film. The *javānmard* protagonist Dash Hasan, played by Muhsinī himself, approaches the scene to calm the driver who almost kills her, an outraged black man who flouts the *lūtī* codes by reprimanding instead of charming and comforting the beautiful Khurvash. (As in *Rivalry in the City,* Dash Hasan eventually marries Khurvash, making her a respectable wife.)

In *Rivalry in the City,* Asghar and Farhad signal two moral ends of the continuum of recognized masculinity, from which the *siyāh,* not unlike the dumbfounded, vestibular black background actor in *The Chivalrous Rogue,* plays an imperceptible foil. The first film in Iranian cinematic history to take place among ordinary people in the streets of Tehran, *Rivalry in the City* passes in large part in café settings, of which Ghafārī and his cowriter Jalāl Muqadam had developed intimate quasi-anthropological knowledge after spending three months immersed in the cultural milieu of South Tehran, to the point of befriending local gang leaders who would guard their film crew during shootings (and who would later turn out to be threats once the film was released).[98]

In the moments just before Leila's *siyāh bāzī* begins in *Rivalry in the City,* camera focalizations frame a stage dancer's body parts as

Figure 6. Scenes from Ghafārī's *Rivalry in the City*. Top: Farhad stares down Asghar at the café where performances take place on a stage. Bottom: Asghar stares down Farhad.

she awkwardly adopts unfamiliar Eastern dance styles (see figure 4). (As part of his aforementioned critique of Ghafārī's filmmaking inconsistencies, the critic Amīr Hūshang Kāvūsī complained about the constant "sweeps" [*jārū*] of the female dancer's stature with his faulty "*découpage*," implicating the film in his anti-*fīlmfārsī* invectives.)[99] In this lead-up to the black play scene, shifting gazes between male rivals huddled and drinking at café tables alternate with the close-ups of the female dancer's moving naked belly. The *siyāh bāzī* scene, while narratively sealed off from the female performances that precede and follow the spectacle, occupies the same physical space. In a shot just prior to Leila's appearance on stage, Efat learns that Asghar demands to see her later that night. Efat's anxious frown cuts

Blackface and the Immemorial « 59 »

to a plump cartoon figure on the wall. Devoid of sexual attributes, the crayoned outline wears a neutral smile, rotund belly punctured by a black point in the middle—a navel. The brief, almost unnoticeable cartoon image marks the scene's focal transition to the café stage, where we ultimately encounter Leila the *siyāh*. By dint of a certain narrative dexterity, the interceding cartoon navel scrawled on the wall invokes *Night of the Hunchback*'s dancing belly. Tracing the winding intricacy and abounding repetition effects of this entropic network, *siyāh bāzī*, like the inscrutable glyph of the navel, recurs in Ghafārī's oeuvre, even throughout his biography, wherein, incidentally, he once penned anonymous film critiques for a Tudeh communist newspaper, signing with the alias M. Mubarak, and later, Ghulām Siyāh—"Black Slave."[100]

A medium frontal shot shows Efat absorbed by the *siyāh bāzī* act on stage, before Farhad approaches her (see figure 5). A rupture in the film obstructs the sequence's cohesion, so as the film is currently preserved, the viewer cannot know what links the *siyāh bāzī* scene in the café to the sequence that proceeds immediately in Efat's home, another movement from the public to the private crossed by the sign of blackness, crossed by the sign of the navel. There, Farhad falls in love with her, launching Efat's liberation from café worker (and possibly, prostitute) to a devoted spouse.[101] This transformation is captured by the beginning and final scenes of the film, which frame Efat as a respectable bourgeois housewife in an affluent North Tehran apartment, from which she narrates her scarlet past in flashback to a neighbor. (The ending was an addition to the script, like the incorporation of the female dancer—not included in the earlier, grittier *South of the City* version.) Ghafārī's original *South of the City* is forever lost. It was screened for four days before its negatives were confiscated, returned to the filmmaker three years later mutilated, torn apart, and then pasted together randomly.[102] Unhappy with the reedited and renamed version in 1964, which included new scenes filmed by Amīr Qāsim Shahr, such as the positively inflected ending, Ghafārī even refused designation as the film's director.[103] The artificial lapse in film between the *siyāh bāzī* scene and Efat's new marital destiny in *Rivalry in the City* may be attributed to the derelict conditions under which the new version of the film was reconstructed. The fissure also reactivates the equally elliptical cut to the inexplicable graffitied cartoon navel that initiates Leila's *siyāh bāzī* scene. The navel is itself a kind of cut. The filmic cut is a navel.

« 60 » Blackface and the Immemorial

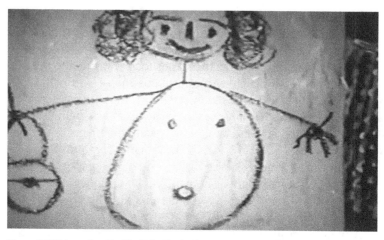

Figure 7. Still from Farukh Ghafārī's *Rivalry in the City*. A stick figure on the wall precedes the staged *siyāh bāzī* performance.

Scholars observe the sexually subversive role that blackface can play in narrative—a break from the prosaic boredom of the heterosexual romantic drama. The black masculinity caricatured in blackface is a riven configuration, in which "the black rapist coexists with the equally resilient image of the black eunuch."[104] In *Black Skin, White Masks*, Frantz Fanon identifies castration as literal and imaginative punishment for the black man's originary guilt. "We know that historically the Negro found guilty of sleeping with a white woman was castrated."[105] Much of Fanon's therapeutic exegesis chronicles the relation between negrophobia, negrophilia, and the black phallus. But if historical details such as "shaved" black eunuchs appear to validate and deepen Fanon's conjectures, it is also the case that the transmedial phenomenon of *siyāh bāzī* suggests that castration, like birth, cannot simply be called historical. For the status of castration, Fanon's originary guilt, is far from mundane, empirical. Similarly, though eunuchism is approached from a historical perspective in contemporary scholarship, eunuchs derive their ultimate roots in a sacred past whose source is impossible to uncover, because bound to secret archaic rituals.[106] Eunuchs were sacralized and chosen to guard the Prophet Muhammad's tomb in mid-twelfth-century Medina, excluded from the earthly realms of natural maturation and procreation, and therefore cast outside of time and history.[107]

Castration, as its sweeping psychoanalytic tropology suggests, cues a mythical, and not merely historical, phenomenon.

Like the mask that disappears the human being through evacuating its distinguishing feature, the face, castration creates a void that resembles death. ("Historically, the [theatrical] mask probably emerged as a death mask.")[108] In *Night of the Hunchback,* the navel consumes the face, functioning like a mask; or rather, the face itself becomes a navel. Trivial, even absurd, the interluding dancing belly sequence in *Night of the Hunchback* and the cartoon navel in *Rivalry in the City* conjure lapses that rescind expectation and disappoint chronology, rearranging symbols and heightening the potency of conflict intrinsic to the filmic shot. As "visual noise" the navel rouses the duplicity of spectacle, activating and interrupting the place of the seer normally obscured by the traditional organization of address and interpellation.[109] Surely erogenous, connected to human origins and reproduction, and thus, the transhistorical control of female bodies, of slaves, Ghafārī's navels articulate fossilized, unintelligible conjunctions between femaleness, enslavement, and blackness. But precisely because it marks an irreversible passage from nonbeing to being, the navel is also the mark of a constitutive enigma, the mark of that which is prior to distinction in general. The navel summons amorphousness and indifference, the origin of being in nondifferentiation; of form in formlessness, originary transitivity that makes difference possible.[110] In being loosened, always already dislodged from context, *siyāh bāzī* is prone to total dissolution.[111]

Black Stasis

A scene from a different kind of black figure in Sāmū'il Khāchikiyān's noiresque *The Midnight Terror* (*Faryād-i nīm-i shab*) sharpens the strange vitality and commodity status of black presence that *siyāh bāzī*'s effluvial history reticulates. After murdering his assistant in the back of a taxi for showing sexual interest in his wife, Zhila, Afshar, a money counterfeiter, lures another man to take his assistant's position. He spots Amir (played by the *filmfārsī* superstar Fardīn) at a bar and invites him to his house the following night after Amir helps Afshar escape a fist fight. When Amir arrives at Afshar's mansion, he is awed by the opulence of the décor, which Afshar informs him Zhila has curated. They banter while Afshar lights Amir's cigarette. Afshar ushers Amir through the rooms, as camera pans absorb the baroque intricacy of the house décor. The frame travels with Afshar until he locates a wine bottle on a bar top, which he uncorks. The density of objects overwhelms the frame. In front of Afshar on the counter sits what appears to be a jug set of elaborate porcelain design; behind him, a sconce, and to the right, a doll-sized figurine resembling a smiling, androgynous, black servant with his or her hand outstretched.

Reminiscent of the black memorabilia and collectibles that circulated during and after the American Reconstruction era, and which both revitalized and mummified the dying practice of blackface minstrelsy at the end of the nineteenth century, the doll in Afshar and Zhila's home is more subtly disfigured than the figurines familiar to Western audiences for promoting racial stereotypes through vivid caricature (hyperbolic smiles, thick red lips, bulging eyes).[112] Peculiarly sized, the doll is too large to be merely decorative, or rather, draws attention to the riddle of the merely ornamental. Its head cocks back and forth from side to side incessantly, as its eyes twitch right and left, a perpetual smile drawn across its face. The black figurine sits cross-legged, wears a white fez, white clothes and a vest, and earrings that look like bells. (In some variations of *siyāh bāzī* where the *siyāh* plays the slave of an Egyptian merchant, the *siyāh* wears a fez instead of a conical hat or crown.)[113]

Film theory has long engaged with mise-en-scène as a locus of enigma, distraction, and subversive communication.[114] For some of the most central theorists of cinema, mise-en-scène—the relation between props, lighting, sets, and actors—even constitutes the very essence of the medium.[115] Afshar and Zhila's labyrinthine living room brims with fanciful oddities and eccentric details: a Greek-style white marble bust, abstract statuettes, picturesque landscape paintings, a library shelf that doubles as a secret door, vases brimming with tall flowers that might be real or fake, defunct furniture. The lurid space intends a wry critique of the petty bourgeoisie. Afshar asks Amir about his fiancée, leading him into a conventional narrative about marriage and financial duty. But the relations of entropy between duplicitous objects overwhelms the men's dialogue, producing effects whose relation to the plot narrative is conspicuous yet unclear. The black doll remains intermittently visible through the interaction between Afshar and Amir that the camera choreographs.

It is not inconsequential that Afshar attributes the household décor to his wife Zhila. The breakdown of gendered spatial distinctions (*andarūnī* and *bīrūnī*—the traditionally partitioned areas of the household) during the post-Qajar period increased female investment in interior design as a form of self-expression.[116] In *Midnight Terror,* Afshar's offhand comment attributes responsibility to Zhila for the presence of the black figurine. The attribution stimulates an analogical force that is propelled by the viewer's new knowledge that the home is tessellated with morbid objects stolen through counterfeit money. Like the figurine, Zhila embodies a certain staticness manifested in her demiurgic femme fatale presence inside the house: "I'm like a bird trapped in a cage of gold," she tells Amir (Fardīn), the first time he refuses her sexual advances. Like the perfidious queens of the *Arabian Nights,* the prototypically wily female figures, Zhila seduces her husband's new assistant from the instant she meets him, urging him to kiss her, touch her, or sleep with her, seductions he virtuously refuses, expressing hidebound commitment to his virginal fiancée.

A musical interlude before Afshar's murder focalizes the significance of the black figurine to Zhila's adulterous inclinations. In glass-heeled slippers and a cheongsam-style dress, Zhila sings amorously to Amir, who looks away distractedly. The camera dances around the characters who move through the dim living room; the black figurine smiles from the background bar top, an extrusion that appears and disappears from the frame. When Zhila threatens Amir as he is about to reject her, the black figurine frames her silhouette on the left, as if charging the depth of field with a demonic force to which her body language gives life: "Stay with me tonight." Amir and Zhila move from the foreground to align with the black figurine's plane of space, which now appears directly between them. A statue of an amorous couple takes up the shaded foreground, before the scene cuts to a thunderbolt. Prerevolutionary Iranian cinema's antirealism achieves a certain thought of the virtual through the most banal articulations of heterosexual intrigue.[117]

Midnight Terror's typical "wiles of woman" narrative communicates a secret with the monument of *The One Thousand and One Nights.* Mirroring the antique clock ticking on the wall across the room, the black figurine timelessly cocks its head and twitches its eyes back and forth, the wily woman's adornment. The androgynous, inanimate black figurine blackens Zhila in the film frame, as

Figure 8. Film stills of Afshar, Zhila, and the black figurine in Sāmū'il Khāchikiyān's *Midnight Terror*.

Mas'ūd blackens Shahriyar's queen in the *Arabian Nights*' frame tale (and Leila the neutered *siyāh* blackens Efat in *Rivalry in the City*). In the cultural lineage of the wiles of women texts, blackness complements and colors female corruption and perversion. But if illicit sexuality is female and blackened, it is equally the case that the black female is absent, "demonic," enfolding within a transaction to which she cannot be present.[118] *Fīlmfārsī*'s absorption of the nebular theatrical *siyāh bāzī* revives the ancient filiation between slavery and the female body. But the black female is nowhere to be seen.

Female Blackface

Film decomposition and the inclement consequences of Pahlavi-era censorship pose perils to recognizing blackface practices in prerevolutionary film, compounding the constitutive ambiguity borne of *siyāh bāzī*'s unverifiable, turgid origins. This is the case especially when black play is not contained as dramatic intradiegetic sequence, like those staged subfabulas in *Night of the Hunchback* and *Rivalry in the City*. On the unstable archival medium of film, facial and object features recoil from recognition, veiled by a penumbral layer of temporal remove. Such is the case with the degraded resolution of the living digitized copies of *Midnight Terror*, in which the black figurine is barely visible. In a film released the year following *Night of the Hunchback*, *siyāh bāzī* black play transforms into full-fledged blackface. Replacing the effeminate blackened male protagonist of *siyāh bāzī*, a masculinized woman in blackface plays a sexually desperate landlord in Riżā Karīmī's *Forced Vacation* (*Murakhaṣī-'i ijbārī*, 1965). While the surviving version of the film makes her blackened face difficult to register, her corpulent silhouette and kerchiefed hair immediately recall the Aunt Jemima stock type character. She plays a needy spinster flattered by a mistaken belief in her tenant's scheming attraction to her.

Compared to the equally decayed version of *Rivalry in the City*, the blackface sequence in *Forced Vacation* is virtually illegible because of its total assimilation into the narrative plot. That is, no longer reflexively contained en abyme as a performance embedded within a performance, *siyāh bāzī* is also no longer recognizable as *siyāh bāzī*. The main character (played by the famous comedian Humāyūn) professes his love to the female landlord in blackface in order to scheme money to save himself from eviction and to pay for a vacation with his partner that the pair cannot otherwise afford. In a conversation in her living room intended as comedic exchange, the landlord (who remains nameless in the film) swoons at Humāyūn's marriage proposal, insisting on kisses that Humāyūn reluctantly offers to prove his sincerity, cringing in direct asides to the spectator. While she leaves the room to retrieve the money he has requested, Humāyūn wonders, in an even more virulent aside, "which coal mine to visit for the honeymoon." When the landlord returns to the frame, a blurry photograph of an African chieftain with a large headdress hangs on the wall and intervenes between the

Figure 9. Female blackface in Rizā Karīmī's *Forced Vacation* (*Murakhaṣī-'i ijbārī*). Hanging on the wall behind Humāyūn and the female landlord in blackface, a painting of an African chieftain, the landlord's "grandfather."

two characters facing each other in profile. "Take good care of it," she urges Humāyūn, referring to her car. "This is the only keepsake I have from my grandfather," she continues, pointing to the photograph. The image of the African chieftain, while barely visible, destabilizes the geographical closure assumed by the Persian-language film, but also ties the blackface gesture to a blackness that is primitive, static. Unlike *Rivalry in the City*'s effeminate slave from Basra or *Night of the Hunchback*'s house-born slave, the *female* blackface character curiously detaches the blackface tradition from any explicit relation to the history of enslavement. (That she is a landlord, rather than a subservient figure, evokes the prevalent "condescending white convention" of characterizing black matriarchal figures with false power.)[119]

Film's resistance to avowing the black female slave figure—and her sexually exploited position—reinforces the antimimetic force of *siyāh bāzī*. Given that, at times, more African women were enslaved than men and exported to Western Asia during the slave trades from Africa to the Arabian Peninsula and Persian Gulf, a faithful historical representation of slavery might take account of this gendered discrepancy.[120] Instead, *siyāh bāzī* dissolves femaleness into maleness, maleness into femaleness, wreaks havoc on gender organization. When, on the rare occasion, *fīlmfārsī* attempts to display the black female body, unlike the typically sexualized Persian *raqāṣ* protagonist, she is not legible as normatively female within the confines of *fīlmfārsī*'s narrative framework, but rather, caricaturized. In *Forced Vacation*, the excessive corporeality of the matriarchal black body conceals her gross abjection from the femininity otherwise enshrined by the narrative's love interest, played by Pūrī Banāyī, another famous *fīlmfārsī* star. Her corpulence also evokes the nurturing, tutelary role of black female slaves and servants as child rearers and surrogate wives. Humāyūn's repulsion, focalized upon the landlord's blackness, which he interprets as ugliness, is intended to generate humor. The reduction of her being to comedy, to cliché, suggests the disavowal of the black female's reproductive capacities as constitutive of the new, normative domestic order, the new, modern, Aryan nation.[121] In both the prerevolutionary Iranian films *Destiny* (*Sarnivisht*, 1977) and *Concubine* (*Kanīz*, 1974) black female characters appear as household servants, and in *Destiny,* the actor Humāyūn plays a cook who sexually harasses the black female housemaid, without the abuse materializing as remarkable, let alone morally apprehensible, plot moments in the film. In *Forced Vacation,* female blackface is illegible, unreadable. Its indecipherability instead sheds light on a gendered order made possible through racial anarchy, and whose spectacle cinematic *siyāh bāzī* both fabulizes and habituates.

Perceptions of *siyāh bāzī* today are divided along ideological lines clothed by unstable logics that attest to the wide-ranging meanings the ritual has accrued over time. Contemporary reactions to *siyāh bāzī* are incensed, whether as protest, or protest *to* protest, spurred for example, by the moral indignation and moral defense surrounding Bahram Beyzai's 2016 Northern California staging of *siyāh bāzī* in his play *Tarabnāmah,* and more recently, in an official decision to ban the *siyāh bāzī* practice of Hājī Fīrūz during the 2021 Persian New Year in Tehran, discussed in the concluding chapter.[122] Contemporary discourse on *siyāh bāzī* signals an anxiety about propriety and stability of perspective that is directly linked to the historical constitution of racial blackness and its relation to global African enslavement. The defensive narrative proclaiming *siyāh bāzī*'s racial innocence denies any antiblack connotations to the practice. In the name of historical specificity, cultural conservatives instead submerge the tradition of the Persian black play in ancient myth, thus protecting it from the history of African enslavement in the Indian Ocean.

But cinema exposes *siyāh bāzī*'s specificity to a radical decontextualization, and thus to a generalization that is itself already inherent in *siyāh bāzī*. (From *takht-i hawẓī* to *pīshpardah,* on the plank plays to precurtain acts, itinerant movement, not immobility characterizes *siyāh bāzī*'s "origin" in the modular.) Meanwhile, by disengaging from the common *siyāh bāzī* preference for a male protagonist in black makeup and instead substituting a female for the *siyāh,* the blackface scene in *Forced Vacation* disrupts the ruse of *siyāh bāzī's* naturalized mythology. The blackface female landlord in *Forced Vacation* is a racial caricature, repeating *siyāh bāzī* in an unambiguously blackface minstrel mode. The blackface female protagonist thus directly translates *siyāh bāzī* into racist blackface minstrelsy. And because she does so within the framework of a Persian-language film, she simultaneously translates racist blackface minstrelsy into *siyāh bāzī,* unhinging distinctions, breaking with the protective cover of context.

Cinematic blackface minstrelsy was already a staple of American cinema when *Forced Vacation* was produced, and for that matter, when *Rivalry in the City* and *Night of the Hunchback* were released. One can only take for granted the explicit or unconscious adoption and influence of antiblack American Hollywood tropes on small national cinemas like Iran's, where Hollywood undoubtedly expressed a decidable force. Sāmū'il Khāchikiyān's penchant for Hollywood genres like the thriller and noir, while enshrining him as a popular filmmaker purportedly capable of instigating traffic jams (his *Midnight Terror* was the highest grossing film of the year), also positioned him for attack from critics who expected a more authentically Iranian cinema.[123] The landlord's kerchiefed hair and grotesque figure in *Forced Vacation* evoke the relationship between blackface minstrelsy and the mass commodification of national food brands, while the black figurine in *Midnight Terror* summons the object, commodity status of the black body in modernity, in particular in post-Reconstruction American consumerist culture. The significance of racialized black stereotypes in American advertising, which had by the 1950s attained a global force, cannot be denied its undoubtedly potent influence on the assimilation of improvisatory *siyāh bāzī* to film.

As with the films discussed in this chapter, the blackface scene in *Forced Vacation* is superficial, peripheral to the main intrigue. The film revolves around the comedian Humāyūn and his business partner's accidental involvement in the life of a female singer (played by the beautiful Banāyī) whom they meet on the road. Having fallen in love with the singer, Humāyūn's partner becomes involved with saving Banāyī from her aunt's witchcraft and design on her inheritance (a paradigmatic parallel wiles of women subplot). The blackface landlord disappears after the early marriage proposal scene in the film, to reappear in the final scene, materializing, as only film

Blackface and the Immemorial « 69 »

can make her do, out of thin air. As Humāyūn, his partner, and their female companions drive off into the horizon, having successfully diverted the wicked aunt's plan for the singer's arranged marriage, the betrayed blackface female landlord inexplicably appears in the back of their car, interrupting the foursome's merry ending with her jealous wrath.

The historical proximity of the filmic *siyāh bāzī* and blackface scenes in *Night of the Hunchback* (1964), *Rivalry in the City* (1964) and in *Forced Vacation* (1965), and the analogous ways in which they produce comedic relief undermine the possibility of an identifiable movement from nonracial *siyāh bāzī* to racial blackface. If such a transition exists, a moment in time when nonracial *siyāh bāzī* "becomes" racial blackface, obviously it cannot be located in the space of a single date. But nor, I have been suggesting, can it simply be located in general, spatialized and stabilized along a chronological line or causal chain. For the very distinction between racial and nonracial *siyāh bāzī* is, finally, made retroactively untenable by its transition to film. On the one hand, by virtue of its form, cinema, and *fīlmfārsī's* unhinged découpage in particular, brings out an original ungroundedness of *siyāh bāzī*. The *siyāh* is a theatergram, modular, movable, metabolic. *Fīlmfārsī* splits, splices, punctures, and affixes a figure that is always already castrated, unmoored from being, alienated from the security of context. The black eunuch, like the hypersexualized black slave, lacks context, history, metaphysical (chronological) time. The black mask, like the time of the laughter it conspires to evoke, is not *of* chronology. The comedy of *siyāh bāzī* is thus exemplary of its temporal anarchy, and it is the comedy of *siyāh bāzī* that *fīlmfārsī* spectacularizes, transforms into a mirror turned toward a future (that is internal to it). Jokes thwart, dislocate the substance of that which they express. In *taqlīd*, comedic improvisatory theater, there is "no border between laughter and provoking laughter."[124] *Siyāh bāzī's* humor depends upon the very laughter that displaces it, repeats it by altering it, and thereby renders it (psychically) real. Lacking physiological explanation, laughter reveals an amassed energy known only through its enigmatic release, the index of schismogenic being.[125] Placed a year apart, the distinction between Persian black *play* (*siyāh bāzī*) and black*face* cannot be adjudicated, managed, analyzed, contained.

On the other hand, in taking historical influence as a point of departure, one could suggest that the entire tradition of Hollywood, and thus American blackface minstrelsy, "derives," or at the very least, has itself been influenced by older traditions like Persian *siyāh bāzī*. One could deduce this from the veering narratives that suggest both *siyāh bāzī* and blackface minstrelsy originate in the Italian tradition of commedia dell'arte, which itself is thought to have borrowed from Near Eastern traditions connecting to histories of African enslavement. The "black-masked comic figure" and "international icon" was "one powerful agent of cultural transmission in emergent formations of race."[126] (Recall, too, the millennium-old but ahistorical, that is, mythic, originarily contaminated oral tradition that fixes the virile black slave jumping from a tree in *Arabian Nights*.)[127]

To be clear, I am not proposing the indefensible, indeed unverifiable, empirical claim that blackface minstrelsy originates in a supposedly older, undocumented tradition of Persian black play. I have been suggesting instead that cinematic *siyāh bāzī*'s formal elements dislocate any such pursuit of univocal origin. Instead, enveloped by the chiasmic figure of the navel, cinematic *siyāh bāzī* evokes a mode of temporality, of the *immemorial,* that the dizzyingly ubiquitous, historically differentiated global imagination of blackness imposes upon thought. In dislodging and proliferating its contexts, in de-contextualizing the practice of *siyāh bāzī,* cinema delivers *siyāh bāzī* back to its own abyssal source, the grounded void of the navel, the omphalic place of a tie to what drives knowledge. Yet *siyāh bāzī* will not itself be known.

Immediately following the *siyāh bāzī* sequence in *Night of the Hunchback,* the troupe gathers in the kitchen to divide the money earned from their hosts for the performance. Foregrounded left, the blackface character in the film de-wigs the dancing navel face. As he peels the shaggy black prop off the inverted pot on which it is fitted, a black actor who plays a tuxedoed servant in the film emerges from behind the performer and walks left to right across the background. He looks briefly toward the camera and smiles as he drifts out of the frame, suspending any possible understanding of how his presence connects or responds to the fraudulent blackness of the blackface scene. A black "extra" in the film, in other words, reaffirms the purely theatrical, nonmimetic nature of *siyāh bāzī* blackness. (Thus, for Gharībpūr, *siyāh bāzī* is very much "*unlike* the reality" of the master-slave relation.)[128] The black extra appears in a frame with the demasked *siyāh,* leaving in the brief wake of these juxtaposed char-

Blackface and the Immemorial « 71 »

acters a question about the sense of a blackness whose truth could be apprehended, seized, represented. This fortuitous synchronicity also poses a broader existential question about the *drive* of blackface. What exactly is it that blackface practices seek to capture?

In Persian, *taqlīd* names the tradition of improvisatory theater, of which *siyāh bāzī* forms merely one genre. *Taqlīd* also means "imitation," mimesis, and is imbued with negative connotation.[129] In his famous tirade against mimesis in *The Republic,* Plato distinguishes between two principles of the human self, a lower principle that is prone to recollection, lament, feeling, and that presents "a great variety of materials for imitation" on the one hand, and another substratum, a "wise and calm temperament, being nearly equable," which is "*not easy to imitate* or to appreciate when imitated."[130] While the passage may be interpreted as a repetition of the familiarly facile, even racialized opposition between reason and emotion,[131] the Platonic attack on theater nevertheless captures something of the doubleness that is characteristic of phenomenological experience. A "variety of materials for imitation" is expressed through "temperate" sameness, just as egoic identity, a sum of identifications, projections, and fantasies, inhabits the finitude of a single, mortal body—a finite self inspirited with infinitude.

Theater, mimicry, and imitation are frightful because they tap into a dubious heterogeneity of the human available to repetition and automation; theater reveals fleshliness through form, variety through sameness. Musing on the structural mise en abyme of the *Arabian Nights,* and in particular upon the "disturbing" night in which all the nights are reflected back to the frame tale, Jorge Luis Borges wonders if "the reader clearly grasp[s] the vast possibility of this interpolation." Perhaps such "inversions suggest that if the characters of a fictional work can be readers or spectators, we, its readers or spectators, can be fictitious."[132] The indulgent emotionalism and litany of clichés delegated prerevolutionary Iranian cinema to the dregs of film criticism. *Fīlmfārsī* is considered one of the basest of twentieth-century cultural forms, just as suspect improvisatory theater once earned the derision of ancient philosophers. For *filmfārsī,* the cinema of clichés, repeats what is revealed by the history of gesture itself: that part of the human that is neither true nor false, authentic nor inauthentic, but imitable, iterable, typological, anachronistic. The "original navel" of the dream offers this final, impossible lesson, the discovery of human as flesh: "You are this—You are

« 72 »   Blackface and the Immemorial

this, which is so far from you, this which is the ultimate formlessness."[133] Flesh is the formlessness that inheres in form. But form is the fleshliness that inheres in the human, and renders difficult to distinguish the singular from the generalizable, the iterable and repeatable. The antiblackness of blackface reduces blackness to flesh and form, projects this generalized truth, that the human *is* flesh and form, onto a racialized, exceptionalized condition. Blackface is the expression of a generalized anxiety about fleshly being, fleshly form, form as flesh. "[We] all enter the Black body," writes Dionne Brand, "take part in its mask."[134]

Siyāh bāzī en abyme describes its self-altering embeddedness in film. It also continues to pose the question of why blackface should signify this fundamental aspect of the human prone to emotivity, affection, gesture, but also and thereby, persona, personhood, ego, identity. Why does blackface so aptly appear to reveal this curiously fraudulent, and yet apparently necessary, dimension of human being known as identity—this many and varied dimension of the human that comedy domesticates and contains under the spell of the trivial, the cliché? *Siyāh bāzī* mocks blackness, addresses blackness as a mode of mockery. But in doing so, it also seems to show that blackness both consolidates and disrupts, reveals and conceals the already disguised doubleness of human being, exemplarily worked over by the most normative and seemingly natural of human orderings: gender and sexuality, race and nationality.[135] Identity is the morphing sign of an immemorial splitting. Thus *siyāh bāzī* recurs like a self-repeating scar, like the omphalic flesh that "remains forever knotted, right on the body."[136] Beyond and before history, at the place of the navel.

« 2 »

Zār and the Anxieties of the Iranian New Wave

Thrashing waves disrupt a calm sea in the first few seconds of Nāṣir Taqvā'ī's' *Wind of Jin* (*Bād-i Jin,* 1969),* an enigmatic twenty-minute black-and-white ethnographic documentary shot on 16 mm that chronicles a *zār* spirit ritual in the Persian Gulf harbor of Bandar Lingih. The sound of the swells continues to rise and fall: "Man is tolerant because of the pain he endures. But when pain becomes unbearable, the blacks of the South perform *zār,*" narrates the poet Ahmad Shāmlū in a Persian voiceover whose lyricism this English translation fails to achieve. Taqvā'ī's initial choice of medium shot and slightly high angle intensifies the disorienting pull of tall waves spraying the camera lens, even though the shot remains constant, anchored to the tenor of the poet's somber voice.

The tropical traction of the sea, as many have suggested, bears a particular weight in the black filmic imagination, intimating African peoples' violently forced dispersions throughout the world since antiquity.[1] Caused by winds blowing over the water's surface, the initial waves in *Wind of Jin* thus embed layers of the film's theme in its very first shot: the "infidel winds" that menace the *ahl-i havā* or "wind afflicted" and spoil the landscape, their connection to the history of African enslavement in the Indian Ocean, and the relationship between a burgeoning anthropology and modernist form.[2] The superimposition of Shāmlū's verse onto the ethnographic images imbues these tropes—the psycho-terrestrial trauma of slavery allegorized in the image of waves, the afflicting winds—with a softly historical connection incommensurable with historiographic closure, just as it complicates the traditional ethnographic procedure, appearing to

---

*While "The Jin Wind" would be a more accurate translation of *Bad-i Jin*, I have opted for the more common English version of the film title.

« 73 »

« 74 »   *Zār* and the Anxieties of the Iranian New Wave

fulfill instead the strange aim of an experimental documentary that is also an alternative, if warped and benighted history telling. Dilating Taqvā'ī's film in context thus reveals a complex of divergent, dizzying levels of meanings and tensions.

Through a reading of the film that magnetizes contiguous artifacts and trends, in this chapter I explore *Wind of Jin*'s aesthetic procedures for pursuing what has been canonized as a modernist form: the Iranian New Wave film.[3] As an ensemble of stylistic strategies oriented primarily toward the refusal of *filmfārsī* hyperbolism—and the broader horizon of ersatz modernity inflecting it—the Iranian New Wave describes a reactive, renewed drive toward the real. The sudden proliferation of ethnographic documentary in the 1960s fueled the inspiration, and "matured" the cinematic language ultimately wielded by the New Wave in service of a critique of accelerated modernization.[4] Indeed, the very documentary gesture at the heart of ethnographic film is itself already an expression of dissatisfaction with modernity that will be more forcefully, if equally indirectly, carried forward by modernist cinema.

Wind of Jin's exemplarity within this configuration of a new cinematographic consciousness pivots around a question about the aesthetic residues of historicity. What are the ethical implications of the aesthetic when its historical subject is slavery? Contemplating the spirit ritual *zār* through one filmmaker's work suggests not only that information about Indian Ocean slavery, like all historical truth, is amenable to distortion, abstraction, errancy, and drift, but that historical fact is at its origin conditioned by the possibility of its own corruption, that at the heart of truth, is an ineradicable inclination toward the false. In the wake of this fundamental duplicity, we are left with the difficulty of proper judgments. Consequently, Iranian cinema of the 1960s and 1970s is at pains to show not only the aggressive turbulences of a Janus-faced modernity, as it has so often been claimed, but too, a more basic, primordial anxiety that ensues in the face of an ever-sought-for, ever-receding real.

Iranian Ethnographic Film

Although its inspiration from Italian neorealism, and to a lesser extent, the French New Wave, receive emphasis in film studies of the Iranian *Mawj-i naw,* it is no exaggeration to state that the New Wave movement developed out of and concomitantly with an ethnographic

Zār and the Anxieties of the Iranian New Wave « 75 »

impulse that was particular to the Iranian intellectual environment of the early to mid-twentieth century. While informative scholars of Iranian film intuit the magnitude of such impulses, the various but often stringently formalist, encyclopedic, or ideological approaches to the study of Iranian film have so far prevented a deeper understanding of the possible meanings of this anthropological impulse. In one of the most magisterial tomes on the history of Iranian cinema, Jamāl Umīd's *Tārīkh-i sīnamā-yi Īrān,* there is barely mention of a single ethnographic film. On the other hand, some commentators frequently cite Furūgh Farukhzād's *The House Is Black (Khānah siyāh ast,* 1962), essentially an ethnographic documentary of a small leper colony in northern Iran, as a seminal New Wave film.[5]

One film scholar qualifies that most midcentury ethnographic sketches did not quite adhere to the strictures of ethnographic documentary.[6] Hamid Naficy similarly coins the term "ethnographic-lite" to signal the fact that although many of the period's films communicated with ethnographic themes, none of the filmmakers attached to the moniker were seriously affiliated with a coherent and institutionalized anthropology. Poetic realism, a favored term among critics for describing works such as Farukhzād's, captures this detachment from scientificity which Iranian ethnographic films never claimed with any earnestness in the first place.[7] Such detachment does not, however, fully disavow the strange effects of even scientificity's aesthetically charged emulation. Indeed, the commitment to observational realism, a constitutive feature of the ethnographic, would become an integral aspect of the germinating New Wave.

The unexplored bond between ethnographic film and literature in the mid-twentieth century leaves dormant an entire aesthetic genealogy that would clarify an understanding of Iranian modernity as deeply anthropological. Anthropology, as we know, is perennially troubled by its history of obscuring a foundational dissymmetry that is its condition of possibility, beholden to naturalized assumptions about the human that inform the history of the concept of race. Equally importantly, here the temporal modernity of ethnographic filmmaking suggests a sensitization to both the sociopolitical *and* philosophical dimensions of modernity connected to loss. Throughout the midcentury Global South, anti-imperialist, anticolonial, generally socialist-oriented, and sometimes religiously charged politics and aesthetics sought ways to mourn the loss of a disintegrating world while molding loss into the locus of a new political subjectivity. It is no coincidence that Karbala, the martyrdom of Imam Husayn, becomes a renewed source of coping with modernity in the works of some of the most influential twentieth-century thinkers, the conceptual architects of the Iranian Revolution (see chapter 3). Nor that the "committed art" (*hunar-i muti'ahid*) of the secular intelligentsia articulates an oppositional politics through "mystical glorification of the masses."[8] In a different way, ethnographic film reconciles the psychic disorientations that ensue from world-disappearance, staging this disappearance by representing the vanishing and shoring up the subject that builds its very raison-d'être upon this world-disintegration. But the unnavigable mire that is continually self-differing difference evades strategies for recalibration, producing in its wake the unabating repetition compulsions of the ethnographic age.

Prosaically, mid-twentieth-century Iranian ethnographic filmmaking grows out of the early years of the Cold War.[9] Between 1945 and 1950, British, Russian, and American embassies all vied to distribute political propaganda through mobile cinema units, leaving in their wake a "nucleus" of directors whose work would later flourish under patronage of the newly developed Ministry of Culture and Arts and National Radio and Television under Muhamad Reza Shah Pahlavi's political reign.[10] Such varicose, politically ambiguous connections attest to the fraught relation between the institutional support for "salvage ethnography" (a form of cultural preservation for indigenous forms of life deemed to be decaying in the throes of modernization), anticommunist sentiment, and the ongoing project of constructing an Iranian nationalism that would buttress the country's international image to stimulate foreign investment and tourism, while curtaining dire internal structural inequalities and mitigating through myriad distractions the unextraordinary durability of royal corruption.[11] For example, measures taken to bolster institutional anthropology in the twentieth century forcefully belied ongoing efforts to homogenize different ethnic tribes and other forms of social, cultural, and linguistic fragmentation into a unified Persian identity that would surrender to administrative hold.[12] (As I show through the postrevolutionary film *Bashu, the Little Stranger* in chapter 4, annihilation and assimilation are two dimensions of the same multicultural habit.)

Ethnography and modernist aesthetics are not only reconcilable but coconstitutive—as we know, surrealism and ethnography have

Zār and the Anxieties of the Iranian New Wave

Figure 10. Film still from the opening of Nāṣir Taqvā'ī's *Wind of Jin* (*Bād-i Jin*, 1969).

historically shared common roots.[13] The figure of the primitive incarnates or assuages modern alienation, denoting the tabula rasa of childhood, premodern intimacy with nature, innocence from mass industrialized culture, and an altered relation to pain.[14] In mid-twentieth-century Persian cultural production, this role is often played by the indigent rural other, whom the urban intellectual, writer, or filmmaker feels tasked with saving from the destructions of modernity through a pull into representation. In Nāṣir Taqvā'ī's films, and in the literary works by Ghulām Ḥusayn Sā'idī upon which they are based, however, the rural is blackened, conflated with the figure of the black slave, and positioned to connote beyond the empiricism of the merely economical or political through a suffusion of realism that is, counterintuitively, also a poetics of abstraction.[15]

"The winds decimated Lingih," announces Shāmlū at the opening of *Wind of Jin*. The figure of the black slave becomes responsible for contamination of the idyllic premodern world he is also charged with embodying, freezing, cutting off from any possible relation to a past or future, dreaming survivor of a global destruction that happens elsewhere. It is no contradiction that black *zār* practitioners enter the ethnographic scene through both the guise of authenticity and the artifice that will destroy it, for blackness is the inhabitation of projected contradictions. The black slave is anthropologized as the most primitive, the most original, the most pure, and at the same time, the most impure, the most corrupting, corrosive force. Through film, this confused causality surfaces as anxiety, an ambivalence toward modernity that exceeds historical eventuality.

Zār and the Long Take

Zār, the assemblage of beliefs in rambunctious and malignant spirits that penetrate the body and psyche, also names the associated rituals intended to "shake the spirits from the skeleton."[16] Because variations on *zār* are practiced primarily among descendants of enslaved Africans in Southwest Asia and North Africa, this ritual is thought to constitute a trace of Indian Ocean and trans-Saharan slavery, for which legible archival documentation is dispersed and often absent, especially for the premodern period. However, as I will suggest later in the chapter, *zār*'s historical itinerary, as well as its status as "trace," is anything but straightforward. Consisting of heterogeneous spirit cosmologies, the winds of *zār* induce myriad ailments that vary in intensity, from headaches, apathy, withdrawal, muteness, and paralysis, to infertility, hysteria, dissociation, and suicidal ideation. (*Zār*'s entry as a "culture-bound syndrome" in the DSM suggests the medicalization of culture as an inevitable outcome of colonial modernity.)[17]

Scholarship has traditionally focused on the predominantly female character of *zār*, but *zār* is indiscriminate, capable of affecting anyone. Its relief consists in the establishment of a lifelong relation with the particular afflicting spirit wind, and takes place in the context of a ceremony involving other members of a *zār* community previously affected by a wind, known as the *ahl-i havā* (people of the wind), or *zārīs*, and organized by a *zār* leader (*māmā* or *bābā zār*). While *zār* ceremonies differ across regions, and even from one neighborhood to another, its central component entails entry into what can only be translated as a kind of trance, accompanied by rhythmic music, through which a wind "descends," that is, makes its identity known.

The identity of name attributed to the rituals, the beliefs, and the possession itself suggests an indistinction between cause and effect.[18] Thus, the "dance is both the effect of the possession and the means of release from it."[19] Unlike other spirits in possession cosmologies, like the unambiguously dangerous Ethiopian *buda* and *ganyen* spirits that must be exorcised, the *zār*, while also dangerous, is open to negotiation, must even take responsibility for healing the very body that it pains.[20] The wind spirit is identified through diverse rituals and preparatory methods, for example, a period of total seclusion (*hijāb*); a protective white cloth that deflects the gaze; ointments

Zār and the Anxieties of the Iranian New Wave   « 79 »

or potions consisting of spices, syrups, and rose water; and finally, kinesis, the perpendicular, frenetic head movements and convulsive body choreography that is activated by singular rhythms. In dance, the identity of person and *zār* spirit merge.[21]

At the level of its form, Taqvāʾīʾs film is divided by what appears as a desire for neutral documentation of *zār* on the one hand, and on the other, an internal resistance to the very possibility of its representation. As a mode of trance, after all, *zār* describes a loss of consciousness and is therefore fundamentally unavailable to perception. One does not perceive one's own loss of consciousness, let alone another's. But neither is it at all evident that consciousness can be, in general, the object of perception, if what we understand by consciousness includes the possibility of perception itself. The visual description of the *zār* ceremony occupies the focal point of *Wind of Jin* and appears in the second half, taking on the architectonic posture of paradigmatic ethnographic documentary: the long take. Both a pillar of ethnographic film and a central stylistic feature of the Iranian New Wave, the long take is also "the schematic and primordial element of cinema."[22] Faith in the long take expresses a commitment to reality as fundamentally continuous, a commitment to reality as fundamentally available, and available only through the uninterrupted, pristine image—analogue for pure perception. The long take's supposed fidelity to reality underlies its centrality to a certain tradition of film theory extended and elaborated by Iranian filmmakers and critics like Feraydūn Rahnamā, who commissioned Taqvāʾīʾs work.[23] It is the desire for the real as a rebellion against modernity's spectacularized pageantry (so exorbitantly channeled by *fīlmfārsī*) that the New Wave shares with its ethnographic supplement and its neorealist inheritance. The long take, and by extension, Iranian ethnographic filmmaking, produces syntax for a critique of modernity that will be recombined and articulated by the New Wave. At the same time, as an expression of the primordial, *zār* furnishes another set of critical resources that stall and disrupt the seamless operation of this same critique, stymieing the observational impulse of the long take. *Zār* thwarts the confidence in reality assumed by the technological force attempting to seize it.

For, if *Wind of Jin* appears caught up in its own illusions of recordability, upon closer scrutiny, strict filmic continuity never materializes, suggesting a reluctant disbelief in neutral archiving and expressing a position that defines a central feature of geographically

« 80 »   *Zār and the Anxieties of the Iranian New Wave*

disparate modernisms, the desire to "merge with the other."[24] This impulse finds expression in Taqvā'ī's own remarks about his strange experiences in Bandar Lingih, his release of conviction in the transmission of verisimilitude while filming there: "In *Wind of Jin* I let go of absolute objectivity."[25] Thus, *Wind of Jin* marks a break with the stylistic tendencies of 1960s statist and propaganda documentary filmmaking, and in particular, its proclivities for linear narrative and monologic narration.[26] The film, as one critic noted at the time (attributing a negative value judgment) elicits attention to its own strange relation, or irreverence for traditional narrative temporality, the hallmark of derealization so central to modernist style.[27] Moreover, the audiovisual compilation of nebulous messages that precede the second, more stationary half of the film disquiet expectations for ethnographic precision. This is true especially because of the degraded quality of the film's preservation, which deprives images of sharpness and shape. The grainy shot of ships docked ashore builds the theme of maritimity incited by the initial scene of waves, and the various connections to esotericism, the inhuman, and violence it conjures: "the curses of the jin winds in the south are many," Shāmlū narrates as the camera draws in focus on three dhows, while waves slap against the dock. The whistle of wind and waves infiltrates a break in the voiceover. A moribund spectrality haunts the film from start to finish. Music punctuates its points of intensification. The melancholic drawl of a folk a cappella accompanies a two-minute montage following a woman kneeling before a tombstone. The camera chooses arbitrary objects on which to rest: a ceramic pot, the open windows of an abandoned mosque, a minaret, a close-up of a crack on the wall. Against *filmfārsī*'s Bollywood-like "cinema of interruptions," New Wave filmmakers tended toward lyrical continuity, eschewing the erraticism of lawless montage in favor of leveled editing.[28] At the same time, this new, alternative cinema does not entirely abandon montage, but rather wields it toward a new disclosure. For all these blank gaps, intervals imperceptibly suturing one image to its successor, subtly gesture toward a field before or beyond vision that is the ground of *zār* itself. *Zār* gives us to wonder whether the common sense that entrusts the image with capacity to represent the real survives the inevitable and relentless passing of the image. For regardless of its languor or speed, its honesty or dissemblance, the image always passes.

Wind of Jin's piecemeal transition to the *zār* ritual occurs through

Zār and the Anxieties of the Iranian New Wave   « 81 »

a simple drumbeat, as film shots remain oriented toward exteriors. Tracking a veiled figure through a sandy landscape, the camera rests on a disfigured tree, bent, as if due to the wind, at an extreme angle: "This tree at the corner of the night is a jin hive," recites Shāmlū. Spirit winds are attracted to trees, and "their world intersects with ours in deserted places, dark areas, doorways, staircases . . . water sources . . . cemeteries," anthropologists inform us.[29] The image cuts to a brick fortress in the distance and the drum's rhythm fades into whistling wind. The camera settles on an extreme long shot of a dome structure. *Zār* houses, called *bayt al-ciddah* (house of instruments) in some Persian Gulf regions, can be visible from far distances, enclosed by sacred perimeters, "time and energy accumulated and stored."[30] Panning right toward a shadow, the frame concludes its movement with a close-up of a wall. Shāmlū ends his prelude. The camera's subtle actions phantasmatically suggest traversal of time and space, translating exteriors into interiors and recapitulating the prototext's findings: that the *ahl-i havā* imagine winds to occupy the most interior corridors of the human body. Too, that like the camera's shapeshifting point of view, *zār* challenges the very idea of corporeal boundary. The drumming picks up again as the camera slowly tilts down to reveal the heads of a group of seated women veiled in black and clapping in time to the rhythm. The frame stabilizes in this downward tilt, contributing to the slightly voyeuristic, disorienting quality of the scene. "*Zār* participants and musicians must be on the same level as the instruments, a powerful symbolism of equality and respect," according to *zār*'s contemporary ethnographers.[31]

Though Nāṣir Taqvā'ī made at least thirteen documentaries throughout his early career, including a second, more realist ethnographic documentary about *zār*, *Music of the South: Zār* (*Mūsiqī-'i Jūnūb: Zār*) discussed below, *Wind of Jin* is worth singling out. First, it foregrounds the anthropological unconscious—as well as the *drive for reality*—sustaining the robust connection between ethnographic filmmaking and the Iranian New Wave, a connection whose implications I draw out further below when I turn to his first feature film, *Tranquility in the Presence of Others* 1970 (*Ārāmish dar Ḥuẓūr-i Dīgarān*). Second, *Wind of Jin* was itself foundational to the surge in Iranian ethnographic film, inspiring a slew of religion and spirituality-themed ethnographic filmmaking that would come to follow it, such as Manūchihr Tayyāb's 1970 *Iran: The Land of Religions* (*Iran: Sarzamīn-i adiyān*); Manūchihr Tabarī's 1973 *A Few Moments with Qadiri Dervishes* (*Laḥaẓātī chand ba darāvīsh-i Qādirī*); Parvīz Kīmīāvī's 1971 *O'Deer Savior* (*Yā ẓamān-i āhū*); and Āṣghar Āṣgharīān's 1976 *The Taʾzīyah of Martyrdom* (*Shabīh-i shahādat*). Ghulām Husayn Tāhirīdūst's 1971 *Red Fire* (*Āzar surkh*), also about the spirit healing ritual *zār* and directly inspired by Taqvāʾī's work, would be deemed by his mentor Jean Rouch the "Iranian *Les Maîtres Fous*," responsible for creating a "new Iranian cinematic language."[32] Third, *Wind of Jin* attests to the potent relation between the history of modern Iranian film and literature, as is reflected in the close resemblance between Ghulām Husayn Sāʿidī's 1966 ethnographic monograph *Ahl-i havā* and Taqvāʾī's filmic rendition, and then in Taqvāʾī's subsequent adaptation of another of Sāʿidī's works for his first feature film, discussed in the following section.[33] Fourth, it romanticizes a founding anthropological object (spirit possession and trance), quintessentializing a crucial aspect of anthropology's connection to modernity's racialized philosophical preoccupations regarding the figures of subjectivity and interiority. Finally, *Wind of Jin* participates in a long history of using blackness as an allegory for universal suffering while ultimately naturalizing the history of slavery that reifies the connection between blackness and abjection, suppressing the meaning of this relation within modernity's material, epistemological, and aesthetic formations. In this sense the film maintains the kind of "idealized knowledge" of slavery characteristic of Southwest Asian societies, and reflected in the paucity of historiographical sources about it.[34] To this day, less than a small handful of texts chronicle the history of slavery in Iran. And yet, if the idealization of Indian Ocean slavery bears roots in the poverty of extant historiography, I am interested in the ways in which the evolution of Taqvāʾī's oeuvre demonstrates that idealization exceeds mere absence of information.

As I will show in my reading of Taqvāʾī's more realist *Music of the South: Zār,* which chronicles an identical phenomenon but prefers limpid rather than vague articulation of facts about *zār*'s relation to slavery, abstraction and aesthetic mediation perform enigmatic functions for historical transmission that are both necessary and aporetic. Mediation is necessary because "pure fact" is always already abstract, conditioned by the possibility of its communication, and thus dependent upon iterability, repetition, on language in its broadest sense, and thus always already susceptible to deviation, distortion, poeisis, and hyperbole. But because the tenuous boundary between abstraction and erasure can neither in advance nor retroactively be adjudicated with authority, this boundary responds to no ethical imperative. Indeed, the border between abstraction and erasure cannot be said to properly exist. Its nonexistence generates boundless turmoil. In Taqvā'ī's oeuvre, the *turmoil of facticity* surfaces as a relentless obsession, a thematic haunting in generically diverse works. The repetition of *zār* in Taqvā'ī's cinema appears to symptomatize the dissolution of slavery in the project of a generalized mourning, that is, in the anguished response to modernity that constitutes modernist ethos. In mystifying causality, the work of mourning dissolves the historical relation between slavery and the modernity (temporalizing mode, philosophical project, epistemological horizon) that is born with and out of slavery.[35] But it also suggests that this historical bond, like fact in general, is originarily, rather than contingently, prone to its own dissolution and forgetting. The precarity of facts incites a disquietude whose effects are, like its source, fully displaced.

Appearing just three years after Ghulām Ḥusayn Sā'idī's ethnographic monograph *People of the Wind (Ahl-i Havā)* and Taqi Modarressi's essay "The Zar Cult in Southern Iran," Taqvā'ī's documentary on *zār* forms part of a mid-twentieth-century anthropological and surrealist infatuation with trance that both transcends and yet remains specific to the Iranian frame.[36] In fact, Taqvā'ī accompanied Sā'idī for portions of his fieldwork, acting as a kind of conduit for southern culture, with which he was familiar because of his own upbringing in the capital of Iran's southwestern province of Khūzistān, Ābādān. In cross-comparing spirit taxonomy in Sā'idī's text, one finds curious resemblances and obvious transformations of African cosmologies. In his taxonomy of winds, for example, Sā'idī writes of Dingomaro. Researchers of the bori ritual in Nigeria identify a spirit by the name of Dangurmu, a native of the Asna—referring to ancient indigenous peoples of the Ader region.[37]

Despite the many interpretations of *zār* throughout Southwest Asia and even within the south of Iran itself, what is more or less common to the tradition is the ubiquitous presence of a drum called *duhul*. (Although, "silent" *zārs* [*sawfrih khāmūsh*] are not uncommon.)[38] As Sā'idī details in his ethnography, the *duhul* awakens the wind spirits from the body of the afflicted, and is also evidence of the celebratory, community-oriented character of *zār*.[39] The introduction to the rhythmic drumming of *duhul* in Taqvā'ī's film accompanies Shāmlū's first insinuation of the *zār* ritual as a form of covert community: "one wind girl wanders around Lingih, bamboo in hand," in search of *ahl-i havā* to gather. Bamboo sticks, sometimes "ornately decorated," are integral paraphernalia of *zār*, as gifts, weapons, and as tools.[40] The *zār* adept scampers around and brandishes her bamboo (*bakol*; *khayzarān*), threatening the wind to leave the afflicted's body. As appeasement, some *zār* winds demand bamboo sticks with golden knots.[41] In certain cases, a "special whip" is used to dislodge the spirit from the body.[42] Aisha Bilkhair Khalifa suggests that such rituals belie a "deep psychological resentment to slavery," because they mimic and trivialize its most important dimension, "the exercise of power."[43] Modarressi observed that some sailors were addicted to bamboo beatings.[44]

Among the features *zār* in Iran shares with contiguous regions is its emphasis on exclusivity and secrecy, and is why it has outlived more public spirit rituals that have sometimes been banned, such as *laywa*. (The amalgamation of *zār* and *laywa* in countries like Oman, following the banning of open-air ritual, has led to a confusion and conflation between these two rituals.)[45] Taqvā'ī admits in an interview that he would not have gained access to the *zār* ceremony had it not been for family connections.[46] *Wind of Jin* in fact marked the first instance of *zār* practitioners consenting to the ritual's recording.[47] The distinction between public and private strengthens a debated anthropological thesis that the exclusivity unique to *zār* in Southwest Asia is related to a generalized alienation, tying its presence to the experience of slavery, dishonor, and exclusion from the social that slave legacy brings with it.[48] Africans have not been the only enslaved people in Iran. But their discernible distinction and the ongoing, seemingly timeless denigration of and association of blackness with servility bears the most inscrutably palpable mark of this legacy. In his study of ethnic minorities, Rasmus Elling points out that it is nearly impossible to distinguish visibly between ethnic minority groups in Iran, apart from "partial exceptions" like the "black African community."[49] The *global* history of African enslavement through time and space, its centrality to the emergence of modernity on a planetary scale, encrypts a relation between blackness and slavery that undermines the purported privilege and self-evidence of statistical logic, as well as the indignation and respectability of minute historical qualifications.[50]

The cinematic techniques Taqvāʾī employs to illustrate *zār* for the viewer suggest why it might be the consistent object of anthropological fascination: possession here visually indexes the perennial modern philosophical problem of the meaning of interiority and exteriority (how to define the self or individual in relation to the body and to the surrounding world; how to formulate a theory of subjectivity and objectivity). The long take is supposed to bring the subject and object closer by steadying both, eliminating the manipulations of discontinuity and conjunction. But as the stylistic tensions of *Wind of Jin* show, the control commanded by sequence shooting does not cure the instability brought on by a kind of image that is intrinsically self-dissolving. As optimists of modernist realism believed, strategies like the long take and deep focus chastely neutralize reality in order to bring out its ambiguity and complexity before the spectator. But in *zār,* the object of perception recoils despite the artist's most earnest efforts. More, *zār* suggests that the discontinuity in the object, the intransigent flickering in the real, is not the simple result of manipulation and duplicitous editing; rather, that the discontinuity of the object is simultaneously a discontinuity that inheres in the subject. Faith in filmic continuity cannot cure a more original discontinuity, no more than faith in truth cures the originariness of the false. *Zār* is an instability in the real, threatening the subject with a therapeutic emptiness that it both fears and desires, perceives as external and intuits as intimate.

In evoking the figure of the slave, Taqvāʾī's film operates the thematic of slavery to subtly elaborate modernist concerns about alienation in an increasingly industrialized and nascently modernizing Iran. But in taking thematic recourse to *zār,* the horizon of redress itself recedes; or rather, the film suggests that modernity elicits just this recess of horizon. For the curse that erodes Bandar Lingih also destroys Iran, has indeed already obliterated it. In the era of nationalist nostalgia for pure, uncontaminated origins, focus upon ruins and ruination acquires ambivalent meanings. In the film, Bandar Lingih and its destruction is a metaphor for the "East" more generally. Ruined interiority pours out into the landscape. Once a booming economic center for pearling and trade, the port used to be called *shahr-i murvārīd* (City of Pearls), and because of its prosperity, *lingih dunyā* (Likeness of the World). One of Lingih's meanings is "singular," "unique" (*tak*).[51] "Lingih has no match!" (Lingih lingih nadasht!), writes Ahmad Mahmūd in his 1981 novel about the port,

Story of a City. Now, we learn from Shāmlū's steady voiceover, "this broken and destroyed port [*bandar-i khurd va kharāb*]" is "a parade for winds [*imrūz jūlan-i bād ast*]." For Taqvā'ī, such dilapidation could only occur in a place where there are no longer any humans. Moralized architecture takes on a meaning irreducible to extant theories of Orientalist imagery.[52] Like the East itself, at the same time as Lingih is imagined as a region of ancient prosperity, it is simultaneously poised for devastation, and both prosperity and destruction appear to have their source in blackness. For at once emblematic of the rich and esoteric reserves of autochthonous culture that modernity has the power to fully annihilate, the primitivized subjects of *zār* spirit possession turn out to be, by an imperceptible shift, the very source of this annihilation, a paradoxically and aboriginally "destructive, healing agent."[53]

As a result of all these metonymic movements and displacements, all that is encompassed in the distribution of *zār* with relation to a history of slavery is itself obscured as a problem for or of modernity. *Wind of Jin*'s ethnographic realism runs up against an unavoidable experimentalism that is demanded by its own object. *Zār*'s presence in Southwest Asia is attributed to the spread of African slavery in the Indian Ocean. In *Wind of Jin,* the uncontrollable slippage between realism and abstraction obscures this attribution, even as it simultaneously inscribes it, rendering slavery's relation to modernity both palpable and imperceptible, static, immobile, immemorial.

In the first minutes after the drumming achieves trance-like uniformity and conjoins the participants' vocal chanting, the camera draws close to the afflicted man in white turban, slumped in the corner of the room, his eyes shut and head tilted forward as if asleep. Though the camera can capture sound and sight, it cannot capture scent, the third most important ingredient in *zār*. In Egypt, devotees inducted to *zār* through heredity are called *ibn* or *bint bukhur* (born into incense). "Attracted by the aroma of incense," possessing spirits make themselves visible by taking over and transforming the body, making the afflicted "sleepy and yawning . . . appearing in her dreams."[54] As the focus expands, the man slowly swerves his bent head from side to side in collusion with the rhythm. Cryptically responding, the music stops and the camera suddenly cuts away from the scene to an image of a broken arched window, revealing darkness between the shattered pattern of its intricate lattice, and evoking nighttime or emptiness with the sound of crickets. When the camera cuts back to the drooping man in the corner, the diegetic music of *duhul* and singing recommence; a second cut away with the same strange crickets effect this time reveals a similar arched window pane, but bare—opening onto black, empty space, suggesting absence in the place of where character interiority might otherwise be elaborated (as in the traditional shot-reverse-shot that simulates dialogue between characters or effects an imagistic monologue through flashback or free association). The enigmatic sequence evokes an earlier sequence in the film, where three times, a blurry image sharpens into the shape of the same arched window: once with its lattice intact, a second time with its lattice partially

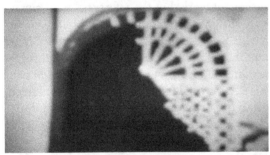

Figure 11. Three shots of an arched window blur in and out of focus in Nāṣir Taqvāī's *Wind of Jin* (*Bād-i Jin*, 1969).

« 88 »   *Zār* and the Anxieties of the Iranian New Wave

broken, and the third time, completely empty. Following the visual parallelism suggests that the *ahl-i havā* is himself the blur that fades in and out of focus.

In the place of a possible meditation on historical conjunction, the abstraction of the slave's imagined suffering (interchangeable in the film with Man's suffering) is exalted into form. Abstraction passes through the evacuation of subjectivity, the imagination of an interiority free for claim, for self-identification. *At the same time,* it is precisely the very possibility, and commonality of such an evacuation of the subject, that *zār* practitioners uphold in their belief in spirit winds that mount, "wear" the body. A possessed person (*malbous*) is worn by the spirit, suggesting the body as a shell, covering, or mask that shelters not a stable essence but vacancy itself.[55] "I feel I am being emptied, I fall apart."[56] Generalizability, fungibility, and emptiness are intrinsic to *zār*. If *zār* is a trace of Indian Ocean slavery, then, it is simultaneously the case that *zār*'s transmission is *also* a path to its own erasure, a movement toward the ongoing dissolution of its own history and meaning. A trace, then, that is not the mark of a past presence, but rather, of a preservation without unwavering, self-identical content, a transmission of absence. The exaltation of *zār* continues to accrue remoter levels of abstraction through Taqvā'ī's subsequent work, but the referentiality of *zār* refuses to fully fade away. This means not only that *zār* itself is a referent, but that, in its particular cosmology of the subject and of time, *zār* is at its core rather a total disorder of reference. Something in the shot refuses to remain still, does not yield to the supposed continuity of perception, remains fundamentally unverifiable, blurred, and, rather than adding to our reserve of knowledge, instead, detracts from it—disabuses the arrogance of quantity, transcendence through epistemological accumulation.

Silence overwhelms the final segment of ceremonial *zār*. ("One who opens his mouth to speak or to yawn is likely to allow the departing evil spirit to slip into his mouth.")[57] As the frame cuts back from the window sequence to the ceremony again, the *ahl-i havā* awakens, strokes his face, and opens his eyes with slight surprise, indicating the arousal of *zār* in his body. Shāmlū's voice returns. Everyone remains seated, as if attending to his ethereal extradiegetic voice:

> The winds have been attributed to the arrival of the blacks from Africa. Prior to the arrival of the blacks for the cost of dates [*pīsh*

az ān kih siyāh bih bahā-ʾi khurmāh biyāyad] the winds existed on the margins of the Gulf; but, like the vital force dormant in a sick body, oil under the seafloor, and intelligence in the mind of a savage, it remained unrecognized. The black tradition, replete with the experience of hunger, recognized the resemblance and brought healing.

African Enslavement in the Indian Ocean

Gratuitous African labor peaked in the Persian Gulf in the late nineteenth century due to the growing demand for commodities like dates and pearls for global markets. Scholarship has often elided the connection between Indian Ocean slavery and the global economy, emphasizing the former's noncapitalist foundation and primarily domestic character. By contrast, transatlantic slavery's centrality to the flourishing of the European capitalist system is comparatively well established. On the one hand, the elision of Indian Ocean slavery's relation to global markets strengthens the typical assumption of its qualitative distinction from the system of mass chattel slavery established in the Americas. On the other hand, the emphasis on Indian Ocean slavery's noncapitalist essence is also thought to mirror the putatively racist tradition of European chroniclers, imperial agents and patrollers who saw slavery in Western Asia as a timeless component of Islamic character even as they intervened in the Gulf to "protect" it from rival monopolistic domination, or, as they wielded abolition as a means of "diplomatic bullying or colonial conquest."[58]

Against formulations that exceptionalize Indian Ocean slavery to divergent moralizing ends, or with divergent moralizing effects, some contemporary scholarship seeks to recognize Indian Ocean slavery's decidedly economic character. In the 1970s and 1980s a number of scholarly monographs argued for the significance of slave labor on the East African coast for the expansion of the French plantation economies, the Omani empire, and the increasing global demand for ivory, cloves, and other commodities in the eighteenth and nineteenth centuries.[59] But only recently has the relationship between slavery and the export economies of the Persian Gulf come under focus. Its precipitous rise in wealth in the twentieth century supports a common "rags-to-riches" narrative that obfuscates the Persian Gulf's history prior to the discovery of oil.[60] But enormous late nineteenth-century value appreciations in pearls attest to "a great internationalization of the Gulf" before its virtually exclusive association with petrol.[61] Just as a modern pearling boom transformed local markets and patterns of settlement in the Persian Gulf, demand for dates generated a vast export industry largely dependent on enslaved African labor. Thus, for Matthew Hopper, "The growth of African communities in the Gulf must not be seen as part of an isolated 'Islamic slave trade,' but rather as part of a labor system that—like its predecessor in the Atlantic—was structured around global economic forces."[62] For William Gervase Clarence-Smith, slavery's dramatic nineteenth-century resurgence, powered by cash crop production and export economies, drew Indian Ocean slavery closer to New World models.[63]

As far back as the publication of *The World and Africa* in 1946, W. E. B. Du Bois helped us to see, through the disturbing image of classical music—a "society darling" delicately stroking her piano keys—a fundamental conjunction between Indian Ocean and transatlantic slavery. According to Du Bois, cotton produced through chattel slavery in the U.S. South generated the wealth in New York and Manchester to purchase ivory from Arab and African slave traders and elephant hunters. Noting that, prior to the nineteenth century, ivory in Africa was primarily sold, along with the slaves who transported it, to "Arabia, Persia, and India" on a moderate scale, around 1840 a renewed demand from Europe transformed the trade into a highly profitable industry, entangling ivory and slave trading in Central Africa with the firearms trade.[64] Like the market for piano keys and billiard balls in the early nineteenth century that intensified the ivory trade, and by extension, slave trading in Africa, international demand for dates and pearls in the 1840s through the 1920s replenished slavery in the Persian Gulf, especially after the collapse of the pearl fisheries in the Red Sea and Ceylon as a result of parasite infestation.

Slavery in the western Indian Ocean is irrevocably connected to modernity, thus contemporary scholarship informs us, offering a corrective to the image of Indian Ocean slavery as static. Yet the reasonable and empirically grounded formulations that tie Indian Ocean slavery to modernity, as well as, therefore, to transatlantic slavery, cannot fully account for the fact that enslaved Africans toiled in the fields of Southwest Asia long before the nineteenth century. References to the relation between slavery and sugar cultivation date

Zār and the Anxieties of the Iranian New Wave   « 91 »

back to antiquity.[65] As Du Bois notes, there is a change in *scale* that transforms the slave trades in Central and East Africa as a result of wealth and consumer habits generated by transatlantic slavery. At the same time, a change in scale is itself unaccountable to the persistence of that which endures its own exponentialization. In order to be what it is, transformation must include, but also repress, sameness. An intemporal kernel survives, gives recognition to something as transformed, and in turn, only gains recognition through this same action. Du Bois notes the bedazzling metamorphosis of Indian Ocean slavery's political economy as a result of wealth generated by transatlantic slavery. And yet, there is nevertheless a mundane, enduring, seemingly untheorizable movement prior to the moment of Indian Ocean slavery's own modernity. Because it verges on timelessness and ahistoricality, scholarship must avoid this intemporal kernel in order to skirt the sin or embarrassment of intellectual error. For the historian, the ahistorical is a kind of moral defect of thought.

Dates have been a staple food of Near Eastern societies long before the advent of Islam, cultivated thousands of years before the first settlements in the plain of the Tigris and Euphrates circa 5000 BCE, just as slavery is endemic to the *origin* of human civilization.[66] Thus, it is not only the case that Indian Ocean slavery dates back millennia, but rather that its origin flouts historiography's twin logics of discovery and consensus. The oblique *bahā-ʿi khurmā* ("for the price of dates") in *Wind of Jin* refers to this deep historical sedimentation, this constitutive opacity of the origin. The difficult translatability of the phrase reflects Shāmlū's poeticization of a fact whose referent is necessarily, rather than contingently, unclear and imprecise. In ethnographic film, cinematic temporality entangles ritualistic time; duration transforms into tension. Thus, the "slow floating" of silence can produce more force than rapid or emphatic movement. There is a special veracity available only to cinema.[67] Trance is a phenomenon that lives "on both sides of the ethnographic contact."[68] The climactic silence in *Wind of Jin* transmits a certain kind of truth, manifested through poetry, as it entices the wind to self-revelation. This doubled sense of waiting produces cinematic affect as confusion. "I once said that my poetry is in no way a continuation of past Persian poetry. My verse takes its roots elsewhere," submits Shāmlū.[69]

To which arrival does the poet refer? Does the *siyāh* (black) arrive in time, or is this another kind of subjunctive coming (*kih biyāyad*)? Shāmlū's phrasing activates a common point of ambiguity

« 92 »   *Zār and the Anxieties of the Iranian New Wave*

in discourse on African presence in the Persian Gulf and in the Indian Ocean world. What is the origin of blackness? And what, were we to know it, could such an origin possibly mean? Appeals to Indian Ocean cosmopolitanism sometimes belie a resistance to acknowledging the violence of slavery.[70] Thus, scholars recall that black presence in the Gulf attests to a timeless free movement of African merchants and travelers from antiquity. According to this line of thought, the conflation of blackness, Africanness, and slavery is only the result of modern impositions, of modern conjunctions that would taint the purity of a truly nonracial, properly differentiated and autonomous Africanness. This line of thought suggests, rightly, that African being has a rootedness in Southwest Asia's antiquity that transcends slavery. At the same time, scholars also concede that "*voluntary migration* to the Gulf from Africa was extremely limited."[71]

The temporal obliquity of Shāmlū's words express and symptomize a general obfuscation inherent to the relationship between racial blackness and Indian Ocean slavery. For this relationship is not, I suggest, merely a temporal, or even economic intimacy—although it is also both of these things. Instead, Indian Ocean slavery's inchoate duration brings to the fore something unrepresentable, immemorial about its own history. This intransigence is reactivated by a blackness whose arrival and meaning cannot be dated (*pīsh az ān kih sīyāh bih bahā-'i khurmā bīyāyad*); or more precisely, whose dating is an insufficient condition of possibility for its meaning.

They came "for the price of dates," goes the euphemistic Persian. *T'āruf,* a feature of Persian language, is a way of politely circumventing undesirable and offensive facts. But the vagueness of temporal markers in Shāmlū's circumlocution reflects the amorphousness of a relation to modernity that is not strictly temporal, of chronology. Does Shāmlū refer to date harvesting in the Persian Gulf in the nineteenth century? Thus tying the presence of blackness in the Gulf to the history of transatlantic slavery and racial blackness? Or does Shāmlū refer to an ancient history of slavery in the Indian Ocean that precedes modernity, and thus, to some extent, activates it? Does his diction even conceal something that could be known? Neither the spectator, nor Shāmlū, knows to which arrival he refers, nor perhaps, whether the arrival of the *siyāh*/black has occurred in the past tense, or is, rather, still occurring, still to come.[72] The (racial) truth of the *siyāh* cannot be extracted from a historical origin, unless we concede the origin is always already conjunctive, fundamentally

Figure 12. The *ahl-i havā* gather for *zār* in Nāṣir Taqvāī's *Wind of Jin* (*Bād-i Jin*, 1969).

unstable. Nonracial blackness does not conceal a sense that is fundamental and whole, but rather derives its purported purity from a racial blackness that equally lacks a stable essence. The dubbed voice, a constitutive feature of prerevolutionary cinema, attains a new level of disembodiment in ethnographic documentary film, endows conjunction with unknown stakes.

The placement of Shāmlū's voiceover toward the end of the film imbues this moment with climactic charge, as if emphasizing the ambivalence of his poetics. They came for the price of dates. In cuneiform inscriptions, the "Drink of Life" refers to an intoxicating beverage furnished by the date palm tree.[73] Having been made to fall, the wind's origin is revealed at the delirious climax of *zār*.[74] After a cut to a mounted mirror reflecting the white shroud-covered wind-afflicted, the music slowly recommences, and the surrounding *ahl-i havā* begin rocking forth and from side to side, seated. Infected, another male participant rises and begins jerking. Eternal hosts of the *zār*, the members of the *ahl-i havā* "may start moving and shaking" when they hear their wind's incantation or rhythm.[75] (In Fahahil one man describes the abnormal jumping of an afflicted man during *zār* as "impossibly high.")[76] When the music ends a final time, it is unclear why; the participants communicate in a cacophony of Gulf dialect, which would have been inscrutable to the majority of urban Iranian audiences at the time of *Wind of Jin*'s release. One of the afflicted appears cured, as he stands up to embrace his fellow *ahl-i havā*. The other one remains covered, his hands bracing his head, and begins screaming while the image cuts again to the initial ocean waves of the film, reasserting a relation between sea and sickness. Against the typical images of the Persian Gulf as fertile, abundant, benevolent, *zār* believers know of an infelicitous wind, Shaykh al-Bahar, or Umm al-Subian, who lives at the bottom of the sea and disappears divers.[77] Some believe *zār* itself is a kind of sea wind.[78] Like the *nūbān* wind, *zār* is African, heathen, wild, subterranean.[79] Wild winds resist incorporation into reciprocity, refuse mediation and flout the community's efforts at humanization. (Thus, to be blind [*kūr*] or seeing [*bīnā*] is indication of a wind's tameability.) "The movements of the mama and baba zars with their white clothes reminded me of the waves of the ocean. The swelling and tempestuous sea," writes one ethnographer. At the *zār* ceremony, fear colored everyone's faces, she reports—"fear of the ship sinking, fear of being sold, fear of cruel masters and fear of the waves."[80] In the nineteenth century, two devastating cyclones on the Batinah coast north of Muscat eviscerated vital date crops and created demand for reconstructing the entire region, renewing and intensifying the slave trade from East Africa.[81] The "images of amorphous phenomena, such as wind spouts, gales . . . are reminiscent of phantasms"; thus, "in many Bantu languages the words which we translate as 'spirit' also mean wind, breath, or waft of air."[82] *Gwati,* a *zār*-like spirit ritual practiced in Baluchistan, derives from *gwat* (wind). Afro-Baluchi practitioners believe that evil spirit winds come from Muscat, where magicians transform strangers into chattel.[83] The occult psychic needs to which slavery was an even more mysterious response remain lodged in a lost topography that surfaces in febrile fantasy.

Anxieties of the Iranian New Wave

The theme of madness that sustains Taqvā'ī's focus on the psychic contagion and terrestrial destruction of African-transmitted *zār* penetrates his contemporaneous and subsequent work, even as Africa continues to dissolve in the spiraling movement of this abstraction. Madness reinvigorates Iranian cinema, minting a new stage of filmmaking that would later become recognizable under the capacious Iranian New Wave, *Mawj-i Naw.* Criticism of the New Wave generally clashes over the precise definition of the movement, whether the movement existed in fact or in a fantasy fulfilled retroactively by critics: "Reviewing the works on the New Wave, either before or after the Revolution, in English or Farsi, we find a sort of confused,

Zār and the Anxieties of the Iranian New Wave « 95 »

disordered, and ambiguous perception."[84] As Golbarg Rekabtalaei notes, a number of different labels were preferred by Iranian filmmakers and critics themselves in the 1970s, including "alterative cinema" (*sīnamā-yi dīgar,* or *sīnamā-yi mutifāvit*); but also "indigenous cinema" (*sīnamā-yi būmī*), "new cinema" (*sīnamā-yi jadīd*), and "cinema of necessity" (*sīnamā-yi zarūrat*).[85] The lack of theoretical precision in its criticism and in its practice reflects the spontaneity, contingency, and ephemerality of the movement, whose underlying unifying feature, if such existed, was above all resistance to the complacency and political impotence of mainstream film culture, generally encompassed by the derogatory neologism *filmfārsī* (see chapter 1) and purportedly inflected by the basest elements of Western consumerism. New Wave films were "closer to omens than artworks."[86]

Taqvāʾīʾs first feature film, produced and released almost simultaneously with *Wind of Jin, Tranquility in the Presence of Others* (1970), is usually categorized as part of the New Wave. Like Ghulām Ḥusayn Sāʿidīʾs more famous screenplay, adapted by Dāryūsh Mihrjūyī in *Cow* (*Gav,* 1969) *Tranquility* explores mental disintegration and the funereal darkness of modernity's alienating forces, breaking with *filmfārsī*ʾs grating Hollywood endings. If *filmfārsī*ʾs affinity for hybridized melodrama trafficked in cabaret scenes, gratuitous sexual imagery, and stilted narratives, Mihrjūyīʾs and Taqvāʾīʾs work was remarkably novel for the period, and, importantly, bridged by the literary-psychiatric figure of Sāʿidī. At the same time, in repudiating *filmfārsī, Tranquility in the Presence of Others,* and the Iranian New Wave in general, was irrevocably tied up with it in an intimate dialectic. (This intimacy is reflected in the generic ambivalence of works like Ghafārīʾs, discussed in chapter 2.) The New Wave rejected a negative imbrication with global modernity (primarily, American-style consumerism and capitalism, and the erosion of cultural singularities) for another, purportedly positive imbrication with global modernity (conceptual dynamism, aesthetic innovation, and meditation on modern subjectivity).[87] Critical of the blithe consumerism promoted by the aspirational example of the royal family, many modernist filmmakers, artists, and intellectuals were trained in Western metropoles whose aesthetic cultures were prized through aspirational Europhilia. Their oppositional, usually leftist stance was paradoxically available to cooptation by the Pahlavi regime, who capitalized on the cultural innovations of leading *rawshanfikr*

Figure 13. Manizheh, the colonel's wife, looking somberly out over the courtyard in Nāṣir Taqvāī's *Tranquility in the Presence of Others* (1970).

(intellectuals) in order to strengthen the "authenticity politics" of official national culture.[88]

About a retired, recently remarried, mentally disturbed colonel who comes to visit his two daughters in the city, *Tranquility* derives from a short story of the same name by Sāʿidī collected in his 1967 anthology, *Unnameable and Invisible Fears* (*Vāhamah'hā'i bī nām va nishān*). Like his films to come, Taqvā'ī's feature *Tranquility* responds to the theme of madness in recognizably modernist ways: through figures of urban disquietude marked by a predominance of closed-form aesthetics, dark interiors, and hospital corridors, counterbalanced by foreboding outdoor scenes, such as the memorable sequence of Akbar Mishkīn (the colonel) marching along a barbed-wire fence in the midday sun, hallucinating the rhythmic music of a military salute.[89] Two long outdoor tracking sequences outside the hospital overwhelmed by the clamor of cawing crows establishes a certain fidelity to the original text and exemplifies the extent to which, as in *Wind of Jin,* worldly and psychic space disquiet and translate one another. The "cinematic-mystical landscape" of Iranian cinema "lures cultural manifestations downward and into the covert beneath."[90] At the same time, in contrast to the ethnographic, primitivized tone of *Wind of Jin,* there is something clinical, medicalized, about the madness in *Tranquility.* Sā'idī showed how the "feelings of fear and insecurity are not peculiar to the village," writes one commentator.[91] The city, as a site of stress, mental illness, drug addiction, disease, and opaque hyperactivity becomes the prized trope of modern alienation in psychiatric discourses of mid-twentieth-century Iran.[92]

Simultaneously playing into and recoiling from the period's demand for sexually exploitative films, the colonel's daughters Maliheh (Partaw Nooriala) and Mahlaqa (Leila Baharan) live alone, command their own household, and date and sleep around.[93] In Taqvā'ī's version, the film opens with a nihilistic conversation between Mahlaqa and her boyfriend about the futility of monogamy, followed by a vivid scene of their lovemaking. Sexuality is a potent theme in *Tranquility,* but one whose prerevolutionary sensationalism has been overtly disfigured. On the surface, the images in the initial sex scene seem like they could have been torn from any typical *filmfārsī* and spliced into *Tranquility.* But in *Tranquility's* lovemaking, perspective abstracts the naked bodies, as the dialogue transforms eroticism into gloom. "What's wrong with you, tonight?," Mahlaqa's boyfriend asks. "I don't know. I've been feeling sad since this morning." The daughters exemplify the dangers of women's liberation in the declining but resolute edifice of Iranian patriarchy. (Like their counterparts in the French New Wave, Iranian New Wave filmmakers often reproduced reactionary gender politics, despite ostensibly revolutionary cultural aims.[94]) "Everyone

« 98 »   *Zār and the Anxieties of the Iranian New Wave*

would freeze in their places when the colonel would walk in," Mishkīn tells his young wife, Manīzhih (Surayā Ghāsimī). "Now, even the servant doesn't listen." The ambiguous consequences of patriarchal degeneration are dramatized in the film adaptation when Maliheh commits suicide as a result of her devolution into depression after a hollow romance ends in betrayal, a somewhat radicalized interpretation of Sā'idī's less sensational ending, which is marked by a journey to an unnamed abroad. Modernity afflicts everyone. Even its imagined beneficiaries (socially liberated, middle-class women) ultimately self-destruct: "All the characters in the film suffer from some form of social anxiety," notes Sara Saljoughi, not just the "odd figure" of the aging colonel.[95] Death in Iranian cinema of the 1960s is the only logical outcome in a society where contradiction has become irresolvable.[96]

When asked why he chose Sā'idī's short story for his first feature-length film, Taqvā'ī admits he was attracted to the mystery inside the story, "The feeling one gets throughout the story . . . something like the ineffable."[97] That sense of the numinous present in *Tranquility* and *Wind of Jin* delineates an undeniable, if unlikely, relation between them. But so does the theme of destruction, atrophy, and apprehension. Admitting his disposal of other elements of Sā'idī's short story, Taqvā'ī submits his retention of the most important theme: anxiety.[98] As Taqvā'ī mentions in a 1986 interview in the Iranian film journal *Sitārih Sīnamā, Wind of Jin* was one of his "dearest" films, specifically because of the novelty of its subject and the "strangeness of its theme."[99] At a private viewing of *Tranquility* in 1971, Taqvā'ī discussed his intense experience of the desolation and ruination of the "jin-ridden" city of Lingih, hinting at a transmutation of atmospheric elements between the two films, and affirming Taqvā'ī's esteem of atmosphere as the ground of art and of history: "Without atmosphere, art is meaningless. . . . Without geography there is no history. . . . The South for me is a very far-reaching geography."[100]

Though the close temporal proximity in both films' productions and identity of the author of both prototexts most obviously strengthens the bizarre affinity between them, there is a more latent dimension to the relationship between *Wind of Jin* and *Tranquility in the Presence of Others. Wind of Jin* is predicated upon a modernity that prompts one to preserve what is unable to survive, to return to authenticity and the rural auratic in the face of the rise of urban simulacrum. *Tranquility,* on the other hand, is a more direct narrative manifestation of modern loss. This loss appears as an exterior

Zār and the Anxieties of the Iranian New Wave   « 99 »

element, an irritant from without that has been interiorized—in medicalized psychosis, in madness, death, and in the ambivalence of the denuded, hypersexualized, consumption-driven female body that desacralizes all social edifice. In *Wind of Jin,* loss, too, surfaces, as a kind of psycho-terrestrial degradation whose source in spirits, in black winds, renders historical causality both superfluous and impossible. The winds come from far-off shores, Sā'idi submits in his ethnography *Ahl-i Havā*: "The Indian and Persian winds, though frightening, do not compare to the enormous and very black winds that come from the coast of Africa."[101]

As with the strange dynamic of the castrated *siyāh* (blackface minstrel) and the female dancer (*raqāṣ*) in *fīlmfārsī* described in the previous chapter, in the more elite, intellectual cinema of the New Wave and the experimental ethnography that subtends it, now the ungendered ahistorical black slave (*Wind of Jin*) and modernity's sexualized, whitening female sacrificiant (*Tranquility in the Presence of Others*) express, embody, but simultaneously cause and propel the loss that is felt as modernity itself. Or rather the figure of the ungendered black slave and the overconsuming, sexually exploited female so prevalent in aesthetic production of the 1960s and 1970s express different modalities of loss and distinct sets of contradictions whose interrelations are dissolved in the distracting play of modernist realism and modernist abstraction.

In its aesthetic decisions and sobriety, *Tranquility* marks a distinct moment in Taqvā'ī's oeuvre and coincides with the evolution of Persian film noir. But *zār's* influence continues to infect Taqvā'ī's other feature films from this decade, such as *Sadiq the Kurd* (*Sādiq Kurdih,* 1972) and *The Curse* (*Nifrīn,* 1973), which may be more convincingly understood through the lens of noir than of the New Wave.[102] The post–White Revolution and land reform era, which greatly shaped the sociopolitical landscape of the 1960s, as well as the disillusionment over the rise in oil prices were "directly mirrored in the sordidness of the urban crime film, which became increasingly dark as the political mood hardened."[103] Both *Sādiq the Kurd* and *The Curse* take place in southern provinces, Khūzistān and Hurmuzgān respectively, bearing subtle and conspicuous traces of *Wind of Jin's* subject: *zār.* In *Sādiq the Kurd,* for example, a woman sings a lullaby identical to the one performed during the montage scene in *Wind of Jin* described above. Sadiq (Saīd Rād)'s wife has just been raped and murdered by a truck driver, launching the protagonist into a murder rampage in search of vengeance for his wife's true killer. Rape in

Iranian film noir, suggests Hamid Reza Sadr, results from a confusion of energies, a deviancy and perversion that is distinct, if not wholly unrelated, to the sexual "absurdity" of *filmfārsī*. The trope of male vengeance "represents an anarchic sense of justice." It is no coincidence that this "sour poetry" is predicated upon the annihilation of the female, transformed into a symbol of male honor. According to this logic, the rape and murder of the female body in film noir, most famously in films like Masūd Kīmiyā'ī's quintessential *Qaysar*, amounts to an extirpation that is distinct from, yet on par, with her annihilation in *filmfārsī*. Noir's perversion diverges from *filmfārsī's* profusion. If the modern, unveiled female body symbolizes a new consumerism, it is also the case that this body itself is consumed, by the sexual overdetermination of a devouring gaze, the camera's "sweep," or *jārū* (Kāvūsī). This female body thus materializes the very act of consumption whose desire she arouses. After one of the colonel's fitful nights in *Tranquility,* Maliheh sits with her father's morose young wife, Manizheh, who notices music wafting. "Are all your records Western?," Manizheh asks. "Yes. Do you like it?," Maliheh responds. "No," says Manizheh. When asked whether she would like to read a European fashion magazine, Manizheh adds, "I don't have the energy." Positioned as a liminal figure between the Westernized youth (the colonel's daughters) and static tradition (the veiled servant), the colonel's wife suffers vicariously. And yet, like all the other characters in the film, her affliction is unidentifiable.

"The global reach of burgeoning consumerism involved the re-creation and commercialization of 'femininity' through growing public exposure of women's voices and bodies."[104] And yet, since the cinematic female in Iranian film is both without referent and overflowing with referents, it is unclear what precisely is being consumed, amputated, in *filmfārsī,* nor in the Iranian New Wave film that attempts to respond but can offer no alternatives to this annihilation, nor in Persian film noir in which nullification is literalized as rape and murder.[105] Is it "the" female that prerevolutionary Iranian film attempts to annihilate, or the effects of modernity, the loss that is mediated by her simulacrum? Iran is feminized in the nineteenth and twentieth centuries, Afsaneh Najmabadi writes, but so is the narrative of modernity, the "deeply felt sentiment of loss" that subtends her figure: "The modernist reconstitution of *vatan* [homeland]," this feminized geobody, "was a grieving moment." For modern Iran is consolidated "not through conquest and consolidation but through successive losses."[106]

Apart from literalizing it in its title, Taqvā'ī's *The Curse* (*Nifrīn*) elevates but also conceals the theme of wind affliction within its narrative core. In the film, a construction worker (Bihrūz Vūsūqī) moves to a small village in Bandar Abbas to help a woman (Fakhrī Khurvash—the star protagonist from Ghafārī's *Rivalry in the City*) repair and repaint her home white. During his stay, the worker observes the dysfunctional relationship between the woman and her husband, who he later learns is the son of the village's deceased sheikh. An alcoholic and opium addict, the village landowner has squandered his family wealth, leaving his wife to manage the estate; the villagers believe he is *"jin-zadih,"* wind stricken. You "would just know . . . from the air [*havā*]. From the way the wind swishes through the leaves at night," one character submits. Considered both a critical and commercial failure (Taqvā'ī never recovered from the financial losses incurred by *The Curse* and was forced into television programming), the filmmaker nevertheless objected to the generalized disdain for the film, defending it as a logical continuation of his oeuvre, the screening of a "catastrophe" about destiny.[107]

The causal relationship between winds, Africa, and destruction is borrowed and repeated from *Wind of Jin*, but the winds' African origins are displaced onto a negligible detail, a fleeting, meaningless moment in *The Curse*. Africanness, its historical relationship to the *zār* complex as it is framed by *Wind of Jin* and its counterpart (*Music of the South*, discussed below) is absorbed by other articulations of blackness that are no less evocative and ambiguous. Taqvā'ī's more famous and critically acclaimed *Captain Sun* (*Nākhudā Khurshīd*,

Figure 14. An out-of-place static shot of two black children kneeling behind crates of fruit in Nāṣir Taqvā'ī's *The Curse* (*Nifrīn*, 1973).

«102»   *Zār* and the Anxieties of the Iranian New Wave

1987) takes place in the same port as *Wind of Jin* (Bandar Lingih), adapts tropes such as belief in jin as the source of Lingih's destruction, and thematizes creolized Persian identity in the Gulf, pearling, and the smuggling of human beings on dhows—thus resonating much more obviously with *Wind of Jin* topically, if less so in style and form. As Malul leads Farhan (Alī Nasīrīyān) through the town in *Captain Sun,* Farhan looks out over a deserted building foundation: "What calamity has befallen this city? An earthquake?" Malul replies, "Can earthquakes cause such destruction? The city has become a jin-hive."

One could thus single out any of Taqvā'ī's feature films as fictionalized extensions and abstractions of *Wind of Jin*'s theme. If there is any reason to insist on *Tranquility*'s privilege, it is due to its uncanny proximity to the production of *Wind of Jin*; because it marks another film adaption of a text written by Sā'idī; because it was chosen by the Ministry of Arts and Culture for the "Week of Iranian Movies" in Paris as a representative of the modern Iranian filmic imagination—thus expressing a conscious articulation of what Iranian (filmic) modernity might look like to the world; and because it is retroactively recognized by critics as a crucial milestone in the New Wave movement and the moral commitment to documentary realism established by the latter. "The blatant and tangible differences between *Tranquility* and the prevalent cinema of the period" explain its box office losses, suggests one commentator.[108] Despite the handicap of its notorious banning and commercial failure, it was one of the first films commissioned for national television and formed part of the resistance movement to *fīlmfārsī*. Parviz Jahid suggests that Taqvā'ī was "forced" to make *Sādiq the Kurd* and *The Curse* in the wake of *Tranquility*'s banning: Taqvā'ī "could probably be called the most important victim of the New Wave; a director that made the most important New Wave film . . . yet failed to continue on the path."[109]

The difference between the quality and kind of madness conjured by *Wind of Jin*'s thematization of the ritualistic and *Tranquility*'s avail of modern ennui does not only separate two cinematic genres, the ethnographic and the New Wave. Rather, this difference impresses a hierarchical distinction in genres of human subjectivity. If for postwar Iranian intellectuals modernity "embodies all that is alien and inhumane," destroying the "mystery of being, and human spirituality," it is also the case that only a modern consciousness can grasp this state of affairs.[110] Thus, in contrast to earlier Iranian cinema, the New Wave exemplifies "self understanding" and "epistemologi-cal maturity [*bulūq-i m'arifatī*]."[111] "Our cultural cinema [*sīnamā-yi farhangī*] is rooted in documentary film," Taqvā'ī announced in a speech at the 1992 Fajr film festival.[112] According to Taqvā'ī, ethno-graphic and art documentary ripened Iranian cinematic language prior to the growth of the New Wave.[113] But if the ethnographic sub-ject offers the raw creative material for articulations of loss caused by modernity, the doubled appearance of madness, as spirit possession in *Wind of Jin* and clinical psychosis in *Tranquility*, also suggests the troubling commonness and universality of altered consciousness, or more precisely, a troubling indecision about any consensus on the character of consciousness in general. This indecision is also a leg-acy of the aesthetic form that *is* cinematic modernism and its tech-nological apparatus.

It can be tempting to attribute *Tranquility*'s distinction to Sā'idī's authorly presence. The striking variation but also resonance in ap-proaches to the study of character in Taqvā'ī's two films can't sim-ply be explained away through recourse to genre distinction—that is, through the difference between experimental documentary and feature-length narrative film. The distinction is curiously mirrored in Sā'idī's two collections of short stories, *Fear and Trembling* (*Tars va Larz*) and *Unnameable and Invisible Fears* (*Vāhamah'hā-yi bī nām va nishān*), in which "Tranquility in the Presence of Others" was published. Both collections appeared just subsequent to Sā'idī's period of field travel and exposure to village life throughout the Ira-nian south and countryside. In fact, the innominate "coastal village" in *Fear and Trembling* is transposed to other imaginary places in Sā'idī's ruralized fiction, in the nonexistent Bayāl in *Mourners of Bayāl* and in Varzīl, from his famous screenplay, "Chūb bi dasthāyi Varzīl."[114] As in his other works, dialogue largely dominates the sto-ries of *Fear and Trembling*—however, dialogue that is muted, flat, and utile, delivered for the relay of information about events and actions, rather than revelatory of thoughts and feelings. The sen-tence construction of his prose is predominantly short, matter-of-fact, and functional. Though anxiety thematically overwhelms both series of stories, in *Fear and Trembling,* anxiety emanates from a naturalized fear of preternatural forces radiating out from physical elements like the sea and air. The "sense of fear in these stories tents the reader's being," suggests one commentator.[115] In "Tranquility" and the larger collection of which it is a part, anxiety appears to surface from human stress about the perceived dissolution and loss of traditional social hierarchies. At the same time, this intuition of causality is unverifiable and belied by the very definition of anxiety, for anxiety lacks a concrete object. Thus, for example, the colonel's development of a psychic condition resembling posttraumatic stress disorder does not result from any empirical war. In an early scene in Taqvā'ī's film, the colonel stares out through the living room window pane into the darkness: "Now it's time for strange thoughts." Maliheh repeatedly inquires about Manizheh's sullenness: "I don't know. Sometimes I just get like this."

In the textual form of *Tranquility in the Presence of Others,* free-indirect discourse and long, winding sentences overflowing with copulas evoke a desultory, subjectless anxiety. "All the characters in the story could conceivably be the patients of their creator, a psychiatrist as well as a creative writer," a commentator suggests, indicating the psychic roundedness of *Tranquility's* characters.[116] But in truth, the modernism of "Tranquility" consists not in the psychologization of characters, but in its evacuation of psychological realism. The absence of depth points toward the elusiveness of the subject, or the difficulty of defining the features of a self, and in this sense bears the potential to say much more, much more convincingly about interiority than the piling up of psychological details, as the genre of modernism in its canonized Anglo-European sense shows. Indeed, as a global project, modernism entails precisely the attenuation or absence of psychological description in favor of radicalized human estrangement, and New Wave films were nothing if not the articulation of this increasing alienation. In Taqvā'ī's adaptation, the interior life of Sā'idī's characters plays out through extensive but enigmatic dialogue, unreadable facial expressions, and lingering close-ups. If close-ups expand space, the facial close-up posits an untappable interiority whose expression is not synonymous with psychology.

In *Fear and Trembling,* psychology is enmeshed by contrast with "primitive beliefs" in "oppressed, backward" places; in these stories, Sā'idī "shows the worst and most unconscious beliefs and superstitions."[117] And released just one year earlier than *Tranquility in the Presence of Others, Wind of Jin's* subjects are spectral characters. Blurs and broken lattices perform the work of depth; they communicate just once in a language unintelligible to an urban Iranian public, and live in a dying, miasmic past, one whose African origins bestow the ultimate profundity to the modernness of the film's form. Thus, if a difference separates the ethnic, ethnographic subjects of *Wind of Jin* from the cosmopolitan fictional characters of *Tranquility in the Presence of Others,* this difference cannot by described in the simple terms of the presence or absence of psychology, nor in the presence or absence of subjectivity. For modernism's abstractions entail as one of their modalities a certain dissolution of the individual that coincides with the disintegration of narrative. Indeed, against the facile and conventional plot scenarios typical of the commercial cinema they decried, New Wave films sought narrative freedom in the form of weakened causality and interpretive ambiguity. This is why they were so disliked by audiences. The rift between high and low culture, between elitist Persian art film and lowbrow *filmfārsī* has often been exemplified by anecdotes of ignorant theater-goers knifing up their seats in protest of the tedious obscurantism of experiment. The commercial failures of New Wave film shore up this rift.

The dissipation of psychological realism in the New Wave thus bodes a certain emptiness that is parallel to, but yet distinct, and implicitly superior to the emptiness of the entranced subjects of ethnographic film. To Manizheh's intransigent sobriety and reticence the colonel's daughters quip, "This is not the countryside. Here, silence is the sign of backwardness." Manizheh's silence is the manifestation of her authenticity, her refusal to adopt the normative desires of the modular West (symbolized through women's magazines and freedom of sexual choice). But her silence is simultaneously the effect of the violence of a modernity that has rendered her authenticity impossible. Manizheh's new silence is the mourning of an old silence, as the psychological emptiness of the modernist character sublates the rudimentary emptiness of the *zārī*. In her "strange silence," she keeps a hidden secret that returns the entire indeterminacy (*ibhām*) of the film back to herself, notes one critic.[118] On the other hand, superstitious and dreaming, *Wind of Jin*'s subjects do not suffer the "unnameable" metaphysical anxieties symptomatic of modern, estranged subjectivity. Their suffering is primal, universal, but also impermanent and flat, vaporous as the self that vanishes with aphasia, the loss of language, or the reduction of meaning to a pure acoustic encounter.

Music of the South: Zār

Part of his locally specific body of cultural influences, *zār* absorbed Taqvāʾī. After filming *Wind of Jin,* he returned to the south to produce

« 106 »   *Zār* and the Anxieties of the Iranian New Wave

another ethnographic documentary about it, this time in the island of Qishm. Unlike *Wind of Jin, Music of the South: Zār* (*Mūsīqī-i Jūnūb: Zār*) relinquishes ellipticism for a scientistic candidness refused in his previous documentary. The film mimics universal ethnographic styles of the period. Taqvā'ī's voice narrates the prosaic geographical and spatial features of the island. We learn, for example, that it is the largest island in the Persian Gulf, that the primary forms of livelihood include sailing between Persian Gulf ports, net weaving, rope braiding, fishing, and shrimp baiting. Still harmonizing with the esoteric subject matter, poetic embellishments mystify more straightforward lines of narration. Framing the sea, then revolving to reveal a leftward pan of the distant port structures' desolate angularity, Taqvā'ī's voice relates: "The jetty is the beating heart of Bandar Qishm. If the jetty is empty, the town is quiet and serene and until another day, until the coming of another dhow, there is no sound but the sound of the breathing sea. Only at night sometimes the sound of the *ahl-i havā's duhul* cuts through the sea's breath." Silence neutralizes the droning wind, replacing the pathos-saturated a cappella lullaby that accompanied the oneiric montage of *Wind of Jin.* The unique juxtaposition of vortical sound and silence leaves a lasting imprint on Iranian soundtracks.[119] A lengthy continuous shot of a *zār* ceremony tightens the homology between *Wind of Jin* and *Music of the South,* both of which ultimately concern the phenomenon of *zār.* However, contrasting with his orchestrated noninterference in *Wind of Jin,* Taqvā'ī's narration guides the viewer through the *zār* ceremony in *Music of the South.* In *Wind of Jin* a confrontation with confusion ensues when the drumming first stops; in *Music of the South,* the audience takes reprieve in the authority of description, rather than the equivocation of poesis, in the voiceover. The *zār* will not leave the woman's body, the narration informs. "The *zār* speaks with Baba Darvish." Baba Darvish shows the woman a ring. Commodity exchanges such as this one commonly color the prosaic economic context of *zār.*

In comparison to *Wind of Jin's* audiovisual thaumaturgy, *Music of the South* delivers an understated but aboveboard narrative about *zār.* We learn of specific names and places. Mama Hanifeh, whom Taqvā'ī introduces as an old mama *zār,* is a well-known practitioner in Qishm.[120] At times, certain lines appear lifted straight from Sā'idī's monograph. Thus, we learn that "The *zār* winds have mostly come from Africa and most of its sufferers are blacks whose long-ago ancestors came to be slaves" [*bih ghulāmī va kanīzī umadand*]. This statement's facticity clearly contrasts with the more poetically inflected "they came for the price of dates" that Shāmlū recites at the climax of *Wind of Jin*.

Whether *Music of the South*'s prosaic forthrightness cost it its success, or whether there were additional causes for its doom to oblivion, the film falls among Taqvāʾī's unknown works. *Wind of Jin* remains a memorable, memorialized film, while there are no traces of *Music of the South*. Unlike *Wind of Jin*, *Tranquility in the Presence of Others*, and *Arbaʿīn* (see chapter 3), all of which were selected as Iranian entries to the 1972 Venice Film Festival, *Music of the South: Zār* left no lasting imprint, evidenced in the near impossibility of its retrieval today and the unfamiliarity of its title, as if it were destined for oblivion. The success of abstraction within the ethnographic film genre is worth remarking and has not, one might argue, yet received its full exploration in either film studies, nor in the anthropology-based scholarship on experimental ethnography. Ethnographic film is "in constant danger of becoming art." But "What kind of art is it?"[121] Does the valorization of abstraction express a desire for a remove from facts or simply inflate facticity's least-appreciated condition of possibility? Facts, that is, are never purely unmediated, passing through, or more accurately, articulating, extending language. Facts depend upon signification, iterability, repetition.

If *Wind of Jin*, and not *Music of the South*, its more factual counterpart, influenced later filmmaking and made a palpable mark upon the cinematic history of Iran, its loss of facticity in comparison to *Music of the South* seems partially responsible. One might hazard such a conclusion based on the evidence: as with *Wind of Jin*, prior to his "comeback" with the television series *Dear Uncle Napoleon* (1976), all of Taqvāʾī's subsequent works *further* abstracted and fictionalized dimensions of the subject of *zār*. Wind possession would return again in 1986. "Malul, my dear, let go of this jin and fairy nonsense," one of the characters in *Captain Sun* pleads. Again, as in *Wind of Jin*, *zār*, metonymically connected to the African slave, is held responsible for desecrating the lawless "no-man's land" of the Persian Gulf port.[122]

To recapitulate: *zār* is a trace of Indian Ocean slavery; *zār* generates a chain of cinematic works. But inside this chain, which delivers

« 108 »   *Zār* and the Anxieties of the Iranian New Wave

various reactions to modernity (salvage documentary and preservationist drive, New Wave anxiety, noir nihilism), Indian Ocean slavery is paradoxically repressed. Indian Ocean slavery is repressed both in its constitutive relation to modernity, that is, as joined to the source of impending destruction, as the source of a certain wished-for salve (*zār*) intended to heal modernity's still-incurring wound, and more troublingly, as a historical fact that the aesthetics of modernist abstraction makes disappear in its very event. By *repression* one cannot simply mean the prevention of some otherwise intact fact from conscious, or full expression. (Each "derivative of the repressed" has "its own special vicissitude."[123]) Though released in 1970, *Tranquility* was immediately banned upon its exhibition. Interpreted as a political critique of the Pahlavi regime, a third of its footage was censored. But there is a more original and enigmatic censorship at work in the translation from *Wind of Jin* to *Tranquility,* and more enigmatically still, an expulsion at work in the recursivity linking *Music of the South* and *Wind of Jin*. Something inherent in Indian Ocean slavery refuses simple transcription. If we can critique the casualty with which Indian Ocean slavery is broached in *Wind of Jin* (*pīsh az ān kih siyāh bih bahā-'i khurmāh biyāyad,* "for the price of dates") it cannot simply be because there is a more faithful film, a more faithful archive, nor more faithful *facts,* elsewhere.

The increasingly elaborate layers of fictionalization unfold laterally, feverishly upon the same generic place, between the ethnographic *Music of the South* and *Wind of Jin,* and between *Wind of Jin* and the slew of fictional feature-length films that begin with *Tranquility in the Presence of Others.* On the one hand then, abstraction begins simply with *zār*'s thematic extension and dispersion as a generalized madness in *Tranquility*.[124] On the other hand, the increasingly complex layers of fictionalization begin with a redacting translation: "The *zār* winds have mostly come from Africa and most of its sufferers are blacks whose long-ago ancestors came to be slaves," in *Music of the South* to *Wind of Jin*'s nebulous "they came for the price of dates." Redaction here embodies a poeisis that cannot simply be described as erasure. Nor can it be simply valorized as poetry, for it bodes a tendentious repression that characterizes Iran's relationship to its own history of slavery. At the same time, the necessity, which is to say, the unavoidability of this repression, is built into the very constitution of facticity. There is never any pure fact if the condition of possibility for fact is its capacity for repetition, recapitulation. And repetition is fundamentally exposure, a path to corruption, contingency and impurity. Like the *duhul*'s drum beat, whose incessant repetition leads the *zārī* into trance, the repetition of fact leads its truth astray into the false. (But the *zārī*'s trance is not only outward travel; it is a return to a more fundamental field, a return to a certain emptiness. Similarly, in its need to be repeated, truth falls back into the refused falsity within.) If the transmission of fact in general *depends* upon iterability, then a certain irresolution bears recursively on the facticity of fact. Nothing is more exemplary of this dimension of facticity than *zār* itself. *Zār*'s historicity is self-eviscerating. If trance is an "anemic communicability," the phenomena of denial and negation surrounding the history of Indian Ocean slavery also suggests that there is something originarily incommunicable, indeed unrepresentable, unrepeatable, seemingly unfactual, about Indian Ocean slavery. "Trancers experience a kind of syncope, an absence, a lapse, a 'cerebral eclipse.'"[125] Historians lament the absence of material archives that would deliver us straight to the facts themselves. But what the unfolding of Taqvā'ī's cinema suggests is that Indian Ocean slavery is both antithetical to fact and simultaneously revelatory of its fundamental structure.

Iranophilia, Realism, and Blackness

Like other global modernist movements, the Iranian New Wave was heavily indebted to the moral commitment to reality known as social realism. Moved by a certain faith in the political potentiality of the image, New Wave realism sought to dislodge the subject from the cult of individualism and attendant fascinations that threatened a collective societal fall into machinism, automatism, and delusion. Anxiety about modernity's destructive, consumerist drive is unsurprisingly expressed in *Tranquility* through the trope of female vanity. "Each person has to save themselves somehow," Maliheh tells her father's new wife as she flips through magazine pages. Manizheh stares blankly ahead. In a future sequence, the three women are seen scurrying down a narrow alley, returning from the salon with voluminous bouffants, but eerie, adrenaline-infused music synched with the scene undermines Maliheh's belief that makeovers would quell the nebulous gloom that "will strangle you." That Maliheh commits suicide at the end of the film suggests, rather unambiguously, that her expressed faith in the salvational value of female self-presentation is, literally, a dead end.

Consumerism—the rampant drive for commodity acquisition—is a theme that runs through the *fīlmfārsī* mode, even when it is an ob-

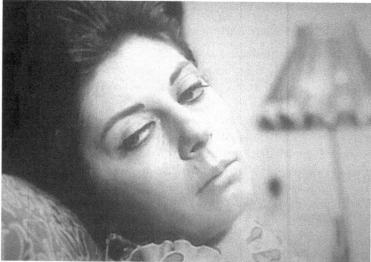

Figure 15. Scenes from Nāṣir Taqvāī's *Tranquility in the Presence of Others* (1970). Top: Maliheh putting on makeup before the party. Bottom: Manizheh, struggling to enjoy herself at the daughters' house party.

ject of critique or moral derision, as in the so-called *jaheli* or "tough-guy" genre, posed against the (usually masculine) spiritualism of traditional Iranian culture. As an expression of desire for pure and limitless expenditure, *filmfārsī*'s penchant for materialism manifests through its proclivity for escapist narratives, fantasy, melodrama, hyperbolic romance, and the omnipresent, usually irrelevant, and unreasonably long sequin-filled song-and-dance sequences that so ruffled its critics. (In modernity, the phantasm becomes buried in the object; henceforth it can only be consumed and destroyed without ever providing satisfaction, without producing experience.) As an antidote to *filmfārsī*'s "dream-weaving," its glorification of the quixotic and the aleatory, but also its compulsive repetition of types, codes, and uninspired binaries, New Wave filmmakers recommended reality. At the same time, faced with endless obstacles hurled at them by the Pahlavi state censorship machine, filmmakers took recourse to symbolism and abstraction, figuring the real through strategies of evasion. In its approach to the real through myth, New Wave strategies dovetailed with those of Persian modernism more generally.

The Iranophilia characteristic of early twentieth-century literati was largely motivated by efforts to rehabilitate the early history of Iranian culture, preserved, it was imagined, in the oral traditions of rural Iranians. Muhammad Alī Jamālzādih's position on the potential for anthropological strategies to serve the project of democratizing Persian literature by reviving authentic Iranian themes testifies to this initial modernist desire, as did Sādiq Hidāyat's pioneering initiatives to embrace Persian folklore. The first Iranian to collect, systematically analyze, and compose methodological guidelines for the study of folk material, encouraging young writers to follow suit, Hidāyat's endeavors were unambiguously charged with racially taxonomic impulse.[126] His *Nayrangistān* divided folklore between the practices of early Indo-Iranian races and non-Iranian ones, for instance.[127] Famously, in abidance with the racial ethos of Pahlavi nationalism, language and customs associated with Arab habits were distinguished from Persian ones and discarded as degenerate. For Hidāyat, the folklore of the people [*mardum-i tūdeh*; *ʿavām*] is the fount [*sarchishmah*] of literature, fine arts and philosophy, and those who drink from this source [*sīrāb shudan*] are the learned [*taḥṣīl kardah*].[128] Hidāyat's syntax in his essay "Folklore, or the Culture of the People," inadvertently suggests a parasitic relation between levels of society that the doubled sense of the term *culture* (*farhang*)

« 112 »   *Zār* and the Anxieties of the Iranian New Wave

conceals. Early twentieth-century approaches to indigenizing modernism bordered on desires for racial and cultural purification present in much nineteenth-century reform discourse.

By contrast, the generation of postwar, post-1953-coup intellectuals defined positions that were ideologically distinct from figures like Hidāyat and Jamālzādih, even as they relied on similar ethnographic strategies for their political expressions. Thus, Shāmlū and Sā'idī are simultaneously folklorists, anthropologists, and treasured seers of the political contemporary. The famous poet and literary critic Reza Barahani named Shāmlū's poetry "a biography of our society."[129] And yet the revival of folklorist themes characteristic of the early twentieth-century wave of literary modernism is impossible to extract from a larger movement of anthropological impetus institutionally supported by both Pahlavi regimes, and refueled by anti-imperialist energies in the 1960s.[130]

Taqvā'ī and Sā'idī were among the group of intellectuals and artists who understood themselves as committed to political transformation and journalistic revelation, and doubtlessly their forays into rural Iran formed part of an intent to chronicle the injustices spawned by Pahlavi-era dysfunction and oppression. "An outstanding psychiatrist, whose profession could have brought him riches," Sā'idī instead "opted to serve the poor in one of the poorest districts of Tehran."[131] (Sā'idī "comes from *sā'id al-mamalik*," offers the author of his own name, "helper of the slaves.")[132] Similarly, Taqvā'ī's earlier involvement with a collective of writers of southern origin who endeavored to articulate Gulf impoverishment in the publication *Gāhnāmah hunar va adabīyāt-i jūnūb* affirms his leftist political orientation. It has been suggested that Taqvā'ī's *Tābistān-i hamān sāl* (*The Summer of That Year*, 1968) informed the nascent trend in modern Iranian literature oriented toward working-class life.[133] Taqvā'ī seems to heighten the impetus toward literary democratization that characterized the modernity of early Iranian twentieth-century literature. If Jamālzādih could lament the Iranian literati's disregard for mass audiences in favor of a sequestered elitism symbolized by baroque language,[134] Taqvā'ī moves this complaint further, relinquishing prose altogether in favor of filmmaking: "There were things in the lives of the people from my birthplace that I saw that I wanted to communicate to others. Story writing wasn't appropriate for these experiences, and this is why I chose cinema."[135]

Taqvā'ī and the artistic cohort to which he belonged regarded

Zār and the Anxieties of the Iranian New Wave « 113 »

film as a means to both connect with and reflect the social ailments of modern Iran. Ethnographic documentary appeared to Taqvāʾī a form of democratic history writing or archiving: in an interview he reveals not only his preference for documentary to feature-film form, because the former could most accurately represent his life experiences, but also that his experiences—presumably of life in the south —were indeed worthy of inscription. It would be "a shame if they weren't recorded."[136] This is a position Taqvāʾī held on to as late as the 1990s.[137] And indeed Taqvāʾī's representation of *zār* has been praised for preserving and transmitting "traditional rites" to new generations.[138] That Taqvāʾī and filmmakers like him were eager in the first place to collude with a political regime that they opposed ideologically testifies to certain hopes and investments in national television's potency as a medium for mass communication. In the same interview Taqvāʾī expresses resentment about the fact that the National Iranian Radio and Television refused to televise his works, despite having ordered some of them to be made and offering him funding to produce them in the first place.[139]

Ethnography, then, in its relationship to the excavation of indigenous culture, funds the source of modernism's politicized, amphibolic drive for the real. Taqvāʾī's ethnographies of *zār* are simultaneously preservationist, and indirectly critical of modernity. It is hardly remarkable that the modernist critique of modernity (consumerism, materialism, machinism, emulation) disregards that the value system under attack also activates and energizes Indian Ocean slavery—that it propels the black slave's arrival to the Persian Gulf coast "for the price of dates." Du Bois's society darling ciphers every Maliheh and Mahlaqa, every Zhila, every middle-class *filmfārsi* housewife and her bourgeois ambitions that the New Wave diagnosed as pathological symptom in need of cure. The unassuming, overconsuming, white-aspiring, narcissistic female, preoccupied with "the enigma of the body," is the figurative source fueling the extractive drive for raw global resources that sustain modern existence and reproduce the violence of desire. Global consumerism repopulates date plantation slavery in the Persian Gulf. Though *fardh* dates were not locally appreciated, "Americans loved the sweet, sticky variety, and grocers stocked and sold millions of pounds of the fruit annually as a holiday confection."[140] The (ungendered) black slave is not just a tool for extractive agriculture, nor for the satiation of extraction's rapacious drive. The black slave also embodies the spiritual and therapeutic resources that supply the modernist critique with its language for grievance. In its double, self-cancelling role, the black slave both bears and reveals modernity's destruction; simultaneously, heals that destruction—mirroring *zār's* peculiarity as pharmakon, disease and cure.

Generically poised to do so, *People of the Wind (Ahl-i Havā)*, Sā'idī's ethnographic monograph, airs political grievance even more explicitly than Taqvā'ī's collection of documentary films. After providing detailed descriptions of various aspects of *zār* belief in the south, Sā'idī declares that *zār* deserves more research, thought, and attention and should not be homogenized or collapsed into the myriad other forms of dealing with spirits; in this region *zār* "may have an economic and sociological dimension."[141] Sā'idī's descriptions of the black communities in the south detail desolation and poverty, conforming to the general project of *adabīyāt-i mutahid,* committed literature of the period. But in addition to their poverty, Sā'idī also notes the segregation that divides black and nonblack, summoning up the reader's indignation at anecdotal antiblackness.[142]

Whatever possible motivations one might attribute to Sā'idī's inclusion of the degrading scenarios he witnessed in his fieldwork, the sparks of indignation and small bids of sympathy collection present in his ethnographic text get lost in the transformation of his observations into his fictional short story writing based upon these very same encounters. The first story of *Fear and Trembling* opens with the main character, Salam Ahmad, who hears his name called out from the sea prior to glimpsing a "strange black man sitting next to a fire with his wooden leg stretched out in a parlor." Upon perceiving the figure of the black man—whose name we never learn—Salam Ahmad immediately believes himself to be possessed by an evil wind and runs to his neighbor for help. The villagers, exemplifying the irrationality and superstition of the characters in *Fear and Trembling,* stone the black man to death in response to Salam Ahmad's accusation. Salam Ahmad finally heals from his curse in the concluding scene of the story when the villagers thrust him near the dead black man's pyre of ashes. The black man whose life is sacrificed in exchange for Salam Ahmad's salvation remains, literally, the "flattest" character of all in this opening story. The author describes only his bizarre literal and figural voraciousness:

> "Even if we kill him, he'll turn up somewhere else," said Zahed.
> "His kind won't stop until the end of time."

Zar and the Anxieties of the Iranian New Wave   « 115 »

"He keeps coming closer. Look at him!" said Zakariya. The black man was very close. His face was quite flat, as if his nose and lips had been gnawed away....

"I'm hungry, I'm hungry," the black man pleaded. The men each picked up a rock and hurled it at the black man.[143]

The anonymous black man is both the cause of Salam Ahmad's wind affliction and the ultimate victim of *zār*; he is stoned, as Ahmad, and the now protected community is healed. In Sā'idī's ethnographic work, black people are impoverished and deserving of the reader's moral sympathy, for they are also discriminated against by other poor people. In Sā'idī's fiction, by contrast, black characters are impoverished, but they are also devious and dangerous, stimulating fears surrounding *zār* and remnants of tradition and sorcery that modernizers and their advocates were eager to eradicate, or aestheticize and taxonomize, to put at a distance for contemplation, preservation, appreciation, and exhibition. Marking a state of innocent being prior to the exposure to industrialization, mass literacy, and modern infrastructure, the rural subject is not merely pitied by the intellectual vanguard. He is simultaneously pitied, envied, and despised. In Sā'idī's work, blackness exposes this ambivalence. And yet, the anxiety that is marked by blackness is not merely an anxiety about generic difference. As the tensions and contradictions of the New Wave and its visual codes suggest, articulated through blackness, modernist angst is anxiety about orientation in general.

It is as if, in airing grievances with the pathological aspects of modernity, Sā'idī also suggests the impossibility of differentiating victim from perpetrator, just as Taqvā'ī's Shāmlū attributes the spirit winds to blacks who came "for the price of dates," yet remarks the winds' antiquity as well as the healing power of an atemporal black arrival, clouding causality. The indistinction between cause and effect also suggests uncertainty about a way out. As the well-known intellectual Daryush Ashuri satirically points out, "Sā'idī thought that tractors were ruining the livelihood of people, but if he went to a village where there were no tractors, he would see that people are really destitute."[144] Plainly, the anti-imperial, anticolonial critique of modernity struggles to reconcile itself to disappearing alternatives. *Fīlmfārsī* elects escapism and repetition compulsion. Alternative cinema chooses death. The turmoil of facticity in *Wind of Jin* makes legible a more general recession of reality that becomes the latent

Figure 16. Film still from the opening of Nāṣir Taqvāī's *Wind of Jin* (*Bād-i Jin*, 1969).

obsession of modernist auteurs and authors. Despite the focus on its empirical dimensions, modernity most profoundly describes the difficulty of orienting oneself toward a real that is always already slipping away, precipitating a generalized anxiety. Scholars suggest that the Iranian New Wave shaped perceptions of the historical process of modernization. But it is perhaps more justly the case that the cinema of the New Wave undermines confidence in perception itself.

It is true that the introduction of new technologies like cinema was itself part of this global destabilization, this globally diminished confidence, refracting in turn myriad sociopolitical eruptions occurring globally: wars, coups, anticolonial revolutions, political defeats. Nevertheless, as the phenomenon of *zār* itself suggests, cinema—the play of conjunction—merely reactivates an original, immemorial dehiscence at the core of signification, at the core of the relation between the subject and object, between context and its void. At the height of *zār*, consciousness lapses, releases itself from the gravitational pull toward a univocal real. If *zār* is a trace of African slavery, it is not a trace in the traditional, indexical sense; *zār* is a disorientation toward history. This disorientation is blackened, dispersed, borrowed, transformed, and is why, rather than a subject for analysis, or the articulation of social grievance, as was the putative goal of many of the modernist works of the era, historical suffering and racial injury quietly sinks into a nontheme of *Wind of Jin*, a subject for abstraction and experiential intuition (as in the initial shot of the waves; the cut from the close-up of ships to the destruction of Bandar Lingih carried over in Shāmlū's narration, blurred images), than of critical reflection. Against Sā'idī's prescriptions in *Ahl-i Havā*, *zār* barely forms a coherent horizon for the exploration of redress, for *zār* is the very dissolution of horizon. As its movement to screen suggests, this corrosion manifests as anxiety, and is why *zār*, though apparently parochial and peripheral to the New Wave (and all that it represents), in fact lies at its heart. By consequence, the dissatisfactions with modernity constitutive of Persian modernism encrypt the history of African slavery that they simultaneously repress, refuse, forget, but also incubate, store for the future.

« 3 »

Irano-Afro-Iran

The Racial Aesthetic

"Every day is ʿāshūrā, every land is Karbālā."
—Shiʾi saying

Pink light scatters on water, reflecting the diminished sun melting into the Persian Gulf's horizon. At once violent and grounding, the sunset image absorbs and projects the memory of blood condensed through the film's restless narrative. Slaves on dhows traveling from Africa's Eastern coast once landed ashore Persian Gulf sunsets such as the one the camera frames. If colors conjure memory, the landscape's crimson doubtless recalls those bobbing lateens no less than it does Husayn's perennial slaughter at Karbala. The disappearance of the light signals the onset of slow, drawn, rhythmic clapping. The movement of time kept by the measured pounding of palms on chests is not, however, orienting, nor does it signal clear temporal passage or direction. Nāṣir Taqvāʾī's experimental documentaries abound with synesthetic effects. Like the ethnographic documentary *Wind of Jin* discussed in the previous chapter, *Arbaʿin* (1970) dispenses a kind of knowledge whose mode of facticity both transcends and fails the hubris of historical fact, confronting instead the dense impurity at the heart of historicity.

Arabic for "forty," *arbaʿin* names a component of the elegiac Shiʾi ritual commemorating the murder of Husayn ibn Ali, Muhammad's grandson, at the infamous seventh-century Battle of Karbala, solidifying a tragic story of origins for the minority Twelver sect of Islam. The Muharram celebrations, of which *arbaʿin* forms an important if underrepresented part in scholarship, mark the original scission between Sunni and Shiʾi Muslims. "While most (Sunni) Muslims

« 119 »

« 120 »   Irano-Afro-Iran

celebrate Muharram as the beginning of a New Year, Shi'i communities wear black and prepare for mourning."[1] Spectacular and controversial in that *arba'īn* and the Muharram rituals to which it belongs can involve, beyond a vital component called *sīnah-zanī* (chest-striking; or *latam* in Arabic), self-flagellation, chain-swinging, and knife-, razor-, or sword-driven bloodletting, variations of *arba'īn* prevail throughout modern-day Iran, home to a majority of Shi'i Muslims. In southern provinces like Būshihr, *arba'īn* acquires what has been recognized as a distinctly black character on account of the scattered African diaspora dispersed along the Gulf for hundreds (or by some accounts, thousands) of years. Descriptions of the ritual stress a qualitative difference in affect and style characterizing regional specificity. In the Iranian south, animation and speed impassion the sobriety more familiar to Shi'i mourning occasions, offering testament to a haphazardly recorded history of movement absorbed in the oblivions of denial, shame, indifference, and time.

One of his better known films from an otherwise more or less forgotten oeuvre of amateur ethnographic documentaries, Taqvā'ī's *Arba'īn* clarifies more than just the singularity of south Iranian Muharram's regional distinction. If the more theatrical Ta'zīyah has received greater attention in academic scholarship on Muharram, Taqvā'ī's choice to focalize the procession of *arba'īn* hints at a subtle recursiveness that thematically dominates his treatment of Muharram as visionary history.[2] For Shi'is, the importance of Husayn's martyrdom at Karbala cannot be overstated. "Every day is 'āshūrā, every land is Karbālā," goes the well known saying. "Every aspect of the pious Shi'i Muslim's life revolves around this anecdotal paradigm and is ordered by it."[3] But if Būshihrī *arba'īn* is exemplary, Taqvā'ī's cinematic *Arba'īn* suggests that it is exemplarily black, and that its blackness exemplarily marks a retroactive interruption to the self-evidence of historical memory.

The film commences with the unique rhythmic *sinj ū damām* musical form that a group of black musicians performs in an alleyway—a call to town dwellers to gather in a shared experience of conflated feeling. Then, shifting to a void, Muharram's narrative loses the anchor of clear expression through flashes of stained glass framed against a pitch black, metonymizing the Dihdāshtī and Bihbihānī mosques where parts of the film take place. Images illustrate floating, disembodied arms shedding drops of blood; a faceless Imam Husayn alights on his white horseback; a dizzying swish pan confusing light and color against black space actualizes a question about spatiotemporal coordinates. Following this transition, the film shows day preparations for the Muharram ritual: men carry construction instruments and hang banners. The actual *arba'īn* procession ensues, an exclusively male gathering for the enactment of *nūhah-khūnī* (dirge singing) and *sīnah-zanī* (chest striking) in the dimmed sacred space where an enclosed Black Iranian singer, the famed Jahānbakhsh Kurdīzādah, more popularly recognized by the nicknames Bakhshū or Bakhshī, receives gifts of colored sashes strewn upon his chest, as he trills tragedy into the microphone, his audience motioning responses to his bellows with powerful body thumps while stepping the circle left.[4] Like a distracted onlooker, the camera cuts away from this neat chronology to seemingly irrelevant elsewheres. This distraction from the collectivity of the fervor magnifies through an interest in lostness expressed as intercut scenes of a veiled black figure ambling down dark corridors of the desolate port city. (Despite its exclusively, even aggressively male exterior, its historiography suggests that *'āshūrā* is an originally feminine mourning.)[5] Spatial devastation and ghostlike vacuity mirrors temporal confusion and recurs in Taqvā'ī's work, and in artifacts of Indian Ocean world port cities more generally.[6]

Known in Iran for popularizing the Būshihrī variant of *arba'īn* throughout the country, Taqvā'ī's experimental documentary provides more to its viewer than mere visual and auditory description about this enigmatic regional component of the Muharram rituals.[7] Taqvā'ī's documentation of *arba'īn* merits focus for the way in which its form and content crystallizes historical inquiry about the blackness of Muharram's elegiac form as practiced and performed around the borders of the Persian Gulf. In my characterization of a pivotal sunset scene in the introduction, I tried to portray both the nebulousness of such inquiry and the unlikelihood of its total satisfaction. In what follows, I suggest that a fuller, more replete historiographical account of blackness may not remedy whatever shortcomings one tends to associate with historical opacity and paucity. Rather, (cinematic) opacity, as it coincides with the rhythmic spacing of *sinj ū damām* and *sīnah-zanī*, is itself constitutive of the philosophical problem of historicity. The space from which meaning arises, the flashing interval that interposes the image, as the silence that intercedes sound, makes inevitable theft, displacement, derangement, and constitutes, simultaneously, an absolute freedom.[8] The question of origin broached and displaced by a *globalized* blackness might be said to exemplify this enigmatic opacity—a resilient force that sustains, coheres common sense, yet discontinuously unsettles knowledge. In the previous chapter I explored how Iranian ethnography's modernism suggests racial blackness as a form of global conjunction. Here I further deliberate upon the cosmically racial dimensions of cultural and aesthetic representation, with focus on the ambivalent relation between conjunction and syncretism that is borne out by the contemporary interest in "Afro-Iran."

A filmic representation of *arba'in* shows how this Shi'i ritual can bear the history of blackness only recursively: through a kind of peeling away, tearing and tarrying, rather than a simple gathering or accumulation of layers of fact. At the same time, taking into account the material conditions of possibility for Taqvā'ī's oeuvre demands that we understand how the racial context of the film connects to and infiltrates the images that comprise it. As an object produced partially in the service of the project of national culture during Iran's twentieth-century racialized dislocative nationalism, Taqvā'ī's *Arba'in* suggests how the aestheticization of religious ritual enacts and appears to resolve the tension between Iran's racial taint and its racial purity.

This tension is expressed primarily and usually through the opposition between Arabness (expressed via Iran's thorough, but continuously if inconsistently disavowed imbrication with Islamicate culture, its complex relation to its own religiosity, its Arabicized language and script) and Iran's Europeanness—a late and cherished discovery of its Indo-European or Aryan essence, its transcendental whiteness. Indo-European affiliation developed from an unlikely origin in nineteenth-century comparative philology and was adopted by Qajar-era Iranian literati and intellectuals, and eventually by both Pahlavi regimes during a formative period of Iranian nationalism that broadly overlaps with the periodization of Taqvā'ī's documentary films. The anti-Arab and anti-Islamic dimensions of early twentieth-century Persian nationalism have been relatively well explored, and perhaps overly emphasized, in Iranian studies scholarship.[9] However, ideals of modern political subjectivity modeled through Shi'i tropes in the mid-twentieth century suggest a deeper sinuosity in the relationship between racial modernity and Islam that troubles the usual emphasis on taxonomic racial distinctions between the Semite and Aryan, Arab and Persian, and that exposes limits to extant narratives on the Iranian inheritance of modern race theory. For, in its antagonism to syncretism, understood as passivity, politicized Shi'ism reactivates more antiquated binaries that flout nationalism theorists' emphasis on the exemplarity and modernity of scientific racism. In other words, in producing its own sets of binary distinctions pivoting around the concept of the human, modernized, politicized Shi'ism itself brings out a certain racial tension inherent in the very notion of (modern) religio-political subjectivity. Put simply, Islam is not merely a racialized object, as has usually been claimed in discourses on Persian nationalism, but simultaneously a racializing force.[10]

And thus, if Taqvā'ī's *Arba'īn* thematizes race, it is not primarily or only because of its protagonist's perceived blackness. The extent to which we are invited to perceive this blackness (as racial) is itself an irresolvable question; the status of the reality or being of blackness in Southwest Asia is always under question or attack, often, but not even always, by those who reap some benefit from disavowing it. Nor is race present in *Arba'īn* because of Islam's perceived Arabness, which reactivates the familiar modern racialized opposition of Aryan and Semite. Rather, the domain that renders legible the documentary as an object of culture funds the source of the *non*racial, unmarked, and universal subject, liberated from the mundane world to which racial categories are bound. This domain is that of the aesthetic, but shares in common with the realm of the political the capacity for and aspiration to universality. Culture is the master symbol of civility and civilization, as *farhang* and *adab* are the conflicting master symbols of *tamadun* (civilization).[11] Aesthetic representations of culture, fueling civilizational (national) pride, are inherently fraught and refractory, racial even where race is nowhere to be perceived according to inherited logics.

This is a strange, winding formulation that I am compelled to develop through sometimes contradictory, intertwined readings of *Arba'īn*. On the one hand, as an artifact that, however dimly, reflects blackness and its history in the south of Iran in a peculiarly cinematic way, *Arba'īn* offers a model of nonnormative historical desire that reckons with the problem of delimiting the conceptual, temporal, and spatial boundaries of Africanness and Blackness, which is also to say, it offers a model of nonnormative historical desire that reckons with the problem of the syncretic structure that holds together the thought of "Afro-Iran." It is nonnormative to the extent that the experimental film, unlike the ethnographic literature surrounding the phenomena it documents, refuses to, or perhaps more simply cannot, take a stance on how the history of blackness ought to be thought, imagined, segregated, or made exceptional. *History* is too strong a word for the kind of knowledge it makes available. The film does not reach for or transmit information. On the other hand, as a chronicle of blackened religious exoticism at a time when Shi'ism was itself birthing a new concept of the political, *Arba'in* shows how the aesthetic reactivates a primally racial distinction between civility and savagery that undergirds this new religio-political subjectivity, as well as the (white) national aesthetic culture to which the film belongs. In fulfilling these different functions, *Arba'in* suggests that the racial is imbricated with *both* the production and refusal of particularity, and is simultaneously constitutive of Iran's filiation with Indo-Europeanness (whiteness), of Shi'i political subjectivity's valorization of activity over passivity (aspiration to universality), and finally, of modernist film's affinity for abstraction (mirror for aesthetic subjectivization). The refusal or disavowal of particularity and affectability is linked to a certain anxiety about the syncretism, hybridity, and enigmatic mixedness that underlies, but also displaces, all being in general. (And therefore, maddeningly, the disavowal of particularity is not distinct from the avowal and reification of particularity.[12]) To the extent that blackness is exemplarily syncretic, exemplarily embodied, ambivalence about particularity is also an anxiety about the force of blackness, an originary cutting into the fantasized integrity of the in-itself.[13]

Arba'in

The Africanness of Iran's southern provinces seems to only recently have come to the fairly sustained critical interest of scholars, artists, activists, and filmmakers. But Taqvā'i's documentary suggests that the festive distinctness of southern Iranian music has a longer genealogy of representation. Decades before the contemporary fascination with "Afro-Iran" broached in the introduction and approached from a different angle in the conclusion, Taqvā'i's film engages the question of South Iranian distinction, while showing how, at every level, the syncretism symbolized by the hyphen marks a threatening implosion.[14] As an artifact of Afro-Iranian life, *Arba'in* thus demands a reckoning with the impossibility of rescuing the bewilderingly facile notion of syncretism from its oppositional presumption of purity. The contested term *syncretism* bears flaws that are uniquely magnified in its application to black cultural forms and speculations about them.[15] It is often acknowledged that the self-evident opposition between pure and mixed models, reifies and stabilizes racial categories themselves.[16] Yet, as a heuristic, syncretism allows at the very least for the appearance of otherwise opaque and submerged ways of being and world inhabitation. These latter can bear no doubt historical and anthropological value, but also philosophical value, so long as the strategies at play risk energization by methodological critique, even and especially where critique results in impasse. In other words, syncretism's deconstructive power is only made possible by putting its own truth to the risk of total annihilation. For if mixedness is always preconditioned by purity (and how could it be otherwise?), we are hopelessly tied up in an irresolvable logic of infinite regress. To say that there is nothing but syncretism, nothing but conjunction, is also to presuppose that there is nothing but purity, nothing but stable essences—at best, like Eisensteinian montage, combined to arrive at third terms. In short, syncretism is impossible. Yet there is nothing but syncretism. In the wake of this radical difficulty, an effusion of origins becomes more tolerable than the absolute displacement of origin that conjunction effects.

Nowhere does this dynamic air its elusiveness more characteristically than through the notion of musical syncretism that *Arba'in* implicitly documents and reflects in and upon through its form. Drawing attention to its subliminal interest, *Arba'in*'s opening high shot condenses the question of African origin at a material level, beckoning with discreetly ethnomusicological strategies for tracking diffusion. Music opens up a certain microcosm that the poet and theorist Amiri Baraka and a twentieth-century anthropological tradition invested in theories of diffusion once identified as the privileged medium for reading African transmutations into blackness.[17] Studies meticulously detail syncretized black spiritual and musical forms abounding throughout the Americas. But far less material, even at the level of bare information, circulates about black musical articulations surviving in the areas covered by what was once a part of the sprawling Indian Ocean trade networks. "Lack of information," as we saw in chapter 2, is not an aberration but constitutive of blackness in the Indian Ocean. Centering on rhythm, which is to say, on silence as much as on sound, blackened music is antithetical but also prior to fact.

« 126 »   Irano-Afro-Iran

Ethnomusicology has long relied upon features of musical instruments as criteria for resemblance in the understanding of cultural diffusion.[18] As if filming from the top of a wall, the camera shows a gathered group of men in an alleyway immersed in a steady beat of cymbals (*sinj*), drums (*damām*), and horns (*būq*). The camera zooms in on one of the drums, drawing attention to its intricate features: tanned goat hide stretched across two ends of its body (*pīp*), suspended by braided bands over an old black man's shoulders. The camera zooms in steadily upon his face bobbing to and fro adjacent to the drum, while the music steadily accelerates. The zoom-in—a technology of instant dramatization—italicizes the frame, which, for a moment holds this adjacency between the musician's face and his drum. In addition to corroborating both historical information about the participation of black musicians in south Iranian ceremonial culture and more recent ethnographic data shoring up its continuity, the zoom-in that holds this juxtaposition evokes the ambiguously syncretic sense of Būshihrī music pursued by Iranian ethnomusicologists.

On the one hand, the close-up of the *damām* gestures toward a recognition of the foreign origins of this membranophonic instrument, which takes center stage during *arba'īn* and other Shi'i ceremonies in the south, and the specific style of rhythm bellowing forth from its body—heavily marked by isochronous pulsing and polyrhythms evocative of African musical cultures, and the myriad realms of expression the "metonymic fallacy" African carries. On the other hand, contradictory claims that the *damām*, this particular drum, originates in *both* ancient Iran and in Africa destabilizes the credibility of any narrative claiming to cement its true itinerary. The *damām*'s conflation with the *damāmah*, an instrument named in texts from the Achaemenid period (eighth to fourth century BCE), clouds the clarity of its origin.[19] Unlike the cymbals (*sinj*) and horns (*būq*), purportedly long staples of traditional Iranian music inscribed in the earliest Persian texts of antiquity, the drum (*damām*) asserts a singular significance within the context of the documentary's unfolding: the question of its "foreignness," its Africanness (thus relation to the long history of African enslavement and of African movement in the western Indian Ocean more generally), but also its tremulous universalism, a paradoxical primordiality that destabilizes the first two of these evocations. Indeed, the *damām* perverts even the supposedly Persian origins of the other instruments along which it is played: "The instruments of '*sinj va damām*' were first brought to this region from Africa and were played by Africans."[20] Catachrestic, the drum cannot help but recall the very emergence of music, if not the emergence of language, the human being.[21] "Without rhythm, no language is possible."[22]

Thus, the *damām,* the drum, a central component of Būshihrī *arbaʿīn,* is both African and Iranian, particular and universal, originless. Contradictory claims about *sinj ū damām* corroborate only the mythicism, almost otherworldly power, rather than the rigid and immutable facticity of the connection between Africa and Iran, at once attesting to a realization of the African origins of the musical style while simultaneously claiming their original Persianness and development from Būshihrī antiquity—as if, in their cosmogony, such simultaneity could be possible without contradiction. Anthropological studies bear out this contest and conflict over musical and ritualistic origins.

The "African-derived" music that sustains *arbaʿīn*'s meaning and soundtrack thus seems to oppose, even as it simultaneously supports, the abstracting movement of the film's modernist form, bearing a tension that can only be resolved by the stillness of an anonymous viewer who, rather than pulsate with the mourners, comprehends the design value of rhythmically, spastically succeeding frames. Accordingly, *Arbaʿīn* less elicits the viewer's empathy with the faithful, as some have suggested, than marks the difference between the observer's capacity to reflect and the participants' unbreakable rapture, between the aesthetic subject of culture and the aesthetic object of culture.[23] This break between observer and participant, subject and object, is made tangible through the blurred presence of a police officer, recognizable only by his cap, standing rigidly alongside the musicians as if guarding the distinctions between participation, management, and observation. The officer's presence suggests that the relation between particular and universal embodied by the *damām* and its bellowing rhythm, elicits a kind of tension that demands policing.

Arbaʿīn and the Muharram rituals more broadly diverge significantly across regional borders.[24] Later, I will suggest that Trinidadian Hosay, a West Indian form of *ʿāshūrā* linked to more familiar processes of creolization, aids us in perceiving what is specifically vexing about blackened versions of Muharram. The percussive tradition of *sinj ū damām* distinguishes Būshihrī mourning culture, perennially attracting the largest number of participants and spectators in Būshihr. Drumming virtuosity distinguishes Būshihrī and other forms of *jūnūbī* (southern) music and infuses the celebratory aura of south Iranian *arba'īn* in a peculiar form of the more widespread practice of dirge singing (*nūhah-khūnī*). Celebration thus seeps into the deepest strata of the often politicized cultures of mourning so integral to Islamic, and specifically Shi'i, ethics and being.[25] For this reason, and like other aspects of the Muharram rituals like self-flagellation which have become the center of controversy amongst the religious elite, the ritual has been as frequently demonized and condemned as it is revered and fetishized.[26] In fact, the controversies surrounding chest striking (*sīnah-zanī*), both in Iran and elsewhere, crystallize a set of polarities evoked by *arba'īn*. These polarities are familiar and obvious, if not elemental: active and passive, abstract and concrete, involved and disinterested, civil and wild. Currents and countercurrents flowing into one other, these oppositions send each other spinning into a rotational fury, losing the distinction of orientation. (Sailors and fishermen from nearby Jafra were enamored with Bakhshū, who would travel to contiguous regions to satisfy yearning listeners with his song: "*Really,* they saw his voice like the sound of thunder that has captivated their ship in the middle of the sea," a witness recounts.[27])

The excitement elicited by the subtle rhythmic accelerandos and the hallucinatory states *sinj ū damām*'s entranced and entrancing performers display contradicts the gravity expected of lamentation traditions, as it symbolizes the distinction between mere religious fervor and staid, policed religious subjectivity, a sonic metaphor for the difference that allows modern subjectivity to appear. Taqvā'ī's film harps upon the perverse contamination of sober mourning with rhythm. The animation is exalted, and thereby rendered further perverse, through the film's editing strategies: quick cuts, unwarranted camera movements, and seemingly senseless images that, like the neorealist New Wave ethos it precedes and shapes, disperses reality.[28] Among the useful if ideologically conflicting theories of montage in film theory strains a certain intuition of montage's capacity to break into relation's invisibility.[29] One might recognize in Taqvā'ī's seemingly irrelevant juxtapositions a challenge to this operation. For the folding back upon itself which the term "Afro-" requires on any anthropological register—that is, one attempting to

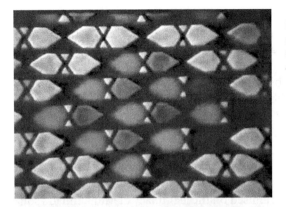

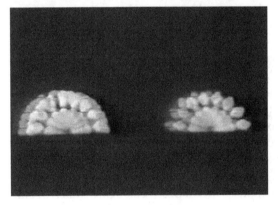

Figure 17. Abstract geometrical imagery at the start of Taqvā'ī's *Arba'īn* (1970).

define a syncretism—experiences a kind of reactive paralysis at every juncture.

The rhythm of Būshihrī Muharram's *sinj ū damām* blends into the syncopation of chest striking (*sīnah-zanī*), thus appearing to integrate the African origins of *sinj ū damām* into the Shi'i origins of *latam*. Participants encircle the *nūhah-khūn*—the dirge singer, or cantor—in a configuration called *bur*. With achingly precise and predetermined rhythm, mourners strike their chests in unison, recreating the sound of a large, collective drum, transmuting African gesture to Shi'i expression, or Shi'i gesture to African expression, confounding the direction of transmutation and transformation, interrupting causality itself. And yet, if the origins of *sinj ū damām* are contested, because double—both Persian and African—so too, does the Muharram practice of chest striking embody the enigma of

Shi'ism's own impossible origin. *Arba'īn*'s all-male *sīnah-zanī* buries the sign of an originally female mourning: forty days after Husayn was killed at the Battle of Karbala, the prisoners of his camp returned to Medina by way of Karbala, and upon the sight of Husayn's gravesite, women "beat their chests and wailed."[30] Shi'ism's traumatic origin lies less in the singular event of Husayn's murder than in the retroactive (female) commemoration and mourning that marks this murder as communally, transhistorically significant. "Every day is 'āshūrā, every land is Karbala." This suggests not only that Shi'ism's origin is belated, but that rhythm, the iterability of *latam* is itself a kind of mourning for the impossibility of the in-itself. For in as much as Shi'ism is premised on the legitimacy of Muhammad's son-in-law Ali, and then his martyred grandson, Husayn, as rightful successors to the caliphate, Shi'ism is premised on faith in the purity of a (kin) relation that sacrally ties the son to the father (Husayn to Ali, Ali to Muhammad) in an uninterrupted chain of transmission and legitimacy.[31] If the "primary figure of the Shi'i trauma" is Husayn, Husayn's murder, the breached caliphate, is also the sign of a metaphysical contamination.[32] And if Būshihrī *arba'īn* is exemplary, it is because blackness exemplarily bears the enigmatic truth of an inadmissible, originary deviation at the heart of Shi'ism itself.

Against the realism of countercinema's documentary drive (see chapter 2), Taqvā'ī's *Arba'īn* wields a sonic montage. Against the usage of the term that denotes harmonious or coherent synthesis, some scholars argue that *syncretism* should be reserved for the coming together of conflicting ideas or practices that do not result in consistency or harmonious unity, but rather, like montage, in dissonance.[33] And yet, this sonic montage, induced through rhythm, intends less the production of discord than an abolition of the autonomy of the single unit. Taqvā'ī's vision affirms the paradoxical suitability of moving sound-images to the ambiguity of historical knowing about African diasporic history and its ensuing residues. If this vision is offered primarily through sound (*sinj ū damām,* Bakhshū's dirges, *sīnah-zanī*'s rhythm), rather than facts, it is not merely due to hierarchical genre distinctions: false cinema, true historiography. But rather, because sound is prior to the ideality required by fact, because rhythm, like silence, is prior to history. Iterability makes facts, and therefore history, possible. Rhythm, repetition, is the basis of history: "Sooner or later [rhythm] encounters the event that arrives

Figure 18. Film still of *bur* from Taqvāī's *Arbaʿīn* (1970).

or rather arises in relation to the sequence or series produced repetitively. In other words: difference."[34] And, "Even if it is difficult to communicate the nature and meaning of rhythm, nature and meaning themselves appear to us through rhythm."[35] Bio-cosmological but never self-same (seasons, circadian rhythms, sound waves, light waves, brain waves), rhythm makes history possible through its inherent exposure to interruption.

Rhythm precedes history, as repetition and sound precede fact. (The condition of ideal meaning or fact, after all, depends upon its capacity for repetition to infinity.) But there is another sense in which the visual rhythm of succeeding static frames, film's ontology, simulates the production of history. Historical knowledge depends upon the absence of the event, as film's materiality depends upon the absented *"having been there"* of represented space, where what synthesizes filmic continuity is distention of the optical trace, "holding on (to) the gone, giving way to the waiting."[36] The film's images summon, as its sonic rhythm appeals, to a realm of possibility prior to the continuity demanded and produced by meaning—a blanking, a spacing, an interval. The single image, the autonomous unit or sign, the individual strike can be lifted from its immediate interlocking chain and cut in elsewhere. This inherent exposure to disembedding is due to a certain absence, a certain silence, and a certain spacing. In the subtle shift from *sinj ū damām* to *latam*, in the space between pounds, in the silence between strikes, as in the blank between frames, lies rhythm's very possibility. This spacing is

« 132 »   Irano-Afro-Iran

the site of leaking context, impending disintegration, capture and theft. In short, if there is a figure that reifies the always extant possibility of decontextualization that spacing, rhythm, enables, it is the figure of the slave.

Pearling Immemorial: The Parcel of Fish Eyes

Among the many oddly placed cuts complementing the serialization of musical ritual in *Arba'īn,* a shot of two bloated, listless, silver fish washed ashore interposes the *bur,* or chest-striking encircling. The concentric circles enclosing the cantor recall the ubiquitous African diasporic tradition of ring shuffling as a kind of ancestral honoring.[37] Elsewhere, *sīnah-zanī* occurs in columns. The booms of chest pounding syncopated with shuffling overlays this image of death and fertilizes the metonymic powers of maritimity. If the sea bears a particular resonance in the Black filmic imagination associated with the history of African enslavement through the Atlantic world, Taqvā'ī's catatonic fish, like his docked dhows in *Wind of Jin* distill lesser understood layers of this history. It also reorients the nation-based ideology of historiography and contemporary Gulf nationalist emphases on Bedouin and desert heritage, in favor of a more conflicted perception of space that remains paradoxically more faithful to the Persian Gulf past's configuration in the Indian Ocean.[38] As Fahad Bishara observes, for medieval historians, "the Gulf did not lie within the sphere of the 'Middle East'. . . . Rather, it occupied a more organic, intermediate space between the Arabian Peninsula, Indian Ocean, and broader world—with its inhabitants mediating between, but also susceptible to shifts in each."[39] In tenth-century geographical accounts like al-Istakhrī's and Ibn Ḥawqal's, the Persian Gulf (*khalīj-i fārs*) might include the entire Indian Ocean (*bahr al-hind*).[40]

Specifically, *Arba'īn's* fish frame evokes the history of pearling that typifies, especially in the modern period, one potent image of enslaved African labor in the Persian Gulf. Pearling's peak in the late nineteenth century exacerbated enslavement.[41] In the period of increasing prosperity driven by global demand for pearls, slave labor saved the pearling economy that had for centuries, even millennia, been integral to the Gulf.[42] Considered to be one of the most physically and emotionally painful of occupations, with risks of "drowning, swordfish and shark attacks, trachoma, anemia, malnutrition, and scurvy,"[43] prior to the discovery of oil and the conflation of the oil industry with the global image of the Persian Gulf, the majority of Gulf inhabitants professed subsistence through some form of connection to the sea, laboring as fishermen, pearl divers, sailors, and shipbuilders. Both free and enslaved divers propelled the hazardous and exploitative Persian Gulf pearling industry. One political agent reported that pearl diving's deleterious effects explained the ongoing disappearance of "middle-aged Africans."[44] Arab, Persian, Indian, and African divers all suffered the perils of ruptured eardrums, blindness, bronchitis, and other respiratory ailments. But primarily Africans, scholars inform us, whether free or enslaved, were perennially exposed to the threat of kidnapping.[45] The ongoing threat of decontextualization is the unique inheritance of blackness in Southwest Asia. (And is exemplified in the very contestation of the *existence* of blackness in Southwest Asia.)[46]

As with the renewed attention to the nineteenth-century date plantation economy discussed in chapter 2, recent scholarship focalizes the connection between Persian Gulf pearling and global commodity circuits, tying African enslavement in the Indian Ocean to modernity. And yet, the fish frame only alludes to and does not secure such a context. The historicity enacted by the film, if there is such, is sensed rather than comprehended, intuited rather than conquered or delivered. *Sīnah-zanī*, chest striking, is enchantment "by the allure of the unarticulated."[47] Such felt historicity connects to deep traditions of both Persian and African forms of transmission that pre-date and outdate the modern inheritance of historiography-as-science—our privileged, naturalized relation to the past. In the Persian Gulf, historical documents that pre-date colonial presence are rare; the indigenous textual genres like *safhat* (literally, pages, leaves) is steeped in an oral narrative culture that moves seamlessly between fact and legend, gathers around the incidental.[48] For centuries, Persian oral storytelling, or *naqqālī*, like the epics it communicated to live audiences, combined religious, mythical, and historical narratives. The storyteller's success depended upon the extent to which he could elicit pathos and audience feeling, rather than deliver consumable, fixed information.[49] As discussed in chapter 1, the introduction of television and television networks, such as the one commissioning Taqvā'ī's films, nearly wiped out the tradition of *naqqālī*, creating a direct link between *Arba'īn* and the storytelling culture that the film's existence both displaces and sublates into a

« 134 »   Irano-Afro-Iran

new form. The cloth banner juxtaposed next to Husayn's figure in the filmic prologue recalls a *naqqālī* spread. In a West African Muslim context, the privileged mode of epistemic transmission is bodily, rather than textual osmosis.[50] Contemporary Islam (conflated with modern, orthodox forms of Sunni Islam like Wahhabism) privileges the textual over the bodily, thereby denigrating African Islam as forged and diluted: "Arab countries . . . [are] presumed by a sort of racial alchemy to preserve the essence of Islam."[51] Scholars of "African Islam" decry the ways in which Islamic practices in the African continent have come to be viewed as derivative, despite being in many cases orthodox. Negative theological judgments about syncretism are charged by anxiety about the contamination of revelation with worldly history, universality with particularity. Given the pre-existing characterization of "African Islam" as inauthentic, Būshihrī *arba'īn* layers, embeds, syncretisms within itself, as if *en abyme*.

In modern consciousness, pearling tends to be associated with the Arabian shore of the Persian Gulf. But in the fourteenth to seventeenth centuries Hurmuz was the major mercantile superpower in the region. During the Safavid era, Persian kings and their successors derived significant revenues from the Gulf's pearl fisheries.[52] Thwarting the orientation of context, the seemingly irrelevant shot of fish evokes the famous "parcel of fish eyes" from Dilmūn (modern-day Bahrain), the cuneiform tablet discovered at Ur and dated to 2,000 BCE. Scholars of Mesopotamian antiquity interpret references to "fish eyes" in ancient artifacts to mean pearls.[53] Though it forges one representation of Indian Ocean slave labor, pearl diving *also* fabricates the Persian Gulf's ancient archetype. Pearling features in regional descriptions over the past seven thousand years and is thought to constitute the substrate of early civilization, fueling one of the world's most enduring economies since prehistoric times.[54] It is in this way that the material history of the Persian Gulf entwines with the cosmic immemorial of the Muharram ritual that *Arba'īn* documents. The immemorial absolves any authoritative recognition of slavery's history and destabilizes its sense for collective memory and citation.[55]

Our extant historiography is indebted either to colonial records or to a genesis in colonial scientificity, and is therefore circumscribed within contrived temporalities. The immemorial is beyond the reach of memory, beyond the reach of forgetting. Taqvā'ī's fish conjures, for it could not possibly cite, such iconicity. In precitational forms of allusion, remnants of slavery—not yet, maybe never, a history—drown in the generality of depthless time. In the port village of Banak residents refer to Black Iranians' "antique presence" (*ghidmat'dār būdan-i anhā*).[56] Like Ahmad Shāmlū's temporally indeterminate voiceover phrase at the height of the *zār* ceremony in *Wind of Jin* (chapter 2), the fish eyes divert the pretense of protected referentiality. The seeming stability of the single shot, the single phrase, the single fact, the single context, is undermined by its vulnerability to disembedding, cutting, its power of authority perforated, exposed to the drone of a surrounding blankness and silence. This is rhythm's reminder. "Can we conceive of a rhythm that, in itself, makes visible what is 'nonrecurrent,' that affirms difference as primary and absolute?"[57] Can we conceive of a rhythm that, in itself, is prior to even the possibility of affirmation? Against common sense, the commemoration of Husayn in *'āshūrā*'s bodily practices is tied to a certain amnesiac dissolution, and not merely a fortification of memory. Thus, an Isfahani elder justifies his abstinence by claiming that Husayn is consigned to oblivion in lamentation ceremonies. In Persian Muharram, it's as if the mourners "want to forget something."[58] Repetition is a necessary path to fact. Repetition is a necessary path to fact's self-erosion.

The industrial origins of cinema in Iran are inextricably connected to the development of an oil industry that obliterated pearling, displaced the already invisible slave. The films produced by the Anglo Iranian Oil Company in Southern oil cities like Abadan sought on the one hand to legitimize the extractive and exploitative practices of a foreign company which had accrued vast swathes of territory as a result of a 1901 concession between Reza Shah and the oil baron William Knox D'Arcy (caricatured in Parvīz Kīmiyāvī's surrealist 1979 *OK Mister*).[59] The agreement has often been interpreted by critics as an indirect form of colonization. The exploitative terms of the contract, which essentially granted the British company exclusive access to one of the world's largest oil refineries, resulted in a series of turbulent political events culminating in the infamous CIA-backed coup of Prime Minister Mossadeq and subsequent consolidation of monarchical power. As discussed in the previous chapter, this political backdrop informs the context for the countercinematic, anti-imperial movement to which Taqvā'ī's films belong.

The Gulistān Film Workshop, run by the well-known writer and

« 136 »   Irano-Afro-Iran

filmmaker Ibrāhīm Gulistān, was funded by the National Iranian Oil Consortium, and many of the films produced through the Gulistān workshop precipitated the poetic realist aesthetic that would become a signature of the New Wave. Taqvā'ī's apprenticeship at the workshop explains Gulistān's stylistic influences on Taqvā'ī's work—in particular, his tendency to humanize landscape in patterns of intercutting that superimpose labor and land. Gulistān's Film Workshop was the first independent nonfiction film studio in Iran. The films it produced aestheticized the transformations that oil extraction exacted on the southern Iranian landscape. Gulistān's famous short film *A Fire* (1961) documents a 1958 oil well explosion that floods a petroleum zone near Khūzistān's capital city Ahvaz. The fire, at first monstrous, rolling with thick, black columns of smoke, soon assimilates, becomes "part of the landscape," as the English voiceover informs. The same year, another well-known filmmaker Farukh Ghafārī, whose feature films I discuss in chapter 1, produces the documentary *Black Veins* (*Rag'hāyi siyāh*) about oil pipelines moving oil from the south to the country's capital.

Oil is "the key element," the unconscious of the Iranian film industry.[60] But it is also the case that pearling—and the slave labor that fueled it—is the unconscious of oil.[61] The collapse of the Persian Gulf's once thriving pearl industry since the discovery of its artificial reproduction has all but obliterated the memory of pearling in popular consciousness.[62] Instead, the emergence of petromodernity replaced slavery as the prime source of the world's surplus capital.[63] The ecological transformations captured and aestheticized by the so-called poetic realism of Gulistān's studio thus encode a disappearance that, unlike the perceptible, detrimental physical effects of oil extraction on land, cannot be made visible or narratable.

Taqvā'ī's cuts between the chest-striking procession inside the dark mosque in *Arba'īn* to bright outdoor images such as the one of beached fish consistently disorient the viewer. Part of the disorientation ensues from the imperceptible shifts from stabilized, if not entirely static, interior shots to trembling, handheld exterior images, whose point of view cannot be localized or logically derived from within the context of the film, despite the aural continuity of dirges, beating. From which perspective appears the bobbing shot of Būshihr's coast, as if filmed from an unanchored spot in the sea? What is "place" and "perspective" from the point of view of water? (For Pasolini, montage is a kind of death, without which there can be no history.[64]) Through movement, the time of *arbaʿīn* is ungrounded from the space of *arbaʿīn*. Such dissociation of time and space is itself intrinsic to the rituals of Muharram. For the Shiʿi community, Husayn's death "provides a focal point from which prior, as well as subsequent, history must be viewed."[65] But unlike the primordial tragedy of Husayn's murder at Karbala, remembered not only perennially ("Every day is ʿāshūrā"), there is no event with which to anchor the history of enslavement in the Persian Gulf to living memory. Unlike the ritualized event of theological time and the contingent event of even the most secular and homogenous of temporalities, one encounters in the place of a history of slavery only fragments that resist assembly into memory, images like omphalic traces of ancestors' daydreams or nightmares, difficult to thread into a story worthy of the telling, especially to the overwhelming forces that prefer, desire, dictate, or merely necessitate forgetting.

The condition of text—written, spoken, sung, filmed—is retention (there would be no sentence, no phrase, no song, no sequence, no *experience* without the possibility of retaining a beginning). But *Arba'in*'s rhythm performs a relentless annihilation, of an origin to be retained, of a text to be synthesized. The film contains no direct information, no dialogue or subtitles, other than that of rhythm; Bakhshū relives the tragedy of Karbala for the participants who self-strike in response, embodying the sensual fervor that form cathects into light. In its incapacity to transmit information about Indian Ocean slavery, film seems to ask instead whether and how slavery can be the object of historical experience. Though Taqvā'ī had originally written a script for the film, he eventually abandoned it. No voice over, rhythm begins as if always belated; the sea's elemental flashes reverberate with no determination or destination, conjuring instead the immemorial, sublime in its whelming.

Where the striking sound moves from its connection to the labor of ritual to coincide with the outdoors (rocky landscapes where a few men carry heavy loads, a lone man at sea, palm tree sheaths shaking) the uncompromising pulse of the human drum sounds more like whip lashes. Būshihrī music embodies toil and labor, pain and hardship, distance and affliction, of these "sea-hearted people [*mardūm-i daryā dil*]."[66] The horn moves in with a new evocation; asserting its own voice, the *būq* demands so capacious a lung capacity that it usually takes more than one musician to play, one person being unable to perform for more than a minute at a time. In descriptions of horn performance, the physical pain of playing surfaces on the body: "so much pressure . . . the muscles of his neck protrude."[67] Like the drum, the horn ferments layers of meaning: the cavernous lung capacity it requires recalls not only the incredible might demanded by diving, evoked by the instrument and the depthless sea that the film chronicles synchronically with its music, but also the deep emotional and physical costs exacted by the occupation itself, on its practitioners and their families, who endured the peak season months in anxiety and fear of no return.[68] In the nineteenth century, enslaved Africans "were forced to dive forty times a day or more," with high mortality rates.[69] A popular lyrical theme in *fijiri,* another Gulf musical tradition connected to African enslavement, included expression of "sorrow at feeling stolen from one's homeland by the pearling life."[70] Common aquaphobia, delusion, and hallucination in the deep sea were understood by enslaved divers as a form of possession.[71] The synesthetic absorption of the visual by the auditory in Taqvā'ī's film thus interrogates the salutatory image of labor that commentators have generally assumed images and scenes like this to suggest.[72] If previous interpretations foreclose the intuition of enslavement evoked, but not cited, by the film, it cannot merely be due to the limitations of subjective interpretation. The memory of African enslavement for which Būshihr served as a portal for centuries is unremembered—and, or *because,* it is self-dissolving. The physiological harshness of drum music overlaying the image of dead fish revives a relation that can barely be called real. In interviews, Taqvā'ī avows consistently the incompatibility of the film form with something like authorial intention.

Evocative, rather than consumable, *Arbaʿīn* does not revive a history of pearling whose "intergenerational transmission is failing."[73] Unlike the sphere of governmental heritage, the film does not attempt to salvage the obliteration of collective memory. *Arbaʿīn* does not revive history. Rather, with his mellifluous song, Bakhshū the cantor returns mourners to a state of deep trance ("you need to experience sorrow that *burns you empty,*" reports one *maddah*).[74] If we can read the materiality of Bakhshū's blackness into this spiraling, burning, healing descent into emptiness, it is not because *Arbaʿīn* revives history, nor because it revives the history of African enslavement in the Indian Ocean. It is rather because *Arbaʿīn* opens up a certain relation to the syncretism, or impossibility of origin, upon which history is based—upon which history succeeds, and fails, to constitute its own coherence. And this syncretism, this blackness, transcending Indian Ocean slavery, is itself older than history.

Zang, Zanj, Zanzibar: Hybridity as Tautology

There is no organic Persian translation for "Afro-Iranian." And yet the directionality and hierarchy of essences inherent to the hyphenation in question is from the outset presumed. Black individuals in Iran do not identify as *Īrānī-i āfrīqā'tabār* (which would be the Persian translation of Afro-Iranian), nor always as *siyāh* or *siyāh pūst* (black, or black-skinned), which, due to its derogatory connotations, is not unequivocally embraced. In fact, much of the anthropological literature on black communities in Southwest Asia and North Africa repeats the truism that black people do not identify as black, but as Iranian, or Arab, or Emirati, or Qatari, and so on.[75] In her description of *zār* in Bandar Abbas, one ethnographer writes: "None of the black Mama or Baba Zars or locals whom I spoke with traced his or her ancestors back to Africa. They all considered themselves Iranian and never made any reference to Africa,"[76] an assertion repeated in Behnaz Mirzai's 2013 documentary, *Afro-Iranian Lives.* (Whether or not it offers a clear picture of reality, this view at least seems to reflect the outsider status of the scholars and ethnographers making such observations.) The subordination of blackness to national identity only mutes the historical trajectories that stabilize and naturalize the supposedly immutable, whole, and hegemonic national identities in question.

For theorists of race, racialization is a despotic process that subsumes, homogenizes, and abstracts, dissolves the particularity of the ethnonym into flat, universal signs. Racialization creates "the 'Black' where once there had been Asante or Ovimbundu, Yoruba, or Bakongo."[77] The term *siyāh* (black) only reflattens other similarly homogenizing historical terms. A common Persian reference to African peoples in early modern historical literature, for example, is the term *Zang* or *Zanj,* which appears superficially to indicate the East African origins of slaves who, along with gold, tortoiseshell, mangrove, ivory, and teakwood were transported by ship to the Persian Gulf since the earliest periods of Persian Empire.[78] The Sasanians (224–651 CE) take credit for integrating the first maritime trading system in the Persian Gulf, and recorded evidence of slaves in the Persian Empire dates back to at least the third century.[79] Trudged through deserts by caravan and on foot to strategic port towns, captives were boarded onto dhows tracing water routes, sometimes with multiple stopovers, to major entrepôts throughout the premodern and modern histories of Indian Ocean maritime trade. Such entrepôts included the ancient city of Sīraf in the province of Būshihr, which dominated trade with East Africa during the ninth and tenth centuries, the island of Kīsh, commercially significant during the twelfth through fourteenth centuries, and Hurmuz in the fourteenth through sixteenth centuries.[80] Būshihr again vied for domination of caravan routes to Iran's interior during the nineteenth and twentieth centuries.[81] At least nine or ten points of departure comprised the system of East African trade, but captives sailing from the coast were not necessarily local natives.[82] Assumptions about linear movements are misleading, as scholars note of tracing slave itineraries across the Atlantic.[83] In addition to exploiting vulnerable territories dominated by Christian or Muslim rulers, slavers may have commonly seized individuals from Central and Southern Africa. This violent theft fueled the East African slave trade to the Persian Gulf from a period long before the nineteenth-century emphasis in modern scholarship. Every single raid and kidnapping could not possibly possess a material correlate or record. Why would slavers have catalogued such acts?[84] Kidnapped slaves were encouraged, by way of sorcery and other forms of psychological violence, to forget their pasts—a phenomenon Saidiya Hartman poignantly describes in *Lose Your Mother: A Journey Along the Atlantic Slave Route.*[85]

Zang, Zangh, Zanj, or *Zinj* (the sound *ng* transcribes into Arabic as *ghayn* or *nūn-jīm*). One commentator hesitates between *fatha, kasra,* and *damma* vowel sounds (*Zanj, Zinj, Zunj*).[86] The proliferating etymological interpretations approximate an entire deranged epistemology. Africanists note that medieval Arab historians use the term *Zang* loosely and without geographical specificity, generating obvious methodological thorns.[87] John Hunwick calls *Zanj* a generic term for Africans: "Although Arab writers treat the term *Zanj* as if it were the name of a specific group, it is clear that nothing unites the *Zanj* other than stereotyped characteristics." And, "There appears to be considerable confusion about the precise location of *Zanj* and all it included."[88] Despite its usual association with Eastern Africa, *Zanj* is applied to a number of different areas in Muslim geographical treatises, spanning out from modern-day Senegal toward Pakistan and Indonesia: "Such transferences of names do not seem to correspond to any real migration of peoples."[89] In the nineteenth-century West African Sahel, the founder of a reformist Islamic state designates some of the region's inhabitants as permanently servile castes, legitimating their enslavement to the new ruler. One of the designations of "servile blackness" is *Zanj*.[90] In a tenth-century Persian geographical treatise, an anonymous author likens the *Zang* to wild animals (*dadagān va bahā'im*) who are "extremely black" (*sakht siyāhand*).[91]

Another scholar's "best indication" is that Arab writers used *Zanj* to refer to eastern Africans, "broadly speaking," since *Bar al-Zanj*, like Zanjibar, indicates "coast of the Zanj." Elsewhere, an early twentieth-century British resident suggests that the name Zanzibar derives "from the Persian root zangh," which he translates as "Negro," and "bar (coast) thus meaning 'Negro coast.'"[92] The formulations that the term *Zanj* refers to Zanzibar and that Zanzibar comes from *Zanj,* and that *Zanj* refers to Eastern Africans because Zanzibar means "Negro coast" create a stream of strangely impenetrable tautologies. (The designation *Sūdanī,* referring to the Sudanese, embodies a similar etymological guard. Sudan, from the Arabic *Bilad-al Sudan,* literally "land of the blacks," shows how the appearance of objective reference immunizes geography from its own racial history.)

Tautology is brought to a head in the following formulations which tie *Zang* to Ethiopian or Kiswahili origins, without giving up on a Persian origin: "Its etymon could be Ethiopian (*zanega* 'to barbarize, prattle, stammer') or Persian (*zang/zangi,* which means 'negro')."[93] *Zengua* means "confused, absurd speech" and is etymologically related *Zanj,* claims one commentator, who presumes that *Zanj* produced the Ethiopian verb and noun.[94] In the opinion of another scholar, the word *zenj* may derive entirely from Kiswahili terms for savage, *ushenzi* or *ushenji,* though "not necessarily associated with blackness in the African context."[95] The oddly racial undertone of *Zanj's* millennial transmission is not only a result of its anachronistic and clearly unstable translation as "Negro." (In a different context, admits Robert Bernasconi, "The question of whether a term like 'Negro' is already a racial term prior to any clear understanding of race is too complex to be considered.")[96] The oscillation between Persian and Kiswahili etymology foretells an anguish that transcends any simple dichotomy between the racial and nonracial, cutting through *Zanj's* ranging meanings and geographical, historical contexts, even where and when it was or is no longer "necessarily associated with blackness." The phrase, "not necessarily associated with blackness," begs the question no one dares ask: How does savagery get *necessarily* associated with blackness?

The deeper one wades into tautology, the more of it one discovers. And the more of it one reproduces. In the sparse scholarship that exists on slavery from the East African coast to the Persian Gulf, one encounters the recurring assumption that the majority of Iranian African slave descendants are East African descended—whether *Zangī* (purportedly, from "Zanzibar") or *Habāshī* (Abyssinian, or Ethiopian), *Sūdanī* (from Sudan), and so forth.[97] The cloudy etymological claims about *Zang* are compounded by yet more pleonasms. Some Swahili inhabitants along the East African coast avow Persian, or Perso-Arab, ancestry. Swahili traditions collectively memorialize late first millennium contact between Persian immigrants and African indigenes as the primal scene of Swahili being. One of these traditions recalls the Persian Ali B. Hasan who emigrated from Shiraz because he was insulted by his brethren due to the fact that his mother was an Abyssinian slave. A version of this tradition claims Hasan outfoxed Muli or Mrimba, the African king, by using the test that was presented him (to surround Kilwa with cloth) to prohibit the king's return access to the island.[98]

Whether due to naiveté or racism (assuming that East African civilization must have been founded by foreigners), colonial historiography took for granted Swahili claims to descent by Persian nobles like Hasan, the supposed ninth-century founders of Swahili settlements, later superseded by Arab rulers. Recent revisions to Shirazi-Swahili and Perso-Arab kinship transparencies instead foreground circuits of contact "with multiple migrations in both directions."[99] Critical of the interplay between history telling and writing, politically and ideologically motivated legend, overreliance on European sources, and racialized attitudes toward the African continent, historians of East Africa have questioned the literalness and veracity of the Shirazi origins of the Swahili. Yet, despite an awareness of the naturalized racism that assumes African incapacity for civilizational structures, it is difficult to reconcile or pass judgment on Swahili inhabitants', indeed entire Swahili villages' own claims to Shirazi descent.[100] The "Shirazi tradition is widespread along the Swahili coast from the Benadir in Somalia to northern Mozambique, the Comoros, and northern Madagascar."[101]

Irano-Afro-Iran « 143 »

The methodological approaches of early twentieth-century scholarship suggest that, in order to substantiate the thesis of Shirazi ancestry, one ought to be able to convincingly isolate adequate and properly Persian architectural and material remains in East African settlements: ceramics with specifically Persian patterns, glass beads, wares, building styles reflective of Iranian architectural design. The excavation of landscape for the discovery of Persian art forms would thus result in the discovery of a Shirazi essence imprinted on and inherited by Swahili being. In the 1980s scholars criticized the "coral rag and mortar" complex driving archaeological pursuits in East African coastal settlements: "Archaeologists ... think ... only in terms of stone," enshrouding a more holistic picture of Swahili history.[102] Civilization is stony, durable, but also a sign of foreignness. If from the view of the Southwest Asian territories bordered by the Persian Gulf, the sea is associated with trivial, uninteresting, and incoherent history in comparison to the epic grandeur of the empire, nation-state, or the history of Islamic civilization, from the Swahili African coast, the opposite is true. Civilization is gifted from the sea, which is to say, from elsewhere; in contrast, the land is tied to the ephemeral, to the *makuti* (impermanent), the humble mud and thatch, the palm frond roofs, all that is perishable, unworthy and also incapable of holding memory. In Swahili material culture, "conceptually stone is linked to the sea and earthen houses to mainland Africa,"[103] holding the fable of African primitiveness and non-African civilization that Swahili architecture appears to make real.[104]

In *Arba'īn,* bobbing shots of coastal land filmed from the perspective of water suggest that the landscape could belong to a territory other than Iran's Būshihr. The liquidity of the movements threaten a sudden mutation in space, or a dissolution of the viewer's orientation, brought on like the "sombre, windy, and depressing tumult" of a southwest monsoon.[105] If Afro-Iranians are East African descended, as has been posited with the fragmented and fallible recensions available, and if East Africans claim, regardless of the claim's motivation, Shirazi or Persian descent, Afro-Iranians would be, so to speak, redundant: Irano-Afro-Iranians. The assumption that origin is inherently monological and sutured to place or to biological causality, argues Mana Kia, derives from modern reasoning that is inappropriate for earlier historical imaginaries.[106] According to the space opened up by this line of thought, there is nothing contradictory in the claim to an origin that is multiple, nor to an origin that is

Figure 19. Scenes from Taqvāī's *Arba'īn* (1970). Top: Fish washed ashore. Bottom: Floating dhows.

not necessarily rooted in geographical space. Just as there is no contradiction, and not even necessarily a concealed disavowal in Black Iranians' refusal of ties to Africa. And yet, there is a way in which the twining tropes of the *Zanj*, like the *siyāh*, in exemplifying the process of homogenization that is central to racial blackness, provoke a rupture with context whose violence eludes neutral rubrics of multiplicity.

Blackness bemuses tautology, "confounds rather than permits the compensatory gestures ... of 'hybridity' and 'syncretism.'"[107] It also coheres notions of cultural purity. Without the chimeric cushion of a region bordering, enclosing, and sealing off the Iranian mainland, there would be nothing to contrast the absoluteness of an Iranian essence supposedly left unadulterated, as its Gulf coasts absorb pollution and creolize from the outside in. The witticism "Irano-Afro-Iran" is no less vexed than the seemingly self-evident hyphenation, Afro-Iran. And the hyphenation Afro-Iran is no less perspicuous than what remains when the first term, and its hyphen, are removed. Irano-Afro-Iran approximates the conceit undertaken more generally by the creole signifier, exposes the false neutrality that is dissimulated by the absence of the creole signifier. The creole is indissociable from the fantasy of purity that undergirds it, even, especially, *despite* the claims that all identities, all cultures are mixed—as the creole's generally felicitous inflection in modern scholarship suggests.[108] What appears before mixture? Where and when does creolization start, and how does it end? Who gains what from temporary, limited, circumscribed exclamations of hybridity, and who and what endures the gaping aporia at its heart?[109]

Creolizing Legend

Arbaʿīn atomizes the Muharram ritual, transmuting its elements into experiments with form, as it severs from normative logic those aspects of our sensibilia, time and space, crucial to any formulation of objectivity and history. The pitch-black background that frames the uncanny flashes of color and floating panels at the beginning of the film also symbolizes the severance of ritual from religious context. Blackness elevates ritual to the status of the image. A new tension between its present and past forms rises, just as the autonomous work of art emerges out of its cultic origin in "first magical, then religious" ritual.[110] *Arbaʿīn*'s formal relation to its content cannot be reduced to a story of release from its Shiʾi origin, but of a reconciliation that departicularizes Iran's Muslim (Arabicized) past by transforming it into experimental art. In turn, its experimentalism is *also* a simulation of the process of aesthetic judgment that conditions the universal, the political.

By absorbing the energies of cultural and historical plurality, the modernist aesthetic emerged as a capable challenge to the hegemony of Shiʾism, guardian of Iran's spiritual realm. Shiʾism has simultaneously, and paradoxically, maintained this dominant status as Iran's spiritual guardian since at least the Safavid period, while being itself at least theoretically antithetical to the very existence of a nation-state and sometimes (though by no means consistently) denigrated as an archaic remnant of the traumatic "Arab invasion."[111] The ethnographic documentaries about Shiʾi ritual appear comfortably alongside other ethnographic documentaries chronicling nomadic tribal life, indigenous technologies, and archeological ruins that attest to the ancient, esteemed Persian civilization imagined to precede Islam and shore up its modern, nationalist aesthetic.[112] Simultaneously, by signaling the rituals' syncretism, *Arbaʿīn* implicitly gestures toward contemporaneous theological judgments about Muharram that mirror the shift from Shi'i passivity to political activity, from aesthesis to the aesthetic, and from sensation to sense, that the filmic representation of the ritual embodies in its modernism.

The drifting stained glass images glowing in rapid motion prior to the start of dirge preparations in Taqvāʾī's film evoke *ʿāshūrā*'s arcane lineage and burial in deep history. For just as South Iranian *arbaʿīn* encrypts African ways of being for Būshihrī inhabitants while exploding the fraught distinction between African and Iranian, the entire constellation of Muharram rituals retroactively ciphers pre-Islamic mythology, pulling attention to the inaccessibility of its core truth. Scholars attribute some of the staggering appeal of the drama of Husayn's martyrdom for Shi'is to its compatibility with the pre-Islamic Iranian myth of the Blood of Siyāvash; both dramas draw from the trope of the "spilled blood of the innocent."[113] (Husayn's piety is re-created in Shi'i memory with the popular usage of the title *mazlūm,* meaning oppressed, but also "gentle and modest," moral virtues.)[114] Some have suggested that the *Shahnamah*'s influence on Husayn's narrative martyrdom reflects the syncretic Persianization of Islamic practices: "Isn't the story of Imam Hossein, as the defining trauma of Shi'ism, just another apocryphal *Shahnamah* story that has not made it into any critical edition, for it has made it into our collective consciousness as our public religion?"[115] At the conclusion of Simin Danishvar's famous 1969 novel *Siyāvashūn,* the mourning of Husayn blends with a scene of mourning for Siyāvash, illustrating their parallels and suggesting the derivation of Taʿzīyah from the much more ancient tradition of *Siyāvashūn.*

In Firdawsī's tenth-century *Shāhnāmah,* or *Book of Kings,* the story of Siyāvash relates the hero's demise. Wrongfully exiled from Iran for accusations of incestuous desire, the prince ultimately fails to assimilate to his diasporic refuge. To illuminate Siyāvash's transcendental chastity, his betrayal recurs transpatially—in his divinely native Iran, where he is ousted by his king father (Kay Khusraw) despite proving his innocence by passing through fire unscathed, and in Turan, Iran's geographical archetype-adversary (sometimes conflated with the land of the Turks) where the leader Afrāsiyāb first embraces, then ultimately murders Siyāvash after new lies about the tragic hero spread. Seduced by his wily stepmother Sūdabeh in Iran, betrayed by his father Kay Khusraw, and again betrayed by his father-in-law, Afrāsiyāb in Turan, like Husayn, the figure of Siyāvash irradiates mythological righteousness, but without the self-conscious dress of historical realism.[116]

In *Arba'īn* geometrical shapes flash neon between suspended images of a figure astride a white horse, recalling Husayn's mythic archetype, Siyāvash, the tragic hero of the Iranian national epic.[117] The horse has a special meaning, endowed with a kind of mysterious knowledge. The riding figure is defaced, rendering the identity of the horseman unrecognizable and commutable, Husayn for Siyāvash and Siyāvash for Husayn; ultimately, a blank space. The momentary disfigurement, combined with the black backdrop against which it arises and suddenly appears, posits an ephemeral space of substitution and parallel. In a Lahore version of *'āshūrā,* a riderless horse follows a procession of men carrying a staff decked with colored cloth: "Its empty saddle reminds watchers of its fallen master, the object of the crowd's adulation."[118] The *Shahnameh*'s poems begin at the origin of creation, prior to history. Scholars observe, but can draw no conclusions, from the symbolic resonances between the pre- and post-Islamic narratives of Siyāvash and Husayn. Yet, we might connect Karbala's "origin" in prehistoric legend to the derogation of its syncretized performance. In lacking a stable beginning, Muharram lacks a permanent essence, is affectable to time. Through reason, the religio-political subject masters its emotional affectability and susceptibility to accretion, as, through disinterest, the aesthetic subject masters the affectability of sensation, aesthesis. The resonance between Husayn and Siyāvash culminates in a disappeared protagonist, realizing through absence the amniotic nonpurity of the Shi'i ritual.

Shi'ism's alterity was mobilized by anticolonial thinkers and philosophers of Islam in pursuit of revolutionary epistemologies in the 1960s. From the majority Sunni position from which Shi'ism deviates, Shi'ism is seen as an impure and false version of Islam, *shirk* (sin of idolatry).[119] Thus, beyond Iran, where a Shi'i-led regime wields repressive, perversely violent, and dictatorial power, Shi'i minorities are sometimes held in ill repute: in spite of the political popularity of Hezbollah in Lebanon, for example, "popular lore has held that Shias have tails; they reproduce too prolifically. . . . In Saudi Arabia, it is said that Shias spit in their food"; in Pakistan, Shi'is are called

Figure 20. Faceless Husayn in Taqvā'ī's *Arba'in* (1970).

mosquitoes. For Sunnis, and increasingly for Shi'is themselves, Shi'is "are too loud in expressing their religiosity."[120] Thus, from the perspective of prominent ulama members, Iranian Muharram reflects an embarrassing hyperbolization, replete with "numerous supernatural, legendary accretions."[121] One need only recall the various ways in which religious syncretism has been perceived as a form of racialized contamination to recognize the facility and commonness of such embarrassment, expressed by the ulama's repudiation of the more animated iterations of Muharram.[122] At the same time, the pre-Islamic, nonpure origin of Shi'ism is subsumed into the very form of historicity that authentic Shi'i cosmology makes possible and elevates above mere historical time: "The spiritual essence of Husayn's great deed existed as a timeless expression of divine grace."[123] For the Shi'i, all earthly creatures participate in the passion of Husayn.

Iran's assimilation of European racial taxonomies supported anti-Islamic attitudes that positioned the advent of Islam in the seventh century as a historical nadir.[124] But while Persian nationalists certainly did espouse viewpoints that denigrated both Islam and Arabness, I have been suggesting that this denigration was premised less forcefully on the superficial taxonomic difference between the Semite and the Aryan than on the binary of civilization and barbarism, and alternatively, passivity and activity that inflects that taxonomy's most profound racial charge.[125] Some of the most important anti-Arab proponents of Persian nationalism unabashedly contrasted the civilization of the pre-Islamic Persians with the savagery of nomadic Arabs. By contrast, Persian nationalists who *incorporated* the Arab and Islamic intellectual traditions within the canon of Persianate intellectual and literary history promoted Islam as a progressive force either equal to or, in some cases, superior to Western civilization. The embrace of Islam was not premised upon the assumption of Arab moral superiority, but upon the notion of Islam's conduciveness to forming proper subjects of civilization, even of modernity. Thus, the nineteenth-century pan-Islamist Sayyid Jamal al-Din 'al-Afghani suggests Islam promoted human characteristics that contributed to the "cause of the progress of the nation," touting particularly those aspects of Muslim subjectivity in line with the idea of a proper subject of civilization; *adab* names the proper conduct leading to good, civil, normative subjectivity.[126] By attending to the ways in which the binary of civility and savagery undergird the nuances of Persian nationalist thought, we see how articulations of racial difference are always more than merely taxonomic, Eurocentric, or modern.

While Persian nationalism sometimes denigrated Arabness and Islam, it is also true that throughout the twentieth century the Shi'i ulama themselves eschewed traditional, that is, hyperbolic, modes of religious practice, as well as its perceived syncretism or contamination by nonreligious forms. The Shi'i modernization of the Muharram rituals shunned its passive, pietistic, purportedly fetishistic character in favor of its rhetorical potential for political subjectivity. For, since at least the mid-twentieth century, intellectuals argued that the early history of Shi'ism renders it amenable to political mobilization, and that further, Shi'ism was a political religion from the outset. The popularization of the Karbala paradigm lent concrete credence to this view. In this sense, the denigration of the syncretic seems to have its source in the denigration of the passive or affectable.

During his speech on the occasion of *arba'in,* Morteza Motahari, an important early Islamic Republic ideologue, admonished chest strikers and chanters, for identification with Karbala ought to elicit heroism, agency and commitment, rather than misery and passivity.[127] Earlier in the century, the controversy over chest striking followed an identical prescription: participants ought to supersede the passivity and emotionalism of weeping and grief with political activism, argued a Shi'i scholar in Lebanon.[128] Muharram's religious reform entailed eliminating its more lively features, such as self-flagellation and chest striking—forms of intensity that compound the rhythmic passion of *arba'in*. According to the logic of this elimination, that which is at odds with "forwardness," being rightly oriented on the scale of objective global time, is neither Shi'ism, nor Islam, but those particular dimensions of it that do not conform to the civilizational image Islam makes available to its adherents. Many Iranian ulama continue to repudiate aspects of Muharram, like the accompanying music of *daf* and *tunbak,* more mainstream parallels of *sinj va damām, maddahs* (effusive narrators), and the "uneducated no-goods [who] get together and chant 'Husayn, Husayn!' . . . beating [their] chests" for hours on end.[129]

The opposition between political and passive religious practice mirrors the opposition between disinterest and elementary sensation at the heart of the subject of the aesthetic.[130] There is a series of odd conceptual parallels here that appear contradictory only on the surface: the Shi'i ulama's call to activate Muharram for political agency; modernist literati's denigration of passive, classical, rule-bound poetry in favor of formally liberated activist prose and poetry (*sh'ir-i naw; adabīyāt-i muti'ahid*); film auteurs' elevation of realism, but also abstract film, and denigration of hyperbolic, melodramatic *fīlmfārsī* (chapter 2).[131] Each of these expresses the aesthetic's valorization of contemplative form as distinct from mere sensation. The aesthetic is to the political what mere sensation (aesthesis) is to bare religious practice, and echoes an archaic human/animal distinction. Thus, the disparaging of older, supposedly cruder iterations of Muharram in favor of its rejuvenated, politicized form mirrors the disavowal of passivity for the capacity for political representation enshrined by the ideology of aesthetic disinterestedness, the movement of the aesthetic from sensation to form.[132]

'*ajam* of the '*Ajam*

The characterization of Shi'ism as an impure version of Islam is helpfully clarified by the term '*ajam.* The Qur'an designates ethnically and linguistically non-Arab Muslims *'ajam* or *'ajamī,* a word used initially to refer primarily to Persians (though the usage of the term *'ajam* itself pre-dates Islamic discourse). Connoting strong ethnolinguistic difference, similar to the Greek labels *ethnos* and *barbaros,* *'ajam* joins together linguistic and communicative competence with moral and civilizational completeness, functioning as a boundary-setting force.[133] Thus, "whereas *'ajam* earlier meant being non-Arabic-speaking, particularly of Persian origin, later the term started to signal speaking the language with difficulty, or speaking it with characteristic interferences from the mother-tongue."[134] In the tenth century, the Arab poet al-Mutanabbi and the phonetician Ibn Jinni both proclaim the prideful symbolism of the Arabic phoneme *dād* (which the Persians do not possess as part of their alphabetical ken, pronouncing a weaker sound—*zād.*) In certain cases, as in Jahiz's theory of language, the *'ajam* is contrasted with *fasīh* (human) as *fasīh* is contrasted with all other members of the animal kingdom capable of oral communication (*'a'jam*).[135] The lexical correlation between *'ajam* and *'a'jam,* suggests Yasir Suleiman, constructs a dichotomy within the category of the human, between Arab and *'ajam,* the human who communicates meaningfully and with clarity (*bayān*) and the human who communicates unintelligibly and unintentionally.[136]

It has been argued that the spread of Islam and the Arabic language to the African continent through its eastern and northern coasts intensified the desire to preserve differences between newly Islamicized regions, as it simultaneously mitigated, without dispelling, the deranged views about Africans preserved in ancient geographical treatises. It is well known that medieval Arab geographers, like their Greek and Persian predecessors, mixed and confused mythology with anthropology in their descriptions of the African continent. Homer interwove ethnographic descriptions of northern Africa with projections of "mythic monsters, dog-headed or headless peoples and humans with eyes in their breasts" living beyond the Tritonian lake, just as the Achaemenid prince Sataspes reported back upon his failed mission to circumnavigate the African continent with dubious observations of "little men who wore palm-leaf raiment."[137] The medieval geographers who absorbed ancient Greek treatises "were loathe to excise information derived from earlier authorities"; thus even where new information was attainable, it was assimilated to older, more fantastical, discreditable frameworks. Based as much on ignorance as fantasy, views about African savagery were rarely properly dispelled by actual encounters that ensued from the Islamic conquests that pre-dated the European "discovery" of Africa by centuries. Rather, such views were refiltered through the enduring distinction between civilization and savagery. As Sylvia Wynter writes with a certain unsettling common sense: "All three monotheisms . . . had been religions instituted by population groups who were white-skinned, or at least, not black-skinned. With the result that the intellectuals of these groups, in developing the symbolic systems of their monotheistic creeds, had come to define these symbols in the terms of their own somatotype norm."[138] And, "The common thread binding Muslim and later Christian imagery was as much a rejection of blackness as it was the outcome of the lighter-skinned ruling class's desire to protect its position of superiority by celebrating its civility."[139]

Persians, while *'ajam,* nevertheless understood and aggressively expounded upon the worth, and in some cases, superiority, of their pre-Islamic heritage. In fact, for some scholars, the *shu'ubiyah,* referring to the eighth- to tenth-century controversy over the position of Arab and non-Arab Muslims in Islamic society, arose in part out of the strengthening force of the Persian Sasanian administrative apparatus during the later Abbasid period, specifically, the new importance given to Iranian clerks whose vague claims to genealogical ties to past Iranian kings had been rendered impotent by Islamic hegemony.[140] While scholars debate the true political scope of the *shu'ubiyah* movement at the historical moment when it was active in print, the very fact that the era's rhetorical sensibilities have survived to the present day suggests a potency to its underlying logic that is irreducible to the unpromising distinction between the political and the literary.[141] Under the Abbasids, the Persian *shu'ubis* protested against the dominant sense of Arab superiority under the previous Umayyad dynasty (661–750 CE). That the *shu'bis* were initially called *ahl al-taswiya* (the levelers) suggests that they demanded to be recognized as equals, if not ultimately superiors, to Arab Muslims, articulating a symmetry in collective archives of pride. A fund of past and present, real or imaginary civilizational achievements (even when conceived of simply as traceable genealogical continuity) fueled the literary diatribes and polemics between groups vying for the right of cultural hegemony in the early Abbasid period.

Yet, the tropes transmitted through Arab and Persian medieval geographers and philosophers by way of the Greek theory of climes preserved the binary of civilization and savagery that would render Africans *'ajam* of the *'ajam*. In the contemporary social hierarchy of Arab Gulf states, third-class Gulf Arabs are *'ajam* or *haulas,* those with Persian filiations, while yet beneath them, the fourth class, are the Africans, or *'abid* [slaves], whose "class is written on the blackness of their skin."[142] Africans, once initiated into the territorial and metaphysical scope of the Islamicate world, were rendered "more" *'ajam* than the Persians, either further back on the continuum between *fasīh* and *'a'jam,* or beyond the continuum altogether.

To this day, Persians self-invoke the term *'ajamī* as a source of pride, marking their triumphant Indo-European difference from Semitic Arabs. Yet such confident invocation belies an ignorance of *'ajam* as a broader historical category encompassing other, non-Arab Muslim groups, including Muslim Africans with whom most Iranians assume little in common.[143] (In yet another intriguing etymological procedure, Pearce suggests the word *Zanj* derives from "the still more ancient name of Azania," a Latinized form of the Arabic "Ajem," once signifying East Africa.[144]) In the Tunisian spirit healing ritual *stambeli, stambeli*'s lyrics are considered " *'ajmī*" due to occasional words borrowed from "Sub-Saharan languages" and the unintelligibility of the words, "which are not explicitly concerned with the (human) listener's comprehension."[145]

Historically, the film *Arba'īn* rendered Būshihr's Muharram rituals exemplary, even if Bakhshū's renown circulated further and more frequently through the medium of the insertless cassette tape, which absolved his blackness by decontextualizing his voice, making it available for plagiarism. The appropriation of Bakhshū's famous elegy, "Layla bigufta ay shah-i lab-i tishnih kamān" ("Layla said 'O king of those with thirsty lips,'") for national and military agitation during the Iran–Iraq War epitomizes this tendency toward sublation.[146] But because of *Arba'īn*'s Bushihri exemplarity, the film's focus on syncretic instrumentation evokes yet another localized Muharram tradition: Trinidadian Hosay (a linguistic modification of Husayn, the protagonist of Muharram). The movement of this Shi'i ritual to yet another geographical context of enslavement follows a trajectory distinct from the one *Arba'īn* chronicles, even as it clarifies the potency of its blackness.

Sonic Blackening and Phobic Mixing: Caribbean Hosay

Shi'i ulama in the early and mid-twentieth century decried overly passionate forms of Muharram. But these positions have shifted over the past two decades in accordance with new political needs. Namely, recognizing the importance of securing the support of more traditional sectors of Iranian society, it is somewhat of an open secret that today, even officials like Ali Khamenei, Iran's supreme leader (head of state), now generally support even the more ostentatious forms of Muharram previously condemned.[147] Senior ulama have had to inflate the emotiveness of traditional *rawzah* (Muharram recitations) in order to compete with the animated energy of dirge singers, Muharram's contemporary celebrities.[148] The contemporary embrace of hyperbolic Muharram may partially explain why Nāṣir Taqvā'ī's *Arba'īn* was screened, under the "Restored Classics" category, at the thirty-sixth Fajr in 2018, Iran's most important annual film festival.

The contradiction inherent in the doubled gesture to shun hyperbolic Muharram rituals and simultaneously embrace and exhibit them to the world is amplified in the West Indian context, where Muharram appears more obviously "creolized" than in Iran. Triangulating Iran and the West Indies with South Asia clarifies the point. Ethnographers of Muharram in South Asia affirm the magnetism of rhythmic drumming that is cinematically documented in Taqvā'ī's *Arba'īn*. Despite religious antagonisms, South Asians of diverse affiliations are attracted to the Muharram festivities, just as Muharram in Būshihr is reported to be one of the most attended and spectacular events in the province, proof of its spellbinding appeal. South Asian Muharram has been particularly shaped by various elements of Hindu culture.[149] In some cases the Sunni majority contests the anthropomorphism of certain Muharram traditions, like the construction of *ta'zīyahs*, the brightly colored, multitiered wooden tomb chambers carried in procession—and passed on to the Trinidadian Hosay tradition under the name *tadjahs*. In other instances, Sunnis are the primary participants, Muharram becomes an occasion for comedy and farce, and Shi'is are alienated from participating.[150]

The presence of Muharram in Iran and India is unsurprising and comes from a long, if sometimes disavowed past of shared history, language, and religion; Persian was the lingua franca of the Indian subcontinent between c. 1000 and 1860 CE. The tendency to imagine Persia and South Asia as entirely separate cultural entities reflects modern nationalism's recursive influence on scholarly practice and popular imagination.[151] The resemblance between south Iranian and South Asian Muharram in particular also suggests the greater integration and representation of South Asian culture into southern, rather than northern Iran. Southern Iranian provinces are sometimes described as a "melting pot" of South Asians, Iranians, Arabs, and (less frequently included or remembered) Africans. Writing about his own experiences of Muharram as a child growing up in Ahvaz, one scholar recalls "a syncretic culture heavily influenced by four concurrent traits: Indian from the east, African from the south, Arabic from the west, and Iranian from the north . . . We are heavily influenced by African, particularly East African, dance and music."[152] The continuities between South Iranian and South Asian Muharram suggest the naturalness, rather than aberrancy, of accretion and transformation. Where the extension of a centralized authority over ritual is attenuated (as in northern India, where Shi'i are a minority of a minority, or in the south of Iran, where modern Iranian youths travel for "a sense of freedom"), excrescences grow not only organically, but seemingly uncontrollably.[153]

South Asian and Iranian Muharram share features that are attributable to geographical and cultural contiguity. Muharram's animation in the Caribbean, by contrast, suggests a proximity to Southwest Asia that cannot be explained through any geographical or linguistic intimacy. Instead, West Indian Hosay articulates a different kind of conjunction. Hosay traces the history of movement from South Asia to the Caribbean as a result of the demand for indentured servants, primarily from India's northern provinces, following the abolition of African enslavement in the Caribbean in the 1830s. Hosay's practice is particularly pronounced in Trinidad and Tobago, British Guyana, Jamaica, and Surinam. For oral historians of the Caribbean, Muharram was carried in the "hearts and memories" of destitute Indian indentured migrants who struggled to maintain cultural norms on New World plantations.[154] This is also why Hosay's transmission remains a mystery, an "obstreperous commemoration," that has survived transformation into occasion for political rioting, postcolonial nationalist discourse, as well as denigrated and beloved carnivalized street celebration.[155] The revival of Muharram, or Hosay, in Trinidad peculiarly repeats the phenomenon of multireligious affiliation characteristic of its South Asian iterations, while making legible a coarticulation of religion and race that is less intelligible in its Indian and Iranian counterparts.

Muharram in Būshihr and Muharram in Trinidad—by way of the North Indian-Caribbean passage—both reflect two implicitly opposing views of syncretism. Trinidadian Hosay italicizes a modality that is left dormant in the Iranian context. On the one hand, in the Caribbean, Hosay syncretism symbolizes modernity as multicultural, preserving and displacing the antagonisms embedded in the encounter that presupposes syncretic possibility. In Trinidad, the metaphor of mixedness refers to a "heterogeneity that connotes democratic (equal) political representation, a cosmopolitan worldview, and therefore consummate modernity in a global context."[156] The modern, positive inflection and international postwar reception of the creole "master symbol" and the image of Caribbean hyperdiversity it represents and transmutes to various, usually unrelated contexts has come to color general academic attitudes toward hybridity in the present.

The contemporary, positively inflected representations of Afro-Iran, which mark both continuity and rupture with the older racist views expressed by contemporaneous commentators of Taqvā'ī's work, uphold this postwar revaluation of the creole signifier. Indeed, most modern representations of Afro-Iran take distance from the negative pole of contamination characteristic of outdated, explicitly racist accounts in favor of the cosmopolitan cool that association with implicitly contemporary, Anglophone blackness offers.[157] The cosmopolitanism, as well as capacity for commodification, of blackness is already evident in the very fact of Būshihrī *arba'īn*'s transformation into an object of experimental, ethnographic art in 1970. As an aesthetic object, an otherwise denigrated ritual is enjoyable, consumable, and celebratable as a sign of national culture. Similarly, the cooptation of Hosay by state narratives about multicultural modernity, as well as its promotion by the West Indian tourist industry, repeats the extension of heritage into both commodity and art, and displaces, but does not absolve, the racial. For the aestheticization of (racialized, religious) ritual produces the unmarked, universal subject of aesthetic culture. Like the modernized political subject, who abjures Shi'ism's exaggerated emotivity in favor of its revolutionary potential, and like the political subject of the multicultural state who outgrows the primitivism of racial antagonism in favor of transracial harmony, the subject of aesthetic culture exemplarily appreciates and upholds the distinction between life and art. The affectable object of aesthetic culture, on the other hand, lives out their indistinction.

If creolité is the new master symbol of the postwar era, its popularization has been largely explained through the paradigm of late capitalist globalization, as well as certain twentieth-century epistemological transformations to the concept of culture: namely, that, like the "hollow category" of tradition, culture lacks the sense of ontological stability once ascribed to it by more archaic models of anthropological thought.[158] But as anthropologists of the Caribbean have argued, the adulatory politics and fashionableness of creolité is far from unambiguous. The word *creole*, from the Portuguese *crioulo*, for example, referred in popular usage to a slave brought up in the master's house, and its catachrestic applications rarely take into account the full politics of the term's universalization.[159]

And yet, the postmodern Caribbeanization or creolization of all culture cannot merely be ascribed to willful ignorance of ethnographic context specificity, nor to naïve or wishful interpretations of hybridity as inherently subversive, as critics like Aisha Khan have insightfully suggested.[160] For at the heart of the celebration of the syncretic lies a recognition of the artifice, the intrinsic lack of the in-itself. If multiculturalism underlies the basis for national identity in the Caribbean, it is because displacement and *de*contextualization, rather than origin and context-truth, are framed as inherently authentic. But because multiculturalism is always already premised on a prior possibility of autonomous, pure, or original culture, its capacity for subversion is destined to tautology and dissonance. Thus, the optimistic undertone of all tropes connoting mixedness (syncretism, creolité, hybridity) is prone, inevitably, constitutively, to devolution into the underlying antagonism and violence that lies at its heart. If the contradictions of mixedness are brought out exemplarily by a certain anxiety about black "antinomian modes of behavior,"[161] and more pointedly, by a certain distaste of rhythm, it is because rhythm's blackness generates an unavoidable confrontation with the blankness, the spacing, the void at the heart of the origin. "[Loss] brings us closer . . . then we become empty," submits one dirge singer.[162]

As if to affirm the way in which blackness produces anxiety about origins, ethnomusicological literature surrounding Būshihrī mourning practices analogizes African presence in Iran to recognizable tropes of cultural deterioration that are more familiarly associated with Arabness. Thus, the syncretism of Būshihrī Arbʾaīn is described as adulterated, polluted with wild African blood: "The influences and changes instigated [by African slaves] not only did not result in the strengthening of the host culture, but weakened and disintegrated it," writes Muḥsin Sharīfīyān, who compares African musical influences effected by slave presence with the seventh-century Arab invasion of Rayshahr that terminated Persian dynastic rule.[163] In one breath, pride of cosmopolitanism decays into nationalist aversion, revealing the guiling displacements at constant play in the representations of Afro-Iran. Like the trope of the Islamic invasion recurrent in Persian nationalist historiography, blackness produces an unyielding amnesic pause; literally, African slaves are imagined to have extinguished historical memory. At the same time, if blackening mirrors Arab/Islamic contamination, this is only when and where Islam is imagined in terms of the uncivilized, nomadic Arab horde. As we have seen, this is only one image of Islam and Arabness in the Persian nationalist imagination. Bifurcated, the imagination of Islam is divided by the opposition between civilization and savagery. (Thus, in Arab Gulf understandings of social standing, nomadism is not automatically collapsed into savagery, but is redeemed through recourse to the notion of a blood transparency that bedouinism necessitates.) What is truly abhorrent is neither Islam, nor the supposed civilizational lack of nomadism, but ultimately, the savagery of kinlessness, the state of bastardization intrinsic to enslavement, the vulnerability to the most radical grafting.[164] Blackness mediates Arab difference through absorbing lack (of capacity for civilization) and representing instead, passivity and enslavement, the affectability of particularity.[165] Blackness thereby also embodies the anxiety produced by the Persian-Islamic encounter.

Similarly, default views about Hosay in the Caribbean, especially up until the independence movement, revolved around belief that "Afro-Caribbeans and rogue individual coolies" brought religion-nullifying festivity to Hosay/Muharram.[166] The celebration of creole culture in Trinidad is fraught with ambivalence about miscegenation that is reflected in Indo-Trinidadians' repeated assertion that "Indian and Negro don't mix," as well as in the confusing simultaneous encouragement of and indignation about non-Muslim Afro-Trinidadians' participation in Muharram.[167] If mixing's embrace is premised on the intuition of progressivism associated with the multicultural and the multiracial, angst ensues from fear of adulteration and deculturation associated with mixing's shadow: blackening. In the Caribbean, as in Southwest Asia, blackening is not merely an ocular but also a sonic process.

It is not without reason that the deflation of authentic Shi'i Muharram is based in worries about rhythmic infusions. The earliest iterations of Hosay on Caribbean plantations were observed through *marsiyahs* (*marcee* or *marsay* in Trini patois), or lamentation songs about Husayn's death, sung by women in Hindi dialects. As the tradition of lyrical female lamentation waned with the colonial absorption and erasure of Hindi by English, the percussive tradition of drumming, accompanied by cymbals (*sinj*) preserved Hosay in sound: the "tradition which remained pervasive in Trinidad, even as 'Indian' declined in usage, was the beating of drums." Rhythm thus subsumes the semiological dimension of Muharram, assuming, as supplement, "esoteric intricacies."[168] As language, as context dissipates, rhythm preserves the interval, the spacing, the silence that allows meaning and context to first appear. Afro-Trinidadians participated in Hosay from the beginning of its observance in the nineteenth century, and their involvement as drummers is obsessively noted by ethnographers.

A profusion of origins (Iran) is superseded in the Caribbean with a profusion of rhythm. Anxiety about its origin and religious legitimacy leads some Trinidadians to circumvent Hosay's religiosity by displacing Shi'ism as the causal force of Muharram altogether. In substituting Shi'ism with the figure of the "memorial"—the memory of enslavement and indenture entwined with the legend of Karbala—practitioners see Hosay, simultaneously, as a ritual of honor for Husayn's martyrdom and, equally importantly, as commemoration of slave and indentured ancestry, a living conduit to plantation history. Anthropologists thus recognize "drum 'talk'" in Hosay as the "melodic encoding" of memory and narrative.[169] But, like the entrancing drumming of *duhul* in *zār*, which brings participants to emptiness (chapter 2), and the repetitive chest striking, or *sīnah-zanī*, in Būshihrī Muharram that "burns you empty," the elaborate rhythms of Hosay do more than simply communicate meaning. Rhythm also returns meaning to the space from which sound, and therefore meaning, narrative, and history become possible. As intervallic strikes and the silence between them, rhythm is the mark of the space from which meaning rises and becomes vulnerable to its own dislocation, and is why blackness, in its violent conflation with slavery, exemplifies the intrinsic terror of this necessary spacing that is otherwise attribute-less, universal, absolutely empty, absolutely free. "The *slave* didn't bring Hosay? How you know they did not, how you know that?" protests a *tadjah* constructor to his ethnographer-interlocutor.[170] Slavery is the historical mark of an ontological disruption that transcends history.

Syncretism's revelations of both cultural crisis and cultural allure reestablish and nourish traditional perspectives on culture as a self-contained ontogenic and historically guaranteed entity. And this is so even when syncretic forms fail to arrest, when they mundanely index rather than spectacularize difference, as in the case of Caribbean cultural festivities, whose creolité has long gone treated rather as a self-evident state of affairs available to perception.[171] But it is equally so when syncretic forms appear exemplary and exceptional, as in south Iranian Muharram, whose blackness appears to hyperbolize a state of cultural mixture that is, in truth, *unexceptional,* ubiquitous, but also, unthought, unthinkable. Blackened, syncopated, suffering sound is sonic disruption to the categories of culture, history, experience itself. *Arba'īn* invokes instead, through its mediatized form, the unyielding repetition of a sign whose referent endlessly loses itself in the flashes between what is there to be sensed.

« 4 »

The Black Maternal and the Interruptive Imagination

Bashu

Gham dārī bābā, zār dārī bābā. ("You have sadness
dear, you have *zār* dear.")

—*zār* saying

Bahram Beyzai's *Bashu, the Little Stranger* was written and produced at the height of the Iran–Iraq War, but war is never directly thematized—one of the many reasons the Islamic Republic of Iran banned the unapologetically pacifist film from domestic distribution for three years and sabotaged its eventual release in 1989.[1] Instead, war is metonymized by explosive displacements, fire, smoke, and burnt flesh. The withdrawal of historical referent inflates the substitutional possibilities of catastrophe, creating an anamorphic image of disaster that is present but oneiric, barely accessible to sense. Arguably, the unspoken wounds figured by the bombs exploding on the Khūzistānī border surface in the spectral form of the main character Bashu's mother, whose incineration inaugurates the film. The mother's ambiguous blackness conjures an unstable state between being and nonbeing, fact and imagination, past and future, magnifying, multiplying, but also dissolving catastrophe's referent. The gravity with which her veiled figure moves through space belies the impermanence of the path she traces—a nameless, nebulous shape sweeping depths of fields, irruptive in her quiescence.

The most famous of Iranian films foregrounding phenotypically inflected racism, Beyzai's *Bashu* brings out the webs of contradictions

« 162 »   The Black Maternal and the Interruptive Imagination

inherent in dominant modes of narrating the historical emergence, and taxonomic containment, of blackness. The film oscillates between two familiar positions. On the one hand, it reduces blackness to a symptom of a more general, universal, transhistorical problematic—difference in general. On the other hand, it secures in place the *exemplarity* of blackness for the articulation of this generalized, universal, and transhistorical difference. *Bashu* vacillates between assimilating and rendering exemplary. And in doing so, the film shows that blackness *exceeds* our historically and culturally variable modes of articulating and framing it.

Bashu demonstrates this excess through three subtly interlocking registers: first, at the representational level, through summoning tropes of Persian and Arab difference that deploy an equivocal blackness for their coherence, thus suggesting the capaciousness of blackness as an anachronic force that absorbs other forms of historically inscribed difference, including most notably race, ethnicity, and nationality. Second, through an abbreviation of the spirit healing ritual *zār*, which exemplifies the precarity, diffuseness, and fundamental resistance to facticity of African slavery's history in the Indian Ocean. And third, through the child-figure's articulation of natal alienation that subtends the longue durée of African enslavement in the Indian Ocean world, but that also suggests a crisis of origin, of the immemorial. To show how these different registers operate in tandem, in the second part of the chapter I turn to another film produced during the same period, Amir Nadiri's *The Runner,* also about a young boy in the south of Iran. Though the main character of *The Runner* is not marked as black, like *Bashu, The Runner* shows interest in the possibility of overcoming the violent effects of racism by positing proper language (and national integration) as a path to full, universal humanity. Together the humanist themes these two films have in common—language, literacy, self-transcendence—dwell upon the intransigent unincorporability of blackness. This unassimilability, I argue, is connected to the difficulty of securing a *proper context* for blackness in Southwest Asia.

Bashu

At its most prosaic, *Bashu* is a story about a displaced ethnically and racially ambiguous child from the southwest of Iran, Khūzistān, whose parents and sister blow up in a bombing that destroys his

The Black Maternal and the Interruptive Imagination   « 163 »

entire village. Bashu escapes into the back of a truck that transports him hundreds of miles up to the verdant border of the Caspian Sea, the northernmost Iranian province of Gīlān. Explosions interpreted as threats literally propel him north. When the pickup driver stops for tea en route, detonations nearby launch Bashu from his nap in the cargo area of the trunk, running through shrubs in order to escape what he perceives as the continuation of the bombings. A series of cinema verité moves like a handheld shot chasing Bashu's bolt through a forest, coupled with extreme long shots of an imperceptible figure fluttering across the frame, demonstrate the temporal intimacy and confusion that mediates the viewer's experience of Bashu's experience of temporality throughout the film. Eventually Bashu runs as far as a rice field where Na'i, played by famous theater actress Susan Taslimi, and her two young children share a meal nearby. Bashu has traveled all the way up to Gīlān. Upon seeing him, Na'i expresses repulsion for Bashu's dark skin color, wondering aloud if he has escaped from a coal mine. Gradually her instincts prompt her to welcome the child into her home, against the objections of extended family and Gīlāni town dwellers, all of whom find Bashu's blackness a subject of derision and comedy. The village shopkeeper insultingly slips Na'i an extra bar of soap. A group of young boys encircle, bully, and parody Bashu at every sighting.

Most commentators who dwell on the theme of racism in the film interpret Bashu's character as ethnically, or culturally, Arab, and this interpretation, though burdened by the undecidable profile of the schism between ethnicity and culture, appears buttressed both by Bashu's rare speech in the film and his portrayal by Adnan Afravian, who was not a professional actor and whom Beyzai chose specifically because of his skin color, which he thought exemplified the coastal Iranian profile. But Arabness is never directly referenced, other than the very few instances when Bashu speaks Arabic, and because he appears to identify as Persian, rather than Arab, the question of his difference transforms, consistently, into a metaphorical one, a placeholder.

At the time of *Bashu's* production, Persian denigration of Arabness was both topical and convenient. It is a longstanding current in Iranian social history, from the neo-Zoroastrian renaissance led by Persians self-exiled in India in the sixteenth century all the way through to more familiar nineteenth- and twentieth-century nationalist discourses. Nationalism shapes and reproduces a narrative

« 164 »   The Black Maternal and the Interruptive Imagination

of Arab invasion and debasement of Persian civilization, promotes extirpation of Arabic vocabulary in Persian poetics and everyday discourse, and revives and popularizes ancient, and thus presumably truly authentic, Iranian history and essence.[2] If a subtle anti-Arabness is illustrated by Beyzai's film, mediated through characters who ostracize the ambiguous Arab/black Bashu,[3] it is also the case that, in the aftermath of the Iranian Revolution of 1979, during the Iran–Iraq War, the Arab, secular Baath Iraqi state also appeared as a substitution for a more permanently existential enemy—the West, metonym for modernity, Pahlavi authoritarianism, and Europhilia, all that Iran had defeated in its embrace of anti-imperialist Shi'i hegemony. In the background of *Bashu,* as in Nadiri's *The Runner,* thus wages not only the war between Iran and Iraq, the Persian and Arab, Shi'i and Sunni, but the ongoing war between Iran and Western modernity. But because modernity itself includes the programmatic articulation and development of the nation-state and the cultural nationalism that subtends it, this war is also simply internal to Iran itself. Iran is at war with itself.

Bashu's unnamed southern origins accommodate his ambiguous, unplaceable Arabness, and because one of the longstanding Persian tropes of Arab difference is a fantasy of impurity that derives from a supposed nomadism of origins, his particular kind of Persianness does not contradict his Arabness. Coastal peoples have long been designated as belonging to a "primitive universe" by Iranian and Arab historians alike, a disprized but indispensable zone undergirded by an imaginary of dilution. This denigration of the coastal is shared amongst Persian Gulf cultures in general.[4] The fourteenth-century Muslim geographer Ibn Khaldūn distinguished between *badawa* and *hadara*; as Miriam Cooke argues, this distinction created an association between nomadism and blood purity, and urbanism and miscegenation, that has been revived in current forms of social categorization in the Gulf.[5] Anti-Arabness encounters anti-Persianness in a seemingly ongoing circulation of localized animus that the invisible backdrop of the Iran–Iraq War, one of the "most impenetrable inter-state conflicts since WWII," assimilates into the deepest strata of the film's representation, resisting any straightforward geopolitical framework.[6] Political power conflicts are just one expression of the struggle with modernity. By subordinating the political to the spiritual, *Bashu* shows how the metaphysical struggle with modernity arises from anxiety with a world that is continually,

The Black Maternal and the Interruptive Imagination   « 165 »

if imperceptibly, disappearing. In the wake of this loss that is modernity itself, film summons blackness, and its spiritual resources, for reassurance, reconciliation, and healing.

Why is it corporeal difference, a perceived "impurity" that appears to surface through the skin, that most satisfies the desire to evoke the experience of difference and of loss? The choice to represent Bashu's difference as one bound up in skin color, despite the lack of even anecdotal claims that Arabs are darker than Iranians, elicits a question about why the history of race, though never exclusively bound to phenotype, and in fact, always imagined in excess of the corporeal, finds its privileged metonym in blackness. In Beyzai's film this blackness is more swarthy than jet, generating ambiguity and problems for recognition and comprehension, yet it is one that stereotypically is claimed to absorb filth and foreignness, even when filth is transvaluated, an alluvial human essence stranded between the terrestrial and the metaphysical, between soil (*khāk*), the pure earth and dirtiness. Toward the end of the film, recapitulating the film's ultimate abstracting gesture, Na'i pronounces that Bashu "like all children, is a child of the sun and the earth." Yet the "dirty" color of Bashu's skin imbues this final rhetorical sleight with ambivalent meanings. In the twentieth century, the word *khāk* (dirt, soil, earth) linked on to *vatan* (homeland). And the idea of Iran as a unified community was "marked by a loss that could not be recovered."[7]

As with other elements in *Bashu,* the positive term *khāk* is under relentless threat by a fear of literal impending invasion, just as it is jeopardized by other possible and contiguous denotations. When Na'i's relatives come to visit her, no one sees Bashu as a child of Iran, a recognizable brother or son, and they cannot resist remarking instead upon Bashu's "charcoal" color. They gather on a carpet, palaver and pass around tea, reprimanding Na'i for her reckless decision to host the foreigner, while various family members molest Bashu. An aunt gropes Bashu's head in search of lice; an uncle demands dental inspection. Bashu's body gradually discomposes itself. His slouching back buckles, his visibly perspiring skin dampens his ragged yellow shirt collar. A small girl he had earlier glimpsed from the window with intrigued curiosity crawls toward him on the carpet and swabs his face with her finger, which she examines, disappointed. Bashu lowers his head in shame.

This bodily discomposure culminates in convulsive fits after Na'i angrily pushes the relatives out of her house. Bashu moans, shivers, and shakes on the ground, the color drained from his lips, sweat soaking his clothes as Na'i panics, unable to interpret his sudden illness. She sprints through the village in search of the local doctor, who soberly informs her his medicine does not cure people "of that color." Later in the film, Na'i herself contracts a fever after a sleepless night searching for runaway Bashu in a downpour. Bashu interprets her illness as *zār* affliction, possession by spirit winds, which Beyzai indexes with minute, fleeting details. Outside, straddling a large inverted pot, and invoking the significance of drumming in *zār,* Bashu pounds out a rhythm, wails and sways. Pasty-faced, Na'i's body awakens from the verge of death, twitches and jerks on her mat as she is jolted to her knees. Performing the signature signs of *zār* possession, her shoulder blades roll, her chest jilts, her torso bounces while closed eyelids and a dropping jaw betray a state beneath or beyond consciousness. She throws a white sheet over her

Figure 21. Scenes from Bahram Beyzai's *Bashu, the Little Stranger* (1989). Right: Bashu drumming outside of Na'i's home when she falls ill. Far right, top: Na'i is feverish after spending a night in the pouring rain searching for Bashu. Far right, bottom: Na'i throws a white sheet over herself and jilts to Bashu's drumming, a signature of *zār*.

The Black Maternal and the Interruptive Imagination   « 167 »

convulsing body as the camera cuts back to Bashu's drumming as it intensifies the acceleration of the rhythm and Na'i's pantomimes. A pan moving away from Bashu's concentrated, grieving face through the blonde rice fields gathers the ethereal dimension of this healing ritual, which results in Na'i's full recovery. Through a kind of hyperbolic parallelism typical for Beyzai the filmmaker, Bashu's interpretation of Na'i's delirium adjusts the viewer's understanding of his own sickness earlier.[8] Bashu, too, has been *zār*-afflicted in Gīlān.

It is not a contradiction that Bashu's blackness is unidentifiable in the film. Neither Persian nor Arab, the idiosyncratic name Bashu has no meaning, does not belong to an identifiable culture. "It's my invention," says Beyzai, "from the word 'to be' [*būdan*] and, essentially, 'to reside' [*bāshīdan*]."[9] "Say something so I can know what language you speak. You're black, you're dumb, you have no name. Every human being has a name," Na'i prods a curled-up Bashu with

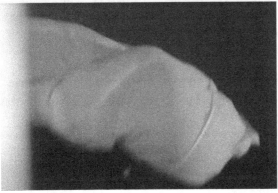

« 168 »   The Black Maternal and the Interruptive Imagination

her stick in their initial encounter. Despite the prevalence of African and African slave descendent communities in the south of Iran, where Bashu is from, neither an African heritage nor a slave heritage is assured by the diegesis; it is rather unjustified. Understandably, perhaps rightly, no commentator has made such a connection between *Bashu* and the history of slavery. Nevertheless, this possibility is embedded in Beyzai's very insistence on sampling a coastal culture that he sees exemplified by Bashu's skin color. And the senselessness of the name Bashu invites, even if it cannot assure, this seemingly out of place connection. In Southwest Asia as elsewhere, renaming individuals with nonhuman names was one means by which masters asserted control over the identity of their slaves. Representing power is integral to reproducing domination, and renaming was one of the most powerful displays of the owner's mastery.

Hortense Spillers writes of the being *"nowhere at all,"* the loss of an attachment to one's name that characterized movement through the Middle Passage.[10] Across the passage from the African mainland to the eastern coast, to the Red Sea and Gulf of Aden, literal castration, the fate of male slaves destined for royal servitude, paralleled the more commonplace castration of the name across gender, across age (see chapter 1). This kind of castration was compensated for with belittling reminders. Slaves were often renamed with floral, spice, and ornamental associations: Lawn Flower (Chaman Gul), New Flower (Taza Gul), Diamond (Almās), Gift (Hidīya), Saffron (Zafarān), Congratulations (Mubārak).[11] In Southeast Asia, "female slaves were given new names by their masters, effectively erasing former identities," or "named simply 'daughters of god,' indicating their kinless status."[12] In Egypt, some black slaves carried "the names of the trade routes they had travelled into slavery."[13] In the Indian Ocean, slaves "almost never carried ordinary Arab personal names, but . . . special names."[14]

The Black Child, the Cinematic Child

Like Bashu's name, the *zār* he performs to heal Na'i literalizes by a kind of cosmological analogy this dispossession of self specific to slavery, and which the narrative of the film reflects through the dispossession of childhood. *Zār* is usually associated with women, with female social denigration, and led primarily by black *māmā zārs,* or spiritual leaders. Thus, a *zār* is sometimes described as a marriage ceremony, and both female and male patients can be adorned like brides.[15] The *zār* sequence between Bashu and Na'i includes or channels Bashu's spectral mother despite her absence, and is just as uncommunicative. "When Bashu drums [*tasht mīzanad*] it's for no one other than his sick mother," Beyzai tells us, leaving ambiguous the question of which mother is sick, for which mother he drums, mourns.[16] At the turn of the twentieth century, the emotive force of *vatan* (homeland), once a fluid term denoting land of birth, is transferred "to the larger, more mediated *Iran'zamin* (terra iranica)." *Vatan* in turn is feminized, maternalized into the image of a sick mother "in need of diagnosis, cure, and care, as a neglected, weak female figure in need of her sons' medical and emotional attention."[17] "What is the message of Na'i's becoming-mother and Bashu's becoming-son in this film?," one cinema-goer wonders.[18] Woman is the most primitive instrument of nationalism, "metonymized as nothing but the birth canal."[19] Coincident with the profusion of sex in the prerevolutionary cinematic imaginary evolves a certain ideology of maternalism, suturing motherhood and care of the child to the nation.[20]

The ubiquitous child protagonist is a striking feature of many cinemas from the Global South. Commentators interpret the prominence of the child-figure in postrevolutionary Iranian cinema variously. After the 1979 Revolution, new restrictions, such as the banning of sex in films and the expulsion of female actresses from the film industry, imposed limitations for what it was possible to display on screen, thus accelerating, but also transforming, an ongoing tradition of child acting. For, as film scholars point out, child focalization in cinema was not novel. The 1969-established governmental organization known as the Center for the Intellectual Development of Children and Young Adolescents produced filmmakers as internationally lauded as Abbas Kiarostami and Beyzai himself. Based primarily around filmmaking of and for children, the center unexpectedly contributed to an alternative genre of elite cinematic modernism described in chapter 2, a movement in rebellion against *filmfārsī*: "unprofessional actors, outdoor locations, small cooperative filming teams, and a documentary-fictional style picturing marginalized and excluded people."[21] Like the National Iranian Radio and Television network, one of the primary establishments for ethnographic filmmaking in Iran, the Center for the Intellectual Development of Children and Young Adolescents provided state-funded support for small-scale documentary and animated films that were

« 170 »   The Black Maternal and the Interruptive Imagination

"somber and philosophical," "free from capital and the box office," and therefore addressed to "intellectual and pedagogical concerns" of artistic film directors.[22]

The meaning of the child protagonist shifted after the 1979 Revolution, and in particular, during the Iran–Iraq War: "the children in Iranian films of the war—attractive, idealized, their innocent faces peering from the screens," approximated the famous, injured martyr of the Sacred Defense genre.[23] On this interpretation, as symbolic war victim, the child protagonist depicts trauma-induced passivity, recalling Gilles Deleuze's famous characterization of the postwar rupture in the history of cinema as an atrophy of capacity and devolution of faith in the human subject's agency toward a passive witnessing.[24] (In Persian, *shahīd*, martyr, is etymologically connected to *shāhid*, witness.) "Children liberated films from the domination of plot."[25] Iranian films propelled by child protagonists implicate us "in a fictional world that is constantly failing."[26] Thus, the cinematic child might suggest political transitions to skepticism and impotence manifested in the tranquil art cinema of a filmmaker like Abbas Kiarostami, who worked on *Bashu* with Beyzai and whose own child-centered "earthquake trilogy" was released during the same quarter decade. Kiarostami's childhood-centered films exemplify the power of the child to generate narrative experiment with forms of subjectification that would be adequate to the political and ethical crises born in the wake of the Iranian Revolution.[27]

A broad and heterogeneous genealogy undergirds the reading of the child protagonist in film studies, inflecting interpretations surrounding the historical specificity of Iranian films. Film scholars understand the child figure more generally as a proxy for the "mental machinery" that is the film-spectator relation. The child is the classic spectatorial figure, because cinema bears witness to the child within. As spectator, the child details self-dispossession in the moment of narrative captivation, absorption in the repetition of the other. A tradition of film theory posits the child as the embodiment of the spectator's naïveté and gullibility, an avatar for the "suggestible subject" seduced into the hypnosis of cinematic viewing: "the borders of the ego relax" in the "narcotic inducement to fantasy" that is cinema.[28] "Cinema is what's bigger than us, to which we have to lift our eyes." Historically, cinema is part of an epistemological configuration and image-making tendency that involves the development of psychoanalysis, hypnosis, and time capture.[29] But naïveté is also a modality of the child's impropriety; to be admitted into adulthood is to achieve propriety, ownership over one's self. (More prosaically and cynically, some commentators emphasize the strategic significance of children's actual naïveté; directors preferred working with nonprofessional actor children not only because it was a logical economical choice but because, "as Kiarostami has shown, children are easier to manipulate.")[30]

It is unsurprising that the child is a recurring cinematic figure as well as a site of proliferating theories of spectatorship. A "national avatar," the child creates a "highly mobile" "intensity of recognition."[31] The child is an obvious choice for pathos stimulation, claim to verisimilitude, and metonym for modernity's pivotal symbolic construct, around which foundational cultural institutions like the school and family rest.[32] But childhood is also a mask, a prophylactic of innocence against the aggression of norms. The child reminds us that conformity to culture is impossible, tempting the unrelenting fantasy of escape and destruction, and the return back to the idyllic abyss. Kojin Karatani comes close to suggesting that this (adult) desire for an imaginary irenic childhood is itself responsible for the very invention of the child. Adults radicalize "the historicity of 'the child.'"[33] Idealized as a human tabula rasa, and thus emptied of knowledge, reason, and form, the child figure also gives way to the eruption of monstrosity.[34]

If the adult is a prototype for the human, the child, as the wild, unformed adult, poses questions about the inhuman that lies within. The child is the capacity to acquire a second nature, to obtain "adult consciousness and reason"; but thereby, the human, the adult, "depends on and presupposes" the child, or that which exists without and prior to culture, a "native lack."[35] Like the enigmatic excess that overspills the humanist theory of development, of *bildung,* cinematic perception repeats the failed imbrication of biology and culture as a tumultuous relation between rapture and automation.

It might thus be possible to see the character Bashu as cinematic *infans*—the state of being without language that marks the limit of what "words can be called upon to tell" and "what *in the image* falls outside" of itself.[36] And certainly, Bashu might also be seen as an allegory for postrevolutionary shock as it worked itself out during the Iran–Iraq War period, a recovery of pure perception in the wake of catastrophe. Narratively, however, the sublation of Bashu as exemplary of the abstract child figure is difficult to maintain, given

« 172 »   The Black Maternal and the Interruptive Imagination

that Bashu is one of many children in Beyzai's film. In scenes, he often appears alongside Na'i's children, Oshin and Gulbisar. Beyzai emphasizes the difference between these three children, and the two kinds of childhood they represent. In one scene, Gulbisar holds up a mirror to herself as she looks back at Bashu sleeping, confirming his deviance from her white skin. When he wakes up, she runs away: the two children have been "forced to confront the illusion of seeing themselves replicated in the images of others."[37] Although Bashu the child seems to invite interpretations that substitute his otherness for a more general ontological difference, his blackness resists universalizations. In another famous scene, Na'i bathes her own children in the river, and then tricks Bashu into the water, furiously scrubbing away at his dark skin and nearly drowning him, hoping to remove his color as if removing a stain: "Sefid nibeh, ki nibeh" (No, he won't become white) (Rahimieh, 243). As black, the film repeatedly suggests, Bashu's childhood marks a dispossession that is not universal, not shared in the same way by all children, nor by a general status of *infans*.

While theories of the cinematic child figure are all apt, Bashu's blackness thus resists full assimilation to them. He represents neither a national structure of feeling nor a stage of paralyzed interwar or postwar witnessing, nor can he merely be read as a metareflection on the position of spectatorship elicited by cinema itself. Rather, Bashu's blackness suggests a certain impossibility of childhood, evoking a racialized natal alienation that gestures back toward the history of African enslavement in Southwest Asia.[38] This blackness is inexplicably summoned to articulate the ethno-national-linguistic distinction between Persian and Arab that it simultaneously blurs and confounds. The tropes through which *Bashu* articulates natal alienation—blackness, orphanhood, Bashu's spectral mother, *zār*—suggest that the history of slavery is itself at its core the most profound philosophical elaboration of a contextlessness that troubles all naturalized claims to identity and that interrupts all familiar models of identification. If there is a historically specific meaning to genealogical isolation, Bashu activates its metaphysical dimension, one that exposes modernity's obsession with forged, especially linguistic, kinships that compensate for loss. But if the loss that modernity *is* produces the racial by reifying difference, then blackness is the remainder that precedes and subtends this loss, thwarting all compensatory gesture.

The Black Maternal and the Interruptive Imagination   « 173 »

Figure 22. Bashu peers through an abyss of sugar cane at the opening of Beyzai's *Bashu, The Little Stranger* (1989).

The pallor of diegetic allusions to the history of enslavement in *Bashu* should indeed cause one to seriously doubt any plausible referential earnestness. Gestures too weak to be named allusions to the history of African enslavement appear in *Bashu* where unintended. The connection to slavery fails to meet even the relatively low threshold for conviction in fictionalized interpretation. At the same time, it is also the case that *only* attenuated diegetic allusiveness can adequately capture the weak facticity, or the resistance to full facticity that shapes Indian Ocean slavery's historicity.

The viewer first glimpses Bashu dramatically peering between two tall strands of an abyss of sugar cane in his southern village. Abetted by its conducive geographical features (bounded by mountains to the north and east, and by the lower Tigris River on the west), Khūzistān was the most important sugar-producing site as early as the Sasanian period, and continued to be until the tenth century.[39] The connection between slave labor and sugar cultivation dips into an undatable chasm that echoes through this scene in the ambiguity of stalk identification. Though, and because, there seems really no conclusion to be drawn from this fact, it is often forgotten that it was through contact with westward-expanding Islamic civilization that Europeans acquired the expertise to transform sugar cultivation into one of the most lucrative and exploitative projects the world had ever

« 174 »   The Black Maternal and the Interruptive Imagination

Figure 23. Scenes from Bahram Beyzai's *Bashu, the Little Stranger* (1989). Top: Bashu's sister seen walking through a desert. Bottom: Two disparate times and spaces intertwine as Na'i is seen crossing paths with Bashu's deceased family.

known. "Persia and India, the regions that had known sugar making for the longest time, were probably where the fundamental processes associated with sugar making had been invented."[40] Like the unread, uninteresting footnote, this detail in the history of sugar cultivation enjoins the entire history of slavery in Southwest Asia and in the Mediterranean to Atlantic slavery.[41] It thereby also gestures toward the economic processes of modernity that scholars like C. L. R. James, Eric Williams, and W. E. B. Du Bois understood as directly powered by chattel slavery in the Caribbean basin. The retrospective work of political memory leaves a large "conceptual gap."[42]

In the scene where Na'i expels her guests for their cruelty to

Bashu, Na'i sarcastically consents to one relative's casual offers to put Bashu "to work." "Please take him," she begs, yanking Bashu's hand. A medium close-up of Bashu, breathless, cuts to a seemingly irrelevant image of a childlike figure in a black veil. Her back moves farther and farther from the viewer in an empty, expansive desert populated with scattered footprints. A cut back to a perplexed Bashu shifting his drifting off-screen gaze from one direction to another signals a boundless dissociation. Na'i's joking gesture to force Bashu on her sister-in-law evokes the gratuitous sundering of familial bond intrinsic to enslavement, and rends his psyche. The female child, probably Bashu's sister, Bimānī (meaning "to stay," Beyzai tells us) wanders through a desolate desert, a convenient metaphor for absolute isolation, but also of origin. Bimānī's silhouette seems to revive a trodden primal scene: the trail of swollen feet, desolation, and death from the African mainland to the Eastern coast. "Whenever the child could be got to recount the history of [her] capture, the tale was almost invariably one of . . . indescribable suffering."[43] Though less lengthy than the Middle Passage, the conditions of passage from continental Africa to Western Asia "were just as awful and the effects equally terrifying."[44] The institution of slavery "depended on brutal raids, pathetic sales of destitute people, traumatic forced marches, dangerous sea journeys, and the demeaning routines of the slave market."[45] And, "as in the Atlantic slave trade, death was a constant companion, with shortages of water and diseases giving the trans-Saharan crossing its particular horrors."[46] The Arabic word 'abd (slave) comes from "treading on the ground to trace a clear, smooth path," writes Mohammad Ennaji. A slave bound to his master for more than three generations was named *al-turtub,* dust.[47]

Umm al-walad, the Slave Mother

Childhood is conditioned upon the promise of a maternal figure nurturing of the *infans.* For in lacking language, the child is threateningly close to nonbeing and death. At the same time as she protects, however, the maternal also bodes a different kind of amputation in her proximity to the social world and the compulsion to enter language, the replacement of the perceptual, the haptic, the sensual, with the verbal, the rational, the logical. (For French feminist theory, her distance from the symbolic assured the maternal's association with the soft semiotic, the denigrated remainder of language.[48])

The child relation, molded by a dependency indistinguishable from love, is most vulnerable to exploitation.[49] "The mother's presence," suggests Zāvan Qūkāsian in his interview with Beyzai, does not appear like a "straight line; the twists and turns of Na'i's relation to Bashu reveals the sense of the mother in all its complex multidimensionality."[50] *Bashu*'s doubled, in fact tripled, maternal figures—Na'i; the spectral, nameless, silent Black mother; and Iran as the maternal homeland—issue three forms of maternity, three proximities to adulthood, and three incommensurable forms of annihilation.

In Negar Mottahedeh's meticulous reading of *Bashu*'s opening scene, consecutive shots of terrestrial explosion, mediated by a synchronous audio track of bombings, is punctuated twice by images of burning women—first Bashu's mother, who flails in orange flames, and then his young sister, Bimānī, swathed and swirling in smoke, attempting to escape from the calamity. For Mottahedeh, the twin combustions found a decisive and enigmatic movement that propels the film's plot forward.[51] Though the author abandons this focused line of thought in her subsequent analysis of the film, Mottahedeh's insight into the destruction of the maternal as a founding moment and subtext is confirmed by the repetition and return of Bashu's spectral mother.

Although commentary on *Bashu* that treats gender is common, Bashu's mother is rarely, if ever, a focus. Instead, critics usually celebrate the character of Na'i, Beyzai's perpetual muse, who no doubt exudes a magnetic presence in the film.[52] Na'i's and Bashu's apparent exclusion from the linguistic community of Persian positions their relationship as one of a mutual recognition of alterity. "Racial" and gender difference is coupled and mediated by a doubly withdrawn figure: Na'i's missing husband, substituted with Persian as the absent formal national language. Na'i is an illiterate peasant. After revealing his secret of Persian literacy in one of the most dramatic scenes of the film, Bashu comes forth to replace the village doctor as Na'i's scribe, transcribing her letters, and thus serving as prosthetic intermediary in the sexual act that epistolarity between Na'i and her distant husband replaces in a cinema dictated by censorship of even prosaic acts of heterosexual romance. In her final letter to her husband who has left the village in search of employment, Na'i dictates, "and little by little, out of every six words he [Bashu] says, I understand three." The translation "understand" used by the English subtitled version of the film does not capture the more idiomatic nuances of

Figure 24. Close up of Susan Taslimi (Na'i) in Bahram Beyzai's *Bashu, the Little Stranger* (1989).

man rā hālīm mīshad, which translated word by word could mean, "gives me sense." Na'i's illiteracy, her minimal competence in the national language, her immersion in Gīlakī, and moreover her ventriloquism of animal sounds, suggests an unthreatening, feminine relation to language that contradicts the virility that psychoanalysis and philosophy, in distinct ways, posit as the threat of the symbolic and the death of the *infans,* singular relation to being.[53]

Instead, Na'i and Bashu switch roles as the *infans.* Na'i's wide, blue-green gaze, which often fixes directly on the camera, was ill received by the censors, who intuited the threat of unabashed female sexuality. The Farabi Cinema Foundation authorities objected to Taslimi's "powerful presence and penetrating eyes," commanding her to look down in subsequent films.[54] Hamid Naficy understands Na'i's initial encounter with the camera as a transgression of "years of entrapment by modesty rules": "In this alignment of gazes, Na'i becomes *halāl* to the spectators and Bashu becomes a substitute for them, ensuring their suture into the diegesis."[55] Rather than sexual seduction, however, Na'i's piercing gaze more accurately appears to evoke the wonder and bewilderment of the child—guileless, uninitiated. Her relation to the symbolic is unclear. Bashu translates her

« 178 »   The Black Maternal and the Interruptive Imagination

Gīlakī speech into written, formal Persian; she translates his Gulf Arabic into intelligible meaning for the villagers. Naʾi's subordinate, peripheral place in the symbolic order is made clear by her subtle laments: "Dast-i tanha bubustam, khaleh jan" (I've been left alone, Auntie). The Gīlakī expression refers literally to "the hand that she has been denied."[56] Despite the common celebration of Naʾi (and Taslimi more generally) as a notable feminist figure in Iranian cinema, as Nasrin Rahimieh points out, Naʾi's aplomb is often undermined by the very language available to her to describe her own relation to the world: "My father called me Naʾi," she tells Bashu, by way of introduction. "Naʾi asserts herself only after she has given due recognition to patriarchy."[57] However, Naʾi's marginality is also *relative* to the black, spectral mother who speaks *no* language and belongs to no symbolic order at all, appearing instead, as an ephemeral trace, abandoned, in truth, unseen, by even the most astute of film commentators. When Bashu sees this "woman wearing clothing from the south," a commentator observes (drawing no further conclusions), Bashu murmurs to himself, "mother" (*mādar*).[58]

Kinship is a regnant analytic in taxonomies of enslavement. Control, manipulation, and prohibition on biological consanguinity defines one of the clearest and most lasting barbarities of Atlantic World slavery, exemplified in the formal vacuity of the parental relation. Although Orlando Patterson's work on natal alienation brings the question of kinship in enslavement to bear most broadly across global systems of slavery, Hortense Spillers's meditations on the enduring diachronic consequences of matrilineal trauma in the transatlantic realm have provided the more sensitive theoretical resource for Black feminist scholarship since the 1980s. But although Spillers herself thinks in terms of the transatlantic, it is usually ignored that her theory of *flesh*—elaborated in part as the violent rupture and loss of horizontal and vertical relation—draws upon historical scholarship on systems of enslavement within continental Africa. Spillers's work therefore bears a deeper global resonance than is suggested by the tendency to view chattel slavery in the Americas as a singular aberration in time and space, a history of slavery ruptured from its past and future (as well as a history of slavery disconnected from the more general problematic of semiosis).[59] As Spillers, quoting the Africanist Claude Meillassoux, showed, the violability of the parent-child slave relation created a situation where "the offspring of the enslaved, 'being unrelated both to their begetters and to their owners ... find themselves in the situation of being orphans.' "[60] The female slave's child does not "belong" to the mother, but to the slave owner, who exercises his incontrovertible right of property. "To be a slave is to be 'excluded from the prerogatives of birth,'" writes Saidiya Hartman: "The mother's only claim—to transfer her dispossession to the child."[61]

Natal alienation, the original site of theft from context, is thus welded to its adjacent concept, genealogical isolation, which shapes polarized attitudes toward different histories of enslavement. But because it is more open to empirical variation, namely, historical programs for slavery *heritability,* genealogical isolation tempers the absolute violence, as well as the universality, of the first term, the first scene of violence. Genealogical isolation, Orlando Patterson's second constituent element of slavery, absorbs, deradicalizes the first constituent element.[62]

In genealogical isolation, heritability and ancestral heritage, voided of all spiritual resonance, are filled with the curse and the nihilism of their own voiding. The implementation of the Virginia law of 1662, *Partus sequitur ventrem* ("offspring follows the belly") revitalized and codified into American law a reproductive logic of enslavement borrowed from ancient Roman practices. By inducing maternal lineagelessness, colonial legislators and slave owners sought to banish the enslaved from codes of normative kinship and human society. Slavery "creates an economic and social agent whose virtue lies in being outside the kinship system."[63]

As Jennifer Morgan argues, the paradigm of *partus sequitur ventrem,* a transference of animal husbandry laws to enslaved women, was both illogical and a profound subversion of traditional patriarchal notions of heritable descent. By comparison with the early modern Southern European pattern of hereditary enslavement, which also borrowed from Roman law, the American inauguration of *partus sequitur ventrem* was anomalous. For the early fourteenth-century judicial rulings in Southern Europe prohibited male European slave owners from selling children they'd fathered with their female slaves, allowing for the assimilation of "Slavic, Berber, Greek, and Muslim slaves into Europe. In other words, the child did *not* in fact always follow the condition of the mother, particularly, it would seem, if that child was seen as assimilable."[64] On the one hand, the appearance of assimilability leads to a rejection of *partus sequitur ventrem* in a Southern European society where Roman law is

« 180 »   The Black Maternal and the Interruptive Imagination

otherwise influential in the practice of slavery. By contrast, in the Americas, where slaves are seen as inassimilable, because black, and where the rule of economic profit purportedly reigns above all other considerations, *partus sequitur ventrem* is invoked to "fix" the otherwise "indeterminate" status of mixed-race children, who are seen "as excess, as both circulating and unregulated, and ultimately as a source of chaos."[65] In trying to comprehend the bizarre logic of matrilineal heritability that defines Atlantic slavery, Morgan points out its total aberrancy: "In essence, slaveowners and slaveowning legislators enacted the legal and material substitution of a thing for a child: no white man's child could be enslaved, while all black women's issue could." The racial corollaries that qualify "child" and "thing" suggest, first, the impossibility of the black child, and by extension, the impossibility of black childhood.[66]

It is indeed a well-known fact that in the so-called Islamic systems of slavery in the Indian Ocean that preceded and coexisted with the late medieval Southern European examples, enslavement was not usually legally heritable through the matrilineal, as long as the father was a free Muslim, and so long as he recognized and acknowledged his paternity. According to tradition, the prohibition of sale on the child of the slave mother and free father was codified during the first era of Islamic hegemony under the caliph 'Umar I.[67] *Umm al-walad* (literally, "mother of the child"), is the title given to slave women who would be freed upon birthing their master's child. A polarization of views divided ideas about how the *umm al-walad's* own freedom ought to be conceived, with one tradition acknowledging her freedom only upon the master's death. Because the status of *umm al-walad* was a religious injunction, like other presumed norms regulating patterns of Indian Ocean enslavement, the extent to which it was put into practice is unclear.[68] Although there is evidence that a version of the *umm al-walad* status might have been practiced under the pre-Islamic Sasanians, it is also the case that the question of the *umm al-walad's* saleability later divided Shi'is and Sunnis, as it fragmented sects within Sunnism. For Shi'is sometimes "adopted traditions ascribed to Ali that the *umm al-walad* could be sold."[69]

In contemporary slavery scholarship, the *umm al-walad* (free mother of the child) is a negative emblem. She negates the atrocity of slave heritability that characterizes transatlantic slavery's cardinal perversion, and instead, models benign, nonheritable "Islamic" slavery. In stark contrast to the abject transatlantic female body reduced to "popped" flesh, a figure "strung from a tree limb" or "bleeding from the breast on any given day of field work,"[70] the *umm al-walad* is the marker of the good, well-treated slave. Some historians go so far as to couch her within the language of "social mobility": "In an attempt to flee the shackles of slavery, slave women would use various sly means to become pregnant by her master and thus gain the status of *umm al-walad*."[71] As Kathryn Hain writes, "Muslim cultural practices provided social mobility to enterprising female slaves."[72] The examples of slaves who became the powerful mothers of caliphs populate the imaginary of the *umm al-walad*. Khayzuran, the Yemeni slave and mother of the quasi-mythological Harun al-Rashid of the Abbasid era, who purportedly influenced three generations of Abbasid caliphs, is one such famous example.

Rightly, the figure of the *umm al-walad* intends to contextualize Indian Ocean slavery by situating it within its own lifeworlds. For historians, distinguishing Indian Ocean slavery from transatlantic slavery is paramount; to fail to make this distinction is to fall prey to anachronism and context perversion. And yet, the economic rhetoric of "social mobility" and "enterprising" is itself strangely anachronistic, evocative of our own (neoliberal) age. By characterizing her as an ideal of social mobility, historians also inadvertently romanticize the heroic narrative of the slave who overcame her lot through cunning her master into inseminating her, linked to the misogynist and antiblack trope of "Black women [who] could use their sexuality to strategically manipulate their 'masters' and better their lives."[73] Despite the fact that scholars concede "most [female] slaves faced lives of dull and physically demanding domestic work," the few stars like Khayzuran curiously "[eclipse] the usual, nameless servitude."[74] The paucity of sources on especially premodern family structure in Islamic societies leads to a situation in which the slaves' positionalities are often sentimentalized and made exceptional.[75] Where information about slavery from the early Islamic period exists at all, it is culled from elite sources: the Qur'an, hadiths, biographies of Muhammad, chronicles, and legal treatises. Thus, even the lives of extraordinary *umm al-walad* are in many ways secondhand fantasies of their observers. Much less is knowable about the majority of female slaves, who lived under the impoverished condition that is the perennial stress of impending sexual violence. But what remains unavailable to contention is that this natural "eclipse" of ordinary, mundane sexual terror is the result of the very archival logic that subtends the historian's own enterprise. There is no way for the annihilated to account for her own annihilation. A "world grounded on the destruction of that which is [its] very essence," is unintelligible for historiography; that is, the destruction, as well as the impossibility, of the document.[76] But at least equally resolute and unavailable to contention are the unnamed codes that animate historiography's fabrications of historical experience and historical subjectivity. For in truth the economic rhetoric of social mobility is no stranger than the more prosaic scholarly desideratum of the slave's (subversive) agency. Is it to be less like an abject slave, and more like a willful agent antithetical to the conceptual economy of slavery, or rather, fully internal to it?

Even where the focus is not on the rare, usually Arab, Persian, or Eurasian female slaves who become caliphal queens, the specter of the *umm al-walad* provides a panacea to the insult and shame imputed to a society whose integrity might be compromised by slavery.[77] As Aysha Hidayatullah points out, inexplicably beatific portraits of the prophet Muhammad's own *umm al-walad,* Mariya the Copt, were informed by efforts to assuage the unseemly fact that Muhammad owned and bore children with female slaves.[78] In scholarship, "elite" slavery produces a conceptual dead zone, not only eclipsing but submitting to a second violence the fate of the ordinary, unexceptional female slave, just as the *umm al-walad* overcompensates for a violence that is beyond humanist mitigations, qualifications, and compensatory claims to anachronism.[79] Elite slavery eclipses mundane, domestic slavery, the way that, as Indian Ocean slavery scholars themselves complain, the spectacular violence of Atlantic slavery clouds the muted historicality of Indian Ocean slavery.[80]

While individual historians contributing to "writing the feminine" in Near Eastern studies may have the most benign of intentions, the revival of the *umm al-walad* often appears motivated by a political imperative (countercolonial history) that must remain blind to the doubled obliteration of "nameless servitude."[81] In Indian Ocean slavery scholarship, the impulse to expose the racist fallibilities of Western colonial accounts of the Indian Ocean slave trades butts up against the impossible task of an uncompromised, uncontaminated reckoning. The *umm al-walad* has often been marginalized, receiving only passive mention in modern studies dealing with slavery. But heretofore lost to the dregs of dusty hadiths, the recent scholarly resuscitation and valorization of the *umm al-walad,* Islam's gift to the female slave and genealogical isolation's foil, also voids the possibility of a radical politics or imagination of freedom. To be sure, such a possibility would have been destroyed before it could ever have been articulated, that is, before it could exist as an archival fact, deadened in its tracks by the slave master's phallus, and later, the historian's recursive pen strokes. As Saidiya Hartman laments of the fate of the female slave in the literature of the Black (masculine) radical tradition, "Marriage and protection rather than sexual freedom and reproductive justice were the only ways conceived to redress her wrongs, or remedy the 'wound dealt to [her] reputation as a human being.'"[82] Hartman writes about the reduction of a politics of female freedom to a nuclear model supposedly healed of slavery's kinship wounds, which "converged on the figure of the (restored) husband-father as the primary breadwinner."[83] After the nominal abolition of slavery in Iran in 1848, the specter of masses of liberated, indigent women created moral crises that heightened the need for procuring protection, usually in the form of marriage. In turn, the marital status of slaves often determined a female slave's eligibility for freedom. Thus already-married slaves seeking emancipation were often denied freedom, no matter how brutal the situation, for "the principle mandate of the state" was to ensure that "liberation would not undermine the moral fiber of society."[84] Indeed, like the wanting narratives of restoration Hartman describes, circumscribed by the fantasy of marriage-as-protection, the so-called freedom of the socially mobile, "enterprising" *umm al-walad* in contemporary scholarship suggests the disappointing limits of a philosophy of emancipation in the archival remains of Indian Ocean world slavery and its historian inheritors, the gatekeepers and narrators of its truth. Historians are the unknowing guardians of metaphysical inheritances that fuel the very drive for history. And thus, the rejection of more legible anachronisms and context-conflations renders imperceptible historiography's own reproduction of inexorable metaphysical truisms. There is no such thing as a reckoning with the past that is not fundamentally contaminated by anachronism—that is, exposed to the *radical* vulnerability of its own context.

The impossibility of black childhood is not only predicated on transatlantic slavery tropes, as the sophisticated caveats to genealogical isolation show. The legacies of Indian Ocean slavery, too, suggest the impossibility of black childhood, first, due to a logic of

« 184 »   The Black Maternal and the Interruptive Imagination

assimilation that conceals the complexities of metaphysical obliteration. (In the nineteenth century, an observer noted the short life expectancy for enslaved Africans in Iran: "Few black slaves reached the age of thirty"; orphans rarely "reached puberty.")[85] But also, because blackness in Southwest Asia is not recognized as an intelligible form of existence. It is rather like an unmatured state, a permanent childhood of (real, racial) blackness. Race is an "Atlantic-derived category," it is most commonly objected, and therefore, "blackness and Africanness are and remain unstable and subjective descriptors."[86] "Fundamentally, should African-descended peoples in South Asia be referred to as 'black'?"[87] Statements like these saturate Indian Ocean slavery scholarship. They suggest the depth of a conflation between race and blackness that renders blackness in Southwest Asia illegible, decontextualized, anachronistic, warped, contaminated. It is no surprise that film scholars struggled for the proper language with which to name Bashu. The public, and private, discomfort about blackness in Southwest Asia and its relation to the legacy of slavery, but also of race, bears witness to the unlikelihood of a proper naming, a proper sense making. Suspended between contexts, periods, and genres of discourse, blackness is rendered false the moment it is pulled into representation, the very sign of an anxiety about falsity.

The explanatory models of absorption and assimilation conjured by sexual flexibility, cultural integration, and the *umm al-walad* produce quasi-dignified meanings for the disappearance, the extinction, as well as the supposed nonexistence of blackness. In Southwest Asia and North Africa, blackness blurs, blends, absconds into the red-brown landscape. The child figure is the primal site of black impossibility, through which scholars posit so many versions of the inopportunely named "ascending miscegenation" thesis.[88] As a black, kinless orphan adopted by a white Gīlānī mother, Bashu articulates both a politics of multiculturalism as well as erasure, annihilation of blackness. As we know, these two strategies are not as distinct as they might appear; ethnic cleansing and multiculturalism are two responses to the (allegedly new, allegedly old) crises of difference produced by the hegemony of the nation-state in modernity.[89]

Ambiguous phrases like "ascending miscegenation" and "generational integration" appear to explain and justify an otherwise unremarkable vanishing, as they prove that the oblivion of slavery was not intentional, thus, not genocidal, but an anticipated outcome of natural human processes: love, reproduction, child rearing.[90] Literally, ascending miscegenation is conflated with the humane nature of slavery in Islamicate societies: "Islamic slavery thus had a built-in process of emancipation. The slave population was constantly drained, creating conditions not only for the perpetuation of the slave trade, but for social integration and assimilation. It provided a window for upward social mobility."[91] And "The comparative smallness of a black diaspora in Islam is evidence not of the small numbers carried by the trade, but of the degree to which large numbers were *absorbed* by the wider population."[92] Criticizing Joseph Harris, the first African American to research slavery in the Indian Ocean, for his lament of a "slow and agonizing process of racial and cultural oblivion," Abdul Sheriff insists instead that slavery in the western Indian Ocean "allowed slaves and their descendants to be integrated into a society fundamentally based not on racial purity but on *cultural integrity*." Any lasting remnants of "racial prejudice" are exceptional "pitfalls."[93] African descendants in India would "eventually, and to various degrees, become *integrated*," another source insists.[94] "African identity seems to lose much of its salience as people seek to integrate themselves into their host society."[95] The "passage of several generations ensured not only social absorption . . . but . . . visible disappearance," Ehud Toledano writes of black invisibility in post-Ottoman society.[96] The recurring trope of fluidity softly buoys the naturalism of the logic. Nonracial blackness is pliable, not rigid, goes the implied logic, because practices of sexuality in Southwest Asia, indeed cultural practices in general, are fluid, unfettered by the draconian ideologies of race that structured North American forms of family under slavery.[97] But the opposition between fluidity and rigidity is no less tenable than the opposition between hypervisibility and absence. Beyond the distraction of uncritical binaries, what these logics in fact reveal is not that nonracial blackness is rigorously distinguishable from racial blackness. But rather, more problematically, more heretically, that blackness itself transcends the very category of race, is not *containable* by history.[98]

Confusingly, against logics of racial harmony and assimilation, other studies—and in some cases, the same studies—repeatedly portray paradigmatically antiblack scenarios in the western Indian Ocean. In the Arabian Peninsula, "strong prohibitions against intermarriage with Africans served to keep slaves and *mawlas* [freedmen] alike apart from the Arab population."[99] When "[Saudis] talk about black people in general, they use the term *'abīd* (slaves) (sing. *'abd*)."[100] In the Shatt al-Arab, ethnographers noted that Black people were "strictly endogamic" and "regarded by outsiders as socially inferior."[101] In Hyderabad "Islam formed a common bond of identity" between former African slaves (Siddis) and Indians; and yet, the Siddis face "considerable marginalization" and are "designated at the bottom of the caste hierarchy, just above the so-called 'Untouchables' or dalits."[102] In South Asia, "discrimination" against African descendants remains "a shared reality."[103] In Tunisia the "government still uses a stamp of a 'Negro head' to denote the lowest grade of silver"; the most "socially acceptable term for black people is *wasfan* (servants)."[104] Though slaves were only "'slaves in name,'" an Emirati native informant insists, "many do not consider Afro-Emiratis true Arabs."[105] "Indeed, the concepts of descent and purity [in Sohar] seem to derive less from positive traditions and identifications with Arab genealogies than from the absence of African somatic features in the family."[106] In nineteenth-century abolition-era Egypt, freed Sudanese female slaves were kidnapped and resold into slavery because "a black woman, wandering the streets of Cairo ... was assumed, by default, to be a slave."[107] Although "the relationship of enslaved communities to hegemonic systems of power varies throughout different periods of history, what remains consistent is the association of Blackness with marginality."[108] There is "clear evidence" of "racial hierarchies that denigrate blackness."[109] The historian Chouki El-Hamel points out that assimilationist discourses in Morocco camouflage the devaluation of blackness.[110] Recourse to "sentimental tropes of reciprocity, domesticity, and kinship" appear to resolve the tension between domination and intimacy, even as they obscure the obvious connections between intimacy and terror so incisively theorized by Black feminist scholars.[111]

The Black Maternal

Consumed by fire during the first scene of the film, Bashu's mother reappears before his eyes in sporadic sequences throughout the subsequent plot, achieving brief scissions between Bashu and the viewer on the one hand, and the film universe as a whole on the other through a free indirect cinematic discourse. The film illustrates this scission through techniques that bring special attention to the off-screen. First as Na'i quarrels with birds, Bashu's mother surfaces on the right-hand side of the frame; as she walks behind Na'i to the

The Black Maternal and the Interruptive Imagination « 187 »

opposite side of the shot, the camera abandons Naʿiʾs actions to wander with the veiled figure off screen. The immediate cut to Bashu running forward toward us signals that it is his apparition we witness. Second, the dramatic medium shot of Bashuʾs mother facing the camera head-on cuts away to Naʿi making bread. The camera again pans away with Bashuʾs mother as she walks past the hearth into the woods. Her veiled black figure ushers the focus on narrative action off screen, magnetizing Bashuʾs attention, which shifts from surprise into panic, and at other times into keening, hysteric bursts.

Almost all commentators on Beyzai note his well-known grounding in traditional Taʿzīyah theater, arguing for its chameleonic expression in his films. Like Asiatic theater more generally—which Beyzai has researched and written about extensively—the Taʿzīyah tradition inverts the Aristotelian hierarchy of time and space: plot does not power action but is rather an excuse or pretext for performance itself. An expert dramaturge who has written over one hundred plays and screenplays, Beyzai did not require recourse to special effects to represent the distinction between reality and hallucination; classic camera techniques clarify this division for the viewer. Significantly, it is her static, at times gestural poise and gait that seem to suspend Bashuʾs mother in the realm of the otherworldly. Her body is both iconic and theatrical. Samuel Weber reflects on the contemporary perseverance, even proliferation, of traditional theater practices in the overwhelming wake of new mediaʾs virtualizing powers and effects. Calling on Walter Benjaminʾs meditations on epic theater, Weber arrives at a crucial distinction between theater and theatricality. He distills the defining quality of theatricality as a power of interruption. Theatricality "brings the plot in its sequence to a standstill and thereby forces the listener to take a position."[112]

Bashuʾs mother interrupts action. Yet whatever demand her theatricality might impose on the viewer dissolves in the brevity of her appearance. She cannot assume the imperative. Rather, she confronts the viewer with a cognitive chiasmus that cannot be bound. The cinematic frame analogizes the borders of the visible, the borders of what is there to be sensed. Her consistent movement off screen, and the cameraʾs inclination to follow her, thus suggests an "off " that is the invisible *gestured toward,* dismantling the partition between inside and outside, an experience of decentering.[113] Stimulating necessary, if involuntary acts of imagination, the off-screen incites a perpetual state of deprivation, dispossession, longing,

« 188 »   The Black Maternal and the Interruptive Imagination

space for thought.[114] The off-screen is relation to contiguous context. Though we can predict what would be seen, the off-screen is definitionally ungiven, definitionally absented of certainty. And therefore, the off-screen is also a relation to the threat of an absence or loss of contiguity, a dissolution of context. In *Bashu,* the black maternal is not a figure for genealogical isolation. For her ubiquitous but unremarked presence ensures that Bashu is never alone. What her movement produces instead is an anxiety about an always-impending theft of context, a theft that has also always already occurred.[115]

More than the character Bashu himself, Bashu's mother is a mystery to perception. Her hijab is stratified, her veilings layered. Her long black *jilabiye* indexes Arabness, possibly Iraqi origin, while her *burighih,* the black mask she wears over her face, is specific to the southern provinces of Iran, by legend, a tradition begun by women attempting to hide their beauty from slave masters. The veiled cinematic female offers a "pre-framed face," which is "difficult to light, difficult to frame, and difficult to move."[116] (For André Bazin, "The screen is not a frame like that of a picture but a mask.")[117] Like her son, Bashu's mother is dark skinned, particularly in contrast with pale, green-eyed Taslimi, with whom she is systematically juxtaposed. Yet, save her temple, eyes, and jaw, her face consistently withdraws itself from this perception. The discourse on black filmic representation highlights the affective force of visual inscription. The black image wavers between erasure and hyperbole.[118] The undecidability introduced by hijab, an equivocal African origin both fused with and veiled by uncertain Arab and Persian markers, aggravates this vacillation, but guides the look beyond the dualism of invisibility and hypervisibility. The veils, instead, like her posture, interrupt the seen, compel and deflect your gaze from the screen, toward what is beyond observation, verification.

The power of the bond between Bashu and his mother erupts in the enjambment of temporalities. Orphaning seems to place the question of kinship at the center of the film. It is a theme that Beyzai pursues in his following feature film, *Maybe Some Other Time* (*Shāyad Vaghtī Dīgar*) made almost simultaneously with *Bashu* and released in 1987. About a tormented middle-class woman, played again by Susan Taslimi (who also plays two other female roles in the same film), *Maybe Some Other Time* chronicles an unraveling marriage, exacerbated by Taslimi's gradual psychic decomposition. Taslimi learns, at the film's climax, that she was abandoned by

The Black Maternal and the Interruptive Imagination « 189 »

Figure 25. Scenes from Bahram Beyzai's *Bashu, the Little Stranger* (1989). Top: Figure of Bashu relaying his mother's burning to Na'i in Arabic. Bottom: Bashu's mother appears in the frame as he is telling his story.

her impoverished single mother as an infant and relives its abrasive spectacle in the film's final and most animated scene, in which Taslimi simultaneously plays herself and her own mother. Indeed, orphanage is a consistent theme of Beyzai's work during his early career; in a short, *The Journey* (*Safar*, 1972), two orphaned boys search among urban debris for their parents.

In the 1987 film, Taslimi is restored to peace after an impossible reminiscence about her own maternal abandonment. But in contrast to the obviously reparative ending of *Maybe Some Other Time*, the severed bonds of kinship remain frayed at the ends by

« 190 »   The Black Maternal and the Interruptive Imagination

the conclusion of *Bashu, the Little Stranger*, which ends on a freeze frame. The freeze frame struggles against the natural progression of the image, a "permutation, a diversion [*dérive*]," setting something adrift.[119] In one of the final scenes, having returned from his search for employment with a lost arm, Na'i's husband quarrels with his wife over the permanent guest, wondering how they can afford to feed another child. The amputated arm is a not-so-subtle reference to the unrepresentable Iran–Iraq War. In cinema, "when the male subject is brought into a traumatic encounter with lack, as in the situation of war," suggests Kaja Silverman, "he often experiences the impairment of his anatomical masculinity." And yet, what is truly at issue in the anatomical is "psychic disintegration—that is, of a bound and armored ego, predicated upon the illusion of coherence and control."[120] Because he is no longer a "full man [*insān-i kāmil*]," Na'i's husband can accept this otherwise intolerable situation: no one in the family is any longer in her right place.[121] Bashu breaks in on the quarrel between Na'i and her husband, which quickly dissipates as Na'i's husband hides his reservations, embracing Bashu's sympathetic hug at the sight of the missing limb. The fate of the transracial family resolves itself in Bashu's unacknowledged acquiescence to work. Na'i scrunches her nose at the threatening whiff of a wild boar, and barks. Na'i, her husband, and Bashu run into the rice fields yelling with sticks, chasing off the feral threats. The plot's motion congeals into a still shot, cresting in ambiguity.

If the interruption of the family dilemma and the final, ambivalent freeze frame foreshadow the impossibility of Bashu's full assimilation into Na'i's family, the freeze frame also suggests that his past, and in particular, his ancestry, never becomes history. Bashu's past cannot become history not only because it is incomprehensible to his addressee, but also because he seems to have no addressee adequate to the task of comprehension. Neither Na'i, nor the Persian viewer of the film, speak his language. Bashu's initial hysteric outburst when trying to explain the catastrophe of his family's incineration in Khūzistān to Na'i emphasizes the frustration produced by the chasmic fractures that frustrate the scene of address. As he delivers his story in emotional Arabic, limbs miming, Na'i stares back agape, confounded. His language is unintelligible to the Gīlāni woman. Beyzai's decision to omit subtitles affirms an impossibility of reception, of comprehension, this "veil" (*hijāb-i zabān*) that cov-

The Black Maternal and the Interruptive Imagination   « 191 »

ers another scene of sense at the heart of language. "In this film, it's as if words play no role."[122]

Bashu's past cannot become history because Bashu's ancestry, and in particular, the figure of the black maternal, is silent. Here, silence does not indicate incapacity of speech. Nor does this silence express that what happened never took place. Rather, silence may mean that the purported addressee (Persian-identifying or international audience) lacks the competence or worthiness of understanding. Against the figure of the female slave that historians resurrect through the sources that speak of, but that cannot speak from, her position (the *umm al-walad*, enshrined in records inscribed by male chroniclers), Bashu's mother remains absolutely silent. No one "remembered her name or recorded the things she said, or observed that she refused to say anything at all,"[123] writes Hartman of a different context for the black female slave. Veiled in palimpsests, speaking of no past, the black maternal is the disruption of the now that occurs through an interruption of space, of the partition between the frame and the off-screen. It is not simply that Bashu's mother does not have a language. And it is not simply that, in translating her obliteration into meaning, narrative can only inevitably misrepresent the absolute senselessness of slavery that archival absence preserves as spectral lack. To write history is to repress history.[124] For Zakkiyah Iman Jackson, the Black maternal, connected to the concept of *mater*, matter, is nonrepresentability itself, haunting "the terms and operations tasked with adjudicating the thought-world

Figure 26. Frontal shot of Bashu's mother.

« 192 »   The Black Maternal and the Interruptive Imagination

correlate or the proper perception of illusion, Reason and its absence, subject and object, science and fiction, speculation and realism." The Black maternal's "ever-present unsettling excess . . . eludes representation" while holding "the potential to transform the terms of reality and feeling . . . rewriting the conditions of possibility of the empirical."[125]

Bashu's black maternal is silent, but not because she is incapable of speech. Her silence is itself a kind of transmission, a patience, a waiting for "right" context that may never arrive, may have never existed. Her inaugural death is a burning by fire, bodes a total rupture with presence, with knowable contexts. Burning by fire in Iranian cinema symbolizes the ultimate sublimation of a causal circuitry. The black maternal's break with context is absolute.

Zār, the Archetypal Tongue

Like the loss of language in the *zār* ritual that it summarily enacts, *Bashu* consistently deflects attention from the omnipresent and convenient moral question of treatment, as well as the indulgent heading of difference (racial, ethnic, national), back to a scene of original, incontrovertible, recurring, if unrepeatable, disruption. *Bashu* also, like *zār*, redirects attention back to the silence, the impossibility of a proper document of this disruption, as well as a proper context for its interpretation. In doing so, *Bashu* calls to mind that *absence* in the archives of Indian Ocean slavery is necessary rather than merely contingent. For only an absence that is absolute can convey slavery's fundamental and constitutive theft—of ipseity, identity, the continuous discontinuity of being one's self, a self with the possibility of a present, however ontologically questionable. *Zār*, like natal alienation, is premised upon a loss of univocity, a break with the unified subject that makes experience possible. And in introducing a fundamental fissure in the relation between experience and fact, *zār* undermines the possibility of full facticity in the archives of Indian Ocean slavery.

Beyzai's elusive reference to the spirit healing ritual *zār* bears a potency belied by the casual brevity and simplification of the sequence. One would miss it altogether without some prior knowledge of *zār*'s distinctive elements—the belief in individuated winds that penetrate the body's interior, cathartic drumming, the striking

The Black Maternal and the Interruptive Imagination   « 193 »

bodily convulsions, horripilation, shuddering and swooning that indicate the wind's awakening in the host body, the presence of a white sheet concealing the wind-ridden's shape from the gaze, the obvious association with Bashu's south Iranian roots. As I emphasized in the introduction, ethnographic information about *zār* is fallible, shifty, changing; nor does the otherwise fascinating scholarship on its etymology illuminate anything about how *zār* asks its perceiver to orient herself toward the very question of its meaning, whether an a priori concept of history is even at play. Like the mask (chapter 1), trance "belongs to divine mystery."[126] I therefore pass neither etymological nor ethnographic findings off as truth, but rather as generative fictions that tap into the falsity that inheres at the very heart of truth. As with the tautology of Afro-Iranian syncretism discussed in the previous chapter, speculations on *zār*'s provenance suggest that recourse to origins will reveal very little about its meaning. *Zār* is anoriginal.

Zār elicits a kind of dispossession that tempts abstraction toward meditations on the ontology of the subject. To heal from *zār,* one has to know the *zār.* Ethnographic accounts of *zār* thus often begin with an invitation to speak, so that the inhabiting wind might reveal itself to the *zār* adept—*māmā* or *bābā zār*—who facilitates negotiation and healing. But, as with other linguistic aspects of *zār,* including the songs that are sung to awaken the spirit, the ritual process does not yield a traditional model of communication. It results instead in "a form, perhaps, of glossolalia."[127] "Frequently, the language is indistinct and difficult to understand."[128] The *zār* adepts produce "strange utterances," singing in a variety of languages they may not "know." In the African Maguzawa songs played in the middle of the night during Afro-Maghrebi *dīwān,* not knowing the meaning of the Kuria lyrics they sing, the musicians' song is bated, restrained, protected under the guise of inarticulateness.[129] An ethnographer in Ethiopia who attempted to deconstruct its language noted that the *zār* argot deforms Amharic root words, suspends the distinction between the semantic and the semiotic, translating the concrete into the abstract.[130] *Rotana* describes *zār*'s incomprehensible language in Sudanese *zār-tambura,* practiced primarily among slave descendent communities.[131] In Moroccan *gnawa,* unintelligible "Sudani" lyrics (associated with West Africa), "highlight the limits of humans' understanding."[132] Black "pneuma," suggests Ashon

« 194 »   The Black Maternal and the Interruptive Imagination

Crawley in his study of Black Pentecostalism, includes speaking in tongues, and reveals the disruptive capacities of black spiritualism, a "range of sensual, affective, material experiences" that "produce a break with the known."[133]

In the language of *zār*, sound is sundered from semantic intent. Contrasted with logos, "*phone* is a confused, continuous, and inarticulate voice . . . akin to 'timbre' or a 'tone,' an 'intonation' or 'inflection.'"[134] *Zār* is "communicability without content."[135] But, like the off-screen, whence our gaze wanders with the silent black maternal, this tear in sense is not mere absence. This deficit of content travels toward an unachievable limit. In "gibberish" and "glossolalia" it is not that there is merely a lack of intention, but rather that the source of intentionality cannot be confined within familiar, knowable senses of "embodiment," nor of consciousness. Something is transmitted, but not comprehended. Sound is uttered but, intended by a force that transcends the singular voice, is not the product of consciousness, an agent, a self-mastered subject. One anthropologist marvels at the implications of the Zanzibari spirit ritual complex, *uganga*. For in *uganga,* an entire community, rather than the unique afflicted individual, transports, carries the voice of the spirit, delivers the knowledge of the spirit's identity to its host: "To speak of the echo of the voice is thus to speak of its resonance in other bodies."[136]

Both Bashu, and then Na'i, are wind afflicted: first Bashu, due to unkind molestation at the hands of the extended family that rejects his color, and much later Na'i, as a result of the very antiblackness that drives her adopted son to disappear. But the *zār* sequences in *Bashu* are too brief to belabor details. They are peripheral to the film's drama, and thus rarely addressed in *Bashu's* fund of commentary. The sequences are, like most mainstream representations of the ritual, sent:tentious, theatrical abstractions that do not even dissimulate ethnographic moments. Instead the plot displaces the linguistic confusion at the heart of *zār* into an edifying and moralizing tale about Iranian polylingualism. In what is often described as a pivotal moment in the film, the ambulatory, taunting cabal fights and pushes Bashu to the ground, before Na'i arrives to intervene. As Na'i chastises the boys, Bashu reaches for a rock nearby, but picks up a fallen school textbook instead. He lifts himself up and begins to read from it in stalling, but passionate formal Persian: "Iran is our homeland. We come from one spring, one soil [*az yik āb va khāk hastīm*].

We are the children of Iran." As the others look at him with surprise and sudden intrigue, Bashu lifts the rock he initially abandoned and pitches it forcefully, the camera tracking its movement in the air until it hits a wooden structure that appears to collapse and explode. In contrast to most character dialogues in the film, all of which emphasize "cultural, racial, and linguistic differences, their lack of unity," only the "language of the book and the use of the standard convention connoting linguistic exchange" communicates national unity. For Mottahedeh, the typical editing strategies that articulate the sequence pose a question about the necessity of standardized cinematic language, like standardized national language, to produce communication.[137] The "collapse of the structure is filmed from three angles, and played three times, in slow motion," notes Kamran Rastegar. Just as the gesture evokes the incinerated schoolhouse in his home village, which Iraqi bombs destroyed, delivering a history he has been unable to tell with verbal language, the physical prowess seems to symbolize Bashu's newly realized power: the transcendence of his blackness through literacy.

This moment in the film thus transitions Bashu into a masculine, adult figure. He can now communicate with Na'i through standard Persian, expressing the power of Persian to cultivate national unity; henceforth Bashu becomes substitute for the absent father-husband, waking with Na'i at dawn to tend the fields. Bashu's ability to read proves his humanity, his Persianness, and his masculinity, suggesting a fungibility of terms. The enunciation of unity in the textbook scene is imposed through the external gaze of the Persian-speaking audience, subjectivized to believe in the unity and naturalness of the community and homeland that Bashu speaks of.[138] This is why his sudden intelligibility is described as a relief. The textbook scene was "highly cathartic" for both its domestic audience and the "Iranian exiles, who," as Hamid Naficy suggests, "tearfully identified with both Bashu and Na'i."[139] And yet, each of Bashu's apparent achievements (literacy, Persian subjectivity, masculinity) remain under constant threat by an irreconcilable blackness that is the site of an enigmatic unincorporability to sense. And despite critics' varying ideas about it, the explosion scene itself resists incorporation into the film's narrative, is a senseless act whose struggle to signify produces a profusion of interpretations. In reverting immediately to a primitive action (hitting, throwing, exploding) just subsequent to having proved his capacity for intelligibility, Bashu regresses to

« 196 »   The Black Maternal and the Interruptive Imagination

gesture. Bashu regresses to an incommunicability that is closer to *zār*'s inscrutable semiosis than to the intelligible, linguistic universality that provides the addressee-spectator relief. *Zār* is ridicule of the archetypal tongue. "My medicine does not cure people of that color," submits the village doctor when Bashu is wind ridden. But what is Bashu's illness? And what is the therapeutics (*zār*) that is applied as a rhythm that empties, as a transmission whose content has been drained of all context?

The Runner

The relationship between literacy, humanity, and race is brought to the fore by another film produced in the same years as *Bashu*, and possibly even influencing it. Beyzai admits to conceiving of *Bashu* during his work editing Amir Nadiri's *The Runner* (*Davandeh*, 1984), which takes place in the southern provinces of Iran, and like *Bashu*, indirectly thematizes the Iran–Iraq War. Amir Nadiri's *The Runner* is often remembered for a climactic slow-motion scene in which a young boy from Abadan (Amiro, played by Majid Niroumand) gloriously lifts a large block of melting white ice and repeatedly slams it against the top of a tin barrel as an oil fire spreads across the landscape around him. Amiro's beaming face tilts up to the smoky black sky as he raises the ice overhead in ecstasy, the liquefying block expressing all the victory tears in the world. Amiro has finally won a sprinting contest, one of the many he and his friends have competed in throughout the film. But the scene is emblematic of much more than just Amiro's eventual athletic feat; within the film's emplotment, the scene is a celebration of Amiro's interiorization of alphabetic script, his achievement of Persian literacy, and thus, accession to full subjectivity.

   The Runner is less narratively driven than *Bashu*. Thus, one film critic finds fault with its "dazzling veneer [*rūkish-i jaz'āb*]," which hides an impoverished story.[140] The film unfolds through a confluence of images, a kind of dream-work. Through *The Runner*'s progression, Amiro, an orphan, works in the trash mounds as a garbage picker, then as a bottle collector in the sea—catching the stray beer bottles tossed overboard by drunken sailors. Later he works as a shoe shiner at a port-side café where blond foreigners in sunglasses come to sip cold beverages and listen to jazz. And then sometimes he walks through the port selling cups of ice water. Throughout

Figure 27. Iconic images of Amiro winning a race in Amir Nadiri's *The Runner* (*Davandeh*, 1984).

these scenes of labor are interspersed scenes of play: Amiro and his Khūzistānī friends play running games where the winner is whoever catches up to the passing train; they race bikes, play street soccer, and climb rocks. Intermittently, between scenes, Amiro stares out into the ocean and fantasizes about being taken away by one of the

« 198 »   The Black Maternal and the Interruptive Imagination

large white ships: "How white . . . how beautiful," he murmurs, smiling out blissfully into the fog. Long shots of the blue ocean and soft coral sunsets outlining the silhouettes of sailboats slow the pace of the film: "At the edges of frames and on the horizon, the world seems to fade into pure light."[141] On his way home to his abandoned boathouse, Amiro sometimes stops at a nearby bookstand to skim the foreign magazines for glossy pictures of helicopters and airplanes: "I can't read [*savād nadāram*]. I just buy them for the pictures." When the magazine merchant suggests to Amiro that he has Persian magazines "for cheaper," since he can't read them anyway, Amiro returns to the seashore in a funk. Whereas long shots of the ocean signify the south's tranquility throughout most of the film, in the last quarter the presence of this new, unwelcomed realization disrupts its beauty. Amiro is "stuck" in the landscape, unable to transcend it through the abstraction of knowledge. He is illiterate. Amiro's elemental lifestyle (*Water, Wind, Dust* [*Ab, Bād, Khāk*, 1989] is the title of another film by Nadiri, also featuring Niroumand) constitutes the film's hazy, surrealist focus.[142] The landscape registers the enormity of the bookseller's comment. The camera sweeps across a magnificent view of the shore streaked by golden hues, which spill forth through the rocks where Amiro, at the shore's border, angrily tears out the pages of the magazines. The intermittent fantasy shots of airplanes flying overhead turn nightmarish; in a vision, a plane closely chases behind Amiro as he furiously pedals away on his bike. In the next shot, Amiro has gone to the local schoolhouse to register his name, but is told he is too old for regular schooling and must return for night classes.

Concerns about racial difference do not appear in Nadiri's film, which is instead predicated on a humanist logic that underscores literacy as value. As in Beyzai, a soft cultural nationalism subtends the film. At the same time, *The Runner* recognizes literacy as a corporal practice, that is, rendered native to the body; artificial, and also, as in *Bashu*, a path to self-transcendence. Toward the end of *The Runner*, Amiro embarks on a mission to learn the alphabet. His night school teacher dictates the letters of the Persian alphabet in military style chant, slamming his stick against each chalked letter as the camera cuts quickly to Amiro's profile in medium-close up. In other scenes, with his back to a soft pink sunset and rippling ocean waves, Amiro sits on a rock and whispers to himself slowly and unsurely, "*alef . . . be . . . pe . . . te.*" In the breathtaking montage sequence that follows, interspersed with similar classroom scenes, Amiro's confidence slowly builds as he paces the seashore, repeating consonant pairs "*re ze re ze re ze re ze . . . sīn shīn sīn shīn sīn shin.*" Legs dangling over the rocky edge and shouting out to the ocean, he repeats, "*ghāf ghāf ghāf ghāf ghāf ghāf . . . ayn ghayn ayn ghayn ayn ghayn . . . dāl zāl dāl zāl dāl zāl dāl zāl*" as the camera slowly tracks toward him at an overhead angle, looking beyond at the coarse waves. Then, finally, a close up profiles Amiro screaming to the sky with wet hair, "*dāl zāl dāl zāl dāl zāl dāl zāl re ze re ze re ze.*" His voice and head elevate with the articulation of each letter, securing an earth-shattering transformation. In a climactic shot, the camera pans the jagged seashore, while Amiro's voice is distantly heard. Finally he is spotted stranded on a rock, pulsating with the alphabet emanating through his small body: "Amiru, the letters of the alphabet, and his natural environment—water, wind, rock—all begin to coagulate into one symphonic crescendo."[143]

Within the various angle arrangements, this cataclysmic long shot announces the achievement of distance, capacity for abstraction, inspired by Amiro's visceral experience of letters. The ensuing fragments of this sequence, dispersed throughout the remainder of the film, recapitulate some of the earlier sequences of Amiro playing with his friends (climbing rock mounds, sprinting after trains). Now in solitude, he achieves individuality through the rehearsal of letters. The interiorization of the alphabet is represented in the film as a bursting out of nature, as emergence from space, as his shaking, verging on hyperventilation, indicates: "The alphabet sequence of *The Runner* remains the most glorious lesson in a literacy beyond words, and it is one of Nadiri's greatest achievements in his virtuoso performances as a sound designer: the noises of water, wind, fire, and dust all collecting momentum to syncopate Amiru's recitations of the Persian alphabet." Amiro is "elemental, elementary, figurative, phenomenal."[144]

The merit of this interiorization is crowned by Amiro's final feat over the once athletically superior, darker-skinned "street urchins." Physical power, like labor, is racialized in the film through the presence of white American and European foreigners who come to the port to get their shoes shined and, juxtaposed with Amiro bent at their feet, reveal his imprisonment within labor. (Wealth distinctions such as these also contradict the images of Abadan once popularized by the Anglo-Iranian Oil Company as a "modern, egalitarian space

« 200 »   The Black Maternal and the Interruptive Imagination

of welfare.")[145] Literacy rescues Amiro from menial labor. For when Amiro learns to read, he also procures the capacity of commensurability. One darkening evening, he beats a drunken American sailor that had earlier in the day falsely accused him of theft. But literacy also rescues Amiro from a descent into blackness as it allows him to triumph both figuratively and literally over an "excessive corporeality," an excessive intimacy with the landscape. (In Oman, suggests Maho Sebiane, Sawahili collapses blackness *with space* [Sawahili, *as-sahil,* of the coast], distinguishing it from the cultural and historical complexity associated with the term *Swahili.*)[146]

Connected to the power of thinking, of developed interiority, of civic identity and modernity, literacy is a weighted trope, suturing alphabetic script to the interiority of the subject and assigning value to the capacity for reason and self-transcendence through knowledge accumulation and knowledge production. The ascendance of the genre of autobiographical literature in Western modernity, as the binding of literacy to the life of the mind, argues Lindon Barrett, is emblematic of the transformation of subjectivity into a foundation for property-owning individuality and other "accelerating civic attachments" bounded to the nation-state project. Literacy recapitulates the redundancy of the material body, the alleged "overwhelming corporeality of blackness."[147] In the wake of the losses connected to the Iran–Iraq War, mobilized in Beyzai and Nadiri through the figure of the fatherless orphan, the aspiration to mastery that is male subjectivity is replaced with the Persian alphabet, a figure for community and communicability, but also for reason, origin, and truth. The alphabet ciphers and erects the borders of the self-contained nation, interiorizes the nation into the self. It assuages the violence of difference experienced as unintelligibility. And this "rock bottom comfort in one's language and one's home" is manipulated, mobilized to transcendentalize the nation.[148]

If postwar films tend to show less that the orchestration of war succeeds in annihilating the enemy than in destroying the positivities of the masculine self, in *The Runner* and *Bashu,* textbook language and the performance of literacy offer putatively therapeutic, reparative powers to the damaged, masculine, revolutionary nation ego, successor to the damaged, masculine imperial ego. (As theorists of Iranian nationalism have repeatedly pointed out, the very engagement with European modernity as an initially militarized endeavor ensues from an experience of imperial loss and defeat.) The mean-

The Black Maternal and the Interruptive Imagination   « 201 »

Figure 28. Scenes from Nadiri's *The Runner* (1984). Top: The schoolteacher traces the letters of the Persian alphabet on the chalkboard. Bottom: Amiro shouts the letters of the alphabet into the ocean.

ing of the Iran–Iraq War, as mobilized by Nadiri and Beyzai, accrues enigma. Against the background of the ideologically dense genre of Sacred Defense cinema, critic after critic praises Beyzai's *Bashu* and Nadiri's *The Runner* for their oblique accounting of war-time Iran, favoring nonrepresentation. *Bashu* "produces a counternarrative to

« 202 »   The Black Maternal and the Interruptive Imagination

the state's project of war memory," while *The Runner* is a "sublimated response" to its effects.[149] Thanks to Beyzai's "seamless and dynamic editing, *The Runner*... [effaces] the war."[150] "Signs of war are nowhere in sight."[151] The war is a repository, an abyss of historical injuries, including the failing 1979 Islamic Revolution that both prompts and serves to perpetuate the Iran–Iraq War, but also, everything that the Revolution stands for: the loss of a real world in whose wake appear only ersatz images, *filmfārsī*, incoherent cinema, the object of virulent revolutionary attack. The war that defends Iran is also the war that defends against the will-to-mastery that is the modern nation-state Iran. Cinema's postrevolutionary period thus shows an unravelling, or, a disorienting *stabilization* of the distinction between the real and the unreal, the concrete and the metaphysical.[152] Thus, Nadiri's *The Runner* "aimlessly drifts" between the allegorical and realist modes, undecided, one critic complains. Amiro ages nonlinearly, stretches the liminality that distinguishes childhood from infancy and adulthood. Neither real nor allegorical, Amiro is "distilled, without time or place"; neither character, nor type.[153] Against the allegorical meanings of homeland (*vatan*) in premodern geographies, "modern Iran was above all a physically defined geobody."[154] Once mediated by the monarch, the territorial and affective relation to Iran is now mediated by the geographical concretization of *khāk* (soil), *vatan* (homeland), and the materiality of an obligatory alphabet, a literacy that literalizes, that attempts to distill an essence from the vaporous taper of words, but remains perennially prone—as *zār* continuously augurs—to drifting reduplication, a mise en abyme of sounds.

Sentiments of loss, conjured by a scene where Amiro reluctantly parts with a friend, suggest the ambivalent nature of literacy, of this escape, this death of childhood, this disappearance of the *infans*. In *Bashu* too, the textbook scene expresses a new masculine virility that is perceived both as achievement as well as a loss of innocence and threat. Na'i looks aghast with large eyes after Bashu explodes the wooden construction with his strong pitch, suddenly apprised of Bashu's hidden strength. The orientation of scholarship on language and literacy in twentieth-century Iran is inflected by the history of Persian nationalism and the integration of the nation-state. Film analyses of *Bashu* therefore rightly focalize the thematic significance of Persian as a universalizing medium in the film, connecting it ideologically to the nationalist project of mass education inaugurated most clearly in Reza Shah's formation of a pedagogic state, perpetuated under his son's reign, and mutated but not fundamentally transformed after the Revolution under an Islamic state. (Although the philosophy of education in Iran changed more or less radically between the Pahlavi and the Islamic Republic eras, the emphasis on Persian language instruction, at the expense of all other languages, remained intact.)[155]

Readers of *Bashu* generally interpret the textbook scene as one in which Persian appears as the language of universal mediation. Between two distant languages, the Gīlānī and the Khūzistānī, the northern and the southern understand each other through a neutralizing, transcendental Persian. This interpretation places Gīlakī (the language spoken in Gīlān) and Khūzī Arabic (Beyzai's term, referring to Bashu's regional Arabic dialect) as languages equally obliterated by the rise of the nation-state and the phantasm of Iranian identity shaped by the modern ideology that sutures Persian language to Iranian nationality and Indo-European race.[156] Purportedly, Gīlakī and Khūzistānī Arabic are equally different languages, identically subjected to the "shared experience of loss." The "mutually incomprehensible nature of the languages forms the central problematic of the film."[157] "What Na'i and Bashu have in common is their status as peripheral to the existing linguistic, social, and cultural systems of signification, which isolate and vilify difference."[158]

But despite commentators' suggestions, Beyzai's own thoughts on language in *Bashu* suggest an important distinction between these languages that reanimates the historical formation of comparative linguistics and its relation to the development of racial science, that is, to the very process that articulates Persianness with nation and race.[159] "Gīlakī is one of the most authentic artifacts of the remains of ancient Persia and many lost words and pure structures [*tarkībhāʾi nāb*] can be found there," explains Beyzai. In some parts of Iran they speak languages that are "one step away from the Pahlavi language [Middle Persian] and its older root, ancient Persian." For Khūzī Arabic, which has been "mixed with Persian and English words" Beyzai has only to dismissively add that we can detect the role of "regional proximity and imperialism" in the mélange of Persian and Arabic, peppered with English words.[160]

Like other languages in Iran, Gīlakī was subordinated to Persian, which became the official language of the country in 1935—the same year that "Persia" was rebranded as "Iran," land of the Aryans. But unlike Khūzī Arabic, Beyzai's comments suggest that Gīlakī shares proximity to a primordial Persianness. The conflation of an

« 204 »   The Black Maternal and the Interruptive Imagination

archetypal language baring spiritual truth with the most original, most perfect form of human being resembles the "romantic ebullience" of the Indo-European hypothesis.[161] In the "comparison of these languages which are all branches of one body, thousands of words and meanings and idioms that have been lost can be retrieved from history."[162] According to Beyzai, knowledge of Gīlakī has the potential to restore the internal purity of Persian. Na'i's animal mimicry, though often read as a dimension of her feminine alterity, also symbolizes the purest, most authentic kind of language: the language of nature. By contrast, contaminated by English words, coastal Persian and coastal Arabic expose the impurity of creole or patois, its susceptibility to contamination and errancy, its affectability—as in the *zār* argot, its deformation of contexts. Though commentators suggest that the Arabness of Bashu's language might have been a "dislocative strategy," troubling the distinction between Arab and Persian that was often mobilized by Iran–Iraq War discourse, it is not only Bashu's Arabness that is at stake but also his susceptibility to permanent, incurable blackness, best epitomized by the famous scene in which Na'i angrily fails to scrub the color off his body.

If racial, ethnic, and linguistic difference are to be resolved by the nation, *Bashu,* like the freeze frame upon which the film concludes, leaves us wondering about a blackness that is the perpetual site of a failure of resolution. This does not merely mean that blackness is a racial-ethnic, therefore modern, difference that cannot be resolved by the (equally modern) nation-state. For, prior to its racialization or biologization, blackness is already the site of a resistance to incorporation, a site of context-perversion. In the medieval era, Arab geographers' categorial terms for African peoples, like *zanj,* augur blackness as the site of an ongoing unmooring from context. The "derivation and meaning of Zandj is still unresolved"[163] (see chapter 3). Blackness is inadequate, anachronistic, imposed, improper to our properly indigenous epistemologies, scholars of Southwest Asia complain. It is not merely that blackness is a modern racial-ethnic difference that cannot be resolved by the modern nation-state. Blackness marks the site of a failure of incorporation into the very categories of the racial and the ethnic, that is, into the categories of difference that have been historically constructed to comprehend, annihilate, and ultimately to transcend it.[164] It is unsurprising that Persian, the formal national language, the language of writing and dissemination, the language of primordial truth, cannot incorporate

Bashu. Failing the symbolic, Bashu "resorts instead to an act that is semiotically open," throwing, shattering, crying.[165] In Persian, Bashu can only parrot clichés. Nor is Persian a path to corporeal transcendence. Bashu's (linguistic) difference is not generic.

Like race's other debated historical precedents (religion, class), and succeeding historical categories (ethnicity, culture) the relationship between language and race is negotiated by scholars in various ways.[166] In the previous chapter, I explored the relationship between language and race through the lens of Orientalist comparative philology, and in medieval Islamic views about the difference between proper and defective speech as expressed by Arabs and Persians' purportedly distinct civilizational capacities. The quest for an "abstract prototype" or primordial tongue between the sixteenth and eighteenth centuries played an important role in the development of race theory. Like Sanskrit, at moments even rivaling it, Persian constituted one of the major sources of linguistic paleontology. In his 1792 speech "The Origin and Families of Nations," William Jones pronounced Iran the cradle of human civilization, identifying the only remaining human family in the wake of the great biblical flood to reside in the northern parts of Iran. The Indo-European thesis suggested a common ancestor linking populations dispersed between India and Western Europe. Tied to a notion of fully human potentiality, capacity, and creativity, Indo-Europeanness expressed the "migratory abilities of Indo-European peoples, who were great conquerors: their diaspora extended from India to the western extremities of Europe."[167] Associated with the figure of the settler, Persian, classified by philologists as an Indo-European language, was renewed as the prized possession of Iranian nationalists in the twentieth century.[168]

Though a migrant and a Persian speaker, Bashu does not fit the figure of the "great conquerors" of Indo-European history. For his blackness conjures instead the slave, the native, or the refugee. (Unlike the trope of the mobile subject typical of road films in which characters appreciate and appropriate the world as spectacle or scenery, Iranian films position children as a "condition of being" rather than an "extension of being.")[169] "Two theories of the origins of [black] people have been advanced," writes one scholar, mimicking a narrative typical of twentieth-century nationalist historiography. The first theory "relates them to the aborigines on the Iranian plateau before the advent of the Indo-Iranians. . . . These

« 206 »   The Black Maternal and the Interruptive Imagination

'ugly natives' were subjugated and enslaved by the invaders."[170] And, "Long before the Elamites [c. 2600–330 B.C.], Khūzistān was the land of black people [*siyāh pūstān*]"; the later arrival of black slaves from Zanzibar and Muscat created an "admixture" [*ikhtilāt*] of the black race [*nizhād-i siyāh*]. Supporters of this idea suggest that the continued poverty of black communities in Iran is justified by an intrinsically "servile stance."[171] The first theory appears to be a version of the Aryan conquest narrative, in which the "tall, light complexioned, meat-eating" Aryans conquer the "short, dark, vegetarian" indigenes. The Rig Vedas describe intertribal tension between the Arya pastoralists and indigenous population, called *pani* and *dasa* in the Vedas, later to mean "slave" in the Sanskritic tradition, while *arya* means "noble," "honorable," or "aristocratic."[172] As in the case of South Asia, while the Indo-European hypothesis allowed Persians to believe they were of the same race as Europeans, it also boded a division of Iranians into superior (Aryan) and inferior (aboriginal, or non-Aryan) Persians. This division reverberates, in a different way, for example, in the contemporary institutional tendency to define the Persian language as an exclusively Iranian spiritual resource, excluding its Afghan, Tajik, and North Indian iterations.

These two specious genealogies, of the white (Indo-European) and the black aboriginal slave, bode two modes of contradiction. The Indo-European thesis is contradictory on the one hand for positioning the figure of the Aryan as simultaneously foreign and indigenous—foreign, because he is a migrating pastoralist, and indigenous, because the Aryan is imagined as the most prototypically Persian, the ancestor of modern Iranians. (As Zia-Ebrahimi notes, it was precisely such contradiction that led to the unstable doctrinal position of Indo-Europeanism in a different context of nationalism. Hindu reformers were ambivalent about a narrative of Aryan migration into India that would ultimately posit them as foreign, similar to "the Muslims to whom they directed their ire." At the same time, the theory "established tribal peoples and low castes as India's 'original' non-Aryan inhabitants."[173] More contemporary revivals of Aryanism contest not the essentialism that makes India Aryan, but the idea that Aryans were foreign invaders.[174]) The Persian historian's narrative of the emergence of the admixed "black race [*nizhād-i siyāh*]," on the other hand, suggests a parallel contradiction whose import is distinct. Black people (*siyāh pūstān*) are also both foreign and indigenous—aboriginal inhabitants of the Iranian plateau (long before the Elamites), and simultaneously foreign slaves. In the relation between white and black contradiction, the settler/slave distinction overrides, cancels the value of indigeneity. The most astute theorists of Indo-Europeanism in Iran emphasize its significance as a carrier of proximity to Europeanness. But, at its core, the Aryan theory was the result of a general *inquiry into origin*. The Indo-European tongue, and the ancestors who spoke it, were the most original, purest humans. Historical migration is irrelevant when the Aryan *is* origin. White people are origin, wherever they travel. By contrast, the black slave, slavery that is blackened, or a blackness that is enslaved, is incurably decontextualized.

Against the compulsion to national, ethnic, racial identification wielded by the politico-phantasmic force of centralized power (and softly diffused through the pedagogical state apparatuses), blackness in *Bashu* inadvertently reveals the inconsistency of universals. Bashu is "stuck to his strangeness [*sakht bih qaribigi'i khud chaspidih ast*]."[175] At the same time, *Bashu* also questions whether inconsistencies and failures (of the national, the racial, the ethnic) can be compensated for by better, more successful identifications. The family, that romanticized microscopic unit that precedes affiliation with the nation, is revealed, too, in the end, to be a fragile, unreliable edifice. Scholarship on the "reverse work" of Persian nationalism suggests the heteronormative family as the logical outcome of the nationalist ruse, not merely its survivor.[176] Bashu's final frozen frame does not settle with confidence on new attachments.

Persian literacy, too, in its connection to national identity, ultimately guarantees nothing to Bashu. It is a structure of association that his blackness places on the verge of collapse: "While his recitation of the communal discourse of the textbook in the common national language of formal Persian promises to end his alienation from the village, the end of the textbook scene seems to set limits on this hopeful outcome."[177] In *zār*, the fall into glosses splinters identity. This black spiritual practice suggests a ruse of the first language, a mother tongue capable of inspiring identification, origin, pride, loyalty, truth. The language "learned first through the infantile mechanism is every language, not just one's own."[178] There is no mother tongue. Iran's mother is black. Iran is a black mother. *Zār* culminates in a silence that is absolute.

In *Bashu*, first Bashu and then Na'i are *zār*-ridden. Bashu is sickened by wounded kinship, an encounter with the antiblack world that proceeds from the originary burning of the black maternal and culminates in assimilation to a world that produces and annihilates blackened experience. Na'i too, the ill mother, the metaphor that recalls the regnant maternal trope of the Iranian nation, is sickened, maddened by her encounter with a blackness, and an antiblackness, that turns out to be more than merely exterior. Bashu soothsays Na'i back to health with his rhythmic drumming, just like the *māmā* and *bābā zārs* heal their *zārīs*. Though "Bashu" has no meaning, "Bashi is a prayer. Every time you call this child you are saying a prayer," submits Beyzai.[179] He cures Na'i, but Bashu cannot nurse the specter of his other mother, the black maternal, back from her condition of silence, of death, of total rupture with proper context. Incessantly moving off the screen, she coaxes the eye beyond the visible frame and the sensible world of diegetic meaning, beyond the sensible world of congruent, restorable contexts. The persistent reappearance of the black maternal in *Bashu* interrupts our self-evident narratives about Indian Ocean slavery, as it arrests our confounded narratives about blackness, nation, language, identity—guiding viewers away from what the plane of the visible confirms as obvious. The black maternal moves us toward a scene that has not yet taken place; perhaps, a scene that cannot take place. If there is a proper way of relating to the past, if there is a proper modality of identification, as the pretension to truth in history, culture, and nation presumes, then above all, *Bashu*'s silent black maternal disrupts any comfortable convictions that we have discovered it.

« CONCLUSION »

The Collective for Black Iranians
On Digital Anamnesia

In a forty-eight-second clip produced by members of the Collective for Black Iranians, the whirring sound of a carousel projector accompanies the colorful flutter of an image appearing to spool erratically through an old machine. Once the jittering stabilizes, the scratched image of a Nowruz spread gradually clears. Despite the low resolution, the objects would be recognizable to anyone familiar with Persian culture: lush, sprouted wheatgrass (*sabzah*); colorful dyed eggs; garlic (*sīr*); and sumac (*sumāq*) in elegant but simple coupe glasses populate the tableclothed surface, the focus of the slightly aged photograph. Nowruz, the Persian New Year, which means literally "New Day" and falls on the Spring equinox, honors renewal, and its celebratory practices include the setting of just such a table spread with seven items that begin with *sīn* (a consonant that phonetically resembles the English "s"). But what is notable about the first image of the photo collage is not the typical *haft sīn* ("seven s's") that it partially depicts, but the performative gesture underlying the old video affect. The image shakes and stutters, suspended between motion and stillness, undecided about its status as photo or film, authentic archival artifact or fabricated simulacrum. Analog nostalgia and the precarious aesthetic more generally recall found footage practices that were popular among avant-garde video artists in the 1990s.[1] The Nowruz spread image is cut with a crisp intertitle announcing the name of this micro "film": "Voices from home, the Childhood series," appears on one side of the black frame; on the other, in slightly faded text, "world edition."

As the clip proceeds to the next image, the familiar hi-hat rhythm and low-key piano refrain of Biggie Smalls's "Juicy" subsumes the gurgle of the rotating motor. Another Nowruz table spread appears:

« 209 »

« 210 »   Conclusion

tall greens, tapered candles, a bowl of glossy red apples, brightly patterned eggs nestled in hay, and three small goldfish swimming in a clear fish bowl construct the mise en-scène. In the foreground, a young boy grins playfully at the camera with his tongue slightly protruding, his head cocked sideways. On the lower right-hand corner of the image, an animated red pin drops: Los Angeles, US. Another Nowruz spread featuring a small child succeeds the frame. This second photograph is stamped "Minab, IR," referring to the small city near Bandar Abbas in the Hurmuzgān province of Iran. The bass enlivens the high hat (the point at which, were this not just a sampling of the instrumentals, the Notorious B.I.G. would start rapping, "It was all a dream.") Amid their succession, the photographs begin to disengage from the strictly Nowruz ambience. And not all of them are properly labeled with geographical locations. In the photographs, bodies freeze in mid-dance; some images are posed, others unstaged. All feature the symbol of the red Google pin at the lower-hand base, but, in lacking a geographical stamp, some of the photographs suggest either technical error or enigmatic omissions. The credits on the last photograph, an image of a visibly black family gathered for a picture, attribute production to the Collective for Black Iranians.

The chapters in this book so far have centered a nonblack Iranian media archive. In certain cases I have focused on this archive's most antiblack moments (in chapter 1, on the *siyāh bāzī*, or blackface scenes in prerevolutionary films), or on its most fetishizing ones (in chapter 2, on ethnographic documentary's fascination with African spirit ritual). At other moments I have turned to the imaginary teleology of racial antagonism and transracial synthesis mediated by the project of Iranian nationalism (chapter 4, on Bahram Beyzai's *Bashu*). The conclusion is distinct from the rest of this book in at least two respects. Here, I turn away from cinema as it is traditionally approached in some strains of film scholarship as a disembodied artifact separate from the set of behaviors and economic circumstances that characterize its existence, to analyze cinema's convergence with embodied media practices in the post-internet age, in which, paradoxically, cinematic ubiquity becomes more and more disembodied, more and more disembedding.[2] Secondly, I turn away from the nonblack archive to focalize the first-ever media project to be authored (primarily) by Black Iranians about being Black and Iranian, and, at the time of this book's writing, largely disseminated

Conclusion

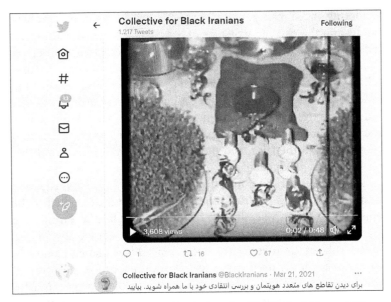

Figure 29. Image from the Collective for Black Iranians' Twitter feed, Nowruz 2021.

through the social media platforms of Instagram and Twitter. (For my ongoing capitalization inconsistencies, please refer to the introduction.) This turn toward the participatory politics of the internet reactivates questions about how cinema lives inside of a continuum with new forms of connective media that reorganize collective desire and racial meaning within a quickly changing, yet seemingly timeless, neoliberal environment.

As scholarship on digital media argues, in the twenty-first century, the internet has entirely redefined the cinematic text, producing novel modes of storytelling and decentralizing traditional hierarchal production and distribution processes. But decades after the popularization of the internet, the extension of cinematic practice into the web is still difficult to theorize. In reinventing and expanding the scope of cultural production, the internet has created new possibilities for the formation of historical narratives of political solidarity, even while it is also connected to the resurgence of articulations of identity politics. If exuberant media theorists of the early internet era once celebrated the seemingly radically democratic potential of new media structures, today, media theorists generally concede, the internet only amplifies and conceals hierarchy, rendering social reality into a "corporate hybrid between handheld media and the psychic structure of the user."[3] Couched within new hybridized forms of telepresence, the potentially emancipatory capacities of social media's purportedly democratic modes of storytelling cannot be fully disambiguated from the perverse vagaries and predatory tendencies of platform capitalism and algorithmic governance. Simply, social media only enhances the deep ambivalence, the simultaneous capacity for truth and for falsehood (for the truth that inheres in the false, and the false that inheres in the true) that characterizes *all* language.

Although its original founder, Priscillia Konkou-Hoveyda, had designs to document stories about Black Iranian life long before the emergence of the Collective for Black Iranians (Ja'mī'at-i Īrāniyān-i sīyah pūst), it is not coincidental that the group was officially formed in the wake of the 2020 resurgence of Black Lives Matter. Famously, Black Lives Matter itself began as a post on Facebook in protest of the 2013 acquittal of George Zimmerman in the Trayvon Martin case, then transformed into a hashtag on the microblogging site Twitter.[4] Critics of Black Lives Matter—in particular, critics of its strategies—attempted from early on to compare the movement's methods to the purportedly nonviolent and assimilationist tactics of the civil rights movement, but as media scholars have suggested, in its deep-rooted symbiosis with social media, as well as its rejection of the "charismatic leadership model," Black Lives Matter is best conceived under a new social movement paradigm.[5] As others have suggested, traditional, efficient, goal-oriented, or utilitarian political activism is not the proper lens through which to understand social media formations in the first place. Indeed, that "digital practitioners engage in 'nonproductive' and 'inefficient' online activities" suggests a libidinal dimension to online relationality that does not fit the constraints of a single framework, nor the facile commitment to binary judgments, including that of success and failure.[6] According to this lens, Black Lives Matter is less oriented toward mobilizing extant resources and institutions than to achieving (potentially enigmatic) communicative goals.

Indeed it is the constitutive and striking hybridity of the Collective for Black Iranians that renders it so unique but also vulnerable to criticism from those who see blackness as an irrevocably foreign, Western, even imperial imposition clouding the reality of what it means to be indigenously black in Southwest Asia, indigenously *siyāh*

Conclusion « 213 »

(black) in Iran, or *daw ragih,* of Iranian *and* African descent. *Daw ragih* is an infrangible term denoting biraciality, and which means literally, "of two veins" (*rag*: vein), thus drawing upon an economy of blood resembling iterations of a more familiar concept of race and that Persian speakers recurrently invoke and simultaneously disavow as organic to their own racial epistemology. Though the Collective of Black Iranians is composed primarily of diasporic Iranians with double ancestry (for example, Iranian and Congolese, Iranian and African American, Iranian and Caribbean, and so on), their content frequently incorporates the stories from black people with generations of roots in Iran. Nevertheless, the Collective has been criticized domestically for the politics of its own positionality, as well as the assumption that its very premise is based in an American understanding of racial blackness that misinterprets the (putatively nonexistent or impossible) status of (racial) blackness in Iran. In other words, the familiar admonition seems to go, the Collective decontextualizes blackness. I will explore such criticisms of the Collective more deeply in the following section, where I discuss backlash against the Collective's unexpectedly inflammatory influence on contemporary Iranian social policies. Suffice it to say that the charge of foreignness wielded by such criticisms of the Collective for Black Iranians paradoxically hypostasizes blackness even though it purports to problematize racial hypostasization itself.

Appearing to rehearse common identity politics critiques, skeptics of "Black Iranian" exchange one mode of identity politics for another. "Even the premise of this profile is fabricated," one Twitter user claims, reposting an image of the Collective for Black Iranians and underlining in red the term *Afro-Iranian.* "In contrast to America, where race is important and racial groups like Afro-American and Latin-American exist, in Iran no such group as Afro-Iranian [*Irānī'i Āfrīqāyī tabār*] exists, and *we are all Iranian.*"[7] This comment is unexceptional, that is, typical of Southwest Asian (and North African) mainstream understandings of indigenous blackness, in which blackness is always subordinate to another identity, whether national, ethnic, or religious.[8] And though the statement does not explicitly accuse the group of identity politics, it extracts and applies the logic of a common identity politics critique, which presumes nationality as a more universal, or rather, less particularist mode of identification than race. Yet as much as critiques of identity politics pretend to issue from an appeal to universality, identity politics

« 214 »   Conclusion

critics never explore what renders national belonging the most appropriate and natural of identificatory forms, in other words, what makes nation any more nonparticularist than race. Blackness is commonly recognized as a mere racial identity, rather than a layered and modular global position/relation comprising opaque historical sedimentations. Blackness can be and certainly is understood as an identity, especially in language often formulated by the Collective itself. And though blackness can and has been wielded in the service of identity politics, Blackness is not only one particular identity among others. I will show how the trope of repetition in certain aesthetics practiced by the Collective exemplifies this singular mode of relationality, or potentiality for conjunction, that blackness embodies and expresses, even where my own readings may contradict the Collective's strong stance on the importance of identity and recognition—signature tropes of identity politics.[9]

The Nowruz clip best exemplifies the rudimentary and self-reproducing narrative of contamination and foreignness that critics of the Collective suggest they have cleverly unveiled. The Notorious B.I.G. song appears to signify a certain brand of Black Americanness, typifying the height of (especially East Coast) hip-hop's entry into mainstream pop culture, and repeating a familiar "hustler to rapper," hood-to-wealth narrative generic to hip-hop lyricism.[10] Biggie's lyrics also paradigmatically embody the aesthetic of what Abdul JanMohamed names the "death-bound subject," a submerged discourse within the tradition of African American literature and culture that grapples with the aporetic formation of a subjectivity incubated inside the always imminent threat of death.[11] Coupled with the images of Persian New Year family gatherings, the audiovisual synthesis announces a most hyperbolic troubling of cultural authenticity, a total catachresis. But a deeper reading of the hip-hop sampling aesthetic at work in the Collective's clip complicates this surface synthesis. For it is rather a sedimentation of terms that the "Juicy" instrumentals in the Nowruz clip cite. Nowruz itself epitomizes this inevitably unplumbable repository that tradition—as locus of the immemorial—bears. In Abu Rayhan al-Biruni's *al-Āthār al-bāqiyah,* or *The Chronology of Ancient Nations,* at least four separate accounts centering on the mythological Persian king Jamshid describe the transformation of the spring equinox into Nowruz.[12] In antiquity, Zoroastrian Nowruz symbolized the "new day" of eternity.[13] (It is no coincidence that Nietzsche selects Zarathustra, or

Zoroaster, the founder of this pre-Islamic religion, as the title character for the work where he develops most profoundly his thinking on eternal return, for "Persians were the first to take a broad and comprehensive view of history.")[14] It is not only, or not primarily, the techno-nostalgia for analog attenuation that the rounded corners and gate weave of the photo collage's successive frames evoke. Rather, an evanescence of origin carries the complex operation *upon* thought that blackness offers *to* thought and is articulated in the common cultural practice of musical sampling, of digital looping, and the philosophies of repetition such gestures carry forth.

Analog nostalgia is no longer the once innovative theoretical framework for interpreting independent video art practices or understanding why the re-creation of "immediate experience in an age when most experience is rendered as information" is so prevalent especially among those who began video production in a fully digital age. Indeed, a quick online search for "old movie effect" or "VHS effect" will now yield a range of postproduction templates that anyone with access to the internet can use. As with most avant-garde practices, the analog nostalgia of the early digital age has long been transformed from a rich expressive aesthetic to yet another commodity peddled on "capitalized machinic interfaces [that] prey on visuality," what social media pessimists dub the "malevolent bathosphere."[15] Perhaps nothing illustrates this commodification of the precarious aesthetic like social media platforms' own sepia and vintage filters and sundry preset options, or the variety of applications that now exist through which you can film à la VHS mode on your own smart phone, replete with analog grain, light streaks, flipped time stamps, and other options for glitchiness.

What stands out in the Nowruz clip, then, is not the longing for indexicality proposed by the first wave theories of contemporary digital media practices, but the poesis of sampling in Biggie Small's "Juicy," which continuously loops a cut from Mtume's 1983 R&B song, "Juicy Fruit." Sampling and mixing are methods taken up by musicians to combine elements of already recorded material into something new, the "incorporation of features from multiple sources," a creative act of regeneration.[16] Sampling is an "architectural blueprint" that organizes "sounds along a course that affirms the histories and communal narratives of Afro-diasporic people."[17] On the one hand, this model of repetition is an address to memory. One repeats to remember, to protect from the eroding forces

« 216 »   Conclusion

of time.[18] In sampling, "linearity and progress yield to a dizzying synchronicity."[19] Musical repeats compel us to linger, fixing a fleeting pattern of sound.[20] Like a cinematic close-up, the sample makes apparent the autonomy of the part, severs, abstracts, disassembles.[21] It is also thereby intrinsically subject to misreadings. But vulnerability to wrong interpretation and miscitation is not only due to sampling's manifested articulation "*inside* the commodity market." Vulnerability to perversion is constitutive of the operation of citation itself. Openness to errancy and corruption, as I argue differently in chapter 2, is indeed the very condition of possibility for citation. Hip-hop samples tend to follow a "logic of rupture and renovation *by means of* repetition."[22] Sampling is not merely a liberation of context, but the exposure of an essential drift of signification. The philosophy of repetition activated by sampling troubles all certainties about knowledge, experience, and history that a dominant model and descriptive statement about the human continues to assure.

Although dozens of songs sample Mtume's "Juicy Fruit," the Notorious B.I.G. version is the most "eager," indeed the most famous, realizing most fully the originality of the first instance of its articulation.[23] Biggie's 1994 "Juicy" both maintains its relation of contiguity to Mtume's 1983 "Juicy," while simultaneously relinquishing, or rather masking, this relation through Total's harmonic eclipse over the eroticism of the original chorus. In the Nowruz photo collage, the chorus never arises to begin with; nor do any lyrics whatsoever. What remains of Juicy (Fruit) is thus the most stripped down register of funk's idiomatic polyrhythmic complexity. The clip does not void Biggie, but in evacuating the "humid clouds of words" that is his signature, the soundtrack necessarily alludes to the older version of the song, and therefore, to the "'aesthetic of deliberate confusion'" that constitutes Black fusion music of the 1970s and 1980s.[24] Whether the sampling of instrumentals without words was dictated by copyright law or inspired by creative license, the abandonment of Juicy's voice in the Collective for Black Iranians' art does not seem like an ordinary repression; it rather heightens the relations of contiguity at the very heart of sampling and paradoxically suggests the irreplaceability or singularity of the lyrical, the "infinitude of unmeaning" expended by what Lindon Barrett called the signing, singing voice.[25]

In addition to the metallic indexicality of the photographs, the repetition of absence connects the 2021 clip to the 1990s song "Juicy,"

Conclusion « 217 »

but also to the 1980s "Juicy Fruit," and thereby, to the 1960s and 1970s, the political milieux—Black Power, Pan-Africanism and third worldism—constituting the Funk, Soul and R&B movements that incubated bands like Mtume. James Mtume, born James Forman, changed, or rather, "received," his stage name Mtume from Maulana Karenga after joining Karenga's Black Nationalist organization, US.[26] Contemporary rap and hip hop in the neoliberal age is often caricaturized as a commercial perversion of its originally politicized iteration, but it is impossible to fully eradicate the historicity of Black Consciousness from even the most seemingly pasteurized of new musical contexts. Like off-frame action, the sonic's historical context can persist, insist, and remain intended, even where it is necessarily absent or unactivated, even contradicted, refuted. Historical acousmaticity is only exaggerated by a now limitless technological hypermobility, through which a viewer and listener receives the Collective's art. Via the tablet or the mobile phone, the "interface is an 'agitation' or generative friction," a "gateway that opens up and allows passage to some place beyond."[27] Our dominant models of thinking rely upon the linearity of chronology for orientation. But Black sound's omnidirectionality imposes a new imagination of context.

Dominant frameworks for theorizing the precarious aesthetic in new media practices valorize modes of invisibility. But there is little evidence based on the totality of the Collective's media production that their artwork generally aims away from visibility. Indeed, again and again, the Collective issues statements about their belief in the *significance* of visibility. The valorization of opacity in European-based film and media theory does not always translate easily across geographical and political contexts.[28] It is unclear whether elusiveness is necessarily a transgressive political strategy in contexts where invisibility and erasure are already the norm. Unlike the recoil from the transparent sovereign subject that the most critical strains of black studies shares with Eurocentric critical theory, the withdrawal from sovereignty expressed by the former issues from a legacy of theft, is not a neutral divestment.[29] But the very *same* antiblack world that produces the longing for recognition also mines recognition for value, speculates on difference, monetizes every online human relation, interaction, and behavior, colonizes the open horizon of human life.[30] Platform capitalism undermines the digital politics of recognition and confirms what the Collective's practice must already know: there is no guarantee that the absolute contours of a context

« 218 » Conclusion

are fully determinable, and neither, therefore, can the meaning of a desire for recognition be fully secured, its laudable intentions protected. That, finally, the ultimate source of light that offers visibility in the form of sovereign self-determination derives, as Eduoard Glissant proposes, from a "fatally proposed" model.[31] Investments in sovereignty, self-determination, and recognition inform one aspect of a certain failure that characterizes the history of Black liberation.[32]

But there is a way in which the Nowruz clip's detour through error and low definition, combined with the sampling aesthetic, eschews the motive of visibility announced by the Collective itself, and alludes instead to the edges of sound, to the recursive restraint of the dystopic. Citation "engenders an infinity of new contexts."[33] The microfossil of the family photograph suggests something radioactive, echoic, about the clip's components, testifying to the deficiencies of recognition. The icons of Persian tradition (Nowruz; *haft sīn*) are transformed through the oblique sonic texture of a famous American hip-hop track. On one reading, critics of the idea of the Black Iranian, or Afro-Iranian, are affirmed in their objection that these terms fabricate nonexistent realities. If the Notorious B.I.G.'s sample imbues these Nowruz images with blackness, it appears to be a foreign kind, American Blackness. This would be one, obvious, but also facile reading. For on the other hand, a deeper interrogation of the sample in question, and of sampling as a general orientation, demonstrates the incontrovertible universality of a blackness assumed to be localized and localizable in the first place. Unlike vision, which is partial, situated, easily bordered, sound is omnidirectional.[34] The 1960s and 1970s era of black fusion music and internationalism, of which Mtume's "Juicy Fruit" is a legatee exemplifies this political conjunctiveness of black sound.

In addition to their media creations focalizing biographical vignettes of Black Iranians, the Collective regularly posts content on Black transnationalism and pan-African history, organized under their "Black is transnational" series. Another fourteen-second clip collates a set of images of Toni Morrison. Black and white photographs of her appear and fade on a single textured, yellowed folio accompanied by phrases in Persian and in English that are assembled together in the final image. A hyperrealistic painted image of Conceição Evaristo celebrates the Black Brazilian author: "Escrevivência: to tell our stories from our perspectives," is scrawled like a rounded halo around the top of Evaristo's curved afro.[35] A looping

Conclusion   « 219 »

animation of Kwame Nkrumah thoughtfully staring off into space as he rests his pen against his notebook includes in the black backdrop of the image the following quote, "I am not African because I was born in Africa but because Africa was born in me," and transforms into Persian translation, *man āfrīqāyī nīstam bih khātir īnkah dar āfrīqāh bih dunyā umadah-am, man āfrīqāyī hastam chūn āfriqāh dar man mutivalid shudah ast.*[36] Other images feature the Zimbabwean author Tsisi Dangarembga, Angela Davis, James Baldwin, Aimé Cesaire, and Frantz Fanon. Another post proclaims in four swipeable frames that formally reflects the poetic function of the stanza, "Blackness is transnational (*siyāh būdan farā milāyatī ast*) / That means you can find Blackness everywhere (*yanī shawmā mītavānīd sīyāhhā rā har jāyī paydā kunīd*)." On the top and bottom lines of each square frame is drawn mirroring geometrical shapes that resemble abstract Islamic floral imagery, anthropomorphized into a black human visage with almond-shaped eyes accentuated with a signature Persian monobrow.

Before there is Black Iranian, but also, before there is Black *American*, before there is any identity whatsoever, there is first and foremost blackness. In her essay "On How We Mistook the Map for the Territory and Reimprisoned Ourselves in the Unbearable Wrongness of Being," Sylvia Wynter historicizes the emergence of the concept of blackness in the 1960s, reviving the connection between the Black Power Movement and the Black Arts movement (which interacted, "by means of the transistor radio") with the Jamaican Rastafari-Reggae religio-cultural movement, the Afro-Cuban and Afro-Antillian movements of the Hispanic Caribbean, Francophone West Africa's Negritude movement, but also the entire "global field of decolonial movements" occurring synchronically throughout the world.[37] Wynter's webbed constellation reminds us of the now-overlooked fact that the term *Black* was not a ubiquitously appreciated descriptor of African Americans before the 1960s, who were previously designated "negro" or "colored," and prior to Reconstruction, "freedmen." (The fight to capitalize Negro in written publications was famously waged by W. E. B. Du Bois, who announced in his first footnote in *The Philadelphia Negro* that "eight million Americans are entitled to a capital letter.")[38] Though this obvious point is often underappreciated, the reanimation of blackness occurs at a particular moment in time. And yet, the reanimation or revalorization of blackness bears a valence that transcends its own

« 220 »   Conclusion

historical context, for it is rooted in a sprawling conjunction of globally disparate emancipatory projects. In *Black Power: The Politics of Liberation,* Kwame Ture insists upon a "growing resentment of the word 'Negro' . . . the invention of our oppressor," and suggests that "many blacks are now calling themselves African-Americans, Afro-Americans or black people."[39] Blackness describes a rebellion against what was perceived as the more assimilationist "Negro," and is an organizing category of political identification against forces of racialization. Blackness is always already racial, political, historical, but in ways that challenge the simplistic chronicity of causality—let alone the normative, well-rehearsed accounts that find the need to retrench over and again its origins. *Negro,* from the Portuguese root, recalls the early involvement of Portuguese merchants in the Atlantic slave trade, but also the Portuguese role in African enslavement in Mediterranean Iberia, where for centuries before 1492, the peninsula was ruled by the Muslim Ummayads: "The racist ideologies of fifteenth-century Iberia grew out of the development of African slavery in the Islamic world,"[40] implies some scholarship. The phrase "Black is beautiful," a ubiquitous expression peppered throughout the Collective for Black Iranians' social media accounts in both English and Persian, emerged at the height of Black Consciousness and is a clear sign of the Collective's debt to this movement. But, contrary to inherited wisdom, the phrase "Black is beautiful" responds not merely or solely to one historical moment (the 1960s) but to a context that necessarily exceeds, because it cannot simply be contained by, historical memory (see chapter 1). Blackness, as the site of a global, collective recognition of *desêtre,* or "wrongness of being" necessitates an affirmation that is by definition a *break* with context.[41] For Wynter, "the systemic devalorization of racial blackness" that called for the political *re*valorization of racial blackness ("Black is beautiful") is "only the map of the real territory," a "dilemma," that resists discovery, diagnosis, or even thinking by means of current regimes of knowledge alone. Racial blackness augurs a demand for (an impossible) break with our present order of context.

Political activists, poets, and artists did not abandon blackness, just as in the 1920s Du Bois would not abandon the denigrated term *Negro,* despite the objections of his interlocutors to the continued usage of this word.[42] In place of abandonment, Blackness, like the term *Negro,* needed to be repeated, and thereby decontextualized, recontextualized. In repetition, in "repercussive revision," blackness recovers the disequilibrium and the irreducibility of its own sense.[43] Repetition testifies to "a refusal to forget," to the persistence of "a burning image" and to the "looping and determined return," forever seeking its own outside.[44] Rap producers, argues Tricia Rose, invert the previous logic that characterized the sampler as an expedient shortcut; rather than masking the sample and burying its origin (previously the norm in music production), rap producers sampled to highlight repetition.[45] What is repeated in sampling is not an original, but the indefinite compulsion to cite, scratch, scrub, X-.[46] "What would a mark be that could not be cited? Or one whose origins would not get lost along the way?"[47] At the same time, suggests Wahneema Lubiano, it is precisely repetition, unprotectable circulation, that creates the demand for origin—and thereby, authenticity—in the first place.[48] Fault, shame, pride, anguish "motivate the idea of an origin."[49] Serial form, suggests Nathaniel Mackey, is dystopic, moving "forward and backward both, repeated by 'back/at/some beginning.'"[50] Repetition is irreducible to easy exuberance, even if, in the "polyphonic affectivity of the ghost . . . there is the trace of what remains to be discovered."[51]

Identity Fetishism

Along with the forty-nine-second Nowruz photo collage posted on Twitter and Instagram, the Collective for Black Iranians posted other informational materials relevant to the occasion of the Persian New Year in March 2021. Another tweet highlights the lyrics of Hājī Fīrūz, the blackface minstrel who appears during the Persian New Year and pronounces lyrics like: "My master, hold your head up high / My master, why don't you laugh? / It's Nowruz, it's one day a year!"[52] The Collective for Black Iranians was likely to thank for a significant ban on Hājī Fīrūz blackface in Tehran. In March 2021 during the Persian New Year, for the first time in history, the deputy mayor of Tehran for social and cultural affairs implemented an interdict upon the practice of Hājī Fīrūz, leading to a wave of protests by resentful Iranian social media users. "I deeply regret reading the lines of this rationale," a Twitter user responded to the publication of the decree. Too bad, he continued, that the city council had overlooked the "towering name of Mihrdād Bahār" (the famous nationalist linguist and mythologist whose writing on Hājī Fīrūz I discuss in chapter 1).[53] Among other conjectures, in his writings on Persian mythology and

« 222 »   Conclusion

ancient culture, Bahār draws a convoluted correlation between Hājī Fīrūz's black face and the Sumerian practice of women blackening their faces in the ancient mourning festival of Dumuzi, which he submits has been transmitted through the Persian pre-Islamic ritual of Sīyāvashūn. Despite the absence of any evidence to corroborate this wildly speculative hypothesis, Bahār's theories about Hājī Fīrūz, and *siyāh bāzī* (black play) more generally, have been enthusiastically incorporated into common consensus about Hājī Fīrūz's origins. Indeed Twitter users responding to the deputy mayor explicitly cited Bahār's theory, which even appeared at one point to have developed its own pseudo-hashtag (#tumūz).[54] Other commentators echoed this lament over the eclipse of Bahār's supposedly impeccable erudition in favor of mediocre, "unscientific" thinking, and "nonsense" that mistakenly interprets Hājī Fīrūz's black face as racist.[55] The cascade of threaded replies that ensued echoed such sentiments.

This backlash against Hājī Fīrūz's banning was unrestricted to a set of conservative, ignorant, or older-generation Iranians, but issued from a wide spectrum of internet users, including liberal and leftist youth. The banning of Hājī Fīrūz induced an outpouring of discourse on Twitter, as well as on the then recently developing and suddenly popular social media site Clubhouse, in addition to more traditional ethnic news programming. Postban outrage was justified through allusions to seemingly related prohibitions on Nowruz. As is well known, Iran's postrevolutionary authoritarian Islamic regime has a long tradition of prohibiting practices it deems "un-Islamic," mandating compulsory head scarves for women, enforcing gender segregation in public spaces, and forbidding alcohol and even musical instruments. In addition, Shi'i ideologues attempted to eradicate aspects of Iranian Nowruz, considered a pre-Islamic tradition, and tried to instill instead emphasis on Islamic holidays like Eyd-i Ghadir and Eyd-i Ghurbān, which are generally less popular in Iran than Eyd-i Nowrūz. Sīzdā bi dar and Chahār shanbah sūrī were neutralized of their pre-Islamic undertones and renamed Rūz-i tabīyat (Nature Day) and Chahār shanbayi ākhar-i sāl (the last Wednesday of the month). Against the Pahlavi nationalist era's de-Islamicization of Persian culture, the postrevolutionary era saw the re-Islamicization and to some extent, de-Persianization of Iran. *Milī-girāyī* (nationalism) is deemed *shirk,* blasphemy. One user's post thus encapsulated the ubiquitous view that the ban on Hājī Fīrūz was an extension of

Conclusion « 223 »

these other earlier repressions of Nowruz: "The problem with Hājī Fīrūz isn't his blackness, the problem with Hājī Fīrūz is his dancing and joyfulness; haven't you heard that being joyful and making joy are prohibited?"[56]

But there was also another subtext to the rage. Over the past decade a new discourse surrounding Iranians' racialized identity has exposed the dated discourse of Pahlavi nationalism and the deluded assumptions of first-generation Iranian immigrants educated during the Pahlavi era about their own racial standing as Indo-European and white, interrupting the cross-generational and transnational transmission of this Aryan myth.[57] Unlike the ruptural "awakening" of other ethnic minorities in the United States and European diaspora in the 1960s and 1970s, Iranian immigrants, perhaps due to their relatively late dispersion, have arguably never experienced a collective moment of recognition of their own racialization vis-à-vis a white world, unless we understand this recognition as the very phenomenon that was the Revolution of 1979, leading up to which, the revalorization of Islam, and specifically Shi'ism in the 1960s and 1970s, paralleled, conjoined, and drew energy from the revalorization of Blackness in the 1960s and 1970s globally.[58]

A popular image on Persian social media at the height of the Black Lives Matter resurgence in May 2020 Arabicized the phrase "*azizam* [my dear], you are not white" in traditional *nastalīq*-like script elongated on a curved geometrical shape reminiscent of Islamic imagery.[59] Here, "white," written in Arabic characters with the consonant *vāv*, is pronounced *vayt* in Persian, and in reflecting a prototypically Persian accent back to readers of Persian script, reminds immigrant Persian language speakers that their accented English is one among other markers of their nonwhiteness and thereby ethnicized and racialized positionality in white Anglo-Saxon Protestant and European society. The circulation of this textual graphic implicitly also addresses Iranian-descended readers and prompts them to reflect on their racial loyalties amid the Trump-era antiblack context framing the Black Lives Matter resurgence in 2020.

The reappearance of this famous image during the Hājī Fīrūz debacle perversely manipulated its original meaning, acquiring a completely different valence. In March 2021, "azizam, you are not *vayt*," generated an adversarial semantic possibility. *You are not white. Therefore,* your *siyāh bāzī* is not racist blackface minstrelsy. Or, and additionally, *You are not white.* Therefore, *you cannot be antiblack.*

« 224 »　　　　　　　　　　　Conclusion

Going further, the user who reposted the phrase in the context of the Hājī Fīrūz debate argued in his caption that dissimulating "Western guilt" for slavery would not make Persians white, just as feeling shame for Jews would not make them Germans.[60] The perverse analogy is that the Hājī Fīrūz ban promotes a demand to feel guilty about Hājī Fīrūz, and more specifically, a desire to *share in the guilt* of white people for the horrors of African slavery and legacies of antiblack violence. To share the guilt of white people is to forge an intimacy with whiteness.

Echoing another common sentiment, a different Twitter user proclaimed, "My pain is that this lens did not come from within. It's an entirely Orientalist gaze. . . . Westerners who had this problem [racism] suddenly turned their eyes toward this part of the world and saw there is something that looks similar on the surface."[61] Another commenter posted an image of the Collective for Black Iranians satirizing Mr. Javadi Yeganeh (the deputy mayor for social and cultural affairs) for posting about the Hājī Fīrūz ban with the caption "Black Lives Matter" in Persian (*jān-i sīyāhān muhim ast*). "Congratulations to Mr. Javadi. . . . You mean that Hājī Fīrūz in Iran is now on equal footing with the West's history of genocide and slavery!"[62] Another internet user wondered why Mr. Javadi suddenly cared so much about what the West thinks about "us." The refusal to allow the "Orientalist gaze" to dictate Iran's stance on slavery has a notable precursor in the very history of abolition in Iran. On purportedly religious grounds, Muhammad Shah Qajar rejected multiple requests by the British that he issue a *firmān* (royal decree) to abolish slavery, arguing, "Between the religions of Europe and our religion [Islam] there is a great distinction and difference."[63] At the same time, in the nineteenth century, the very abolition of slavery in other predominantly Muslim countries and then, decades later, the Ahmadiyya Muslim movement in Europe and America wielded Islam's "categorical ban on racism and slavery" as an attribute of Islam's purportedly enlightened and tolerant, but more importantly monolithic, character as a universal religion.[64] Slavery's history is irrevocably modulated by globality.

Underlying and unifying the variegated lay critiques of Hājī Fīrūz's ban, and the Collective's role in it, is the assumption that, in Iran and in Southwest Asia more generally, blackness is out of place, has been dislodged from its proper context. Critics and skeptics of "Black Iranian" masquerade as context police, assuming the authority mantle of the historian. But in doing so, they misrecognize the unregulatable sense of repetition, decontextualization, and recontextualization that blackness always already bodes, prior to its capture by the discourse-genre of history. Sylvia Wynter historicizes the global (re)formulation of racial blackness in the 1960s. But her exposition aims less to reify along a timeline or geographical plane than to show how blackness drives emancipatory potential forward *through its own dislocation,* its irruptive break with context. Like the sampling and citation aesthetics the Collective employs in creation, blackness is intrinsically self-repeating, both remembering and risking itself in repetition, drifting, absconding from the capture of context, the "grid's continuous burn."[65]

Repetition is not the reactivation of a former present. Nor is it an arbitrary manner of external practice, an overdetermined cultural homogenization, an "indeterminate mélange of sounds and signifiers,"[66] the hypnotic stimulus, obsessive pulse and reiteration, "consumption compulsion" that are markers of new media and of our time. Repetition is a poesis that echoes a "profound internal repetition within the singular."[67] To repeat blackness is not to repeat identity. Repetition is the creative movement propelled by an originary gap within what is unique and *unrepeatable*—a seismic force and original fracture that stalls the misguided overconfidence of the repeatedly disintegrating *I.* The accumulative nature of Black digital repositories, argues Lauren McLeod Cramer, demands that "we make these objects . . . strange."[68] The "blackest" of black aesthetics anticipates the unimaginable.[69]

Blackness as Content, Slavery as Information

Though perhaps one of the most recent, the Collective for Black Iranians is just one of a number of different digital collectives organized by Black Southwest Asian and North African activists over the past decade. Antiracist organizations and informal coalitions led by Black Maghrebi activists have been prevalent throughout North Africa since the Arab Spring of 2011. In 2014, for example, Moroccan activists forged the national campaign *Je ne m'appelle 'azzi* or *Ma smitish 'azzi* (I am not a Negro), which later expanded into a North-Africa-wide effort.[70] Imazi-noirs, or blackmoroccans, a French and Arabic language Instagram account, first posted their mission in June 2020 and describe some of their goals as follows: to provide a space for Black Moroccans to exchange and testify to their experiences, to bring to light the African slave trade in Morocco and its consequences, to denounce all forms of racial discrimination in Morocco, and to bring awareness (*Sensibiliser, sensibiliser, et encore sensibiliser,* they emphasize) about antiblackness in North Africa (*négrophobie*). Voix des Femmes Tunisiennes Noires (Voices of Black Tunisian Women) operates primarily through Facebook (at the time of the writing of this book), and according to one of its founders, Khawla Ksiksi, largely informally: "We refuse the juridical status of an association," and "are constituted horizontally"; "We speak in the name of a collective."[71] Formed on January 23, 2020—a symbolic date, referring to Tunisia's January 23 abolition of slavery in 1846—part of the impetus for the group's formation pertains to the failure of a law against racial discrimination implemented in Tunisia in 2018, but which, according to Huda Mzioudet, one of Voix's founders, has only exacerbated the prevalence of everyday antiblack attacks.[72] The implementation of the law against racial discrimination in Tunisia was itself facilitated by another grassroots organization, M'nemty (My Dream), formed in 2012 and founded by the Black Tunisian female activist Saadia Mosbah, attesting to the largely female leadership of antiracist work in Tunisia.[73]

The scope of activism in Southwest Asia and North Africa is transregional. Even so, as the titles of the different collectives demonstrate, the demand to be recognized as *part* of a national identity (Black Iranian, Black Moroccan, Black Tunisian) appears unavoidable. The inevitable hegemony of the national is difficult to disentangle from the politics and history of nationalism that have rendered the nation-state our hegemonic form of identification and analysis in the first place. "The territorial truth of a nation has an obviousness that is deeply contingent historically and politically."[74] The Collective for Black Iranians seeks to unsettle Iranian identity by reinserting the existence of Black people in Iran. But the mediatized form of this reinsertion is fraught with a necessary naturalization of national identity on the one hand, and on the other, fused with the difficulty of its distinction from a globalized brand of pluralist multiculturalism that proliferates difference and ultimately extracts difference for value. The two terms in the formulation, Black and Iranian, exist in tension with each other. (See chapter 3, on the tautologies of "Afro-Iran.") In chapter 3, "Afro" and "Iranian" reinforce the tautology

Conclusion   « 227 »

that *is* hybridity. Similarly, in *Black Iranian,* the "second word of the phrase is given a problematic inflection by the first."[75] For in its originarily political valence that the Collective reactivates in their practice, blackness is the very challenge to the ethnic signifier that is affirmed by the second term. That is, in its 1960s revalorization that the Collective consistently evokes with the phrase *Black is beautiful,* Blackness challenged the "spectacle of ethnicity" institutionalized by a depoliticized neoliberal multiculturalism in order to emphasize something broader than particularistic cultural content—the fuel of the content industries, of the Content Age. My intention here is not to undermine self-identification, nor to erroneously position racial self-nomination as a simple choice, but rather to bring attention to the way that the very sense of "Black Iranian" rekindles the tensions inherent in the pressures of compulsory self-identification and self-realization that constitute our globalized inheritance of the subject. As Sylvia Wynter notes, it was the liberal humanist "reterritorialization" and assimilation of blackness into the ethnic and the multicultural that, like the institutional sanitization and translation of black studies into African American Studies, marked the "eventual defeat" of Black radicalism.[76] Beyond its force as a mere mode of identification that one hyphenates, blackness is a question for the matrices that produce identification as natural, necessary, desirable, just as it is a question for the very configuration that produces context as coherent, closed, autonomous.

The "Narges" thread that featured serially from November 2020 to February 2021 described the story of a "dark-skinned Black woman named Narges" (pronounced Naar-gess) who was the free daughter of an enslaved mother and free Muslim father, wrongly purchased by a prominent merchant for his wife in 1906 Tehran. The ten-part Twitter and Instagram threads follow Narges's escape from the couple who initially purchase her and her eventual refuge with Haji Naneh, a freed black woman in Tehran who helped enslaved women escape to freedom. Perhaps as a result of social media's general character quota, each "part" is only a few sentences long, written in both English and Persian, and accompanied by one colorful looping graphic illustration (GIF) depicting a scene from Narges's journey. In the last part of the series, an illustrated image shows Narges and Haji Naneh sitting under a pomegranate tree on a red geometrical carpet, with small glasses of tea in their hands.[77]

« 228 »   Conclusion

Figure 30. Narges achieves freedom with the help of Haji Naneh in the final illustration of the Narges thread in the Collective for Black Iranians Twitter feed.

Excerpted from the dissertation of the Collective's resident historian, the story itself is somewhat reminiscent of the genre of emancipated slave narratives one finds in the few existing historiography monographs on Indian Ocean slavery centered on the modern period. Ehud Toledano's *As If Silent and Absent,* which focuses on the Tanzimat period (1839–1871) of the Ottoman Empire, describes a number of case studies of kidnapped, enslaved Africans escaping to the British consulate in anticipation of freedom. Such stories of seeking protection from the state resonate with the narrative arc of Narges's story. According to the final Twitter post, Narges's narrative ultimately ends after she secures her "papers" at the Iranian Parliament, after which "No one could attempt to enslave her—and try to get away with it—again," the Twitter and Instagram threads read. Though the story's ending might be read as an unintentional affirmation of the state as a benign and benevolent actor, in the illustrations it seems clear that the Collective wishes to stress Haji Naneh's role in protecting Narges, and the role of black women as community protectors more generally, not the state as savior. Mutual protection and care of freed slaves is also a known historical feature of the Ottoman Empire, where freed female African slaves (named

Conclusion   « 229 »

kolbaşı or *godya/godiya*) ran a network of "lodges" that doubled as sites of spiritual healing—in some cases, of *zār*.[78] Compared to our information about slavery in the Ottoman Empire, stories about Iran's legacies of slavery are far rarer.

Though inspired by the dense and colorful aesthetics of the Persian miniature, the digital illustrations accompanying the Narges thread express a tendency toward minimalist design. Created by the artist Mina Jafari, the lines of the composition are strong, clear, angular, and descriptive, mirroring the geometrical sensibilities of the Persian miniature but eschewing the saturation and bright palette of the medieval miniaturist style for a bare modernism and subdued, earthy color scheme. Entirely digital, the images also retain traces of the extempore hand-drawn sketch. The symmetrical parallel lines of a brick wall, or the repeating curves of a carpet tendril might suddenly tend toward the rough unfinishedness of pencil's charcoaled abrasion, belying the pristine clarity of the digital's discrete numerical form, the perfect string of 1s and 0s encoding and decoding the GIF form.

While unique in its appropriation of Persian aesthetic, Jafari's animation style is typical of digital art practices ubiquitous on social media that favor clarity and immediate delivery of consumable, digestible information. This is so despite the fact that the actual means by which such art is produced is paradoxically obscure, occult.[79] The beautiful aesthetic supports the narrative arc that emplots Narges's life drama, spreading a beginning, middle, climax, and quasi-cheery end over the serial course of a hashtag's brief lifespan. In short, through her transformation into a Twitter and Instagram character, Narges, the formerly enslaved African woman in the nineteenth century, reaches thousands of people in the new millennium. (At the time I was writing this chapter, her GIF illustrations had been viewed over four thousand times.) Narges's dissemination, the conversion of her life into narrative, thus occurs as she is transformed into information, into consumable content. Narges is momentarily transformed from a human commodity on the illegal black slave market of 1920s Iran into a virtual, ephemeral commodity in the information economy of the twenty-first century.

In previous chapters, I suggest that academic, primarily historiographic engagements with Indian Ocean slavery are never politically neutral, are implicitly dependent on strategies for truth production whose self-evidence is presumed and sealed. The Collective for

« 230 »   Conclusion

Black Iranians renders apparent a community of receivers for this history whose presence has heretofore been deemed nonexistent or irrelevant. The appearance of the Collective for Black Iranians, and of other Black Southwest Asian and North African digital coalitions, does not make the contemporary production of the history of Indian Ocean and trans-Saharan slavery any more politically neutral or objective. (Indeed, no study of slavery is ideologically neutral, politically innocent, as the famous historian of ancient slavery, Moses Finley, once compellingly argued.)[80] The emergence of such groups only heightens the instability of the supposed consensus underlying the self-sufficiency of objective historiography. But in their necessary proximity to the content industries and the adoption of its popular aesthetics, best exemplified by the labor of the Collective for Black Iranians, a question is renewed: *can* Indian Ocean slavery be delivered as anything other than information? Transcending the logic of documentary paucity that has traditionally structured narratives about Indian Ocean slavery, and uprooting the logic of dispersion and lack, the future discovery of new sources, as well as the appearance of a larger body of interested inheritors is already making the history of Indian Ocean slavery "better known." And yet, if, as I have suggested throughout this book, Indian Ocean slavery, like all history, is naturally, intrinsically, prone to distortion and drift, so too, will its future discovery be inevitably dictated by the occult extraction logics of our contemporary information economy. "The subaltern speaks, and somewhere an algorithm listens."[81]

Narges, the free daughter of an enslaved mother and Muslim father, was wrongly purchased by a merchant for his wife. After seeking refuge with a local mullah, she is again betrayed, the Collective's feed informs us. For the mullah sells Narges to another couple, and she is reenslaved. In the nineteenth-century Persian Gulf, blacks, whether free or enslaved, were perennially exposed to the threat of kidnapping. Testimonies of enslaved people shows that theft of context—ongoing displacement—was a normal condition. Saeeda bint Sadem, a former female slave in the Persian Gulf, attested in the early twentieth century to being sold at a very young age to a "Yamani," who, "after eight days," sold her to another man. Six years later she was sold to a third man, and after another ten days, to a master in Qatar, where she was resold and taken to Bahrain.[82] Despite their eventual concentration in the south, in Iran, enslaved people "rarely stayed in one location after their capture." Thus, in a testimony Jamila Habashi reported being

Conclusion   « 231 »

enslaved in Ethiopia, sold in Mecca, then Basra, then Muhammara, and later Shiraz, to an Arab broker, a Persian broker, a merchant, and then two additional masters.[83] In Tunisian *stambeli*'s spirit cosmology, unlike black spirits, white spirits "do not possess their hosts, but rather 'take them away.'"[84] Blackness is exposure to the ongoing threat of decontextualization.

It is not only the case that slavery cannot remain intact in its conversion to information, in the injury to its context committed by the equalizing simulacra of new media. "There is no time in the mass image."[85] In the practice of the spirit ritual *zār*, forgetting is brought to a radical indecision as the self suspends itself in loss. *Zār* is the recurring relinquishment of information gathering, a total abandonment that exceeds the oppositional logic of truth and falsehood. Both the amnesia and now, the digital *anamnesis,* the recovered and recovering memory of Indian Ocean slavery are necessarily inflected, informed by other histories that dictate the conditions for the conversion of the past into reality (historiography), and of reality into information (the information age). The Dutch etymology for "platform," *platte vorm,* suggests "the flat form as a level surface that operates as a gigantic equalizer of different forces and streams."[86] Social media isn't the only locus of our information age, only a particularly ubiquitous example of its crystallization. Under platform capitalism—on the academic platform, on the social media platform—where knowledge is endlessly gathered, stored, and mobilized in the service of production, truth is not merely errant. The originary errancy of truth is itself vulnerable to extraction, to the production of surplus.

At the same time, crafted as seconds-long looping GIFs, the Collective's media art implicitly excerpts formless, intangible phenomena. In their succinctness, this media art leads viewers into the ambivalent hypnosis of a polyvalent repetition. The GIF compensates for its brevity and denaturation of temporal flow through the repetition of its own lack. The repetitive mode of the GIF "plunges its viewer into a trance-like fascination," a "nondestructive innervation."[87] It is true that one "breaks-in another human living being by making them repeat." The military model of the nation-state, which creates an unbroken link between modernity and antiquity, pushes repetition to the point of automatism.[88] But inside the interval of an always potentially violent repetition is an "absence by which the phenomenal is articulated" and which opens up the possibility for a redirection of norms, of a reconstitution of the subject, of the not in-between.[89] What also opens up, as ever present, is the formlessness that is the very ground of form—for the interval realizes not only the capacity for reinvention and regeneration but more fundamentally, a perpetual tendency toward disintegration, an unabating movement toward emptiness. There is a beyond that even seriality and repetition, that even the resistance to information, seeks. It calls toward another kind of freedom.

Notes

INTRODUCTION

1. Because I engage blackness in a context where it is only in the process of being recognized as such, *black* and *blackness* are not consistently capitalized throughout this book. The capacity for capitalization, and thus, hierarchical distinction between upper and lowercase characters, is not a universal property of all alphabetical systems. (In Persian, the term for black [*siyāh*] cannot be capitalized, because no words can be capitalized.) My inconsistency and ambivalence with capitalization reflects a concern about the ways in which processes of recognition coincide with processes of factification that ultimately curtail the universality of blackness as a form of existence.
2. In this book, I will usually refer to what has been traditionally known as the Middle East (a colonial invention) through the more geographically neutralized term *Southwest Asia*. This is in line with emerging academic practice critical of the Orientalist roots of the term *Middle East*. With regard to scholarship on slavery in Iran, Behnaz Mirzai's 2017 *A History of Slavery and Emancipation in Iran, 1800–1929* is a notable exception to the lack of historiography on slavery in Iran. For an important critique of Mirzai's approach, see Amy Motlagh's forthcoming manuscript, *Invisible Men: A Cultural History of Racial Thinking in Modern Iran and the Diaspora*. Another forthcoming scholarly work on the history of slavery in Iran is Beeta Baghoolizadeh's *The Color Black: Enslavement and Erasure in Iran*.
3. On some contemporary scholarship on sexuality and slavery in the Indian Ocean across periods, see for example Gwyn Campbell and Elizabeth Elbourne, eds., *Sex, Power, and Slavery*; Kecia Ali, *Marriage and Slavery in Early Islam*; Matthew S. Gordon and Kathryn A. Hain, *Concubines and Courtesans: Women and Slavery in Islamic History*; Fuad Matthew Caswell, *The Slave Girls of Baghdad: the Qiyān in the Early Abbasid Era*; Madeline C. Zilfi, *Women and Slavery in the Late Ottoman Empire: The Design of Difference*; George H. Junne, *The Black Eunuchs of the Ottoman Empire: Networks of Power in the Court of the Sultan*. For North Africa, see Mary Ann Fay, *Unveiling the Harem: Elite Women and the Paradox of Seclusion in Eighteenth-Century Cairo*.

« 233 »

« 234 »   Notes to Introduction

4. For military slavery in Iran during the Safavid period, see Sussan Babaie et al., *Slaves of the Shah: New Elites of Safavid Iran*. The literature on military slavery in Muslim polities more generally is extensive. See for example Patricia Crone, *Slaves on Horses: The Evolution of the Islamic Polity*.

5. Benjamin Reilly, *Slavery, Agriculture, and Malaria in the Arabian Peninsula*; Matthew S. Hopper, *Slaves of One Master: Globalization and Slavery in Arabia in the Age of Empire*; Kenneth M. Cuno, "African Slaves in Nineteenth-Century Egypt: A Preliminary Assessment," in Terence Walz and Kenneth M. Cuno, *Race and Slavery in the Middle East*.

6. By "transracial" I refer to the significance of the enslavement of peoples from the Caucasus in the history of Indian Ocean slavery, especially in the medieval period. The scare quotes express my awareness that racial terminology during this period is anachronistic.

7. With the exception of scholarship that is primarily concerned with European power in the Indian Ocean, such as French-driven chattel slavery in the Mascarene islands.

8. For a critique of the idea of Indian Ocean "world," which suggests "holistic entirety and self-sufficiency," see Nile Green, "Rethinking the 'Middle East' after the Oceanic Turn," 558. For the Indian Ocean as an "imaginal unit," see Edward A. Alpers, *The Indian Ocean in World History*, 6. Michael Pearson once called for renaming the Indian Ocean the "Afrasian Sea." Himanshu Prabha Ray and Edward A. Alpers, *Cross Currents and Community Networks: The History of the Indian Ocean World*, 2; Michael Pearson, *Port Cities and Intruders: The Swahili Coast, India, and Portugal in the Early Modern Era*, 36–38.

9. Gwyn Campbell, ed., *The Structure of Slavery in Indian Ocean Africa and Asia*, x. See also, James L. Watson, *Asian and African Systems of Slavery*, 1–16; Suzanne Miers and Igor Kopytoff, *Slavery in Africa: Historical and Anthropological Perspectives*, 3–12; Martin A. Klein, *Breaking the Chains: Slavery, Bondage, and Emancipation in Modern Africa and Asia*, 3–37.

10. Elsewhere, I have reflected on the comparative drive at the heart of Indian Ocean slavery scholarship. See Parisa Vaziri, "No One's Memory: Blackness at the Limits of Comparative Slavery." On hyperspecialization as a problem for the study of global African diaspora, see Pier Larson, "Reconsidering Trauma, Identity, and the African Diaspora: Enslavement and Historical Memory in Nineteenth-Century Highland Madagascar," 336–37. For a more general critique of African diaspora studies as a field of study, see R. A. Judy, "Beside the Two Camps: Paul Gilroy and the Critique of Raciology."

11. Edward A. Alpers, "The Other Middle Passage: The African Slave

Notes to Introduction « 235 »

Trade in the Indian Ocean," in *Many Middle Passages: Forced Migration and the Making of the Modern World*, 20, 35.

12. Indrani Chatterjee and Richard M. Eaton, *Slavery and South Asian History*, xii, 20. The "fragmented administrative superstructure" belies any underlying unity of the Indian Ocean world system, "making archival research a formidable task to any serious scholar" (Markus Vink, " 'The World's Oldest Trade': Dutch Slavery and Slave Trade in the Indian Ocean in the Seventeenth Century," 131–77).

13. Campbell, *The Structure of Slavery*, ix. See also Abdul Sheriff, *Dhow Cultures of the Indian Ocean: Cosmopolitanism, Commerce and Islam*, 218–19; William Gervase Clarence-Smith, *The Economics of the Indian Ocean Slave Trade in the Nineteenth Century*, 67–69.

14. Historians of the Indian Ocean are reluctant to "acknowledge that trans-oceanic slave trading was of far greater antiquity in the Indian Ocean basin than it was in the Atlantic" (Richard Allen, *European Slave Trading in the Indian Ocean, 1500–1800*, 4).

15. Burkhard Schnepel and Julia Verne, *Cargoes in Motion: Materiality and Connectivity Across the Indian Ocean*, 7–8; John Wright, *The Trans-Saharan Slave Trade*, 130; Gwyn Campbell, "Servitude and the Changing Face of the Demand for Labor in the Indian Ocean World, c. 1800–1900," in Robert Harms, David W. Blight, and Bernard K. Freamon, *Indian Ocean Slavery in the Age of Abolition*, 31.

16. I refer to Ralph Austin's frequently cited estimates. For an example of the considerable variability in numerical estimations in Indian Ocean slavery, see Gwyn Campbell's remarks regarding the debate on nineteenth-century demand for slavery in the Persian Gulf. Gwyn Campbell, ed. *Abolition and Its Aftermath in Indian Ocean Africa and Asia*, 5. See also Paul E. Lovejoy, *Transformations in Slavery: A History of Slavery in Africa*, 21–25.

17. Anjali Arondekar, *For the Record: On Sexuality and the Colonial Archive in India*, 15; Ariella Aïsha Azoulay, *Potential History: Unlearning Imperialism*, 169; Ann Laura Stoler, "Colonial Archives and the Arts of Governance"; Achille Mbembe, "The Power of the Archive and Its Limits," in Carolyn Hamilton, ed., *Refiguring the Archive*, 19–20.

18. Thomas Osborne, "The Ordinariness of the Archive," 52.

19. Azoulay, *Potential History*,. 43.

20. Throughout this book, when I invoke facticity, I mean simply the quality, state, or capacity of being a fact. This is distinct from the more complex philosophical lineage of the word that is usually associated with phenomenology, and in particular, with the work of Martin Heidegger. In Heidegger, facticity is a constitutive feature of *Dasein* that is distorted by modernity's obsession with the incontestably real. Heideggerian facticity is thus already resistance to facticity. Martin

« 236 »   Notes to Introduction

Heidegger, *Ontology—The Hermeneutics of Facticity*. See also François Raffoul and Eric Sean Nelson, eds., *Rethinking Facticity*; Scott M. Campbell, *The Early Heidegger's Philosophy of Life: Facticity, Being, and Language*; Eric Sean Nelson, "Questioning Practice: Heidegger, Historicity, and the Hermeneutics of Facticity."

21. Joseph C. Miller, *The Problem of Slavery as History: A Global Approach*, 20.

22. Parisa Vaziri, "False Differends: Racial Slavery and the Genocidal Example."

23. Antonin Artaud, "The Premature Old Age of Cinema," in *Antonin Artaud, Selected Writings*, 312.

24. For a discussion of the historical debate surrounding the appropriateness of the "New Wave" label, see Golbarg Rekabtalaei, *Iranian Cosmopolitanism: A Cinematic History*, 245–47. I use "alternative cinema" and "New Wave" interchangeably but tend toward the "New Wave" label because of its present legibility and its communication with other global cinematic movements. For a compelling material history of the eccentric sampling practices and circulation flows in prerevolutionary Iranian film culture, see Kaveh Askari, *Relaying Cinema in Midcentury Iran: Material Cultures in Transit*.

25. A touchstone for film philosophy is Gilles Deleuze's two volumes on cinema, *Cinema I: The Movement-Image* and *Cinema II: The Time-Image*. Methodologically disparate recent examples of film philosophy include Davide Panagia, *Impressions of Hume: Cinematic Thinking and the Politics of Discontinuity*; Robert B. Pippin, *Filmed Thought: Cinema as Reflective Form*; David Yacavone, *Film Worlds: A Philosophical Aesthetics of Cinema*; Daniel Frampton, *Filmosophy*; Bernd Herzogenrath, *Film as Philosophy*; Richard Allen and Murray Smith, eds., *Film Theory and Philosophy*; Craig Fox and Britt Harrison, eds. *Philosophy of Film Without Theory*; Nico Baumbach, *Cinema/Politics/Philosophy*. The list is far from exhaustive. For philosophical approaches to cinema in the context of Black critical thought, see Frank Wilderson, *Red, White & Black: Cinema and the Structure of U.S. Antagonisms*; David Marriott, *Haunted Life: Visual Culture and Black Modernity*; Marriott, "Waiting to Fall." For a critique of national origin as a basis for taxonomizing cinema, see Dudley Andrew, "An Atlas of World Cinema," in Stephanie Dennison and Song Hwee Lim, *Remapping World Cinema*.

26. Bernard Stiegler, *Technics and Time, Vol. II: Disorientation*, 32.

27. Gilles Deleuze, *Negotiations: 1972–1990*, 44. See also Amy Villarejo, "& Mediation," in Richard Grusin and Jocelyn Szczepaniak-Gillece, *Ends of Cinema*, 182–84.

28. Henri Diamant-Berger, "Le Filmage"; Christian Metz, "Ponctuations et démarcations dans le film de diègese"; Robert Bresson, *Notes on the*

Cinematograph, 5; Gilles Deleuze, *Cinema II: The Time-Image,* 25; Deleuze, *Negotiations,* 52.

29. Amīr Hūshang Kāvūsī, in the film journal *Sitārah sīnamā* (1957), quoted in Jamāl Umīd, *Tārīkh-i sīnamā-yi Īrān: 1279–1357,* 298.

30. Hamid Naficy, *A Social History of Iranian Cinema, Volume 2,* 351. On the global reach of neorealism, see Saverio Giovacchini and Robert Sklar, *Global Neorealism: The Transnational History of a Film Style*; and Laura Ruberto and Kristi Wilson, *Italian Neorealism and Global Cinema.*

31. André Bazin purported to call the neorealist image a "fact-image." Bazin, "An Aesthetic of Reality: Cinematic Realism and the Italian School of the Liberation," in *What Is Cinema?, Vol. 2,* 16-41; Deleuze, *Cinema II,* 1; Cezar Gheorghe, "Bazin Meets Deleuze: The Fact-Image and Pure Optical Situations in Italian Neo-Realism."

32. Matthew Soloman, "Sergei Eisenstein: Attractions/Montage/Animation," in Murray Pomerance and R. Barton Palmer, eds., *Thinking in the Dark,* 91.

33. Friedrich A. Kittler, *Gramophone, Film, Typewriter,* 117. For early twentieth-century discourses on the psychological implications of cinema's constitutive machinic discontinuities, see Jeffrey West Kirkwood, *Endless Intervals: Cinema, Psychology, and Semiotechnics around 1900.*

34. Bernard Stiegler and Stephen Francis Barker, *Technics and Time, 3: Cinematic Time and the Question of Malaise,* 87. One only has to recall the myriad technological innovations surrounding the cinema in the decades that precede and antecede it.

35. Jonathan Beller, *The Cinematic Mode of Production: Attention Economy and the Society of the Spectacle,* 26.

36. Thus, observes Miriam Hansen, film responds to an adaptation of technology that has already failed. See Miriam Hansen, *Cinema and Experience: Siegfried Kracauer, Walter Benjamin, and Theodor W. Adorno,* 79. Cinema makes the subject adequate to a new reality of exchangeability and flow.

37. Franco "Bifo" Berardi thus distinguishes "conjunction" from "connection," associating the latter with semiocapitalism. See Berardi, *And: Phenomenology of the End: Sensibility and Connective Mutation,* 21–23.

38. There is considerable debate surrounding cinema's relation to or origins in a drive for scientific certitude, perhaps most famously associated with André Bazin's "The Myth of Total Cinema." But the distinction between science and the "maniacal," as Bazin characterizes cinema's early founders, conceals the fact that there is always something of the antiscientific at the heart of science; thus, something antiscientific at the heart of cinema's scientificity. See André Bazin,

"The Myth of Total Cinema," in *What Is Cinema? Vol. 1*, 17–22. See also Jonathan Crary's critique of the tendency to conflate precinematic optical technologies in a "vague collective drive to higher and higher standards of verisimilitude." Jonathan Crary, *Techniques of the Observer: On Vision and Modernity in the Nineteenth Century*, 110.

39. For an elaboration of the distinction between second and third cinema, see Mike Wayne, *Political Film: The Dialectics of Third Cinema*. See also Robert Stam and Toby Miller, *Film and Theory: An Anthology*; Anthony R. Guneratne and Wimal Dissanayake, *Rethinking Third Cinema*; Hamid Naficy, *An Accented Cinema: Exilic and Diasporic Filmmaking*.

40. James Tweedie, *The Age of New Waves: Art Cinema and the Staging of Globalization*, 6; Geoffrey Nowell-Smith, *Making Waves: New Cinemas of the 1960s*; Peter Cowie, *Revolution! The Explosion of World Cinema in the Sixties*; Surajit Chakravarty, "Discontents of Modernity: Space, Consumption and Loss in Hong Kong New Wave and Bombay Parallel Cinema." On South Asian cinema as an imaginative repository for navigating accelerated modernization, see Iftikhar Dadi, *Lahore Cinema: Between Realism and Fable*.

41. Amīr Hūshang Kāvūsī, in the journal *Firdawsī* (1958), cited in Umīd, *Tārīkh-i Sīnamā-yi Īrān*, 308. In his analysis of Iranian cult cinema, Babak Tabarraee suggests that precisely the collage-like aesthetic of prerevolutionary commercial cinema shaped part of its appeal for viewers. See Tabarraee, "Iranian Cult Cinema," 98.

42. Shāhrukh Gulistān, *Fānūs-i khiyāl: Sarguzasht-i sīnimā-yi Īrān az āghāz tā pīrūzī-i inqilāb-i islāmī, bih ravāyat-i bī. bī. si*, 140; Sajjād Aydinlū, "Muqadamah'i bar naqqālī." Mahroo Rashidirostami argues for the global ubiquity of such indigenous story-telling practices, likening the *naqqāl* to the Arabic *hakawati*, Turkish *aşik*, and Kurdish *denbêj* or *şair*. Rashidirostami, "Performance Traditions of Kurdistan," 280.

43. Khatereh Sheibani, *The Poetics of Iranian Cinema: Aesthetics, Modernity and Film after the Revolution*, 1.

44. Daniel Frampton, *Filmosophy*, 3. Regis Debray distinguishes cinema from television according to the former's production of a "discontinuity of everyday space and time." Regis Debray, *Media Manifestos: On the Technological Transmission of Cultural Forms*, 143. For Sarah Keller, anxiety about desire for cinema is shaped by the volatility of the medium itself. Keller, *Anxious Cinephilia: Pleasure and Peril at the Movies*.

45. Antonin Artaud, "Sorcery and Cinema," 104; Siegfried Kracauer, *Theory of Film: The Redemption of Physical Reality*, 163; Robert Sinnerbrink, "Hugo Münsterberg, Film, and Philosophy," in Herzogenrath, ed., *Film as Philosophy*, 28. On cinema as a cultural technique of

Notes to Introduction   « 239 »

trance, see Ute Hall, *Cinema, Trance, and Cybernetics*; Arnd Schneider and Caterina Pasqualino, *Experimental Film and Anthropology*.

46. Because many leading intellectuals in Iranian society were also artists, writers, and filmmakers, Iran's aesthetic landscape in the twentieth century is deeply colored by its modern intellectual history.

47. Negar Mottahedeh, "Crude Extractions: The Voice in Iranian Cinema," 227. On the coevolution of cinema and oil industrialization, see Mona Dalmuji, "The Image World of Middle Eastern Oil," in Hannah Appel, Arthur Mason, and Michael Watts, eds., *Subterranean Estates*. On the relation between oil, transnationalism, and neorealism, see Georgiana Banita, "From Isfahan to Ingolstadt: Bertolucci's *La Via Del Petrolio* and the Global Culture of Neorealism," in Ross Barrett, ed., *Oil Culture*. On the relationship between realism and global cinema more generally, see Lúcia Nagib, *World Cinema and the Ethics of Realism*.

48. Ervand Abrahamian, *Oil Crisis in Iran: From Nationalism to Coup d'Etat*. The 1921 Abadan Oil Refinery strike is considered the first major event of industrial unrest in Iran, setting the stage for the working-class agitations that would come to generate an eventual revolution in politics (Stephanie Cronin, *Soldiers, Shahs and Subalterns in Iran*).

49. Mona Dalmuji, "The Oil City in Focus: The Cinematic Spaces of Abadan in the Anglo-Iranian Oil Company's Persian Story." (Early negotiations concentrated extractions to the southwest of Iran, in the province of Khūzistān, where the world's largest oil refinery was established and managed by the British-engineered Anglo-Iranian Oil Company.) On the relationship between British colonial networks and the introduction of cinema in the Persian Gulf, see Firat Oruc, "Petrocolonial Circulations and Cinema's Arrival in the Gulf," and "Space and Agency in the Petrocolonial Genealogies of Cinema in the Gulf." On the relationship between oil, imagination, and aesthetics, see Stephanie LeMenager, *Living Oil: Petroleum Culture in the American Century*.

50. Indeed, at the height of domestic film output in Iran, 60 percent of Iran's revenue was contingent on its oil reserves. Ervand Abrahamian, *A History of Modern Iran*, 127. See also Roy Armes, *Third World Filmmaking and the West*, 191.

51. Behnaz Mirzai, *A History of Slavery and Emancipation*, 70. Mirzai's reference is to Mary Sheil's *Glimpses of Life and Manners in Persia*, a nineteenth-century travelogue written by the wife of a British envoy, Justin Sheil. But all Lady Sheil posits on this account, writing in the 1850s, is that compared to the north of Iran, in the south, slaves are "doubtless in greater numbers, and particularly in the low, level tract bordering the coast." Lady Mary Leonora Woulfe Sheil, *Glimpses of Life and Manners in Persia*, 244. Ports on the southern coast of Iran

« 240 »   Notes to Introduction

were also stopovers for further travel to Arabian and Ottoman markets. For example, according to the British envoys in the Persian Gulf, of the thousands of slaves that arrived yearly in Bushehr in the 1840s, the majority were "sent on to Muhammarah and Basra." Charles Issawi, *The Economic History of Iran: 1800–1914*, 124. See also J. B. Kelly, *Britain and the Persian Gulf: 1795–1880.*

52. Andrew Nikiforuk, *Tar Sands: Dirty Oil and the Future of a Continent*, 206. On the continuities between historical trades in enslaved humans and petroleum, see Hannah Appel, *The Licit Life of Capitalism: US Oil in Equatorial Guinea*, 95. On transformations to slavery as a result of palm oil exportation on the West African coast, see Kristin Mann, *Slavery and the Birth of an African City: Lagos, 1760–1900.*

53. W. E. B. Du Bois, *The World and Africa: An Inquiry into the Part Which Africa Has Played in World History*, 71.

54. Philip D. Curtin, *Cross-Cultural Trade in World History*, 34–38; Edward A. Alpers, *Ivory and Slaves: Changing Pattern of International Trade in East Central Africa to the Later Nineteenth Century*; Philip Gooding, "The Ivory Trade and Political Power in Nineteenth-Century East Africa"; Abdul Sheriff, *Slaves, Spices, and Ivory in Zanzibar: Integration of an East African Commercial Empire into the World Economy, 1770–1873*, 77–109; Jan Lindström, *Muted Memories: Heritage-Making, Bagamoyo, and the East African Caravan Trade*, 143–76.

55. J. H. Galloway, "The Mediterranean Sugar Industry." There are many gaps in the historical record pertaining to sugar production in antiquity, but most medieval Arab geographers agree upon the importance of its cultivation in the Tigris-Euphrates delta. In his *Masālik va mamālik* the tenth-century Muslim geographer al-Istakhri remarks on the abundance of sugarcane in Khūzistān. Ibrahim ibn Muhammad al-Istakhri, *Masālik va mamālik*, 73. In the anonymous tenth-century geographical work *Hudūd al-ʿĀlam* (*Regions of the World*), it is claimed that all the sugar in the world comes from ʿAskar-i Mukram, in Khūzistān. *Hudūd al-ʿĀlam: 'The Regions of the World,' A Persian Geography 37 A.H.-982 A.D.*, 130. See also Noel Deerr, *The History of Sugar.*

56. Robert William Fogel, *The Slavery Debates: 1952–1990: A Retrospective*, 22.

57. Azoulay, *Potential History*, 167. For the idea that the discreteness of the "Atlantic" and "Indian Ocean" is a recent emergence indebted to European imperialism, see Isabel Hofmeyr, "The Sodden Archive: Africa, the Atlantic and the Indian Ocean," in Pedro Machado, ed., *Indian Ocean Histories*, 34; and Martin W. Lewis, "Dividing the Ocean Sea."

58. Deborah Kapchan, *Traveling Spirit Masters: Moroccan Gnawa Trance and Music in the Global Marketplace*, 35.

Notes to Introduction « 241 »

59. On the idea that blackness is associated with the "sin of unbelief," see John Hunwick, "Islamic Law and Polemics over Race and Slavery in North and West Africa (16th–19th Century)," 43. See also Ismael M. Montana, "Bori Practice among Enslaved West Africans of Ottoman Tunis: Unbelief (*Kufr*) or another Dimension of the African Diaspora?"

60. Taghi Modarressi, "The Zar Cult in South Iran," 154.

61. Maria Sabaye Moghaddam, "Zâr Beliefs and Practices in Bandar Abbâs and Qeshm Island in Iran," 26. William Beeman, "Understanding the Zar: An African-Iranian Healing Dance Ritual," 78; Anita Adam, "A Saar Gaamuri in Somalia: Spirit Possession as Expression of Women's Autonomy?," 148.

62. Stephan Prochazka and Bahram Gharedaghi-Kloucheh, "The Zār Cult in the Shatt al-'Arab/Arvand Region."

63. Tamara Turner, "The 'Right' Kind of *Hāl*: Feeling and Foregrounding Atmospheric Identity in an Algerian Music Ritual," 124; Richard C. Jankowsky, *Stambeli: Music, Trance, and Alterity in Tunisia*, 4.

64. Aishia Bilkhair Khalifa, "Spirit Possession and Its Practices in Dubai," 35. The dating of *zār*'s diffusion is notoriously unreliable, based as it is predominantly upon European accounts from the nineteenth century. Richard Natvig, "Oromos, Slaves, and the Zar Spirits: A Contribution to the History of the Zar Cult," 669.

65. Hager El Hadidi, *Zar: Spirit Possession, Music, and Healing Rituals in Egypt*, 16, 9.

66. Pamela Constantinides, "The History of Zar in the Sudan," 84. The etymology for the word *gnawa*, a North African Black healing ritual, is similarly convoluted. See Cynthia Becker, *Blackness in Morocco: Gnawa Identity through Music and Visual Culture*, 237.

67. Taghi Modarressi, "The Zar Cult in South Iran." Modarressi conceived of *zār* as the Persian name attributed to a ritual introduced to Iran by African sailors in the sixteenth century. The theory alludes to the sixteenth-century Portuguese invasion of the islands of Kish, Hingam, and Hurmuz during Portugal's initial attempts to gain hegemony over the lucrative Indian Ocean sea trade routes. Modarressi hypothesized that African members of a ship's sailing crew had stayed behind after King Abbas had burned Portuguese vessels and driven them out of the islands.

68. Christian Snouck Hurgronje, *Mekka in the Latter Part of the Nineteenth Century*, 100.

69. Wolf Leslau, "An Ethiopian Argot of People Possessed by a Spirit," 211.

70. Natvig, "Oromos, Slaves, and the Zar Spirits," 686; Tiziana Battain, "Osservazioni sul rito zār di possessione degli spiriti in Yemen," 117.

71. Constantinides, "The History of Zar in the Sudan," 84; Duncan B. Macdonald, "Emotional Religion in Islam as Affected by Music and

« 242 » Notes to Introduction

Singing. Being a Translation of a Book of the Ihyā ʿUlūm ad-Dīn of al-Ghazzālī with Analysis, Annotation, and Appendices," 239.

72. Daniel Heller-Roazen, "Glossolalia: From the Unity of the Word to Plurality of Tongues," 594–95.

73. Dionne Brand, *A Map to the Door of No Return: Notes on Belonging,* 5.

74. I am thankful to Fred Moten for the inspiration to rethink the difficulty of *zār*'s causality.

75. A by now well-known postcolonial lineage has critiqued traditional models of historiography whose implicit focal point is the liberal, bourgeois subject. See for example Dipesh Chakrabarty, *Provincializing Europe: Postcolonial Thought and Historical Difference* and Ranajit Guha, *History at the Limit of World History.*

76. For the concept of melancholic historicism, see Stephen Best, *None Like Us: Blackness, Belonging, Aesthetic Life,* 65–78.

77. Jankowsky, *Stambeli,* 28.

78. Thus, numbers may be expressed by other numbers; one year may represent fifteen years (Leslau, "An Ethiopian Argot of People," 210).

79. Frantz Fanon, *The Wretched of the Earth,* 19; 212–18. See also Fred Moten, "The Case of Blackness."

80. In the nineteenth century, French plans for colonial management of Algeria included proposals of Algerian genocide, supplemented with the purchase and resettlement of militarized, African slave "settlers" to fulfill increasing labor needs. Benjamin Claude Brower, *A Desert Named Peace: The Violence of France's Empire in the Algerian Sahara, 1844–1902,* 159–80; Brower, "Rethinking Abolition in Algeria. Slavery and the 'Indigenous Question'"; John Wright, *The Trans-Saharan Slave Trade,* 134–47. Most pre-nineteenth-century Algerian archives have "vanished." John E. Lavers, "Trans-Saharan Trade before 1800: Towards Quantification," 258.

81. It is well known that the Portuguese "discovery" of Cape Bojador and the subsumption of West Africa into mercantile exchange was motivated, among other things, by desires to hedge Islamic trans-Saharan monopoly over the gold trade and to uncover a new route to the "Indies." Sylvia Wynter, "1492: A New World," 9–11; Cedric Robinson, *Black Marxism: The Making of the Black Radical Tradition,* 91–93; A. J. Russell-Wood, *The Portuguese Empire, 1415–1808: A World on the Move,* 8–26. Abdul Sheriff, "Globalisation with a Difference: An Overview," in Abdul Sheriff and Engseng Ho, eds., *The Indian Ocean.*

82. Jean Khalfa, "Fanon, Phenomenology and Psychiatry," talk at Institute of Comparative Modernities, Cornell University, March 21, 2022.

83. Jared Sexton, "The Social Life of Social Death: On Afro-Pessimism and Black Optimism," 21.

84. Maria Sabaye Moghaddam, *Zār dar Īrān va kishvarhāyi dīgar,* 56. And everyone in the south of Iran, insists Nader Aghakhani, knows some-

Notes to Introduction « 243 »

one who has a wind. Aghakhani, *Les "gens de l'air," "jeux" de guérison dans le sud de l'Iran: Une étude d'anthropologie psychanalytique*, 31.

85. Edward A. Alpers, "The African Diaspora in the Indian Ocean," 33. Moghaddam, "Zâr Beliefs and Practices in Bandar Abbâs," 28. "In Kuwait, non-African middle-class women, struggling to cope with rapid modernization, were the primary practitioners of zār" (Zubaida Ashkanani, "Zar Cult in Kuwait"). In Baluchistan, "the officiants are African Baluchis, but the participants are of all origins" (Jean During, "African Winds and Muslim Djinns: Trance, Healing, and Devotion in Baluchistan," 39).

86. Leslau, "An Ethiopian Argot," 204.

87. Iraj Bashiri, "Muslims or Shamans: Blacks of the Persian Gulf," 7; Kaveh Safa, "Reading Saedi's Ahl-e Hava: Pattern and Significance in Spirit Possession Beliefs on the Southern Coasts of Iran," 90; Lisa Urkevich, "Incoming Arts: African and Persian," 147.

88. David Lloyd, *Under Representation: The Racial Regime of Aesthetics*, 121.

89. The loss of native context, of native culture and civilization, presages the loss of ipseity, as many of these architects of postcolonial thought believed. And thus the cacophony of calls for a return to authenticity in the wake of Western modernity's voracious consumption of indigenous life. On Shari'atī and the Iranian Revolution, see Siavash Saffari, *Beyond Shariati: Modernity, Cosmopolitanism, and Islam in Iranian Political Thought*; Dustin J. Byrd and Seyed Javad Miri, *Ali Shariati and the Future of Social Theory: Religion, Revolution, and the Role of the Intellectual*; Abdollah Zahiri, "Frantz Fanon in Iran: Darling of the Right and the Left in the 1960s and 1970s." For an insightful exploration of Shari'atī's engagement with Fanon, see Arash Davari, "A Return to Which Self? Ali Shari'ati and Frantz Fanon on the Political Ethics of Insurrectionary Violence." See also Ali Mirsepassi, *Transnationalism in Iranian Political Thought: The Life and Times of Ahmad Fardid*.

90. Firoozeh Kashani-Sabet, "The Anti-Aryan Moment: Decolonization, Diplomacy, and Race in Late Pahlavi Iran." See also Amy Motlagh's forthcoming *Invisible Men*.

91. Ricciotto Canudo, "The Triumph of the Cinema," in Casetti, Alovisio, and Mazzei, eds., *Early Film Theories in Italy: 1896–1922*.

92. In modernity, "Time is no longer the benign phenomenon most easily grasped by the notion of flow but a troublesome and anxiety-producing entity that must be thought in relation to management, regulation, storage, and representation. One of the most important apparatuses for regulating and storing time was the cinema" (Mary Ann Doane, *The Emergence of Cinematic Time: Modernity, Contingency, the Archive*, 33–34).

« 244 »   Notes to Introduction

93. For the historical subtleties in distinction between the terms Indo-European and Aryan, see Stefan Arvidsson, *Aryan Idols: Indo-European Mythology as Ideology and Science*, 13–62.

94. Mohamad Tavakoli-Targhi, *Refashioning Iran: Orientalism, Occidentalism, and Historiography*; Reza Zia-Ebrahimi, *The Emergence of Iranian Nationalism: Race and the Politics of Dislocation*; Neda Maghbouleh, *The Limits of Whiteness: Iranian Americans and the Everyday Politics of Race*.

95. Reza Zia-Ebrahimi, "Self-Orientalization and Dislocation: The Uses and Abuses of the 'Aryan' Discourse in Iran," 446.

96. There is a spate of scholarship, especially published in the last decade or so, that seeks to undermine this orthodoxy, attending to race's residual forms in adjacent concepts and periods.

97. Īraj Afshār Sīstānī, *Khūzistān va tamadun-i dīrīnīyah ān*, vol. 1, 474; Hasan Pīrniyā, *Īrān-i bāstān, ya tarīkh-i mufaṣal Īrān-i qadīm*, 157.

98. Behnaz Mirzai, *Afro-Iranian Lives* (2013).

99. Ababu Minda Yimene, *An African Indian Community in Hyderabad: Siddi Identity, Its Maintenance and Change*, 72; Henry John Drewal, "Aliens and Homelands: Identity, Agency and the Arts among the Siddis of Uttara Kannada," in Amy Catlin-Jairazbhoy and Edward A. Alpers, *Sidis and Scholars: Essays on African Indians*, 145.

100. Jankowsky, *Stambeli*, 16.

101. Ismael M. Montana, "Enslavable Infidels: Sudan-Tunis as a Classificatory Categorization for a New Wave of Enslaved Africans in the Regency of Tunis," 79.

102. Isaac Julien and Kobena Mercer, "De Margin and de Centre," 2–11; Stuart Hall, "What Is This 'Black' in Black Popular Culture?"; Houston A. Baker Jr., Manthia Diawara, and Ruth H. Lindeborg, *Black British Cultural Studies: A Reader*; Valerie Smith, ed., *Representing Blackness: Issues in Film and Video*.

103. Lewis Gordon, "Race, Sex, and Matrices of Desire in an Antiblack World: An Essay in Phenomenology and Social Role."

104. Jemima Pierre, "Slavery, Anthropological Knowledge, and the Racialization of Africans," 221.

105. For the idea that race is a process of homogenization, see Omi and Winant: "Where once there had been Asante or Ovimbundu, Yoruba, or Bakongo," racial slavery "created the 'Black." Michael Omi and Howard Winant, *Racial Formation in the United States*, 131. For a critique of racial formation theory as an iteration of white sociology, see P. Khalil Saucier and Tryon P. Woods, *Conceptual Aphasia in Black: Displacing Racial Formation*. For medieval models of Africanness, see Paulo Fernando de Moraes Farias, "Models of the World and Categorial Models: The 'Enslavable Barbarian' as a Mobile Classificatory Label," 31–33; John Hunwick, "A Region of the

Notes to Introduction « 245 »

Mind: Medieval Arab Views of African Geography and Ethnography and Their Legacy." Moreover, color-as-metonymy does not appear to be exclusively modern. Though their origins are "shrouded in mystery," and the meaning of their name is "in dispute," the label given to the *ḥarāṭīn* could derive from a Berber word meaning "black." Hunwick, "Islamic Law and Polemics over Race and Slavery," 57, 68; D. Jacques-Meunié, "Hiérarchiee sociale au Maroc présaharien," 252. A more thorough etymological overview can be found in Chouki El Hamel, *Black Morocco: A History of Slavery, Race, and Islam,* 111, and El Hamel, "Race, Slavery and Islam in Maghribi Mediterranean Thought: The Question of the Haratin in Morocco," 38–39. Mohamad Hassan Mohamed suggests that the usage of *ḥarāṭīn* can "hardly be traced past the eighteenth century," where such groups are described in premodern Arabic texts as "*sudan, suud,* or *sumr . . .* blacks, brown." Mohamed Hassan Mohamed vehemently contests the scholarly conflation of "African," with "black," and as Other to the "Islamic world as a whole and the Maghrib in particular." But the author can merely attribute this conflation to irresponsible postcolonial Anglophone Africanists, offering no account of why the *ḥarāṭīn* are in fact discriminated against in the Maghreb. Mohamed, "Africanists and Africans of the Maghrib: Casualties of Analogy." See also Rachel Schine, "Race and Blackness in Premodern Arabic Literature." For the interchangeability of terms for black slaves in seventeenth-century Ottoman Cyprus, see Ronald C. Jennings, "Black Slaves in Ottoman Cyprus, 1590–1640."

106. Sylvia Wynter, "Unsettling the Coloniality of Being/Power/Truth/Freedom: Towards the Human, After Man, Its Overrepresentation—An Argument." For "affectability" as a racializing attribute that pertains to the inability to transcend one's context, which is to say, to transcend natural law, see Denise Ferreira da Silva, *Toward a Global Idea of Race.*

107. Tapji Paul Garba and Sara-Maria Sorentino, "Blackness before Race and Race as Reoccupation: Reading Sylvia Wynter with Hans Blumenberg."

108. Sylvia Wynter, "On How We Mistook the Map for the Territory, and Re-Imprisoned Ourselves in Our Unbearable Wrongness of Being, of *Désêtre*: Black Studies Toward the Human Project," 108–10.

109. And if the absolute, exceptional degradation of the enslaved is the exemplary model through which to think slavery's horrors, as the historian of comparative slavery righteously complains, "what is the nothingness, which is to say the blackness, of the slave?" (Fred Moten, "Blackness and Nothingness: Mysticism in the Flesh," 744.)

110. One commentator, for example, only describes the transition as "seamless." Ghulām Ḥaydarī, *Trāzhidī-i sīnamā-yi kumidī-i Īrān,* 97.

« 246 »   Notes to Introduction

111. See for example, Blake Atwood, *Underground: The Secret Life of Videocassettes in Iran*; Hamid Naficy, *Making of Exilic Culture: Iranian Television in Los Angeles*.

112. Fogel, *The Slavery Debates*; Alpers, "Recollecting Africa: Diasporic Memory in the Indian Ocean World."

113. Ehud Toledano, *Slavery and Abolition in the Ottoman Middle East*, 158.

1. BLACKFACE AND THE IMMEMORIAL

1. The film was released in early February 1964 (the solar month of Esfand)—one of the worst times of year for film premieres. Jamāl Umīd, *Tārīkh-i sīnamā-yi Īrān: 1279–1357*, 370.

2. Elizabeth Bronfen, "Death, The Navel of the Image," 83. See also Maaike Bleeker, *Visuality in the Theatre: The Locus of Looking*, 91. Sigmund Freud's dream of Irma's injection, whence the "navel of the dream" phrase, is one of the most fecund texts in psychoanalytic discourse and commentary.

3. On the navel as a mythical reminder of the origins of human desire, see Plato, *Symposium*, 191a.

4. On the navel of the dream as a figure for invisible, foundational flesh, see Jacques Lacan, *Seminar II: The Ego in Freud's Theory and in the Technique of Psychoanalysis 1954–1955*, 154. See also Jacques Derrida, "Resistances," in *Resistances of Psychoanalysis*, 27.

5. For an explanation of my capitalization practices, please see the introduction.

6. Simon Morgan Wortham, "Resistances—after Derrida after Freud," 55.

7. Paulo Lemos Horta, ed., *The Annotated Arabian Nights: Tales from 1001 Nights*.

8. Farukh Ghafārī, "Interview with Akbar Etemad."

9. Parvīz Javād, *Nivishtan bā dūrbīn: rū dar rū bā Ibrāhīm Gulistān*, 79.

10. On "middle-ness" in *Arabian Nights*, see Paulo Lemos Horta, *Marvelous Thieves: Secret Authors of the Arabian Nights*, 4.

11. Claire Cooley, "Soundscape of a National Cinema Industry: *Filmfarsi* and Its Sonic Connections with Egyptian and Indian Cinemas: 1940s–1960s." Egyptian melodramas regularly infiltrated Iran's domestic film market prior to the full consolidation of *filmfārsī* in the 1960s and undoubtedly helped shape the Iranian genre. See also Maysam Amānī, "T'asīr-i sīnamā-yi mawj-i naw-i Īrān dar junbishhā-yi ijtimā'i sālhā-yi 1257–1347": "We must understand *filmfārsī* as the child of an American father and an Indian mother" (5). On postwar Indian cinema's transnationalism, see Samhita Sunya, *Sirens of Modernity: World Cinema via Bombay*.

Notes to Chapter 1 « 247 »

12. Jalāl Umīd, *Tārīkh-i sīnamā-yi Īrān,* 307. Though the term is usually attributed to Amīr Hūshang, who purportedly coined *fīlmfārsī* in the 1950s in the Iranian film journal *Firdūsī,* Pedram Partovi points out that the usage of the term probably dates earlier in the promotion of foreign features dubbed in Persian (*Popular Iranian Cinema before the Revolution: Family and Nation in* Filmfarsi, 4). See also Husayn Mu'azzizīniyā, *Fīlmfārsī Chīst?,* 8.

13. Parvīz Jāhid, *Directory of World Cinema: Iran,* 73–74. Masu'd Mihrābī calls *Night of the Hunchback* the "only source of light" in 1964, a year in which filmmakers continued to make "substance-less" films for the masses. See Mihrābī, *Tarīkh-i sīnamāyi Īrān az āghāz ta 1357,* 122.

14. In his famous work of literary theory, *Poétique de la Prose,* Tzvetan Todorov differentiated this type of causality from a more familiar form of causality developed by the psychological novel. Using the example of the *Arabian Nights* generally, and the "Hunchback" cycle specifically, he connected the famous narrative embedding (*l'enchâssement*) structure of the *Nights* with the term used by modern linguistics to describe syntactical subordination of clauses. On retroaction in the causality of mise en abyme, see André Gide, *Journals, Volume I: 1889–1913,* 30.

15. Kaveh Askari's meticulous material history of prerevolutionary Iranian cinema shows the prevalence of idiosyncratic found recording practices. Kaveh Askari, *Relaying Cinema,* 81–103.

16. Hamid Reza Sadr, *Iranian Cinema: A Political History,* 125.

17. On cinema's "necessarily recorded status," and thus, necessarily being-toward-the future as what distinguishes it from television and radio, see Todd McGowan, *Out of Time: Desire in Atemporal Cinema,* 5. On the difficulty of film's medium specificity, see Garrett Stewart, *Between Film and Screen: Modernism's Photo Synthesis* and *Framed Time: Toward a Postfilmic Cinema.*

18. Reza Zia-Ebrahimi, *The Emergence of Iranian Nationalism: Race and the Politics of Dislocation.*

19. This is a partial explanation for the ban on Islamic rituals like *ta'zīyah* under Reza Shah. See Kamran Scot Aghaie, *The Martyrs of Karbala: Shi'i Symbols and Rituals in Modern Iran,* 51. On the evolving relationship between the Iranian state and indigenous rituals, see Babak Rahimi, *Theater State and the Formation of Early Modern Public Sphere in Iran.* Pahlavi racial nationalism also included the religious deactivation of traditionally sacred sites like mosques, and the construction of new secular sites of pilgrimage. See Talinn Grigor, *Building Iran: Modernism, Architecture, and National Heritage under the Pahlavi Monarchs,* 34–41.

20. William O. Beeman, "Why Do They Laugh?: An Interactional Approach to Humor in Traditional Iranian Improvisatory Theater: Performance and Its Effects," 524.

Notes to Chapter 1

21. Parviz Osanlu's *Hasan Siyah* features such a scene, which is repurposed for Mariyam Khakipour's 2004 documentary about *siyāh bāzī*, *The Joymakers*. William Beeman suggests children take the greatest delight in *siyāh bāzī* because of their vulnerable social status in "Why Do They Laugh?," 524.

22. Muhammad Bāqir Anṣārī, *Namāyish-i rūhawzī: zamīnah va 'anāṣir-i khandah'sāz*, 51.

23. Angelita D. Reyes, "Performativity and Representation in Transnational Blackface: Mammy (USA), Zwarte Piet (Netherlands), and Haji Firuz (Iran)."

24. Obviously, there is a long lineage of scholars who have taken (primarily American) blackface minstrelsy as a serious object of historical inquiry.

25. Though Bahram Beyzai dates improvisatory theater to the mid-Safavid period, Willem Floor believes *tamāshaw* (comedy) and *taqlīd* started much earlier in the pre-Islamic era. See Willem Floor, *History of Theater in Iran*, 41.

26. Mihrdād Bahār, *Pazhūhishī dar asāṭīr-i Īrān: pārah-'i nakhust va pārah-'i duyyum*; Hāshim Razī, *Jashnhā'yi āb: nawrūz savābiq-i tarikhī ta imrūz jashnhā-yi tīrgān va āb-pashan*; Muhammad Bāqir Anṣārī, *Namāyish-i Rūhawzī*.

27. Kathy Foley, "Commedia Counterparts: Middle Eastern and Asian Connections," 467.

28. Parisa Vaziri, "Thaumaturgic, Cartoon Blackface."

29. Mihrdād Bahār, *Pazhūhishī dar āsāṭīr-i Īrān*, 194–95.

30. Mahmoud Haery, "*Ru-howzi*: The Iranian Traditional Improvisatory Theatre," 72. See also Davūd Fathalī Baygī, "Barkhī istlāhāt takht hawzī," in *Dar bārah-'i ta'zīyah va ti'ātr*.

31. Beeta Baghoolizadeh, "The Myths of Haji Firuz: The Racist Contours of the Iranian Minstrel." Baghoolizadeh draws a connection between *siyāh bāzī* and eunuchism in the Safavid era. Hāshim Razī, citing the tenth-century scholar al-Masūdi in *Muruj ul-Zahab* (*Meadows of Gold*), suggests that the tradition of Hājī Fīrūz, a particular iteration of *siyāh bāzī*, emerges out of the practices of black slave entertainers during the Sasanian era (third to seventh century CE). Hāshim Razī, *Jashnhā'yi Āb*, 201–2.

32. Saidiya Hartman, *Scenes of Subjection: Terror, Slavery, and Self-Making in Nineteenth-Century America*, 21.

33. Michel-Rolph Trouillot, *Silencing the Past: Power and the Production of History*, 6.

34. Parisa Vaziri, "Antiblack Joy: Transmedial Siyāh Bāzī and Global Public Spheres."

35. Antonio Fava, *The Comic Mask in the Commedia dell'Arte: Actor Training, Improvisation, and the Poetics of Survival*, 5.

Notes to Chapter 1 « 249 »

36. Erith Jaffe-Berg, ed. *Commedia dell'Arte and the Mediterranean: Charting Journeys and Mapping 'Others,'* 14. On Harlequin as the blackface minstrel's prototype, see Henry Louis Gates Jr., *Figures in Black: Words, Signs, and the 'Racial' Self,* 51, and Robert Hornback, *Racism and Early Blackface Comic Traditions: From the Old World to the New,* 27. For the resemblance between Persian *rūhawżī* and Turkish *ortaoyunu,* see Anthony Shay, *The Dangerous Lives of Public Performers,* 182–83.

37. Ali Nasīrīyān, *Bungāh-i ti'ātrāl,* 23.

38. Mustafā Uskū'ī suggests support of minstrelsy under Reza Shah was directly connected to the suppression of intellectuals (*rawshanfikr*), thus, of antistate, communist discourse. Mustafā Uskī'i, *Sayrī dar tarīkh-i ti'ātr-i Īran.* On minstrels in Iranian history as messengers between the sovereign and the public, see Soodabeh Malekzadeh, "Minstrels: The Wise Teachers of Ancient Iran," in Babak Rahimi, ed., *Performing Iran: Culture, Performance, Theatre,* 39–44.

39. Lauren Berlant and Sianne Ngai, "Comedy Has Issues," 235.

40. On the spectatorial relation inherent in theatrical reference, see Sylvie Bissonnette, "Committed Theatricality," 143. On the theatrical impulse of melodrama, see Peter Brooks, *The Melodramatic Imagination,* 12. Melodrama is not synonymous with *fīlmfārsī,* but *fīlmfārsī's* predominant genre is melodrama. For the complex history of the relation between melodrama and modernity studies, see Ben Singer, *Melodrama and Modernity: Early Sensational Cinema and Its Contexts.*

41. On comic blackface figures as theatergrams, see Robert Hornback, "Harlequin as Theatergram," in *Racism and Early Blackface Comic Traditions.* On the concept of "interpenetration" in film, see Donato Totaro, "Time, Bergson, and the Cinematographical Mechanism."

42. Alain Badiou, *Rhapsody for the Theatre,* 188.

43. Cedric Robinson, *Forgeries of Memory and Meaning: Blacks and the Regimes of Race in American Theater and Film Before World War II,* 4.

44. Stanley Cavell, *The World Viewed: Reflections on the Ontology of Film,* 35.

45. Sudabeh Fazaeli, "Fīrūz-i muqadas: bahsī dar namād shināsī-yi 'hājī fīrūz' talāyī dar nowrūz va bahār."

46. Haery, "Ru-howzi," 23; Ida Meftahi, *Gender and Dance in Modern Iran: Biopolitics on Stage,* 49.

47. Fatema Mernissi, *Scheherazade Goes West: Different Cultures, Different Harems,* 70.

48. Here, I refer to American blackface minstrelsy, whose roots in the appropriation of Black culture has been argued by numerous scholars. See for example Dale Cockrell, *Demons of Disorder: Early Blackface Minstrels and Their World*; Eric Lott, *Love and Theft: Blackface Minstrelsy and the American Working Class*; and W. T. Lhamon, *Raising Cain: Blackface Performance from Jim Crow to Hip Hop.*

Notes to Chapter 1

49. Meftahi dates the bifurcation of café spaces along class lines to the 1950s. See Meftahi, *Gender and Dance,* 71. For a history of coffeehouse culture in Iran, see ʿAlī Bulūkbāshī, *Qahvahkhānah'hā-yi Īrān.*

50. Alice Maurice, "The Essence of Motion: Figure, Frame, and the Racial Body in Early Silent Cinema," 131. See also Anna Everett, *Returning the Gaze, A Genealogy of Black Film Criticism, 1909–1949,* 12–13.

51. On Iran's relationship to American jazz in the twentieth century, see G. J. Breyley, "From the 'Sultan' to the Persian Side: Jazz in Iran and Iranian Jazz since the 1920s."

52. Afsaneh Najmabadi, *Women with Mustaches and Men Without Beards: Gender and Sexual Anxieties of Iranian Modernity,* 132–55.

53. Samuel Weber, *The Legend of Freud,* 113.

54. Meftahi, *Gender and Dance,* 102; Anthony Shay and Barbara Sellers-Young, *Belly Dance: Orientalism, Transnationalism, and Harem Fantasy,* 2.

55. Ghafārī, "Interview with Akbar Etemad."

56. Siro Ferrone, "La Vendita del teatro," quoted in Árpád Szakolczai, *Comedy and the Public Sphere: The Rebirth of Theatre as Comedy and the Genealogy of the Modern Public Arena.*

57. George Rehin, "Harlequin Jim Crow: Continuity and Convergence in Blackface Clowning," 682.

58. Calvin Warren, "Improper Bodies: A Nihilistic Meditation on Sexuality, the Black Belly, and Sexual Difference," 36.

59. On the significance of figural contiguity in film semiotics, see Dudley Andrew, *Concepts in Film Theory,* 160–62.

60. Kecia Ali, *Marriage and Slavery in Early Islam*; see also Fatima Mernissi, *Women's Rebellion and Islamic Memory,* for an argument about the impact of slavery on heterosexual relations in Islamicate societies; Mohammed Ennaji, *Slavery, the State, and Islam.*

61. Ali, *Marriage and Slavery in Early Islam,* 7.

62. Mia Gerhardt, *The Art of Story-Telling: A Literary Study of the Thousand and One Nights,* 46.

63. The transgression occurs in a garden orgy with twenty other male and female slaves, ten white and ten black (according to some versions). After witnessing the adulterous scene, Shahriyar vows to kill every virgin in his kingdom. When the vizier in charge of presenting Shahriyar with his victims runs out of virgins for Shahriyar to rape and kill, the vizier consents, by her own request, to allow his daughter Shahrazad to marry Shahriyar.

64. Tarek Shamma, "Women and Slaves: Gender Politics in the Arabian Nights," 243.

65. Jennifer Thorn, "The Work of Writing Race: Galland, Burton, and the Arabian Nights," in *Monstrous Dreams of Reason: Body, Self, and Other in the Enlightenment.* Thorn argues that translations of "blackness"

Notes to Chapter 1 « 251 »

evolved over the course of the *Nights*' various translations into English in line with hardening views about race in the nineteenth century. But the changes in the *Nights*' modern English translations do not account for a more "original" antiblackness that resists its own historicization. On black stereotypes in the *Arabian Nights,* see Ulrich Marzolph and Richard van Leeuwen, *The Arabian Nights Encyclopedia,* 500.

66. Nabia Abbott, "A Ninth-Century Fragment of the 'Thousand Nights': New Light on the Early History of the Arabian Nights"; Robert Irwin, *The Arabian Nights: A Companion,* 1–9.

67. Najmabadi, "Reading 'Wiles of Women' Stories as Fictions of Masculinity," 148. See also Abdelwahab Bouhdiba, *Sexuality in Islam, and* Fedwa Malti-Douglas, *Woman's Body, Woman's Word: Gender and Discourse in Arabo-Islamic Writing.* The centrality of *makr-i zanān* to the conceptualization of female sexuality from its pre-Islamic cultural presence through the entire scriptural body of medieval literature suggests a dense misogyny irreducible and unspecific to Islam, and yet renewed by the institutionalized forms of monotheism. As bell hooks notes, the brutal treatment of black women under chattel slavery was a direct consequence of fundamentalist Christian teachings that portrayed women as evil sexual temptresses. The rape of black female slaves combined hatred of women with hatred of blackness. bell hooks, "Sexism and the Black Female Slave Experience," in *Ain't I a Woman: Black Women and Feminism,* 29.

68. Kamran Rastegar, "The Changing Value of *Alf Laylah wa Laylah* for Nineteenth-Century Arabic, Persian, and English Readerships," 283. The treatment of the *Nights* as an opportunity for public edification by its translators has a long history. See also Ulrich Marzolph, "The Persian Nights: Links between the Arabian Nights and Iranian Culture," in *The Arabian Nights in Transnational Perspective.*

69. Daniel Beaumont, *Slave of Desire: Sex, Love, and Death in* The 1001 Nights, 46; Julie Meisami, "Allegorical Gardens in the Persian Poetic Tradition."

70. Maryam Khakipour, dir., *The Joymakers* (2004).

71. Kenneth Goings notes a similar tension between the black stereotypes of "sambo" and the "brute" in the American racial imaginary (*Mammy and Uncle Mose: Black Collectibles and American Stereotyping,* xix).

72. Ya'qūb Āzhand, *Namāyishnāmah'nivīsī dar Īrān.*

73. Haery, *Ru-howzi,* 56.

74. Cedric Robinson, *Forgeries of Memory and Meaning,* 128.

75. Henri Bergson, *Laughter: An Essay on the Meaning of the Comic,* 50.

76. Robinson, *Forgeries of Memory and Meaning,* 127.

77. See Baghoolizadeh, "The Myths of Haji Firuz."

78. Rudi Matthee, "Boom and Bust: The Port of Basra in the Sixteenth and Seventeenth Centuries," 105; Willem Floor, "Bushehr: Southern

« 252 »   Notes to Chapter 1

Gateway to Iran"; Behnaz A. Mirzai, *A History of Slavery and Emancipation in Iran*, 56; Hala Mundhir Fattah, *The Politics of Regional Trade in Iraq, Arabia, and the Gulf: 1745–1900*, 69–70; Thabit Abdullah, *Merchants, Mamluks, and Murder: The Political Economy of Trade in Eighteenth-Century Basra*, 64–65; Reidar Visser, *Basra, the Failed Gulf State: Separatism and Nationalism in Southern Iraq*, 16.

79. In commedia dell'arte, the *zanni* wears gaudy, tricolored clothing, which the French writer Jean Pierre Florian attributed to the story of an African orphan who was clothed by the three sons of a cloth merchant. Henry Louis Gates Jr, using such eighteenth-century sources that model the Harlequin's origin on the African slave figure, recognizes the inconclusive import of the connection: "These are all, of course, myths of origins. Nevertheless, the visual evidence does suggest at least the myth of an African connection with the origins of Harlequin's mask, in terms of both its features and its color" (*Figures in Black*, 51.) Robert Hornback, following Pastoureau, traces the connection between the patch-clothes of the Harlequin to the Renaissance fool (*Racism and Early Blackface*, 27); while the trope of colorful and mismatching rags can also be traced to the black Semar in Javanese *wayang* (puppet performances).

80. Al-Munsif bin Hasan, *Al-'abīd wa-al-jawārī fī hikāyāt Alf Laylah wa-Laylah*, 32.

81. Persian documentary-literary sources, like the eleventh-century *Qābūsnāmah*, or *Mirror for Princes*, communicate that enslaved Africans were deemed particularly suitable for positions as harem guards. Kaykāvūs ibn Iskandar ibn Qābus, 'Unsur al-a'ālī, and Sa'īd Nafīsī, *Kitāb-i Nasīhatnāmah: ma'rūf bih Qābūsnāmah*. See also Parisa Vaziri, "On 'Saidiya.'"

82. Guity Nashat, "Women in Pre-Islamic and Early Islamic Iran," 12; Sussan Babaie et al., *Slaves of the Shah: New Elites of Safavid Iran*; Jane Hathaway, *The Chief Eunuch of the Ottoman Empire: From African Slave to Power-Broker*, 4.

83. Toru Miura and John Edward Philips, *Slave Elites in the Middle East and Africa: A Comparative Study*.

84. Hortense J. Spillers, "Mama's Baby, Papa's Maybe: An American Grammar Book," 72.

85. Miura and Philips, *Slave Elites*, 43. Islam forbids participation in the act of castration. See also Kwesi Kwaa Prah, *Reflections on Arab-Led Slavery of Africans*, 114–16.

86. Suzanne Miers, *Britain and the Ending of the Slave Trade*, 57; Miura and Philips, *Slave Elites*, 48–50; Humphrey J. Fisher, *Slavery in the History of Muslim Black Africa*, 280; John Ralph Willis, ed., *Slaves and Slavery in Muslim Africa: Vol. 2: The Servile Estate*, 55. Eunuchs were "universally highly prized." Gwyn Campbell, "The Question of Slavery in Indian Ocean World History," in Abdul Sheriff and Engseng Ho,

Notes to Chapter 1 « 253 »

eds., *The Indian Ocean: Oceanic Connections and the Creation of New Societies,* 127.

87. Shaun Marmon, *Eunuchs and Sacred Boundaries in Islamic Societies,* 8.

88. Hathaway, *The Chief Eunuch,* 7. See also Sussan Babaie, Kathryn Babayan, Ina Baghdiantz-MacCabe, and Massumeh Farhad, *Slaves of the Shah: New Elites of Safavid Iran,* 20–49.

89. Ayse Osmanoğlu, *Babam Abdulham,* cited in Ehud Toledano, "The Imperial Eunuchs of Istanbul: From Africa to the Heart of Islam," 382.

90. Jateen Lad, "Panoptic Bodies: Black Eunuchs as Guardians of the Top-kapi Harem," 171. John Hunwick and Eve Trout Powell, "Eunuchs and Concubines," in *The African Diaspora in the Mediterranean Lands of Islam.*

91. George Junne, *The Black Eunuchs of the Ottoman Empire: Networks of Power in the Court of the Sultan,* 114; Ronald Segal, *Islam's Black Slaves: The Other Black Diaspora,* 52; John Laffin, *The Arabs as Master Slavers,* 17. See Sarga Moussa, "The Figure of the Eunuch in the Lettres persanes: Re-evaluation and Resistance," for the European sources of this observation, in Mary Ann Fay, *Slavery in the Islamic World.* On the strange relation between color terminology and categories of castration, see Gavin Hambly, "A Note on the Trade in Eunuchs in Mughal Bengal."

92. For an argument against the genealogical isolation of the eunuch, see Ehud Toledano, "Ottoman Elite Enslavement and 'Social Death,'" in John Bodel, *On Human Bondage: After Slavery and Social Death.*

93. Spillers, "Mama's Baby, Papa's Maybe," 67.

94. Peter Brooks intended the term "moral occult" as an analogy for the "unconscious mind" that the melodramatic genre taps into (*The Melodramatic Imagination,* 4–5), and describes pantomime as a primitive but constitutive phase of melodrama (14). On the relationship between pantomime and commedia dell'arte, see Szakolczai, *Comedy and the Public Sphere.*

95. On the distinction between *lūti* and *jāhil,* see Naficy, *A Social History of Iranian Cinema, Vol. 2,* 281–82 and Jāhid, *Directory of World Cinema,* 74. See also Kaveh Bassiri, "Masculinity in Iranian Cinema," in Howard Chiang et al., eds., *The Global Encyclopedia of Lesbian, Gay, Bisexual, Transgender, and Queer (LGBTQ) History,* 1018–23.

96. Minoo Moallem, "Aestheticizing Religion." See also Moallem, *Between Warrior Brother and Veiled Sister: Islamic Fundamentalism and the Politics of Patriarchy in Iran.* Meanwhile, the introduction and circulation of television into the Iranian economy ravaged the careers of *naqqāls,* while foregrounding audiovisual media as a new site of such technological, gendered configurations. Shāhrukh Gulistān, *Fānūs-i Khiyāl: Sarguzasht-i sīnimā-yi Īrān az āghāz tā pīrūzī-i Inqilāb-i islāmī, bih ravāyat-i bī. bī. sī,* 140.

« 254 » Notes to Chapter 1

97. Partovi, *Popular Iranian Cinema Before the Revolution*, 63.
98. They were unhappy with their romanticized representations, implying a misplacement in Ghafārī's attempt at an avant-gardist revision of the lumpenproletariat stereotype.
99. Umīd, *Tārīkh-i sīnamā-yi Īrān*, 308.
100. Ghafārī, "Interview with Akbar Etemad."
101. For female prostitution connoting a "blackness within" in early Hollywood maternal melodramas, see Mary Ann Doane, *Femmes Fatales: Feminism, Film Theory, Psychoanalysis*, 209–49.
102. The government had taken offense to Ghafārī's meticulously researched portrayals of poverty in the dilapidated South End. Having learned of recent Soviet attempts to stimulate procommunist sentiment through funding of political projects, they feared the film's participation in the arousal of class consciousness.
103. Gulistān, *Fānūs-i khiyāl*, 107.
104. Susan Gubar, *Racechanges: White Skin, Black Face in American Culture*, 170; Ed Guerrero, *Framing Blackness: The African-American Image in Film*, 123.
105. Frantz Fanon, *Black Skin, White Masks*, 53. Later wondering why anti-Semites kill but do not castrate the Jews they hate: "The Jew is killed or sterilized. The black man, however, is castrated. The penis, symbol of virility, is eliminated; in other words, it is denied" (140).
106. Piotr O. Scholz, *Eunuchs and Castrati: A Cultural History*, ix.
107. William D. Phillips Jr., *Slavery from Roman Times to the Early Transatlantic Trade*, 86; Kathryn M. Ringrose, *The Perfect Servant: Eunuchs and the Social Construction of Gender in Byzantium*.
108. Szakolczai, *Comedy and the Public Sphere*, 35.
109. Bleeker, "Navel Gazing as Critical Practice," in *Visuality in the Theater*, 89–90. On the idea that opposing forces keep the cinematic text from cohering, see Kristen Thompson, "The Concept of Cinematic Excess," in Philip Rosen, *Narrative, Apparatus, Ideology*.
110. As Claire Colebrook argues, transitivity and indifference precedes gender differentiation, and not the other way around. Claire Colebrook, "What Is It Like to Be a Human?" See also C. Riley Snorton, *Black on Both Sides: A Racial History of Trans Identity*, 5.
111. For more politically specific reasons, its contemporary practitioners lament *siyāh bāzī*'s impending demise. See Maryam Khakipour, *The Joymakers*.
112. Cedric Robinson suggests that the translation of blackface minstrelsy to the market of commodities saved the former from its impending obsolescence (*Forgeries of Memory and Meaning*, 136). Kenneth Goings estimates tens of thousands of such objects were produced and disseminated between the 1880s and late 1950s and

Notes to Chapter 1 « 255 »

argues that subtle changes in stereotypes reflected in black figurines correspond to shifting racial attitudes throughout the nineteenth- and twentieth-century United States (Goings, *Mammy and Uncle Mose*). On racial stereotypes in visual culture, see David Levinthal and Manthia Diawara, "The Blackface Stereotype"; Donald Bogle, *Toms, Coons, Mulattoes, Mammies & Bucks: An Interpretive History of Blacks in American Films*; James Snead, *White Screens/Black Images: Hollywood from the Dark Side*. On critiques of earlier studies of racial stereotypes, see Wahneema Lubiano, *Representing Blackness; Issues in Film and Video*.

113. Pidrām Laʾl Bakhsh, "Barrisī tatbīqī rīshah'hā, darūnmāyah'hā va kar kard'hāʾī sīyāh bazi Irānī va Amrikayi," 53.

114. Homay King, for example, has drawn a compelling connection between exotic mise-en scène and the circulation of Orientalist tropes in cinema. See Homay King, *Lost in Translation: Orientalism, Cinema, and the Enigmatic Signifer*.

115. James Tweedie, *The Age of New Waves: Art Cinema and the Staging of Globalization*, 46–83; Jim Hillier, *Cahiers du Cinéma: The 1950s, Neo-Realism, Hollywood, New Wave*, 1–21; Michel Mourlet, *Sur un art ignoré: La mise en scène comme langage*; Jacques Aumont, *Le cinéma et la mise en scène*.

116. Pamela Karimi, *Domesticity and Consumer Culture in Iran: Interior Revolutions of the Modern Era*, 12.

117. See Vaziri, "Slavery and the Virtual Archive: On Iran's Dash Ākul."

118. Zakiyyah Iman Jackson, *Becoming Human: Matter and Meaning in an Antiblack World*, 93. What would happen to our understanding of the human "if black women legitimately inhabited our world?," wonders Katherine McKittrick, in *Demonic Grounds: Black Women and the Cartographies of Struggle*, xxv.

119. Diane Roberts, *The Myth of Aunt Jemima: Representations of Race and Region*, 176. See also Maurice Manring, *Slave in a Box: The Strange Career of Aunt Jemima*. As Kenneth Goings points out, in white American imagery of blacks, "the emasculation of African-American males was part of a process that masculinized African-American women" (*Mammy and Uncle Mose*, xxi).

120. John Wright, *The Trans-Saharan Slave Trade*, 29; Ronald Segal, *Islam's Black Slaves*, 4. Though this trend was not consistent over time, with the ratio reversing in favor of males in the case of the Arabian coast in the late nineteenth century. Matthew Hopper, "Slavery, Family Life, and the African Diaspora in the Arabian Gulf, 1880–1940," 174. For Iran, from the Safavid to the Qajar periods, "a perpetual imbalance" in the gender ratio favored female slaves (Janet Afary, *Sexual Politics in Modern Iran*, 55–56). Gwyn Campbell argues female slaves were the "major victims" of "non-Western bondage."

« 256 »   Notes to Chapter 1

Campbell, "Female Bondage and Agency in the Indian Ocean World," in Toledano, *African Communities in Asia,* 38.

121. Amy Motlagh, *Burying the Beloved: Marriage, Realism, and Reform in Modern Iran,* 59–93.

122. Maziar Shirazi, "A Review of Tarabnameh, or, Why Are Iranian-Americans Laughing at Blackface in 2016?"

123. Umīd, *Tārīkh-i sīnamā-yi Īrān,* 335.

124. Ali Gholipoor, "Photographic Documentation of Ta'zieh and Taqlid," 14.

125. Charles Baudelaire, *De L'essence du Rire.*

126. Hornback, *Racism and Early Blackface Comic Traditions,* 36.

127. Or, for example, Hikayat forty of Sa'dī's thirteenth-century *Gulistān,* in which a king presents his Chinese slave girl (*kanīzakī chīnī*) to a "black" (*sīyāh*), and then disavows the girl after she has slept with the *sīyāhī,* because "the thirsty does not wish for limpid water / which has been touched by a rotten mouth" (tishnah rāh dil nakhāhad āb-i zalāl/ nīm khūrd dahān-i gandīdah).

128. Bihrūz Gharībpūr, *Ti'ātr dar Īrān,* 53.

129. Unlike *tashabuh,* for example, which has a similar meaning. For a reading of their difference, see Ali Gholipoor, "Photographic Documentation of Ta'zieh and Taqlid," 5–41.

130. Plato, *The Republic,* 604e, my emphasis.

131. Samuel Weber, *Theatricality as Medium,* 38.

132. Jorge Luis Borges, "Partial Magic in the Quixote," 195–96.

133. Jacques Lacan and Jacques-Alain Miller, *The Psychoses: The Seminar of Jacques Lacan Book III 1955–1956,* 154. Lacan reads Freud's dream of Irma's injection, specifically the infamous image in which he peers down her throat, as an ultimate confrontation with flesh, with "the other side of the head . . . at the very heart of the mystery."

134. Dionne Brand, *A Map to the Door of No Return,* 45, 39.

135. Henri Bergson: "And why does one laugh at a negro? . . . the notion of disguise has passed on something of its comic quality to instances in which there is actually no disguise" (*Laughter,* 41).

136. Derrida, "Resistances," 11.

2. *ZĀR* AND THE ANXIETIES OF THE IRANIAN NEW WAVE

1. See, for example, Christina Sharpe, *In the Wake: On Blackness and Being,* 21.

2. The Persian term for "wind-afflicted" refers to all the individuals that belong to a *zār* community and have established life-long relationships with the winds. The ambiguity caused by the lack of a differentiation between the singular and plural in *ahl-i havā* will be clarified by context.

Notes to Chapter 2 « 257 »

3. Periodized roughly between 1969 through 1979. These films, like much of the literature of the time period, were critical of the social conditions promulgated by the Pahlavi regime's domestic modernization policies, even as they were informed stylistically by modernist forms of cinema abroad.

4. Muhammad Tahāmī-nijād, "Insān shināsī başarī dar sīnamāyi mustanad-i Īran, 'āmil shinakht ya mawzu'yi shinākht"; Ghulām Riżā Jalālī, "Buḥrān-i m'arafatī dar sīnamāyi millī-i Īrān," 220.

5. Farukhzād (1935–67) is commemorated as one of Iran's preeminent poets of the twentieth century.

6. Humayūn Imāmī, *Sīnimā-yi mardum shinakhtī-i Īran.*

7. See Dominic Parviz Brookshaw and Nasrin Rahimieh, eds. *Forugh Farrokhzad, Poet of Modern Iran: Iconic Woman and Feminine Pioneer of New Persian Poetry,* and, for a more ideologically oriented critique, Hamid Dabashi, *Masters and Masterpieces of Iranian Cinema.*

8. Hamid Dabashi, "The Poetics of Politics: Commitment in Modern Persian Literature," 155.

9. An earlier tradition of ethnography heralded by foreign anthropologists popularized the study of nomadic tribes. The American filmmakers Merian Cooper, Ernst Schoedsack, and Marguerite Harrison filmed the nomadic Bakhtiari tribe in the 1920s in their film *Grass*— one of the first ethnographic films made in Iran, and often cited by anthropologists as an archetype of the ethnographic film genre.

10. Mohammad A. Issari, *Cinema in Iran: 1900–1979,* 164–93. Close relatives of both the shah and his wife Farah headed both the Ministry of Culture and Arts and National Iranian Radio and Television, ensuring tight political surveillance. See Hamid Naficy, *A Social History of Iranian Cinema: Vol. 2: The Industrializing Years, 1941–1978,* 69.

11. As George Stocking notes, historically ethnography and anthropology have been used in non-European contexts in the service of nationalism. Stocking, "Afterword, a View from the Center."

12. Stephanie Cronin, *Tribal Politics in Iran: Rural Conflict and the New State, 1921–1941.*

13. The fact that the very earliest films were ethnographic works lends further support to this claim. In literature, the relationship between the development of anthropology and the ascendency of modernism (particularly with regard to surrealism) has been amply explored. For a well-known example, see James Clifford, "On Ethnographic Surrealism." More recent studies on this moment reflect upon the very boundedness of present genre distinctions, asking how the once less rigidly defined fields of literature and anthropology informed each other in the late nineteenth and early twentieth century. See Paul Peppis, *Sciences of Modernism: Ethnography, Sexology, and Psychology.* Many film scholars and visual anthropologists go so far as to

« 258 »   Notes to Chapter 2

claim that the cinema was invented for anthropological purposes, that is, to observe the physical behavior of humans. See David Mac-Dougall, "Beyond Observational Cinema." Lumière's earliest short films, for example, featured Ashanti women and children engaging in daily activities, while Edison's earliest studies pictured Native Americans, African American dancers, Kanakan divers, and Hopi snake dancers. See Assenka Oksiloff, *Picturing the Primitive: Visual Culture, Ethnography, and Early German Cinema.* See also Fatimah Tobing Rony, *The Third Eye: Race, Cinema, and Ethnographic Spectacle.*

14. Catherine Russel, *Experimental Ethnography: The Work of Film in the Age of Video,* 194. In practice, the alienation of a less figural, more literal Other has always lent material substance to this fantasy. David Marriott, "Response to Race and the Poetic Avant-Garde."

15. At the same time as he is romanticized, the salvage paradigm turns the salvaged back against himself. Eric Santner, *Stranded Objects: Mourning, Memory, and Film in Postwar Germany,* 86. See also George E. Marcus, "Contemporary Problems of Ethnography in the Modern World System."

16. Ghulām Ḥusayn Sā'idī, *Ahl-i Havā,* 5.

17. Fahimeh Mianji and Yousef Semnani, "Zār Spirit Possession in Iran and African Countries: Group Distress, Culture-Bound Syndrome, or Cultural Concept of Distress?"

18. Tiziana Battain, "Osservazioni sul rito *Zār* di possessione degli spiriti in Yemen," 118.

19. Anita Adam, "A Saar Gaamuri in Somalia: Spirit Possession as Expression of Women's Autonomy?," 195.

20. Yael Kahana, "The Zar Spirits, A Category of Magic in the System of Mental Health Care in Ethiopia."

21. Hager El Hadidi, *Zar: Spirit Possession, Music, and Healing Rituals in Egypt,* 2.

22. Pier Paulo Pasolini, "Observations on the Long Take," 4.

23. On the problem of filmic truth, Feraydūn Rahnamāh's own dissertation on film reveals important transactions between French film theory and Persian discourse on film. Feraydūn Rahnamāh and Faridah Rahnamāh, *Vāqi'iyat girāyī-i film.* See also, André Bazin, *What Is Cinema? Vol. 1.* Neorealism serves as a primary model for Bazin's valorization of the long take and disdain for montage.

24. Hamid Naficy, *Fīlm-i mustanad, vol. 2, tarīkh-i sīnamā-yi mustanad,* 325. Simon Gikandi, "Africa and the Epiphany of Modernism."

25. Ghulām Ḥaydarī, ed. *Mu'arrifī va shinākht-i Nāṣir Taqvā'i,* 204.

26. At the same time, although Taqvā'i's choice of a famous poet to narrate the film imbues the ethnographic content of the film with reflexivity, in another sense, the documentary is completely aligned with the

Notes to Chapter 2　　《 259 》

state-ordained mandates of the period that ethnographic films appoint for voiceover narration a "'person with a recognizable high-class or good Persian accent,' not a person with a minority accent" (Naficy, *A Social History of Iranian Cinema, Volume 2*, 73).

27. Javād Mujābī, "Successful but Short," in Ḥaydarī, *Muʿarrifī va Shinākht*, 145.

28. Naficy, *A Social History of Iranian Cinema, Volume 2*, 246. See also Lalitha Gopalan, *Cinema of Interruptions: Action Genres in Contemporary Indian Cinema*.

29. Manīzhih Maqsūdī, "Bādhā-yi kāfir va duhul-i sih sar dar khalīj-i Fārs: marāsim-i āyīnī-i darmānī-i zār," *Pazhūhishhayih insān shināsī-i Īrān*, 131; El-Hadidi, *Zar*, 39.

30. Aisha Bilkhair Khalifa, "Spirit Possession and Its Practices in Dubai," 53.

31. William O. Beeman, "Understanding the Zār: An African-Iranian Healing Dance Ritual," 73. Bilkhair Khalifa, "Spirit Possession," 53.

32. Muhammad Tahāmī-nijād, "Insān shināsī baṣarī dar sīnamāyi mustanad-i Īran, ʿamil-i shinākht ya mawẓūʿ shinākht."

33. The list of collaborations between New Wave directors and modernist authors is endless. For instance, Davūd Mulāpūr's *Ahu's Husband* (1966) was based on a story by the same name written by the novelist ʿAlī Muhamad Afghānī; the New Wave film script for Dāryūsh Mihrjūyī's *Cow* (1969) was based off of a short story from Ghulām Husayn Sāʿidī' s *Mourners of Bayal*; Bahman Farmānārā's *Prince Ehtejab* (1974) and his *The Tall Shadows of the Wind* (1978) were both based on stories by the modern novelist Hūshang Golshīrī; Masʿūd Kīmiyāʾī's *Dash Akol* (1974) was based on a short story by the same name by Sādiq Hidāyat; Kīmiyāʾī's *Earth* (1973) was based on a story by contemporary author Mahmūd Dawlatʿābādī; Amīr Nādirī's *Tangsir* (1973) was written by modern author Sādiq Chūbak, etc.

34. Bernard Freamon, "Straight, No Chaser: Slavery, Abolition, and Modern Islamic Thought," in Harms, Blight, and Freamon, eds., *Indian Ocean Slavery*, 62.

35. For slavery as an enduring theory of relation, see João H. Costa Vargas, *The Denial of Antiblackness: Multiracial Redemption and Black Suffering*.

36. "The Period of Trances" in Maurice Nadeau, *History of Surrealism*. Though it is often assumed that surrealism was cultivated primarily in Europe, Nadeau emphasizes that no artistic movement previous to surrealism shared its international scope, and that it was in fact surrealism's burgeoning life in Asia and Africa that sustained its life as one of the most significant movements of the twentieth century.

37. Nicole Echard, "The Hausa *Bori* Possession Cult in the Ader Region of Niger: Its Origins and Present-Day Function." *Zār-bori* is often invoked in studies of the ritual in African contexts, *bori* constituting a related but

« 260 »   Notes to Chapter 2

distinct phenomenon prevalent in West Africa. See also Ismael M. Montana, "Bori Practice among Enslaved West Africans of Ottoman Tunis: Unbelief (Kufr) or another Dimension of the African Diaspora?."

38. Maria Sabaye Moghaddam, *Zār dar Īrān va kishvarhā-yi dīgar*, 21; El Hadidi, *Zar*, 52.

39. The "remedy for winds are not drugs and shots," but *duhul* (Sāʻidī, *Ahl-i Havā*, 32).

40. Adam, "A Saar Gaamuri in Somalia," 193.

41. Iraj Bashiri, "Muslims or Shamans," 5, 6. Prochazka and Gharedaghi-Kloucheh refer to the bamboo as *asā* (cane). See Stephan Prochazka and Bahram Gharedaghi-Kloucheh, "The Zār Cult in the Shatt al-ʻArab/Arvand Region."

42. Kahana, "The Zar Spirits," 136.

43. Bilkhair Khalifa, "Spirit Possession and Its Practices in Dubai," 60.

44. Taghi Modarressi, "The Zar Cult in South Iran," 155; Beeman, "Understanding the Zār: An African-Iranian Healing Dance Ritual," 76.

45. Maho Sebiane, "Entre l'Afrique et l'Arabie: les esprits de possession sawahili et leurs frontières." See also Shihan de Silva Jayasuriya, *Sounds of Identity: The Music of Afro-Asians*, xiv–xv.

46. Ḥaydarī, *Muʻarrifī va naqd*, 203.

47. Muḥamad Chahārmahalī, *Malakūt; nuqtiyi atf-i rīʾālism-i jādūyī-i dar Īrān*, 78.

48. Raymond Prince, ed. *Trance and Possession States*, 36; Jean Rouch, *Cine-Ethnography*, 88.

49. Rasmus Christian Elling, *Minorities in Iran: Nationalism and Ethnicity after Khomeini*, 22.

50. Parisa Vaziri, "No One's Memory: Blackness at the Limits of Comparative Slavery." Historiography turns slavery into a problem that can be "solved through the progressive, sequential manipulation of data." Hortense Spillers, "Peter's Pans: Eating in the Diaspora," in *Black, White, and in Color*, 19.

51. Bahman Shujāʾīnasab, "Naqsh-i iqtisādī-i Bandar Lingih dar hawẓih-ʻi -ʻi khalīj-i Fārs," 25–34.

52. See for example, Linda Nochlin, "The Imaginary Orient," 33–59.

53. Fred Moten, "The Case of Blackness," 186.

54. El Hadidi, *Zar*, 43, 47; Martin Zillinger, "Absence and the Mediation of the Audiovisual Unconscious," 83.

55. El Hadidi, *Zar*, 39.

56. A participant reports in reference to the stambeli ritual. Eli Somer and Meir Saadon, "Stambali: Dissociative Possession and Trance in a Tunisian Healing Dance," 590.

57. Bashiri, "Muslims or Shamans," 7.

58. William Gervase Clarence-Smith, *Islam and the Abolition of Slavery*, 98; Matthew S. Hopper, *Slaves of One Master: Globalization and Slavery in*

Arabia in the Age of Empire, 7; Guillemette Crouzet, "A Golden Harvest: exploitation et mondialisation des perles du golfe Arabo-Persique (vers 1870–vers 1910)," 329; Jerzy Zdanowski, *Slavery and Manumission: British Policy in the Red Sea and the Persian Gulf in the First Half of the 20th Century*; Behnaz Mirzai, "The 1848 Abolitionist Farmān: A Step towards Ending the Slave Trade in Iran," in Gwyn Campbell, *Abolition and its Aftermath,* 94–102. See also Claude Markovits, Jacques Pouchepadass, and Sanjay Subrahmanyam, *Society and Circulation: Mobile People and Itinerant Cultures in South Asia, 1750–1950.*

59. Frederick Cooper, *Plantation Slavery on the East Coast of Africa;* Cooper, *From Slaves to Squatters: Plantation Labor and Agriculture in Zanzibar and Coastal Kenya, 1890–1925;* Abdul Sheriff, *Slaves, Spices & Ivory in Zanzibar: Integration of an East African Commercial Empire into the World Economy, 1770–1973;* Edward Alpers, *Ivory and Slaves: Changing Pattern of International Trade in East Central Africa to the Later Nineteenth Century;* Jonathon Glassman, *Feasts and Riot: Revelry, Rebellion, and Popular Consciousness on the Swahili Coast, 1856–1888.*

60. Hopper, *Slaves of One Master,* 6.

61. Guillemette Crouzet, "A Golden Harvest," 313, 343; Nelida Fuccaro, *Histories of City and State in the Persian Gulf,* 43–72; Pedro Machado, Steve Mullins, and Joseph Christensen, eds., *Pearls, People, and Power: Pearling and Indian Ocean Worlds.*

62. Robert Harms, Bernard K. Freamon, and David W. Blight, eds., *Indian Ocean Slavery in the Age of Abolition,* 224–25.

63. Clarence-Smith, *Islam and the Abolition of Slavery,* 9.

64. W. E. B. Du Bois, *The World and Africa: An Inquiry into the Part Which Africa Has Played in World History,* 71.

65. Barbara L. Solow. "Capitalism and Slavery in the Exceedingly Long Run," 712; Maurice Lombard, *The Golden Age of Islam,* 167; William D. Phillips Jr., "Sugar in Iberia," 299, and *Slavery from Roman Times to the Early Transatlantic Trade,* 68.

66. Paul Popenoe and Henry Field, *The Date Palm,* 5. On the idiosyncratic temporality of unfree labor in the Indian Ocean, see Alessandro Stanziani, *Sailors, Slaves, and Immigrants: Bondage in the Indian Ocean World, 1750–1914,* 1–13.

67. Ute Hall, "Trance Techniques, Cinema, and Cybernetics," in *Trance Mediums and New Media,* 278; Maya Deren, "Creative Cutting," 204; Catherine Russell, *Experimental Ethnography: The Work of Film in the Age of Video,* 220; Gilberto Perez, *The Material Ghost: Films and Their Medium,* 39.

68. Marshall McLuhan, *Understanding Media: The Extensions of Man,* 56.

69. Girdhari L. Tikku and Alireza Anushiravani, *A Conversation with Modern Persian Poets,* 16.

« 262 »   Notes to Chapter 2

70. "Where Gilroy recovers the most wretched of subaltern histories," Shanti Moorthy and Ashraf Jamal write in their 2010 volume on Indian Ocean studies, referring to Paul Gilroy's well-known intervention in the triumphalist narrative of Euro-American exchange across the Atlantic, "Indian Ocean studies reveals . . . 'subaltern cosmopolitanism.'" Shanti Moorthy and Ashraf Jamal, eds. *Indian Ocean Studies: Cultural, Social, and Political Perspectives*, 2. For a critique of Indian Ocean cosmopolitanism, see Edward Simpson and Kai Kresse, *Struggling with History: Islam and Cosmopolitanism in the Western Indian Ocean*, 13–15.

71. Omar H. Ali, *Islam in the Indian Ocean: A Brief History with Documents*, 14; Matthew Hopper, "The African Presence in Eastern Arabia," 329.

72. On an analysis of the concepts through which Frantz Fanon articulated blackness as a future tense, see David Marriott, *Whither Fanon? Studies in the Blackness of Being*.

73. Popenoe and Field, *The Date Palm*, 5.

74. Kaveh Safa, "Reading Saedi's Ahl-e Hava: Pattern and Significance in Spirit Possession Beliefs on the Southern Coasts of Iran," 92.

75. Mianji and Semnani, "Zār Spirit Possession in Iran," 229.

76. Lisa Urkevich, "Incoming Arts: African and Persian," 149.

77. Bashiri, "Muslims," 9; Bilkhair Khalifa, "Spirit Possession," 59.

78. Muḥamad Chahārmahalī, *Malakūt: nuqtiyi atf-i rī'ālism-i jādūyi-i Īran*, 77.

79. Leïla Babès, "Folie douce, vent des ancêtres: la trance au Maghreb," 464.

80. Manīzhih Maqsūdī, "Bādhā-yi kāfir va duhul-i sih sar dar khalīj-i Fārs: marāsim-i āyīnī-i darmānī-i zār," 101–35. Similarly, Susan Kenyon argues "zar acts as a mnemonic version of past events and memories" (*Spirits and Slaves in Central Sudan: The Red Wind of Sennar*, 9.)

81. Matthew Hopper, *Slaves of One Master*, 65–67.

82. Fritz W. Kramer, *The Red Fez: Art and Spirit Possession in Africa*, 65-69.

83. Jean During, "African Winds and Muslim Djinns: Trance, Healing, and Devotion in Baluchistan," 40, 54. On Africans' understanding of slavery as cannibalistic, see Stephen Palmié, *Wizards and Scientists: Explorations in Afro-Cuban Modernity and Tradition*, 168–70.

84. Parviz Jahid, *Directory of World Cinema: Iran*, 85.

85. Golbarg Rekabtalaei, *Iranian Cosmopolitanism: A Cinematic History*, 245–47.

86. Jason Bahbak Mohaghegh, *Insurgent, Poet, Mystic, Sectarian: The Four Masks of an Eastern Postmodernism*, 213.

87. James Tweedie, *The Age of New Waves: Art Cinema and the Staging of Globalization*, 2; Robert Phillip Kolker, *The Altering Eye: Contempo-*

Notes to Chapter 2 « 263 »

rary International Cinema, 89–197; András Bálint Kovács, *Screening Modernism: European Art Cinema, 1950–1980*.

88. Afshin Matin-Asgari, *Both Eastern and Western: An Intellectual History of Iranian Modernity*, 190; Jamsheed Akrami, "The Blighted Spring: Iranian Cinema and Politics in the 1970s," in *Film and Politics in the Third World*, 132.

89. Saʿīd Nūrī suggests spatial difference exemplifies the split between generations. Saʿīd Nūrī, "Khānah dar fīlmhāyi Nāṣir Taqvāʿī," 53.

90. Mohaghegh, *Insurgent*, 214.

91. G. R. Sabri-Tabrizi, "Gholam-Hoseyn Saʿedi: A Voice for the Poor," 12.

92. Cyrus Schayegh, *Who Is Knowledgeable, Is Strong: Science, Class, and the Formation of Modern Iranian Society: 1900–1950*, 78. Friedrich Kittler, "The City is a Medium," in *The Truth of the Technological World: Essays on the Genealogy of Presence*, 138–51.

93. For sex in 1970s Iranian cinema, see Blake Atwood, "When the Sun Goes Down: Sex, Desire and Cinema in 1970s Tehran."

94. Geneviève Sellier, *La Nouvelle Vague: Un Cinéma au Masculin Singulier*.

95. Sara Saljoughi, "Political Cinema, Revolution, and Failure: The Iranian New Wave, 1962–79," 365.

96. Nādia Maqūlī, "Taḥlīl-i jāmiʿih shinākhtī-i mafhūm-i marg dar mūj-i naw," 139; Hamid Reza Sadr, *Iranian Cinema: A Political History*, 137.

97. Ḥaydarī, *Muʿarrifī va naqd*, 207.

98. Hamid Naficy, *A Social History of Iranian Cinema, Volume 2*, 370; Jamāl Umīd, *Tārīkh-i sīnamā-yi Īrān*, 643.

99. Ḥaydarī, *Muʿarrifī va naqd*, 203.

100. Ḥaydarī, *Muʿarrifī va shinākht*, 37.

101. Sāʿidī, *Ahl-i Havā*, 22.

102. Though such genre distinctions are necessarily unstable. Sāmū'il Khāchikiyān is one of the few directors whose films are described as "noir," but also, at other times, "action" or "thriller" films. Thus, a film festival in Bologna curated by Ehsan Khoshbakht in 2017 was entitled "Tehran Noir: The Thrillers of Samuel Khachikian." Hamid Naficy sometimes describes noir as a subgenre of the "stewpot" film, which is itself described as a subgenre of *fīlmfārsī* (Naficy, *A Social History of Iranian Cinema, Volume 2*, 305).

103. Hamid Reza Sadr, *Iranian Cinema*, 136.

104. Liora Hendelman-Baavur, *Creating the Modern Iranian Woman: Popular Culture between Two Revolutions*, 155.

105. Eldad J. Pardo, "Iranian Cinema, 1968–1978: Female Characters and Social Dilemmas on the Eve of the Revolution," 30.

106. Afsaneh Najmabadi, *Women with Mustaches and Men without Beards*, 105, 111.

« 264 » Notes to Chapter 2

107. Umīd, *Tārīkh-i sīnamā-yi Īrān*, 646.
108. Muhsin Sayf, "Āhistah va amīgh birān," 50.
109. Jahid, *Directory of World Cinema*, 105. Like virtually all of Taqvā'ī's ethnographic films, which were sponsored by National Iranian Radio and Television, *Tranquility* was produced by Telfilm, the institution's production arm. Just as Taqvā'ī's ethnographic work and his urban-centered *Tranquility* display two polarized versions of modernity—desolate Bandar Lingih and cosmopolitan Tehran—thus cementing the picture of a "squalid and disintegrating society," the National Iranian Radio and Television's programming channeled the heightening gulf in wealth in the 1970s, leading to "mixed sentiments, envy and outrage" among viewing publics. Pardo, "Iranian Cinema, 1968–1978," 43; Sadr, *Iranian Cinema*, 159.
110. Ali Mirsepassi and Mehdi Faraji, "Iranian Cinema's 'Quiet Revolution,' 1960–1978," 411; Saljoughi, "Political Cinema, Revolution, and Failure," 395.
111. Ghulām Rizā Jalālī, "Buḥrān-i m'arifatī dar sīnamāyi milī-i Īrān," 220.
112. Husayn Sulṭānmuhammadi, "Ruydād," 185.
113. Muhammad Tahāmī-nijād, "Insān shināsī baṣarī dar sīnamāyi mustanad-i Īran."
114. Muhamad Rizā Ṣālihī Māzandarānī and Nasrīn Gabanchī, "Naqd-i ravānkāvaneh-yi bāvarhā va kunishhāyi 'āmīyanih dar majmu'i-'ih dāstān-i azādārān-i bayal-i Ghulām Husayn Sā'idī," 44.
115. Ṣālihī and Gabanchī, "Naqd-i ravānkāvaneh," 44.
116. Rivanne Sandler, "Literary Developments in Iran in the 1960s and the 1970s Prior to the 1978 Revolution," 248.
117. Ṣālihī and Gabanchī, "Naqd-i ravānkāvaneh," 47.
118. Hasan Banīhāshimī, qtd. in Umīd, *Tarikh-i sinama-yi Iran*, 644.
119. Vandād Jalālī, "Az *Bād-i Jin* tā nārinjī pūsh yā arzyābī-i intiqādī-i khat mūsīqī dar sīnamā-yi Īrān," 141.
120. Maria Moghaddam, "Zār Beliefs and Practices in Bandar Abbâs and Qeshm Island in Iran," 24.
121. Catherine Russell, *Experimental Ethnography: The Work of Film in the Age of Video*, 14.
122. Naficy, "Iranian Cinema," in *Companion Encyclopedia of Middle Eastern and North African Film*, 213.
123. Sigmund Freud, quoted in Derrida, *Writing and Difference*, 210.
124. According to Ali Issari, *Tranquility*'s banning deprived it of the opportunity to achieve a level of fame analogous to the most famous New Wave film about madness, Dāryūsh Mihrjūyī's *Cow*. Issari, *Cinema in Iran*, 216; Naficy, "Iranian Cinema," 212.
125. Judith Becker, *Deep Listeners: Music, Emotion, and Trancing*, 25.
126. Nematollah Fazeli, *Politics of Culture in Iran: Anthropology, Politics, and Society in the Twentieth Century*, 67. On the relationship

Notes to Chapter 2 « 265 »

between the aesthetic and the anthropological see Nasser Fakouhi, "Making and Remaking an Academic Tradition: Towards an Indigenous Anthropology in Iran," in Shahnaz R. Nadjmabadi, ed., *Conceptualizing Iranian Anthropology*.

127. Mohamad Tavakoli-Targhi, "Narrative Identity in the Works of Hedayat and His Contemporaries."

128. Sādiq Hidāyat, "Fuklur yā farhang-i tūdeh," in *Farhang-i āmīyānah-yi mardum-i Īran*, 234.

129. Qtd. in Leonardo P. Alishan, "Ahmad Shamlu: The Rebel Poet in Search of an Audience," 375.

130. Thus, what is sometimes referred to as the Persian anticipation of Said's *Orientalism*, Jalāl al-i Ahmad's *Westtoxification* (*Qarbzadigī*, 1962), took inspiration from al-i Ahmad's ethnographic writings, *Awrazān* and *Jazīri-'i Kharg*. While Jalāl al-i Ahmad's reputation as one of the most provocative thinkers of the 1960s is well known, it is often less appreciated that his ethnographic works earned al-i Ahmad a reputation as an ethnographer; his ethnographic works in turn influenced al-i Ahmad's fiction. Fazeli, *Politics of Culture*, 114; Menahem Merhavi, "'True Muslims Must Always Be Tidy and Clean': Exoticism of the Countryside in Late Pahlavi Iran," in Meir Litvak, ed., *Constructing Nationalism*, 164.

131. Sabri-Tabrizi, "Gholam-Hoseyn Sa'edi," 11.

132. Ghulām Husayn Sā'idī, "An Autobiographical Sketch," 253.

133. Haydarī, *Mu'arrifī va naqd*, 5.

134. Nasrin Rahimieh, "Four Iterations of Persian Literary Nationalism," in Meir Litvak, ed., *Constructing Nationalism in Iran*, 44.

135. Haydarī, *Mu'arrifī va naqd*, 46.

136. Haydarī, *Mu'arrifī va naqd*, 202.

137. Sultānmuhammadi, "Ruydād," 185.

138. Hamīd Abdulāhīyān, "Bāznamāyī-i marāsim-i ahl-i havā dar film-i mustanad-i *Bād-i Jīn*," 306.

139. "The films I made about the traditional livelihoods of the people were meant to produce knowledge and familiarity with this wonderful society." If the Censorship Bureau foreclosed distribution of his films in Iran, he lamented, why wouldn't they at least allow the films to flourish outside the country? Abdulāhīyān, "Bāznamāyī-i marāsim-i ahl-i havā," 200.

140. Hopper, *Slaves of One Master*, 54.

141. Sā'idī, *Ahl-i Havā*, 10.

142. Narrates Sā'idī of the village of Kalāt, "a man with a white beard said to an old black man who was sitting near us, 'He's from the jungle, like an animal'. The black man replied 'Yes, I'm from the jungle, like an animal', and laughed." And "during a circumcision gathering, a few black fishermen were standing nearby watching, and a peddler

« 266 »   Notes to Chapter 2

pointed to them and said, 'They are cows.' And the blacks nodded" (Sāʿidī, *Ahl-i Havā*, 6–7).

143. Ghulām Ḥusayn Sāʿidī, *Fear and Trembling*, 12.

144. Mehdī Jāmī, *Mā va Mudirnīyat: Guft ū gū ba Daryūsh Āshūrī*, 22.

3. IRANO-AFRO-IRAN

1. Younes Saramifar, "Circling Around the Really Real in Iran: Ethnography of Muharram Laments among Shiʿi Volunteer Militants in the Middle East," 79.

2. In his study of the historical evolution of the rituals, Ali Hussain recovers a curious developmental chronology, where the celebration of Husayn's death forty days postmortem (*arbaʿīn*), in fact forms the ground for what are thought to be more central elements of the Muharram rituals, like Taʾzīyah. Ali J. Hussain, "The Mourning of History and the History of Mourning: The Evolution of Ritual Commemoration of the Battle of Karbala," 80.

3. Frank Korom, *Hosay Trinidad: Muharram Performances in an Indo-Carribean Diaspora*, 17.

4. It is believed that after the Battle of Karbala, Husayn's family was robbed of their belongings; thus, like the ribbons strewn over Bakhshū, observers donate cloth to the *shaddeh*, the uppermost pole extending from a large wooden lattice called *nakhl*.

5. For the centrality of women to Muharram, see Kamran Scot Aghaie, *The Women of Karbala: Ritual Performance and Symbolic Discourses in Modern Shiʿi Islam*; Karen G. Ruffle, *Gender, Sainthood, and Everyday Practice in South Asian Shiʿism*; Pedram Khosronejad, ed. *Women's Rituals and Ceremonies in Shiite Iran and Muslim Communities*; David Pinault, *Horse of Karbala: Muslim Devotional Life in India*, 57–87.

6. Alexis Wick, *The Red Sea: In Search of Lost Space*, 30; John Meloy, *Imperial Power and Maritime Trade: Mecca and Cairo in the Later Middle Ages*, 45.

7. According to Muḥsin Sharīfīyān's account the screening of Taqvāʾī's *Arbaʿīn* was pivotal for the history of *nūhah-khūnī* in Iran (*Ahl-i mātam*, 179). More than any other tradition Būshihrī *arbaʾīn* has influenced the collective mourning culture of Iran; near identical rituals prevail in two other southern provinces: Khūzistān and Hurmuzgān.

8. For a reading of the cinematic interval as an impossible space of liberation, see Kara Keeling, "'In the Interval': Frantz Fanon and the 'Problems' of Visual Representation": "Liberation, if there is such a thing, is possible in the interval as a present impossibility, an expansion that explodes even the interval in which we wait" (110). See also David Marriott, "Waiting to Fall."

Notes to Chapter 3 « 267 »

9. Until recently, Pahlavi nationalism was viewed as unequivocally anti-Islamic, but a number of scholars have overturned this assumption. See for example Farzin Vejdani, "The Place of Islam in Interwar Iranian Nationalist Historiography." Nationalist historiography, which was, with exceptions, the only Iranian historiography that existed through the 1979 Revolution, largely framed Iran's relationship to Islam as one of "forced miscegenation" with a Semitic Other. On the ideological underpinnings of twentieth-century Iranian historiography, see Abbas Amanat, "The Study of History in Post-Revolutionary Iran: Nostalgia, Illusion, or Historical Awareness?," 67–82. On the framing of Islam as an Arab invasion, see Zia-Ebrahimi, *The Emergence of Persian Nationalism*, 114.

10. The collapse of distinction between religion and tradition and usual intellectual focus on religious content vis-à-vis form forecloses insights into the ways in which religion's alignment with modernity bears implications for the concept of the political in general. See Ali Mirsepassi, *Political Islam, Iran, and the Enlightenment: Philosophies of Hope and Despair*.

11. For the importance of *tamadun* as an organizing principle of history, see Vejdani, "The Place of Islam in Interwar Nationalist Historiography," in Kamran Scot Aghaie and Afshin Marashi, eds., *Rethinking Iranian Nationalism and Modernity*, 211.

12. Thus, when syncretic forms are affirmed, it is usually because the valorization of purity has been substituted for the valorization of authenticity and uniqueness. Rosalind Shaw and Charles Stewart, "Introduction: Problematizing Syncretism," in *Syncretism/Anti-Syncretism*, 7.

13. For blackness as an exemplary figure for the problematization of historical process, rather than a simple identity that can be "related" to another identity, see Nahum Dmitri Chandler, "Of Exorbitance: The Problem of the Negro as a Problem for Thought," in *X: The Problem of the Negro as a Problem for Thought*.

14. Syncretism is often associated with religious amalgamation in Christian contexts, but has also come to refer more generally to interactions and intermixture in religious practice and belief. I use the term in the broadest sense possible, as a loose synonym for hybridity, mixedness, and other models of amalgamation. See Ross Kane, *Syncretism and Christian Tradition: Race and Revelation in the Study of Religious Mixture*; Mika Vähäkangas and Patrik Fridlund, *Philosophical and Theological Responses to Syncretism: Beyond the Mirage of Pure Religion*; Anita Maria Leopold and Jeppe Sinding Jensen, *Syncretism in Religion: A Reader*. See also Charles Stewart and Rosalind Shaw, *Syncretism/Anti-Syncretism: The Politics of Religious Synthesis*.

15. See Stephen Palmié, "Against Syncretism," in Richard Fardon, ed.,

« 268 »   Notes to Chapter 3

Counterworks, and *The Cooking of History: How Not to Study Afro-Cuban Religion.*

16. And in as much as there is no rigorous, scientific concept of the concept, race, like religion, like the political, is itself a syncretic category, drawing from various discursive formations and histories.

17. Amiri Baraka's *Blues People* remains one of the most original studies of this kind detailing the complex and rich history of black music, its transfigurations of contrapuntality, ellipsis, obliquity, antiphonality, and the contradictions of jovial black sound. In a more contemporary continuation of this tradition, Fred Moten's writing on the originary sound of Aunt Hester's screams in the *Narrative of the Life of Frederick Douglass* guides Moten's moving meditations on the exemplary nature of historical transmission in black music. The trace or echo of the slave's suffering—in works of jazz, for example (Abby Lincoln and Max Roach's "Protest" serves vividly his point)—deprives the listener of a tenable, stable distinction between pleasure and terror, bearing implications for commonplace thinking about reproduction and reproducibility. Fred Moten, *In the Break: Aesthetics of the Black Radical Tradition.*

18. Allan P. Merriam, *The Anthropology of Music.*

19. In an in-depth description of instruments in the history of Persian music, for example, there is only mention of the *damāmah,* but not *damām.* Rūḥangīz Rāhgānī, *Tārīkh-i mūsīqī-yi Īrān.* See also Roger Blench, "Using Diverse Sources of Evidence for Reconstructing the Past History of Musical Exchanges in the Indian Ocean," 678.

20. Muḥsin Sharīfīyān, *Ahl-i mātam: āvā'hā va āyīn-i ṣūgvārī dar Būshihr,* 91.

21. John Mowitt, *Percussion: Drumming, Beating, Striking,* 6.

22. Roland Barthes, "Ecoute," in *L'obvie et l'obtus.*

23. Humayūn Imāmī, "Ta'mmulī dar tajalī-'i maẕhab dar sīnamā-yi mustanad-i Īrān," 205–11.

24. Common to most Muharram cultures in regions with a palpable Shi'i presence (Iran, Iraq, Lebanon) are the following: memorial services; the visitation of Husayn's tomb in Karbala, particularly on the tenth day of *'āshūrā* and the fortieth day after the battle; the public mourning processions; the theatrical representation of the battle; and various forms of flagellation. Yitzhak Nakash, "An Attempt to Trace the Origin of the Rituals of 'Āshūrā,'" 163.

25. David Pinault, "Lamentation Rituals: Shiite Justifications for Matam (Acts of Mourning and Self-Mortification)"; Ruffle, *Gender, Sainthood, and Everyday Practice.*

26. On the prohibition on self-flagellation in Iran see Murtiẓā Muṭaharī, *Ihyā-yi Tafākur-i Islāmī,* 90. On the history of the condemnation of *'āshūrā* bloodletting in Lebanon, see Lara Deeb, "Living Ashura in

Notes to Chapter 3 « 269 »

Lebanon: Mourning Transformed to Sacrifice." On speculations on the development of Muharram self-flagellation more generally see Hussain, "The Mourning of History," 86; Nakash, "An Attempt to Trace the Origin," 163. See also Wener Ende, "The Flagellations of Muḥarram and the Shi'ite 'Ulamā.'"

27. Muhammad Rizā Marzūghī, dir., *Bakhshū* (Iran, 2008).

28. For André Bazin, neorealist style fractures reality into "facts" or ambiguous fragments whose meaning emerges only retroactively (*What Is Cinema?, Vol. 2*, 35–56).

29. Christian Suhr and Rane Willerslev, eds, *Transcultural Montage*, 2.

30. Hussain, "The Mourning of History," 81.

31. On the significance of blood and kinship to the question of the schism between Sunnis and Shi'is, see Wilfred Madelung, *The Succession to Muḥammad: A Study of The Early Caliphate*; Hamid Mavani, *Religious Authority and Political Thought in Twelver Shi'ism*, 33–65. See also Mohammad Ali Amir-Moezzi, *The Divine Guide in Early Shi'ism: The Sources of Esotericism in Islam*.

32. Hamid Dabashi, *Shi'ism: A Religion of Protest*, 14.

33. Robert D. Baird, "Interpretative Categories and the History of Religions."

34. Henri Lefebvre, *Rhythmanalysis: Space, Time and Everyday Life*, 7.

35. Alexandria Eikelboom, *Rhythm: A Theological Category*, 2.

36. Garrett Stewart, *Between Film and Screen: Modernism's Photo Synthesis*, 5, 8.

37. "The use of the circle for religious purposes in slavery was so consistent and profound that one could argue that it was what gave form and meaning to black religion and art." Sterling Stuckey, *Slave Culture: Nationalist Theory and the Foundations of Black America*, 11. See also LeRhonda S. Manigault-Bryant, *Talking to the Dead: Religion, Music, and Lived Memory Among Gullah/Geechee Women*.

38. Nation-driven historiography's denigration of the hydrographic received substantive response in French historian Ferdinand Braudel's *The Mediterranean and the Mediterranean World in the Age of Philip II*, an illumination of the sea's place in world history that inspired the first generation of significant Indian Ocean World studies, like K. N. Chaudhuri's *Asia Before Europe: Economy and Civilisation of the Indian Ocean from the Rise of Islam to 1750*. But while the work of this Braudel-inspired coterie paid homage primarily to economic history (often covering such technical minutiae as boat construction, sailing techniques, and climatological details regarding monsoon winds), slavery, and more specifically African servitude, figured rarely into their analyses of labor. Chaudhuri's two volumes cover primarily four major moments in the history of the Indian Ocean World: the rise of Islam in the seventh century to the rise of European colonialism in

« 270 » Notes to Chapter 3

eighteenth; Chinese civilization; periodic migration of peoples from central Asia; and the growth of European maritime power. In a more recent contribution to Indian Ocean World studies, Shanti Moorthy and Ashraf Jamal note Chaudhuri's "scandalous disregard" for any mention of Southern and Eastern Africa in the role of exchange. Shanti Moorthy and Ashraf Jamal, eds., *Indian Ocean Studies: Cultural, Social, and Political Perspectives,* 16. Ralph Callebert similarly notices this strange elision: Callebert, "African Mobility and Labor in Global History," 117. Such responses abound through more contemporary scholarship on the Persian Gulf. See Frederick F. Anscombe, "An Anational Society: Eastern Arabia in the Ottoman Period," in Madawi Al-Rasheed, ed., *Transnational Connections and the Arab Gulf,* 26.

39. Fahad Ahmad Bishara, "Narrative and the Historian's Craft in the Arabic Historiography of the Gulf," in Lawrence G. Potter, ed., *The Persian Gulf in Modern Times,* 65.

40. Thomas Ricks, "Persian Gulf Seafaring and East Africa: Ninth–Twelfth Centuries," 339.

41. By the mid-nineteenth century, African divers in the Gulf numbered approximately one-third of divers. Matthew Hopper, "Slaves of One Master: Globalization and the African Diaspora in Arabia in the Age of Empire," 226. See also Hopper, "Slavery, Family Life, And the African Diaspora in the Arabian Gulf, 1880–1940," in Gwyn Campbell and Elizabeth Elbourne, eds., *Sex, Power, and Slavery*; Hopper, *Slaves of One Master*; Beatrice Nicolini, "The Makran-Baluch-African Network in Zanzibar and East Africa During the XIXth Century," 350.

42. Frauke Heard-Bey, *From Trucial States to United Arab Emirates: a Society in Transition.*

43. Jasim Harban, *L'Fjeri: Silsilat al-fann al-sha'bi fi al-Bahrayn.*

44. Joseph Harris, "The Sea Voyage, Slave Marts, and Dispersian in Asia," in *The African Presence in Asia,* 37.

45. Hopper, *Slaves of One Master,* 104, 117, 206.

46. The perception of blackness is predicated on cultural frameworks that are themselves difficult to historicize. Jon Cruz, *Culture on the Margins: The Black Spiritual and the Rise of American Cultural Interpretation,* 20.

47. Saramifar, "Circling Around the Really Real," 77.

48. As Bishara notes, the *safhat* genre of history writing still awaits its proper theorist. Bishara, "Narrative and the Historian's Craft," 56. For Parvaneh Pourshariati, there is little consensus on what constitutes early Persian historiography ("Local Historiography in Early Medieval Iran and the Tārīkh-i Bayhaq.") On story-telling as the predominant form of relating to the past prior to modernity, see Jacques Le Goff,

Notes to Chapter 3

« 271 »

History and Memory, and Michel de Certeau, "L'Opération historique," in Jacques Le Goff, ed., *Faire de l'Histoire.*

49. Naqqālī's date of origin is unknown. Some scholars agree on its existence from at least the Safavid era. See Kumiko Yamamoto, *The Oral Background of Persian Epics: Storytelling and Poetry,* 20.

50. And the distinction between embodied and textual knowledge constructs "African Islam" as inauthentic, argues Rudolph Ware III. See Ware, *The Walking Qur'an: Islamic Education, Embodied Knowledge, and History in West Africa,* 1–38.

51. Ware, *The Walking Qur'an,* 16.

52. Robert A. Carter, *Sea of Pearls: Seven Thousand Years of the Industry That Shaped the Gulf,* 91.

53. Richard LeBaron Bowen Jr., "The Pearl Fisheries of the Persian Gulf," 161.

54. Bowen Jr., "Pearl Fisheries," 161; Andrew Lawler, "The Pearl Trade," 46. In *Arab Seafaring in the Indian Ocean,* Hourani and Carswell trace diving and seafaring activities in the Persian Gulf back to the third millennium BCE. See also Carter, *Sea of Pearls* and Shamlan, *Pearling in the Arabian Gulf.*

55. I develop this point about Muharram temporality in relation to Firdawsī's *Shāhnāmah* later in the chapter.

56. Sharīfīyān, *Mardūm shināsī va mūsīqī navār-sāḥilī-i Shībkūh,* 112.

57. Domietta Torlasco, *The Rhythm of Images: Cinema Beyond Measure,* 3.

58. Saramifar, "Circling Around the Really Real," 81.

59. Mona Dalmuji, "The Oil City in Focus: The Cinematic Spaces of Abadan in the Anglo-Iranian Oil Company's Persian Story," 78.

60. Negar Mottahedeh, "Crude Extractions: The Voice in Iranian Cinema," in Tom Whittaker and Sarah Wright, eds., *Locating the Voice in Film,* 227.

61. On slavery as the archetypical economy of extraction before the era of fossil fuels, see Kathryn Yusoff, *A Billion Black Anthropocenes or None.*

62. Many slave owners were forced to emancipate their slaves in the wake of impoverished economic conditions, leaving—especially women—in "desperate condition without the means of subsistence." Peter Lienhardt, *Shaikhdoms of Eastern Arabia,* 8. Although, as Aisha Bilkhair Khalifa points out by contrast, in many cases slave owners refused to manumit despite desperate economic conditions. Because slaves could be used as a form of credit, the loss of one's slaves threatened bankruptcy (Bilkhair Khalifa, "African Influence on Culture and Music in Dubai," 228.)

63. Andrew Nikiforuk, *Tar Sands: Dirty Oil and the Future of a Continent,* 206.

64. Pier Paulo Pasolini, "Observations on the Long Take."

« 272 »   Notes to Chapter 3

65. Mahmoud M. Ayoub, *Redemptive Suffering in Islam*, 93.
66. Sharīfīyān, *Mūsīqi-i Būshihr*, 29. Unlike more casual *sīnah zanī* practices, the film's stylized, predetermined meter and highly organized hitting belies its seeming organicity and spontaneity. "In the authentic, Black Bushihri *sinah-zani* . . . if there is even a small mistake, the cantor gets confused" (Marzūghī, *Bakhshū*).
67. Sharīfīyān, *Mūsīqi-i Būshihr*, 34. Contemporary sound studies inquire into how the physiological dimension of music-making embodies or activates histories of violence. Mowitt, *Percussion: Drumming, Beating, Striking*.
68. Nasser Al-Taee, "'Enough, Enough, Oh Ocean': Music of the Pearl Divers in the Arabian Gulf," 21.
69. Nicolini, "The Makran-Baluch-African Network in Zanzibar," 350.
70. Hopper, *Slaves of One Master*, 90.
71. Khalifa, "Spirit Possession in Dubai," 58.
72. Hamid Naficy writes, for example, that the ubiquitous images of sailboats and freight ships indicate the identity of the laborers in the south and the participants of *arba'īn* as represented in the film's chronicle of the ritual: "Shots of farmers working in fields and fishermen going about their business . . . both integrates the ceremony into daily lives and demonstrates that these passionate, artistic people are the same ones who ordinarily farm and fish" (*A Social History of Iranian Cinema, Volume 2*, 104).
73. Dionisius A. Agius, John P. Cooper, Lucy Semaan, Chiara Zazzaro, and Robert Carter, "Remembering the Sea: Personal and Communal Recollections of Maritime Life in Jizan and the Farasan Islands, Saudi Arabia," 127.
74. Saramifar, "Circling Around the Really Real," 85.
75. Gwyn Campbell, "The African-Asian Diaspora: Myth or Reality?"; A. Montigny, F. Le Guennec-Coppens, and S. Mery, "L'Afrique Oubliée"; Lawrence G. Potter, *The Persian Gulf in Modern Times: People, Ports, and History*, 1–23; Abdul Sheriff, *Afro-Arab Interaction in the Indian Ocean: Social Consequences of the Dhow Trade*, 20; Susan Beckerleg, "African Bedouin in Palestine," 293; Edward A. Alpers, "Recollecting Africa: Diasporic Memory in the Indian Ocean World." See also Mahmood Kooria, *Narrating Africa in South Asia*.
76. Maria Sabaye Moghaddam, "Zâr Beliefs and Practices in Bandar Abbâs," 23.
77. Michael Omi and Howard Winant, *Racial Formation*, 131. For a critique of racial formation theory as an iteration of white sociology, see Khalil Saucier and Tryon Woods, *Conceptual Aphasia in Black: Displacing Racial Formation*.
78. Joseph E. Harris, "Africans in Asian History," 325; Maurice Lombard,

The Golden Age of Islam, 167; Andrew M. Watson, *Agricultural Innovation in the Early Islamic World,* 26.

79. Thomas Ricks, "Slaves and Slave Trading in Shi'i Iran AD 1500–1900," 407–8; Redha Bhacker, "The Cultural Unity of the Gulf and the Indian Ocean: A Longue Durée Historical Perspective," 169; Randall L. Pouwels, "Eastern Africa and the Indian Ocean to 1800: Reviewing Relations in Historical Perspective," 391. The Sasanians extended economic activities as far as Aden, which they occupied in the sixth century, while dominating trade with Sri Lanka in the East (Hourani and Carswell, *Arab Sea-Faring in the Indian Ocean,* 140–41).

80. Thomas Ricks, "Persian Gulf Seafaring," 357.

81. Willem Floor, "Bushehr: Southern Gateway to Iran."

82. Paul E. Lovejoy, *Transformations in Slavery: A History of Slavery in Africa,* 25. For an account of slave origins in Ethiopia in the medieval period, see Ayda Bouanga, "Gold, Slaves, and Trading Routes in the Southern Blue Nile (Abbay) Societies, Ethiopia, 13th–16th Centuries."

83. Ross W. Jamieson, "Material Culture and Social Death: African-American Burial Practices," 44.

84. Joseph Harris, "The Sea Voyage, Slave Marts, and Dispersion in Asia," 32.

85. Saidiya V. Hartman, *Lose Your Mother: A Journey Along the Atlantic Slave Route,* 155. On the myriad rites of passage in which slaves were "cleansed of natal ties," see Orlando Patterson, *Slavery and Social Death,* 51–62.

86. Alexandre Popović, *The Revolt of African Slaves in Iraq in the 3rd/9th Century,* 15.

87. Pouwels, "Eastern Africa and the Indian Ocean to 1800," 395.

88. John O. Hunwick, "A Region of the Mind: Medieval Arab Views of African Geography and Ethnography and Their Legacy," 121. Kyle Anderson suggests that *zunūj,* plural for *Zanj,* referred to slaves taken from the highlands of Tanzania and Kenya in classical Arabic. Anderson, *The Egyptian Labor Corps: Race, Place, and Space in the First World War,* 168.

89. John Ralph Willis, ed. *Slaves and Slavery in Muslim Africa: Vol. 2: The Servile Estate.* London: Routledge, 1985, 115–31.

90. Bruce Hall notes that this usage probably derived from familiarity with al-Tabari's medieval writings (*A History of Race in Muslim West Africa,* 71). Hunwick suggests that, in the West African context, *Zanj* may have been interchangeable for *sorko,* fishermen and hippopotamus hunters. See John O. Hunwick, "Back to West African *Zanj* Again: A Document of Sale from Timbuktu," 53.

« 274 »   Notes to Chapter 3

91. *Hudūd al-ʾĀlam: 'The Regions of the World,' A Persian Geography 37 A.H.–982 A.D.*, 163.
92. Francis Pearce, *Zanzibar: The Island Metropolis of Eastern Africa*, 4; G. Peter Forster, Michael Hitchcock, and Francis F. Lyimo, *Race and Ethnicity in East Africa*, 80.
93. Shihan de Silva Jayasuriya, "Identifying Africans in Asia: What's in a Name?," 7.
94. Louis Marcel Devic, *Le pays des Zandjs ou la côte orientale d'Afrique au Moyen Age d'après les écrivains arabes*, 16.
95. James de vere Allen, "Swahili Culture and the Nature of East Coast Settlement," 316; Jonathon Glassman, *Feasts and Riots: Revelry, Rebellion, and Popular Consciousness on the Swahili Coast, 1856–1888*, 125.
96. Robert Bernasconi, "Crossed Lines in the Racialization Process: Race as a Border Concept," 214.
97. Behnaz Mirzai, *A History of Slavery and Emancipation in Iran*, 25. It is worth noting that Mirzai's conclusion about this "fact" is indicative of the overall contradictory logic of much of her analyses: "The fluidity of these terms not only indicates that the identity of enslaved people could be transformed, but that they were not confined to static position within the system and could, in fact, elevate their statuses" (25). See also Abdul Sheriff, "The Persian Gulf and the Swahili Coast: A History of Acculturation Over the Longue Durée."
98. Pouwels, "Eastern Africa and the Indian Ocean," 404. For different versions of the Kilwa Chronicle, see Neville Chittick, "The 'Shirazi' Colonization of East Africa."
99. Richard Pankhurst, "Across the Red Sea and Gulf of Aden: Ethiopia's Ties with Yaman"; Daniel Ayana, "The Northern Zanj, Demadim, Yamyam, Yam/Yamjam, Habasha/Ahabish, Zanj-Ahabish, and Zanj ed-Damadam—The Horn of Africa between the Ninth and Fifteenth Centuries."
100. Kelly Askew, *Performing the Nation: Swahili Music and Cultural Politics in Tanzania*, 32.
101. Sheriff, "The Persian Gulf and the Swahili Coast," 180.
102. James de Vere Allen, "Swahili Culture and the Nature of East Coast Settlement," 309.
103. Sandy Prita Meier, *Swahili Port Cities: The Architecture of Elsewhere*, 28.
104. Myers understands social "hierarchy" as "gradient," but arrives at similar conclusions: "*permanence* of structure was the most visible symbol of social power." See Garth Myers, "Sticks and Stones: Colonialism and Zanzibari Housing," 253. Glassman observes that racial assumptions undergirded the idea that "Africans could not

Notes to Chapter 3 « 275 »

be conceived to have had the ability to build in stone" (*Feasts and Riots*, 34.)

105. Alan Villiers, *The Indian Ocean*, 100.

106. Mana Kia, *Persianate Selves: Memories of Place and Origin Before Nationalism*, 97–194.

107. Zakiyyah Iman Jackson, *Becoming Human: Matter and Meaning in an Antiblack World*, 118.

108. Aisha Khan, "Journey to the Center of the Earth: The Caribbean as Master Symbol."

109. Thus, a recent picture essay in the British *The Guardian*, subtitled "The Hippie Spirit of Iran's South" presents the "*jonob*" [South] as liberal haven. But whose liberal haven? https://www.theguardian .com/world/2020/mar/16/in-search-of-junub-the-hippie-spirit-of -irans-south.

110. Walter Benjamin, "The Work of Art in the Era of its Technological Reproducibility," in *Illuminations*.

111. On the relation between Shi'ism and the nation-state, see Chibli Mallat, *The Renewal of Islamic Law: Muhammad Baqer as-Sadr, Najaf and the Shi'i International*, 22–23, 225.

112. Thus within the span of a decade and a half, filmmakers in Taqvā'ī's cohort produced films about important religious shrines (such as Parvīz Kīmīāvī's 1971 *O'Deer Savior*), about tribal migrations (such as Hūshang Shaftī's 1962 *The Flaming Poppies*), about ancient underground irrigation systems (Riżā Mīrbahā's 1976 *The Qanat Tradition*), and about Iran's archeological ruins (Feraydūn Rahnamā's 1960 *Persepolis* and Ibrāhīm Gulistān's 1963 *The Hills of Marlik*), without these distinctions in subject matter fundamentally affecting their similarities of form. Naficy, *A Social History of Iranian Cinema: Volume 2*, 75–95.

113. Hamid Inayat, *Modern Islamic Political Thought: The Response of the Shi'i and Sunni Muslims to the Twentieth Century*, 181. Mahnia Nematollahi Mahani highlights two other pre-Islamic traditions that are much less frequently referenced: the "tragedy of Mitra" and the murder of Zarir, inherited from Parthian history. Mahani, *The Holy Drama: Persian Passion Play in Modern Iran*, 24.

114. Inayat, *Modern Islamic Political Thought*, 183.

115. Hamid Dabashi, *The Shahnamah: The Persian Epic as World Literature*, 176.

116. On the seductive stepmother figure Sūdābeh, see Afsaneh Najmabadi, "Reading 'Wiles of Women' Stories as Fictions of Masculinity," 157. Siyāvash's murder at the hands of Afrāsiyāb's brother creates a structural parallel between the significance of bloodline and of spatial sovereignty, argues Edmund Hayes ("The Death of Kings: Group

« 276 »   Notes to Chapter 3

Identity and the Tragedy of Nezhād in Ferdowsi's Shahnameh," 369–93).

117. Siyāvash's name means literally "the one with a black horse."

118. Vali Nasr, *The Shia Revival: How Conflicts within Islam Will Shape the Future*, 33.

119. Islam itself has historically been imagined as plagiaristic, imposter-like, "judged to be a fraudulent new version of some previous experience . . . Christianity," argued Edward Said (*Orientalism*, 59).

120. Nasr, *The Shia Revival*, 23.

121. Inayat, *Modern Islamic Political Thought*, 185.

122. Kane, *Syncretism and Christian Tradition*.

123. Kamran Scot Aghaie, *The Martyrs of Karbala: Shi'i Symbols and Rituals in Modern Iran*, 93; Nasr, *The Shia Revival*, 50.

124. For example, 'Abdulḥusayn Zarrīnkūb, *Daw qarn sukūt: sarguzasht-i havādis va awza'-i tarīkhī-i Īrān dar daw qarn-i avval-i Islām az hamlah-'i 'Arāb ta zuhār-i davlat-i tahīrīyān*.

125. The origins of racial theory, could be after all, based upon a profoundly primordial dualism. Peter Robb, *The Concept of Race in South Asia*, 14.

126. On the distinction between *adab, akhlāq*, and civilization, see Kia, "Moral Refinement and Manhood in Persian," in Margrit Pernau et al., eds., *Civilizing Emotions*, 3. At other times, this same thinker seems to reproduce a version of the anti-Arabness characteristic of the work of Ākhūndzādah, calling Islam unscientific. Margaret Kohn attempts to reconcile these two dimensions of Afghani's work through recourse to Afghani's engagement with the work of Ibn Khaldun and the French historian Guizot Kohn, "Afghani on Empire, Islam, and Civilization."

127. Motahari even challenged the reliability of canonical sources that Husayn's family mourned his death at Karbala after his martyrdom. See Hamid Dabashi, *Theology of Discontent: The Ideological Foundation of the Islamic Revolution in Iran*, 147–215.

128. Deeb, "Living Ashura in Lebanon: Mourning Transformed to Sacrifice," 124.

129. Hojjatol Islam Mehdi Daneshmand, qtd. in Nacim Pak-Shiraz, *Shi'i Islam in Iranian Cinema: Religion and Spirituality in Film*, 125–26.

130. David Lloyd, *Under Representation: The Racial Regime of Aesthetics*. On the racialization of sensory experience, see also Erica Fretwell, *Sensory Experiments: Psychophysics, Race, and the Aesthetics of Feeling*.

131. The polemics against classical poetry that shaped the literary landscape of free-form, "committed" new poetry (*sh'ir-i naw*) depended upon an opposition between form and content that cast the

political as form, as free, as universal, and the classical as content, as bound, as inexorably, baroquely particular. See Fateme Montazeri, "A Predestined Break from the Past: Shi'r-i Naw, History, and Hermeneutics." Similarly, the anti-Sufi sentiment that charged one version of the nineteenth- and twentieth-century polemics against classical Persian poetry mobilized an understanding of Sufi poetic apoliticism as slavishly passive and puerile. See Ahmad Kasravī, *Sūfīgarī*; Lloyd V. J. Ridgeon, *Sufi Castigator: Ahmad Kasravi and the Iranian Mystical Tradition.*

132. Lloyd, *Under Representation: The Racial Regime of Aesthetics.* By linking religious calls to political activism with analogical forcefields connected to modernism in the realm of art, I do not mean to suggest these terms ought to be valuated in identical ways, or that there are no differences between them. It should go without saying that religious calls for political activism in the context of contemporary Shi'i history have had disappointing, if not violently deleterious, lethal effects. The virtue-value complex that renders political activism an unqualified positive term in the context of academic liberalism ought to be assessed against the full ground of its complex and contradictory history, just as the academic conservatism that renders *apoliticism* and disinterestedness unquestioned and unqualified virtues ought to be assessed against the full ground of its complex and contradictory histories. I mean to reopen spaces for understanding the evolution of religious, aesthetic and political practices as *not* disconnected from the racial—as cliché and often disingenuous reassertions of "one umma" coerce us to do. In a discussion of "white flight" within Minneapolis mosques in the face of increasing Somali attendance at these spaces of worship, Ramla Bile reports that non-Black Muslims tend to disavow Somali claims about antiblackness within the Muslim community through recourse to the cliché of "one umma." ("English Panel: Anti-Black Racism in SW Asia/N Africa + Diaspora." 7.10. 2020.) The entire conceptual apparatus of a Muslim world is a serious point of debate among scholars (Cemil Aydin, *The Idea of the Muslim World*).

133. Yasir Suleiman, *The Arabic Language and National Identity: A Study in Ideology*, 55–57.

134. Suleiman, *The Arabic Language and National Identity*, 58.

135. Yasir Suleiman, *Arabic in the Fray: Language Ideology and Cultural Politics*, 68.

136. See also C. E. Bosworth, "'AJAM," *Encyclopædia Iranica*, I/7, 700–701. Bosworth suggests that *ajama* is the antonym of *'araba*, "to speak clearly."

137. Valentin Y. Mudibme, *The Idea of Africa.* On the influence of Greek

« 278 »   Notes to Chapter 3

and Roman descriptions of Africa on medieval Arab views of blacks, see Stephen King, "Black Arabs and African Migrants: Between Slavery and Racism in North Africa."

138. Sylvia Wynter, "Unsettling the Coloniality of Being/Power/Truth/ Freedom: Towards the Human, After Man, Its Overrepresentation— An Argument," 301.

139. James Sweet, "The Iberian Roots of American Racist Thought," 147.

140. Roy Mottahedeh, "The Shu'ubiyah Controversy and the Social History of Early Islamic Iran."

141. The anti-Arab sentiment of the *shu'ubiyah* is well known by historians of Iranian nationalism, but *shu'ubiyah* memory is alive as a divisive force within Arab nationalism as well. The term is a "deeply wounding insult," somewhat synonymous with "traitor," to groups or individuals who affirm local solidarities over the principle of Arab nationalism (Sharabi, *Nationalism and Revolution in the Arab World*, 100). The term was used by the Iraqi Ba'thist regime in the 1980s to designate Iranians. Hanna and Gardner go so far as to suggest "an actual trend line linking the eighth and the twentieth centuries" (*Arab Socialism*, 81). Suleiman has a more nuanced articulation: "a web of language-identity conceptualisations in the past that resonate with similar ones in the present" (Suleiman, *Arabic in the Fray*, 55). Gibb believed *al-shu'ubiyyah* was ultimately "a struggle to determine the destinies of the Islamic culture as a whole" (Gibb, *Studies on the Civilization of Islam*, 62).

142. Miriam Cooke, *Tribal Modern: Branding New Nations in the Arab Gulf*, 61.

143. For an argument for *'ajami* as a transregional comparative category of analysis and expression of literary self-consciousness, see Annette Damayanti Lienau, "Reframing Vernacular Culture on Arabic Fault Lines: Bamba, Senghor, and Sembene's Translingual Legacies in French West Africa."

144. Azania is alluded to in *Periplus of the Erythraean Sea*; finding the word more beautiful than East Africa, he proposes that the sultan reinstate it. Pearce, *Zanzibar*, 205.

145. Richard C. Jankowsky, *Stambeli: Music, Trance, and Alterity in Tunisia*, 4.

146. On this point see Beeta Baghoolizadeh, "From Religious Eulogy to War Anthem: Kurdizadeh's 'Layla Bigufta' and Blackness in Late Twentieth-Century Iran."

147. For Muharram of 2022, the Islamic Republic of Iran's state television network even began airing a reality show series on *maddahs* ("Husayniyah-i mu'ali").

148. As Younes Saramifar observes in his contemporary ethnography in Isfahan, participants tend to base their Muharram plans through al-

Notes to Chapter 3 « 279 »

legiance to a particular *maddah* (singer), rather than affiliation with a clergy member. Saramifar, "Circling Around the Really Real," 84.

149. Richard K. Wolf, *The Voice in the Drum: Music, Language, and Emotion in Islamicate South Asia*, 116–44. See also Pushkar Sohoni and Torsten Tschacher, eds. *Non-Shia Practices of Muharram in South Asia and the Diaspora*.

150. Korom, *Hosay Trinidad*, 57.

151. Mana Kia's analysis of the way in which nationalist thought inadvertently affects even the most critical forms of modern scholarship on Iran and South Asia demonstrates the extent to which our methodological starting points are hopelessly mired in inherited categories that are difficult to think our way out of (*Persianate Selves*, 1–29).

152. Dabashi, *Shi'ism: A Religion of Protest*, 4.

153. Mykolas Juodele, "In Search of Junub."

154. Korom, *Hosay Trinidad*, 100.

155. On the mysterious nature of Hosay's preservation, Donald Wood suggests "it is by no means clear why Hosein should have become so popular in Trinidad but in other colonies as well" (*Trinidad in Transition*, 151).

156. Aisha Khan, *Callaloo Nation: Metaphors of Race and Religious Identity among South Asians in Trinidad*, 8. See also Stefano Harney, *Nationalism and Identity: Culture and the Imagination in a Caribbean Diaspora*.

157. Thus, for example, the multi-billion-dollar streaming company Netflix has expressed interest in working with—or capitalizing off of—storytelling about blackness in Iran produced by the Collective for Black Iranians, discussed in the conclusion.

158. Palmié, "Against Syncretism," 86; Stewart and Shaw, *Syncretism/Anti-Syncretism*, 1–26.

159. Charles Stewart, "Syncretism and Its Synonyms: Reflections on Cultural Mixture," 44.

160. See Aisha Khan, "Journey to the Center of the Earth," and Khan, "Sacred Subversions? Syncretic Creoles, the Indo-Caribbean, and 'Culture's In-Between.'"

161. Korom, "Memory, Innovation, and Emergent Ethnicity: The Creolization of an Indo-Trinidadian Performance," 141.

162. Saramifar, "Circling Around the Really Real," 85.

163. Sharīfīyān, *Ahl-i mātam*, 30.

164. Cooke, *Tribal Modern*, 31.

165. Blackness, lacking a robust or systematized repertoire of iconography in Western Asia, gets subsumed into Arabness wherever the Arab is conceived as a racial other; in Turkey, for example, "*Arap*" is a derogatory term for black. And yet, this cannot explain why Arabs have their own repertoire of denigrating iconography for blackness,

« 280 » Notes to Chapter 3

which is to say: taking the Arab or the Semite as *the* symbol of other-ness in the Persian imaginary, as many scholars of Iranian national-ism have done, not only naturalizes the modern nation as a coherent unit of inquiry, but more importantly, eclipses thoroughly the black perspective from which it is possible for the "Persian," "Arab," and indeed "Turkish" and "Indian" imaginaries to oppress, erase, and denigrate blackness. See, for example, Mustafa Olpak, *Biographie d'une famille d'escalves,* for antiblackness in Turkey.

166. Aisha Khan, *The Deepest Dye: Obeah, Hosay, and Race in the Atlantic World,* 149.

167. Khan, *Callaloo Nation: Metaphors of Race and Religious Identity among South Asians in Trinidad,* 9.

168. Frank Korom, "The Transformation of Language to Rhythm: The Hosay Drums of Trinidad," 83, 76. See also Richard Wolf, "Em-bodiment and Ambivalence: Emotion in South Asian Muharram Drumming." For the significance of *marsiyahs* performances for maintaining Shi'i identity in Kashmir, see Hakim Sameer Hamdani, *Shi'ism in Kashmir: A History of Sunni-Shi'i Rivalry and Reconcilia-tion,* 59–65.

169. Korom, "Transformation of Language," 70, 76.

170. Khan, *The Deepest Dye,* 163.

171. Khan, "Journey to the Center of the Earth."

4. THE BLACK MATERNAL AND THE INTERRUPTIVE IMAGINATION

1. Prematurely showing it on public television the night before its anticipated first screening.

2. Mohamad Tavakoli-Targhi, *Refashioning Iran: Orientalism, Occiden-talism, and Historiography,* 77–96.

3. Hamid Naficy calls Bashu a "black Arab boy," while another film histo-rian calls him a "dark-skinned, foreign-speaking boy." Naficy, *A Social History of Iranian Cinema, Volume 4,* 36; Hamid Reza Sadr, *Iranian Cinema: A Political History,* 207. Except, see Zavier Wingham, who identifies Bashu as Afro-Iranian ("Blackness on the Iranian Periphery: Ethnicity, Language, and Nation in *Bashu, the Little Stranger*"). As Kamran Rastegar points out, the remoteness of the village setting in *Bashu* "allows for the villagers to display a degree of ethnoracial preju-dice toward the darker-skinned Bashu, but frees their relationship of the problematic dialectic of Persian and Arab that itself underscored the war's national divisions." Rastegar, *Surviving Images: Cinema, War, and Cultural Memory in the Middle East,* 147.

4. Nelida Fuccaro, "Rethinking the History of Port Cities in the Gulf," in Lawrence G. Potter, ed., *The Persian Gulf in Modern Times,* 24.

Notes to Chapter 4 « 281 »

5. Miriam Cooke, *Tribal Modern: Branding New Nations in the Arab Gulf*, 30. On the complexities of racialization histories in the Persian Gulf, see Ahmed Kanna, Amélie Le Renard, and Neha Vora, *Beyond Exception: New Interpretations of the Arabian Peninsula*.

6. Shahram Chubin and Charles Tripp, *Iran and Iraq at War*, 1; David Menashri, "Iran: Doctrine and Reality," in Efraim Karsh, ed., *The Iran-Iraq War*, 51; Farzad Cyrus Sharifi-Yazdi, *Arab-Iranian Rivalry in the Persian Gulf*.

7. Afsaneh Najmabadi, *Women with Mustaches and Men without Beards*, 111.

8. David Bordwell suggests the term "scanning" for a loosely related kind of comparison between stylistic events (*Narration in the Fiction Film*, 287).

9. Zāvan Qūkāsiyān, *Guft u gū bā Bahrām Bayzāyī*, 224.

10. Hortense J. Spillers, "Mama's Baby, Papa's Maybe: An American Grammar Book," 72.

11. Behnaz A. Mirzai, *A History of Slavery and Emancipation, 1800–1929*, 101; Ehud R. Toledano, *As if Silent and Absent: Bonds of Enslavement in the Islamic Middle East*, 67; Matthew Hopper, *Slaves of One Master: Globalization and Slavery in Arabia in the Age of Empire*, 5.

12. Indrani Chatterjee and Richard M. Eaton, *Slavery and South Asian History*, xxx. On the collective memory of slavery among Sidi women, see Helene Basu, "A Gendered Indian Ocean Site: Mai Mishra, African Spirit Possession and Sidi Women in Gujarat," in Basu, *Journeys and Dwellings: Indian Ocean Themes in South Asia*.

13. Judith Tucker, *Women in Nineteenth Century Egypt*, 167.

14. Edward Alpers, "Recollecting Africa: Diasporic Memory in the Indian Ocean World," 89; Lodewijk Willem Christiaan Berg, *Le Ḥadhramout et les colonies arabes dans l'Archipel indien*, 70.

15. John G. Kennedy, "Nubian Zar Ceremonies as Psychotherapy," 187; Fahimeh Mianji and Yousef Semnani, "Zār Spirit Possession in Iran and African Countries," 226.

16. Qūkāsiyān, *Guft u gū*, 233.

17. Najmabadi, *Women with Mustaches and Men without Beards*, 99, 123. For the etymological shift in the sense of *vatan* to include territorial Iran, rather than one's birthplace, see Mohamad Tavakoli-Targhi, "Refashioning Iran: Language and Culture during the Constitutional Revolution," 76. See also Firoozeh Kashani-Sabet, *Conceiving Citizens: Women and the Politics of Motherhood in Iran*, 31–32; Camron Michael Amin, "Selling and Saving 'Mother Iran': Gender and the Iranian Press in the 1940s."

18. Najm Ābādī, "Sīnamā: andīshah hāyi darbārih-'i 'Bāshu Gharībeh-'i Kūchak.' "

« 282 »   Notes to Chapter 4

19. Gayatri Spivak, "Nationalism and the Imagination," 80. On women's reproductive capacity in service of modernity's epistemological formations, see Alys Eve Weinbaum, *Wayward Reproductions: Genealogies of Race and Nation in Transatlantic Modern Thought*.

20. Kashani-Sabet, *Conceiving Citizens*; Jasamin Rostam-Kolayi, "Expanding Agendas for the 'New' Iranian Woman"; Janet Afary, *Sexual Politics in Modern Iran*, 109–74.

21. Farshad Zahedi, "The Myth of Bastoor and the Children of Iranian Independent Cinema," 24.

22. Hamid Naficy, *A Social History of Iranian Cinema, Volume 2*, 405.

23. Hamid Reza Sadr, "Children in Iranian Post-Revolutionary Cinema," 231. On blackness in Sacred Defense cinema, see Parisa Vaziri, "Ultimate Slaves in the Dead Zone: Blackness in Iranian Sacred Defense Cinema."

24. Gilles Deleuze, *Cinema II: The Time Image*.

25. Sadr, *Iranian Cinema*, 230.

26. Farhang Erfani, "Committed Perception: Merleau-Ponty, Carroll, and Iranian Cinema," 328.

27. Darian Soheil Rahnamaye Rabbani and Julio Groppa Aquino, "A Infância no Cinema de Abbas Kiarostami."

28. Vicky Lebeau, *Childhood and Cinema* and *Psychoanalysis and Cinema: The Play of Shadows*; Lynne Kirby, *Parallel Tracks: The Railroad and Silent Cinema*, 154.

29. Chris Marker, qtd. in Raymond Bellour, "The Cinematic Spectator: A Special Memory," 15; Janet Bergstrom, "Alternation, Segmentation, Hypnosis: Interview with Raymond Bellour," 102.

30. Zeydabadi-Nejad refers to a shot where a child actor was asked to cry in one of Kiarostami's films: "Early in the filming of *Where is the Friend's House?*, Kiarostami took a Polaroid photo of a child, who carried the photo everywhere with him. Just before a particular shot when the child was supposed to cry, Kiarostami ripped the photo and the child began to sob, creating the realism he desired." Saeed Zeydabadi-Nejad, "Iranian Intellectuals and Contact with the West," 384.

31. Stephanie Donald, Emma Wilson, and Sarah Wright, eds. *Childhood and Nation in Contemporary World Cinema: Borders and Encounters*, 3. See also Zhen Zhang, "Transnational Melodrama, *Wenyi*, and the Orphan Imagination," in Christine Gledhill and Linda Williams, eds., *Melodrama Unbound*.

32. Jessica Balanzategui, *The Uncanny Child in Transnational Cinema: Ghosts of Futurity at the Turn of the Twenty-First Century*, 9. For the child as claim to verisimilitude see Lebeau, *Childhood and Cinema*, 27.

33. Kojin Karatani, "The Discovery of the Child," 115.

34. Thus, children often appear as ghosts or demons, the centerpiece of

the horror genre in the 1960s and 1970s. Attention to gender dynamics shows that narratives of female child possession in films often cipher crises in adult masculinity associated with the breakdown and conversion of reason to intuition and imagination. Karen Lury, *The Child in Film*, 6; Andrew Scahill, *The Revolting Child in Horror Cinema: Youth Rebellion and Queer Spectatorship*, 31–56; Karen J. Renner, "Evil Children in Film and Literature," 3; Balanzategui, *The Uncanny Child*, 10; Sarah Thomas, *Inhabiting the In-Between: Childhood and Cinema in Spain's Long Tradition.*

35. Jean-François Lyotard, *The Inhuman: Reflections on Time*, 3.

36. Lebeau, *Childhood and Cinema*, 11–12.

37. Nasrin Rahimieh, "Marking Gender and Difference in the Myth of the Nation," in Richard Tapper, ed., *The New Iranian Cinema*, 243.

38. The "impossibility" of black childhood in contemporary black studies is often interpreted through the analytic of sexualization. See Rebecca Epstein, Jamilia Blake, and Thalia Gonzalez, "Girlhood Interrupted: The Erasure of Black Girls' Childhood"; Tezeru Teshome and K. Wayne Yang, "Not Child but Meager: Sexualization and Negation of Black Childhood." On the other hand, as Toby Rollo points out, it is also because blackness is conflated with childhood that it is "historically identified as the archetypal site of naturalized violence and servitude." See Toby Rollo, "The Color of Childhood: The Role of the Child/Human Binary in the Production of Anti-Black Racism."

39. One etymology attributes the name of the province to *kūz*, for sugar, according to which Khūzistān means "land of sugar."

40. Sidney W. Mintz, *Sweetness and Power: The Place of Sugar in Modern History*, 23.

41. Barbara L. Solow, "Capitalism and Slavery in the Exceedingly Long Run," 712; William D. Phillips Jr., *Slavery from Roman Times to the Early Transatlantic Trade*, 68; Maurice Lombard, *The Golden Age of Islam*, 167; Stuart B. Schwartz, *Tropical Babylons*, 29. Lombard calls the "labourers" "Bantu (Zanj) slaves from the east coast of Africa, who made their way to Khūzistān via southern Arabia, Oman, and the Iranian coast" (25). Elsewhere Lombard notes the cultivation of cotton by African slaves, and the "three-fold connection" (black slaves, cotton, sugar) "later repeated in the Mediterranean and Caribbean" (122).

42. Nell Irvin Painter, *The History of White People*, 40. As Alexander Weheliye writes, "Slavery undergirds humanity's current sucralose surplus crisis" (*Habeas Viscus: Racializing Assemblages, Biopolitics, and Black Feminist Theories of the Human*, 129).

43. Edward Alpers, "The Other Middle Passage: The African Slave Trade in the Indian Ocean," in *Many Middle Passages*, 23. See also Kwesi Kwaa Prah, *Reflections on Arab-Led Slavery of Africans*, 111–16.

« 284 »   Notes to Chapter 4

44. Edward Alpers, *The Indian Ocean in World History*, 108.
45. William Gervase Clarence-Smith, *Islam and the Abolition of Slavery*, 5.
46. George Michael La Rue, "'My Ninth Master was a European': Enslaved Blacks in European Households in Egypt, 1798–1848," 103.
47. Mohammad Ennaji, *Slavery, the State and Islam*, 48.
48. See for example, Julia Kristeva, *Desire in Language: A Semiotic Approach to Literature and Art* and *Revolution in Poetic Language*; Hélène Cixous, "The Laugh of the Medusa."
49. Judith Butler, *The Psychic Life of Power: Theories in Subjection*, 7.
50. Qūkāsiyān, *Guft u gū*, 232.
51. Negar Mottahedeh, *Displaced Allegories: Post-revolutionary Iranian Cinema*, 23–25.
52. Beyzai sometimes insinuates that the film *Bashu* truly belongs to Susan Taslimi (Na'i). Qūkāsiyān, *Guft u gū*, 237.
53. For a critique of this ubiquitous interpretation of the symbolic, see Tracy McNulty, *Wrestling with the Angel: Experiments in Symbolic Life.*
54. Qtd. in Naficy, *A Social History of Iranian Cinema, Volume 2*, 39.
55. Hamid Naficy, *A Social History of Iranian Cinema, Volume 4*, 141.
56. Rahimieh, "Marking Gender and Difference in the Myth of the Nation," 245.
57. Rahimieh, "Marking Gender and Difference in the Myth of the Nation," 245.
58. Najm Ābādī, "Sīnamā: andīshah hāyi darbārih-'i 'Bāshu Gharībeh-'i Kūchak.'" 208.
59. On Spillers's intervention into the ground of theory, see M. Ty, "The Riot of the Literal."
60. Spillers, "Mama's Baby," 74.
61. Saidiya V. Hartman, "The Belly of the World: A Note on Black Women's Labors," 166.
62. Orlando Patterson, *Slavery and Social Death*, 1–35.
63. Claude Meillassoux, "Female Slavery," in Claire C. Robertson and Martin A. Klein, eds., *Women and Slavery in Africa*, 50.
64. Jennifer L. Morgan, "Partus sequitur ventrem: Law, Race, and Reproduction in Colonial Slavery," 5.
65. Morgan, "Partus sequitur ventrem," 5–6. See also Sally McKee, "Inherited Status and Slavery in Late Medieval Italy and Venetian Crete."
66. In historicizing the relationship between childhood and innocence, Robin Bernstein suggests that this seemingly natural, pathos-filled figure of childhood was first and foremost "raced white." See Bernstein, *Racial Innocence: Performing American Childhood from Slavery to Civil Rights*, 4.
67. Though the change is attributed to 'Umar I, scholars disagree on the

veracity of this origin. Khalil 'Athamina, "How Did Islam Contribute to Change the Legal Status of Women: The Case of the Jawārī or the Female Slaves," 386.

68. Matthew Gordon, "Unhappy Offspring? Concubines and Their Sons in Early Abbasid Society," 156.

69. Mustafā Husaynī Tabatabāyī, *Bardigi az dīd-gah-i Islām*, 17; Younis Y. Mirza, "Remembering the Umm al-walad: Ibn Kathir's Treatise on the Sale of the Concubine," 303; Schacht, *The Origins of Muhammadan Jurisprudence*, 265.

70. Spillers, "Mama's Baby," 68.

71. 'Athamina, "How Did Islam Contribute," 387.

72. Kathryn A. Hain, "Avenues to Social Mobility Available to Courtesans and Concubines," in Matthew Gordon and Kathryn A. Hain, eds., *Concubines and Courtesans*, 326.

73. Cynthia J. Becker, *Blackness in Morocco: Gnawa Identity through Music and Visual Culture*, 4.

74. Hain, "Avenues to Social Mobility," 326.

75. Cristina de La Puente González, "Free Fathers, Slave Mothers and Their Children: A Contribution to the Study of Family Structures in Al-Andalus," 31.

76. Marc Nichanian, *The Historiographic Perversion*, 41.

77. Ana Miranda, "Al-Dalfa and the Political Role of the Umm al-Walad in the Late Umayyad Caliphate of Al-Andalus," 171–82.

78. Aysha Hidayatullah, "Māriyya the Copt: Gender, Sex and Heritage in the Legacy of Muhammad's umm walad."

79. Mirza, "Remembering the Umm al-walad." On elite slavery as a conceptual dead zone, see Vaziri, "Ultimate Slaves in the Dead Zone."

80. "Other slave trades, both throughout history and around the world, are . . . silenced by the overwhelming and overpowering horror of the transatlantic trade." Andrea Major, *Slavery, Abolitionism, and Empire in India, 1772–1843*, 18.

81. "Many nameless slaves, of course, perished from the hard toil of menial labor. . . . However, many also rose from the depths of human suffering to put their own stamp on the societies of their adoption." (Abdul Sheriff, *Dhow Cultures of the Indian Ocean: Cosmopolitanism, Commerce and Islam*, 230.) On colonial writings on Indian Ocean slavery as an ideological project, see Sheriff, *Dhow Cultures*, 218.

82. Saidiya Hartman, "The Belly of the World: A Note on Black Women's Labors," 167.

83. Hartman, "The Belly of the World," 169.

84. Mirzai, *A History of Slavery*, 200; Janet Afary, *Sexual Politics in Modern Iran*, 56.

85. Afary, *Sexual Politics in Modern Iran*, 56.

86. Madeline C. Zilfi, *Women and Slavery in the Late Ottoman Empire*, xii.
87. Omar H. Ali, Kennth X. Robbins, Beheroze Shroff, and Jazmin Graves, "Introduction: Afro-South Asia in the Global African Diaspora," in *African Diasporan Communities Across South Asia*, 17.
88. Ali Mazrui, quoted in Abdul Sheriff, "The Slave Trade and Slavery in the Western Indian Ocean: Significant Contrasts," 44.
89. Peter Osborne and Stella Stanford, *Philosophies of Race and Ethnicity*, 8.
90. Chatterjee and Eaton, *Slavery and South Asian History*, 9.
91. Sheriff, "The Slave Trade and Slavery in the Western Indian Ocean," 44.
92. Ronald Segal, *Islam's Black Slaves: The Other Black Diaspora*, 9, my emphasis.
93. Sheriff, "The Slave Trade and Slavery in the Western Indian Ocean," 44.
94. Omar H. Ali et al., "Introduction: Afro-South Asia in the Global African Diaspora," 12.
95. Edward Alpers, "The African Diaspora in the Indian Ocean: A Comparative Perspective," 32.
96. Toledano, *As if Silent and Absent*, 12.
97. The language of hardness and softness, rigidity and fluidity still implicitly dominates all discourse on the historical continuum of difference upon which conceptually proper, real racial blackness is located.
98. Tapji Paul Garba and Sara-Maria Sorentino, "Blackness Before Race and Race as Reoccupation: Reading Sylvia Wynter with Hans Blumenberg."
99. Benjamin Reilly, *Slavery, Agriculture, and Malaria in the Arabian Peninsula*, 50. See also Benjamin Reilly, "Revisiting Consanguineous Marriage in the Greater Middle East: Milk, Blood, and Bedouins."
100. Chanfi Ahmed, *AfroMecca in History: African Societies, Anti-Black Racism, and Teaching in al-Haram Mosque in Mecca*, 123.
101. Stephan Prochazka and Bahram Gharedaghi-Kloucheh, "The Zār Cult in the Shatt al-'Arab/Arvand Region."
102. Khatija Khader, "Mobile Communities of the Indian Ocean: A Brief Study of Siddi and Hadrami Diaspora in Hyderabad City, India," 81; Charles Camara, "The Siddis of Uttara Kanada: History, Identity and Change among African Descendants in Contemporary Karnataka," in Amy Catlin-Jairazbhoy and Edward A. Alpers, eds., *Sidis and Scholars*, 104. On racial signifiers as guarantors of endogamy among Sidis, see Helene Basu, "A Gendered Indian Ocean Site," in *Journeys and Dwellings*, 230.
103. Ali, Robbins, Shroff, and Graves, "Introduction: Afro-South Asia in the Global African Diaspora," 14.

Notes to Chapter 4 « 287 »

104. Richard Jankowsky, *Stambeli: Music, Trance, and Alterity in Tunisia*, 17.
105. Jo Tatchell, *A Diamond in the Desert: Behind the Scenes in Abu Dhabi, the World's Richest City*, 178.
106. Fredrik Barth, *Sohar, Culture and Society in an Omani Town*, 48.
107. Liat Kozma, "Black, Kinless, and Hungry: Manumitted Female Slaves in Khedival Egypt," in Terence Walz and Kenneth M. Cuno, eds., *Race and Slavery in the Middle East*, 207.
108. Becker, *Blackness in Morocco*, 9.
109. Alpers, "The African Diaspora in the Indian Ocean," 32.
110. Chouki El Hamel, *Black Morocco: A History of Slavery, Race, and Islam*, 301.
111. Saidiya Hartman, *Scenes of Subjection*, 30; Christina Sharpe, *Monstrous Intimacies: Making Post-Slavery Subjects*.
112. Samuel Weber, *Theatricality as Medium*, 114.
113. Eyal Peretz, *The Off-Screen: An Investigation of the Cinematic Frame*; Daniel Frampton, *Filmosophy*, 40; Giles Deleuze, *Cinema II: The Time-Image*, 16.
114. Daniel Dayan, "The Tutor-Code of Classical Cinema"; Stanley Cavell, *The World Viewed: Reflections on the Ontology of Film*, 24.
115. M. Nourbese Philip, "Dis Place—The Space Between," in *A Genealogy of Resistance*.
116. Negar Mottahedeh, "Where Are Kiarostami's Women?," 310.
117. André Bazin, "Theatre and Cinema," in *What Is Cinema? Vol. 1*, 105.
118. Nicole R. Fleetwood, *Troubling Vision: Performance, Visuality, and Blackness*.
119. Raymond Bellour, *Between-the-Images*, 25.
120. Kaja Silverman, *Male Subjectivity at the Margins*, 62.
121. Najm Ābādī, "Sīnamā: andīshah hāyi darbārih-yi ʿBāshu Gharībeh-ʾi Kūchak.ʾ " 209.
122. Qūkāsiyān, *Guft u gū*, 226.
123. Saidiya Hartman writing of ubiquitous and anonymous "Black Venus" in the Atlantic context ("Venus in Two Acts," 2).
124. "If it is true that historical knowledge demands that its object be isolated and withdrawn from any libidinal investment come from the historian, then it is certain that the only result of this way of ʿputting down' [*rédiger*] history would be to 'put it down' [*réduire*]." Lyotard, *The Inhuman*, 30.
125. Zakiyyah Iman Jackson, *Becoming Human: Matter and Meaning in an Antiblack World*, 89–91, 101.
126. Tamara Dee Turner, "Music and Trance as Methods for Engaging with Suffering," 81.
127. Kaveh Safa, "Reading Saedi's Ahl-e Hava: Patterns and Significance in Spirit Possession Beliefs on the Southern Coast of Iran," 93.

« 288 »   Notes to Chapter 4

128. William Beeman, "Understanding the Zār: An African-Iranian Healing Dance Ritual," 74.

129. Tamara Turner, "The 'Right' Kind of *Hāl*: Feeling and Foregrounding Atmospheric Identity in an Algerian Music Ritual," 124.

130. Wolf Leslau, "An Ethiopian Argot of People Possessed by a Spirit," 206.

131. Pamela Constantinides, "The History of Zar in Sudan," 98.

132. Becker, *Blackness in Morocco*, 145.

133. Ashon Crawley, *Blackpentecostal Breath: The Aesthetics of Possibility*, 4.

134. Claire Nouvet, "The Inarticulate Affect: Lyotard and Psychoanalytic Testimony," 112.

135. Daniel Heller-Roazen, "Glossolalia: From the Unity of the Word to Plurality of Tongues," 594.

136. Marco Motta, "L'echo de la voix," 101.

137. Mottahedeh, *Displaced Allegories*, 34.

138. As Afshin Marashi points out, the first Persian textbooks under Reza Pahlavi Shah were symbolically conspicuous markers of modernity (Marashi, *Nationalizing Iran: Culture Power and the State 1870–1940*).

139. Naficy, *A Social History of Iranian Cinema, Volume 4*, 37.

140. Jahānbakhsh Nūrāyī, "Parvāz bih Nākujā Ābād," 463.

141. Alla Gadassik, "A National Filmmaker without a Home: Home and Displacement in the Films of Amir Naderi," 477.

142. As film historians have shown, Amiro largely reflects Nadiri's own upbringing, who grew up as a poor orphan in Abadan, infatuated, like Amiro, with foreign magazines, ships, and airplanes (Naficy, *An Accented Cinema: Exilic and Diasporic Filmmaking*, 245).

143. Hamid Dabashi, *Masters and Masterpieces of Iranian Cinema*, 242.

144. Dabashi, *Masters and Masterpieces*, 242.

145. Rasmus Elling, "War of Clubs: Struggle for Space in Abadan and the 1945 Oil Strike."

146. Maho Sebiane, "Entre l'Afrique et l'Arabie," 52. On the relationship between racialization and space, as it is captured by the term *affectability*, see Denise Ferreira da Silva, *Toward a Global Idea of Race*.

147. Lindon Barrett, *Racial Blackness and the Discontinuity of Western Modernity*, 47; Lindon Barrett, *Blackness and Value: Seeing Double*, 132.

148. Spivak, "Nationalism and the Imagination," 79. See also Arshin Adib-Moghaddam, *Psycho-Nationalism*.

149. Rastegar, *Surviving Images*, 144, 146.

150. Naficy, *A Social History of Iranian Cinema, Volume 4*, 31.

151. Gadassik, "A National Filmmaker," 477.

152. Milad Odabaei, "Sickness of the Revolution: Loss, Fetishism, and the Impossibility of Politics."

153. Jahānbakhsh Nūrāyī, "Parvāz bih Nākujā Ābād," 464.

Notes to Chapter 4   « 289 »

154. Najmabadi, *Women with Mustaches and Men without Beards,* 104.

155. See Bahram Mohsenpour, "Philosophy of Education in Postrevolutionary Iran," for differences in philosophical orientation between the two eras. See Golnar Mehran, "Social Implications of Literacy in Iran," for consistencies, including the continued emphasis on Persian as the national language of literacy. For Pahlavi centralization of elementary education, see A. Reza Arasteh, *Education and Social Awakening in Iran,* 55. For the Islamic Republic's literacy campaign, see Mehran, "Social Implications of Literacy in Iran."

156. British residents referred to the languages spoken in the Persian Gulf as "Abbasi patois." Abdul Sheriff, "The Slave Trade and Its Fallout in the Persian Gulf," in Gwyn Campbell, ed., *Abolition and Its Aftermath in Indian Ocean Africa and Asia,* 109.

157. Rastegar, *Surviving Images,* 152, 146.

158. Rahimieh, "Marking Gender and Difference," 241.

159. Maurice Olender, *The Languages of Paradise: Race, Religion, and Philology in the Nineteenth Century,* 7; Geoffrey Galt Harpham, "Roots, Races, and the Return to Philology."

160. Qūkāsiyān, *Guft u gū,* 226–27.

161. Maurice Olender, *Race and Erudition,* 42.

162. Qūkāsiyān, *Guft u gū,* 227.

163. Y. Talib, "The African Diaspora in Asia," in M. El Fasi, ed., *General History of Africa, vol. 3,* 712.

164. E.g., the post-civil rights "multiracial" backlash against racial blackness. See Jared Sexton, *Amalgamation Schemes: Antiblackness and the Critique of Multiculturalism;* João H. Costa Vargas, *The Denial of Antiblackness: Multiracial Redemption and Black Suffering.*

165. Rastegar, *Surviving Images,* 149

166. For the nineteenth-century discursive deployment of race as exceeding the corporeal, see Barnor Hesse, "Racialized Modernity: An Analytics of White Mythologies." On the relation between the categories of race and religion, the literature is rather vast and primarily concerned with the relationship between Christianity and race. Jay Kameron Carter, *Race: A Theological Account;* Geraldine Heng, *The Invention of Race in the European Middle Ages;* Denise K. Buell, *Why This New Race: Ethnic Reasoning in Early Christianity;* Joseph Ziegler, "Physiognomy, Science, and Proto-Racism 1200–1500," in Miriam Eliav-Feldon, Benjamin Isaac, and Joseph Ziegler, eds., *The Origins of Racism;* Margaret R. Greer, Walter D. Mignolo, and Maureen Quilligan, *Rereading the Black Legend: The Discourses of Religious and Racial Difference in the Renaissance Empires;* Stephen Epstein, *Purity Lost: Transgressing Boundaries in the Eastern Mediterranean, 1000–1400;* Gil Anidjar, *Semites: Race, Religion, Literature;* Ania Loomba, "Race and the Possibilities of Comparative Critique." On the importance of language, as

« 290 »   Notes to Chapter 4

opposed to physiognomy, in the historical development of the concept
of race, see Peter Fenves, "What 'Progresses' Has Race-Theory Made
Since the Times of Leibniz and Wolff?" The becoming-culture of race,
similarly vast, is memorably articulated in Etienne Balibar's essay, "Is
There a Neo-Racism?."

167. Olender, *Languages of Paradise*, 12.

168. For an argument about Persian involvement in Orientalist comparative philology prior to its European "discovery," see Tavakoli-Targhi,
Refashioning Iran. See also Carol A. Breckenridge and Peter van der
Veer, *Orientalism and the Postcolonial Predicament: Perspectives
on South Asia*. For the relationship between philology and historiography, see James Turner, *Philology: The Forgotten Origins of the
Modern Humanities*.

169. Karen Lury, "Children in an Open World: Mobility as Ontology in
New Iranian and Turkish Cinema," 289; Dimitris Eleftheriotis, *Cinematic Journeys: Film and Movement*, 142–61.

170. Iraj Bashiri, "Muslims or Shamans: Blacks of the Persian Gulf," 3;
Hasan Pīrniyā, *Īrān-i Bāstān*, 157.

171. Īraj Afshār Sīstānī, *Khūzistān va tamaddun-i dīrīnī-i ān*, vol. 1, 474.
Similar narratives in other parts of Western Asia and North Africa
describe the historical emergence of blackness in parallel ways. In
Morocco, the *ḥarāṭīn*—"descendants of black people who inhabited
the Draa valley since time immemorial" are juxtaposed with black
people in northwest Africa who were originally slaves. See El Hamel,
Black Morocco, 109.

172. Tony Ballantyne, *Orientalism and Race: Aryanism and the British
Empire*, 50, 170.

173. Reza Zia-Ebrahimi, *The Emergence of Iranian Nationalism*, 8. Indo-
Europeanism, or the "Aryan Invasion Theory," was put to work in
various ways depending on the thinker. See also Ballantyne, *Orien-
talism and Race*, 181–87; Tapan Raychaudhuri, *Europe Reconsidered:
Perceptions of the West in Nineteenth-Century Bengal*; Thomas R.
Trautmann, *Aryans and British India*.

174. S. K. Biswas, *Autochthon of India and the Aryan Invasion*; David
Frawley, *The Myth of the Aryan Invasion of India*.

175. Najm Ābādī, "Sīnamā: andīshah hāyi darbārih-'i 'Bāshu Gharībeh-'i
Kūchak.' " 208.

176. Najmabadi, *Women with Mustaches and Men without Beards*, 100;
Amy Motlagh, *Burying the Beloved: Marriage, Realism, and Reform
in Modern Iran*.

177. Rastegar, *Surviving Images*, 149.

178. Spivak, "Nationalism and the Imagination," 83.

179. Qūkāsiyān, *Guft u gū*, 224.

CONCLUSION

1. Laura Marks, "Video's Body, Analog and Digital," in *Touch: Sensuous Theory and Multisensory Media*; Arild Fetveit, "Death, Beauty, and Iconoclastic Nostalgia: Precarious Aesthetics and Lana Del Rey."

2. Michelle Langford, "Iranian Cinema and Social Media," 253. On cinema's fading memory as the basis for contemporary art, see D. N. Rodowick, *What Philosophy Wants from Images*, 11.

3. A brief survey of the literature on internet culture from the 1990s onward indicates an early propensity toward celebration of the democratic potential of cybernetic interactivity, followed by a swelling wave of deep platform nihilism. Geert Lovink, *Sad by Design: On Platform Nihilism*, 1, 45.

4. In addition to Alicia Garza and Patrisse Cullors, Opal Tometi is also responsible for galvanizing the formation of the early social media movement.

5. Frederick C. Harris, "The Next Civil Rights Movement?," 36. Thus, under the reconceptualization of social movement that social media has enabled, signifying identity has become "an end unto itself." Alvin B. Tillery Jr., "What Kind of a Movement Is Black Lives Matter? The View from Twitter."

6. André Brock Jr., *Distributed Blackness: African American Cybercultures*, 34. As Riché Richardson's analysis of the role of social networking platforms in the Trayvon Martin case demonstrates, social media contributed to building public literacy and political outrage over his murder, while at the same time playing a decisive role in criminalizing Martin by supplying fodder for the exploitation and miscontextualization of information from his Facebook and Twitter accounts. Riché Richardson, "E-Raced: #Touré, Twitter, and Trayvon," 100–101. See also Simone Browne, *Dark Matters: On the Surveillance of Blackness*.

7. Ario, Twitter post. March 23, 2021. http://twitter.com/Arrio_B, my emphasis.

8. Thus, Black Moroccan artist M'Barek confesses in an interview that "Today, I am in a phase in which doubt sometimes takes over me. . . . When presenting my projects in the country, I can hear the echo that is projected towards me from Moroccan audiences, which make me dive into a frustrating duality. I am often told 'But, but this doesn't exist,' 'We are all Moroccans, there is no such thing as a Black Moroccan.'"

9. At the time I was writing this book, on the About section on their website the Collective described themselves as "a chapter-based, not-for profit organization with the mission to amplify Black and Afro-Iranians' voices within the Iranian diaspora, educate on the connections between Africanness/Blackness and Iranian identity as well as advocate for the representation of Black and Afro-Iranians

in Iranian narratives." Most of the Collective's energy thus appears invested in producing positive representations of Black Iranians, and more basically, to simply assert their existence and identity as Black and Iranian. At the same time, what distinguishes the practices of the Collective from a mere form of identity politics (with which they can easily become conflated) is the sometimes latent, sometimes explicit insistence on antiblackness that accompanies their assertions of self-existence. See Todd McGowan, *Universality and Identity Politics*.

10. Eithne Quinn, *Nuthin' but a 'G' Thang: The Culture and Commerce of Gangsta Rap*, 202.

11. Abdul R. JanMohamed, *The Death-Bound Subject: Richard Wright's Archeology of Death*. The relation between blackness and death has been perhaps most compellingly articulated in the contemporary discourse known as Afropessimism. See Frank B. Wilderson III, *Afropessimism* and *Red, White & Black: Cinema and the Structure of U.S. Antagonisms*.

12. Muḥammad ibn Aḥmad Bīrūnī, *The Chronology of Ancient Nations*, 200–202.

13. Mary Boyce, *Textual Sources for the Study of Zoroastrianism*, 67.

14. Elisabeth Förster-Nietzsche, "Introduction: How Zarathustra Came into Being," in Friedrich Nietzsche, *Thus Spake Zarathustra*, 2. In the Christian salvational paradigm undergirding the concept of time that renaissance historiography laicized into our modern-day, global inheritance, history both progresses and returns, simultaneously, "one great detour to reach in the end the beginning," centered on the accomplished advent, the *kairos* of Jesus Christ. It is only "because of our habit of thinking in terms of the Christian tradition that the formal division of all historical time into past, present, and future times seems so entirely natural and self-evident." Karl Löwith, *Meaning in History: The Theological Implications of the Philosophy of History*, 182–86.

15. Jonathan Beller, *The Cinematic Mode of Production: Attention Economy and the Society of the Spectacle*, 2, 7.

16. Marina Terkourafi, *The Languages of Global Hip Hop*, 15.

17. Tricia Rose, *Black Noise: Rap Music and Black Culture in Contemporary America*, 84.

18. Carol Vernallis, *Unruly Media: YouTube, Music Video, and the New Digital Cinema*, 105, 134.

19. Houston A. Baker Jr., *Black Studies, Rap, and the Academy*, 89.

20. Peter Kivy, *The Fine Art of Repetition: Essays in the Philosophy of Music*, 352.

21. Davide Panagia, *Impressions of Hume: Cinematic Thinking and the Politics of Discontinuity*.

22. Steven Shaviro, "Supa Dupa Fly: Black Women as Cyborgs in Hiphop Videos," 173.

Notes to Conclusion « 293 »

23. Shea Serrano, *The Rap Year Book: The Most Important Rap Song from Every Year since 1979, Discussed, Debated, and Deconstructed*, 222.
24. Kevin Fellezs, *Birds of Fire: Jazz, Rock, Funk, and the Creation of Fusion*, 56.
25. Lindon Barrett, *Blackness and Value: Seeing Double*, 84. On "repression" in Black aesthetics, see Fred Moten, *In the Break: The Aesthetics of the Black Radical Tradition*, 1–24.
26. Scot Brown, *Fighting for US: Maulana Karenga, the US Organization, and Black Cultural Nationalism*, 59.
27. Alexander Galloway, *The Interface Effect*, 30–31.
28. Laura U. Marks, *Hanan al-Cinema: Affections for the Moving Image*, 73.
29. Alessandra Raengo and Laurel Ahnert, "Blackness at the Heart: Extruding Sovereignty in Nancy's and Denis's *The Intruder*," 145.
30. Nick Couldry and Ulises A. Mejias, *The Costs of Connection: How Data Is Colonizing Human Life and Appropriating it for Capitalism*.
31. Édouard Glissant, *Caribbean Discourse: Selected Essays*, 161.
32. Denise Ferreira da Silva, *Toward a Global Idea of Race*, 1–17.
33. Jacques Derrida, "Signature, Event, Content," 65.
34. Michel Chion, *The Voice in Cinema*, 17.
35. Collective for Black Iranians. Twitter post, April 14, 2021, 11:49 pm. http://Twitter.com/collectiveforblackiranians.
36. Collective for Black Iranians. Twitter post, November 26, 2020, 11:49 pm. http://Twitter.com/collectiveforblackiranians.
37. Sylvia Wynter, "On How We Mistook the Map for the Territory and Reimprisoned Ourselves in Our Unbearable Wrongness of Being, of *Desêtre*: Black Studies toward the Human Project," 112.
38. W. E. B. Du Bois, Isabel Eaton, and Elijah Anderson, *The Philadelphia Negro: A Social Study*, 1.
39. Kwame Ture and Charles V. Hamilton, *Black Power: The Politics of Liberation*, 37. For more on the debate between the terms Black and Negro, see Vincent Harding, "Beyond Chaos: Black History and the Search for the New Land," in *Amistad*, 1267–92.
40. James Sweet, "The Iberian Roots of American Racist Thought," 145. Despite inherited wisdoms, the tethering of blackness to negation and abjection is nonexclusive to modern Western thought, as the political labor of contemporary Black Southwest Asian and North African activists demonstrates, as well as the "potent" traditions in Arabic, Turkish, and Persian literature promulgating antiblack tropes. Edward E. Curtis IV, *The Call of Bilal: Islam in the African Diaspora*, 23; Rachel Schine, "Race and Blackness in Premodern Arabic Literature"; Minoo Southgate, "The Negative Images of Blacks in Some Medieval Iranian Writings"; Mustafa Olpak, *Biographie d'une famille d'esclaves: Kenya, Crete, Istanbul.* The point of Wynter's passage, I would like to suggest, is less that antiblackness has, or can have, a simple origin, or that it is

geographically and historically localizable, confineable to a context, but that *decontextualization* and constant recontextualization drives forward the "emancipatory explosion" that blackness is, that blackness can be (Wynter, "On How We Mistook the Map," 112).

41. Wynter, "On How We Mistook the Map," 115–16.
42. For a meditation on W. E. B. Du Bois's decision to preserve, reanimate, and capitalize the term *Negro* in the 1920s, see R. A Judy, *Sentient Flesh: Thinking in Disorder, Poiēsis in Black*, 27–28.
43. Fred Moten, "The Case of Blackness," 200.
44. Kimberly Juanita Brown, *The Repeating Body: Slavery's Visual Resonance in the Contemporary*, 13–14.
45. Rose, *Black Noise*, 92.
46. Baker Jr., *Black Studies, Rap, and the Academy*, 34–37.
47. Derrida, "Signature, Event, Context," 12.
48. "Authenticity is produced by circulation. . . . Absent the presence of a dominant group, there would be no originary status, no necessary group 'belonging' to protect." Wahneema Lubiano, foreword to Ronald A. T. Judy, *(Dis)Forming the American Canon: African-Arabic Slave Narratives and the Vernacular*, xx.
49. Jean-Francois Lyotard, "Rewriting Modernity," in *The Inhuman: Reflections on Time*, 23.
50. Nathaniel Mackey, *Splay Anthem*, xi.
51. Fred Moten, "Black Mo'nin'," in David Eng and David Kazanjian, eds., *Loss: The Politics of Mourning*, 22.
52. Collective for Black Iranians, Twitter post, March 22, 2021, http:// twitter.com/blackiranians.
53. See also Parisa Vaziri, "Antiblack Joy."
54. Sanaz Rahmani, Twitter post, March 22, 2021, http://twitter.com/ sanazrahmani.
55. "*sat-i savād kisāni ki siyāhī-i sūrat-i hājī fīrūz rā nizhādparastānih mīdānand.*" Saam Givrad, Twitter post, March 22, 2021, http://twitter .com/saamgivrad.
56. Jalal Zaree, Twitter post, March 23, 2021, http://twitter.com/jalalzaree.
57. See, for example, Neda Maghbouleh, *The Limits of Whiteness: Iranian Americans and the Everyday Politics of Race*; Reza Zia-Ebrahimi, *The Emergence of Iranian Nationalism: Race and the Politics of Dislocation*. In 2017, my colleagues penned an open letter to Iranian and Iranian-American academics continuing to propagate and use the myth of a white Iran to support alt-right political agendas. Amy Tahani-Bidmeshki, M. Shadee Malaklou, Nasrin Rahimieh, and Parisa Vaziri, "An Open Letter to Iranian/American Academics and Scholars in the United States," *Medium*, September 14, 2017, https://medium.com/ @amytahanibidmeshki/an-open-letter-to-iranian-american -academics-and-scholars-in-the-united-states-3c25bd1f7051.

Notes to Conclusion « 295 »

58. By contrast, for example, Stuart Hall notes that the first wave of Afro-Caribbean and Asian immigration to the United States in the 1950s and 1960s marked the beginning of the end of the assimilationist dream of liberal humanism. Hall, *The Fateful Triangle: Race, Ethnicity, Nation,* 87–88.

59. Safaneh Neyshabouri, Twitter post, May 31, 2020, http://twitter.com/safanehneyshabouri. I believe the retweeted artwork is attributable to the artist Mina Jafari.

60. Ehsan Mansouri, Twitter post, March 23, 2021, http://twitter.com/ehsamansuri.

61. KEYMOL, Twitter post, March 24, 2021, http://twitter.com/keymolthe2nd.

62. Mirza Gilani, Twitter post, March 25, 2021, http://twitter.com/sekoozhad.

63. Meerza Aghassee to Justin Sheil, cited in Behnaz A. Mirzai, *A History of Slavery and Emancipation in Iran,* 137. Sir A. Ryan to Sir John Simon similarly observes of the King of Saudi Arabia that the latter "looks at the slavery question when it is raised by foreign Powers, not from the point of view of morality or internal policy but from that of his desire to safeguard his independence."

64. Cemil Aydin, *The Idea of the Muslim World: A Global Intellectual History,* 10, 15.

65. Vernallis, *Unruly Media,* 130–32, 137.

66. Laurel Westrup and David Laderman, "Into the Remix: The Culture of Sampling," 5.

67. Gilles Deleuze, *Difference and Repetition,* 2.

68. Although I have chosen the Collective for Black Iranians as a focalizing media object with which to conclude this book, the unending accumulation and always inherently unfinished quality of a project such as theirs in fact exposes the conceit that could be a conclusion. In writing of methodological questions surrounding the study of Black digital culture, Lauren McLeod Cramer grapples with the unmanageability of the digital: "What happens when ten new images are posted the next day?" Lauren McLeod Cramer, "'A Very Black Project': A Method for Digital Visual Culture," 125.

69. Margo Natalie Crawford, *Black Post-Blackness: The Black Arts Movement and Twenty-First-Century Aesthetics,* 1–18.

70. Stephen J. King, "Black Arabs and African Migrants: Between Slavery and Racism in North Africa"; Laura Menin, "'Dans la Peau d'un Noir': Senegalese Students and Young Professionals in Rabat"; Eric Hahonou, "Blackness, Slavery and Anti-Racism Activism in Contemporary North Africa."

71. Khawla Ksiksi, "Faire face au racisme en Tunisie : Entretien avec Khawla Ksiksi." Mrad Dali Inès observes a number of such Facebook

pages created since 2009–2010 (Inès, "Les mobilisations des 'Noirs tunisiens' au lendemain de la révolte de 2011," 61).

72. Safa Bannani, "Un movement contre 'l'invisibilité' des femmes noires en Tunisie est né."

73. Inès, "Les mobilisations des 'Noirs tunisiens' "; Stephen J. King, "Democracy and Progress towards Racial Equality in Tunisia: Interview with Zied Rouine."

74. Mana Kia, *Persianate Selves: Memories of Place and Origin before Nationalism*, 5.

75. As Stuart Hall wrote of a different racial-national concatenation, "black British." (Hall, *The Fateful Triangle: Race, Ethnicity, Nation*, 99). See also Hortense Spillers, "Peter's Pans: Eating in the Diaspora," in *Black, White, and in Color*.

76. See also Cecil Brown, *Dude, Where's My Black Studies Department?*

77. The Collective for Black Iranians, Twitter post, February 5, 2021. http://twitter.com/blackiranians.

78. Y. Hakan Erdem, *Slavery in the Ottoman Empire and Its Demise: 1800–1909*; Ehud Toledano, *As If Silent and Absent*, 204–39; Yannis Spyropoulos, "Beys, Sheikhs, Kolbasis, and Godiyas: Some Notes on the Leading Figures of the Ottoman-African Diaspora."

79. Artists' "reluctance to describe the technological processes behind digital artworks" gestures toward technological obscurity. Ann-Sophie Lehmann, "Hidden Practice: Artists' Working Spaces, Tools, and Materials in the Digital Domain," in Marianna van den Boomen et al., eds., *Digital Material: Tracing New Media in Everyday Life and Technology*, 270.

80. Moses Finley, *Ancient Slavery and Modern Ideology*.

81. Alexander Galloway, "Does the Whatever Speak?," in Lisa Nakamura and Peter A. Chow-White, eds., *Race After the Internet*, 122.

82. Saeedah bint Sadam, qtd. in Jerzy Zdanowski, "Contesting Enslavement: Voices of the Female Slaves from the Persian Gulf," 73.

83. Mirzai, *A History of Slavery and Emancipation*, 70.

84. Richard C. Jankowsky, *Stambeli: Music, Trance, and Alterity in Tunisia*, 75.

85. Sean Cubitt, *Anecdotal Evidence: Ecocritique from Hollywood to the Mass Image*, 225.

86. Lovink, *Sad by Design: On Platform Nihilism*, 67.

87. Graig Uhlin, "Playing in the Gif(t) Economy," 521–22; Karl Schoonover, "Sinkholes, GIFS, and Cinematic Ecocatastrophe," in Karen Redrobe and Jeff Scheible, eds., *Deep Mediations*, 204.

88. Henri Lefebvre, *Rhythmanalysis: Space, Time and Everyday Life*, 48.

89. Judith Butler, *The Psychic Life of Power: Theories in Subjection*, 127; Fred Moten, *Black and Blur*, 1–18.

Bibliography

Ābādī, Najm. "Sīnamā: andīshah hāyi darbārih-'i 'Bāshu Gharībeh-'i Kūchak.'" *Hunar va mi'mārī* 13 (1992): 206–9.

Abbott, Nabia. "A Ninth-Century Fragment of the 'Thousand Nights': New Light on the Early History of the Arabian Nights." *Journal of Near Eastern Studies* 8, no. 3 (1949): 129–64.

Abdulāhīyān, Ḥamīd. "Bāznamāyī-i marāsim-i ahl-i havā dar film-i mustanad-i *Bād-i Jīn*." *Muṭāli'āt-i jāmi'i shinākhtī* 49 (2006): 305–21.

Abdullah, Thabit. *Merchants, Mamluks, and Murder: The Political Economy of Trade in Eighteenth Century Basra.* Albany: State University of New York Press, 2001.

Abrahamian, Ervand. *A History of Modern Iran.* Cambridge: Cambridge University Press, 2018.

Abrahamian, Ervand. *Oil Crisis in Iran: From Nationalism to Coup d'Etat.* Cambridge: Cambridge University Press, 2021.

Adam, Anita. "A Saar Gaamuri in Somalia: Spirit Possession as Expression of Women's Autonomy?" In *Peace and Milk, Drought and War: Somali Culture, Society, and Politics: Essays in Honour of I. M. Lewis,* edited by Markus V. Hoehne and Virginia Luling. New York: Columbia University Press, 2010.

Adib-Moghaddam, Arshin. *Psycho-Nationalism: Global Thought, Iranian Imaginations.* Cambridge: Cambridge University Press, 2018.

Afary, Janet. *Sexual Politics in Modern Iran.* Cambridge: Cambridge University Press, 2009.

Aghaie, Kamran Scot. *The Martyrs of Karbala: Shi'i Symbols and Rituals in Modern Iran.* Seattle: University of Washington Press, 2004.

Aghaie, Kamran Scot. *The Women of Karbala: Ritual Performance and Symbolic Discourses in Modern Shi'i Islam.* Austin: University of Texas Press, 2005.

Aghakhani, Nader. *Les "gens de l'air," "jeux" de guérison dans le sud de l'Iran: Une étude d'anthropologie psychanalytique.* Paris: L'Harmattan, 2014.

Agius, Dionisius A., John P. Cooper, Lucy Semaan, Chiara Zazzaro, and Robert Carter. "Remembering the Sea: Personal and Communal Recollections of Maritime Life in Jizan and the Farasan Islands, Saudi Arabia." *Journal of Maritime Archaeology* 11, no. 2 (2016): 127–77.

« 298 » Bibliography

Ahmed, Chanfi. *AfroMecca in History: African Societies, Anti-Black Racism, and Teaching in Al-Haram Mosque in Mecca.* Newcastle-upon-Tyne, UK: Cambridge Scholars, 2019.

Akomfrah, John, Lina Gopaul, David Lawson, Stuart Hall, Dewald Aukema, Nse Asuquo, Trevor Mathison, and Miles Davis. *The Stuart Hall Project.* DVD. London: BFI, 2014.

Akrami, Jamsheed. "The Blighted Spring: Iranian Cinema and Politics in the 1970s." In *Film and Politics in the Third World,* edited by John D. H. Downing. New York: Praeger, 1987.

Ali, Kecia. *Marriage and Slavery in Early Islam.* Cambridge, Mass.: Harvard University Press, 2010.

Ali, Omar H., ed. *Islam in the Indian Ocean World: A Brief History with Documents.* Boston: Bedford/St. Martin's, 2016.

Ali, Omar H., Kenneth X. Robbins, Beheroze Shroff, and Jazmin Graves. "Introduction: Afro-South Asia in the Global African Diaspora." In *African Diasporan Communities Across South Asia.* Greensboro: University of North Carolina at Greensboro, 2020.

Alishan, Leonardo P. "Ahmad Shamlu: The Rebel Poet in Search of an Audience." *Iranian Studies* 18, no. 2–4 (1985): 375–422.

Allen, James de Vere. "Swahili Culture and the Nature of East Coast Settlement." *International Journal of African Historical Studies* 14, no. 2 (1981).

Allen, Richard. *European Slave Trading in the Indian Ocean, 1500–1800.* Athens: Ohio University Press, 2014.

Allen, Richard, and Murray Smith, eds. *Film Theory and Philosophy.* Oxford: Oxford University Press, 1997.

Al-Munsif bin Hasan. *Al-ʿabīd wa-al-jawārī fī ḥikāyāt Alf Laylah wa-Laylah.* Tunisia: Sirash lil-Nashr, 1994.

Alpers, Edward A. "The African Diaspora in the Indian Ocean: A Comparative Perspective." In *The African Diaspora in the Indian Ocean,* edited by Shihan de S. Jayasuriya and Richard Pankhurst, 19–52. Trenton, N.J.: Africa World Press, 2003.

Alpers, Edward A. *The Indian Ocean in World History.* New York: Oxford University Press, 2014.

Alpers, Edward A. *Ivory and Slaves: Changing Pattern of International Trade in East Central Africa to the Later Nineteenth Century.* Berkeley: University of California Press, 1975.

Alpers, Edward A. "The Other Middle Passage: The African Slave Trade in the Indian Ocean." In *Many Middle Passages: Forced Migration and the Making of the Modern World,* edited by Emma Christopher, Cassandra Pybus, and Marcus Rediker, 20–38. Berkeley: University of California Press, 2007.

Alpers, Edward A. "Recollecting Africa: Diasporic Memory in the Indian Ocean World." *African Studies Review* 43, no. 1 (2000): 83–99.

Amanat, Abbas. "The Study of History in Post-Revolutionary Iran:

Nostalgia, Illusion, or Historical Awareness?" *Iranian Studies* 22, no. 4 (1989): 3–18.

Amānī, Maysam. "Ta'sīr-i sīnamā-yi mawj-i naw-yi Īrān dar junbishhā-yi ijtimā'ī-i sālhā-yi 1257–1347." *Khurdnamah* 12 (2014): 1–26.

Amin, Camron Michael. "Selling and Saving 'Mother Iran': Gender and the Iranian Press in the 1940s." *International Journal of Middle East Studies* 33, no. 3 (2001): 335–61.

Amir-Moezzi, Mohammad Ali. *The Divine Guide in Early Shi'ism: The Sources of Esotericism in Islam.* Albany: State University of New York Press, 1994.

Anderson, Kyle J. *The Egyptian Labor Corps: Race, Space, and Place in the First World War.* Austin: University of Texas Press, 2021.

Andrew, Dudley. *Concepts in Film Theory.* Oxford: Oxford University Press, 1984.

Anidjar, Gil. *Semites: Race, Religion, Literature.* Stanford, Calif.: Stanford University Press, 2008.

Anṣārī, Muḥammad Bāqir. *Namāyish-i rūḥawzī: zamīnah va 'anāṣir-i khandah'sāz.* Tehran: Shirkat-i Intishārāt-i Sūrah-yi Mihr, 2008.

Appel, Hannah. *The Licit Life of Capitalism: US Oil in Equatorial Guinea.* Durham, N.C.: Duke University Press, 2019.

Arasteh, A. Reza. *Education and Social Awakening in Iran, 1850–1960.* Leiden: Brill, 1962.

Armes, Roy. *Third World Filmmaking and the West.* Berkeley: University of California Press, 1987.

Arondekar, Anjali R. *For the Record: On Sexuality and the Colonial Archive in India.* Durham, N.C.: Duke University Press, 2009.

Artaud, Antonin. *Antonin Artaud, Selected Writings,* edited by Susan Sontag. Berkeley: University of California Press, 1988.

Artaud, Antonin. "Sorcery and Cinema." In *The Shadow and Its Shadow: Surrealist Writings on the Cinema,* edited by Paul Hammond. San Francisco: City Lights Books, 2000.

Arvidsson, Stefan. *Aryan Idols: Indo-European Mythology as Ideology and Science.* Translated by Sonia Wichmann. Chicago: University of Chicago Press, 2006.

Ashkanani, Zubaida. "Zar Cult in Kuwait." In *Women's Medicine: The Zar-Bori Cult in Africa and Beyond,* edited by I. M. Lewis. Edinburgh: Edinburgh University Press, 1991.

Askari, Kaveh. *Relaying Cinema in Midcentury Iran: Material Cultures in Transit.* Oakland: University of California Press, 2022.

Askew, Kelly. *Performing the Nation: Swahili Music and Cultural Politics in Tanzania.* Chicago: University of Chicago Press, 2002.

'Athamina, Khalil. "How Did Islam Contribute to Change the Legal Status of Women: The Case of the Jawārī or the Female Slaves." *Al-qantara: Revista de estudios árabes* 28, no. 2 (2007): 383–408.

Atwood, Blake. "When the Sun Goes Down: Sex, Desire and Cinema in 1970s Tehran." *Asian Cinema* 27, no. 2 (2016): 127–50.

Atwood, Blake. *Underground: The Secret Life of Videocassettes in Iran.* Cambridge: MIT Press, 2021.

Aumont, Jacques. *Le cinéma et la mise en scène.* Paris: Armand Colin, 2010.

Ayana, Daniel. "The Northern *Zanj*, Demadim, Yamyam, Yam/Yamjam, Habasha/Ahabish, Zanj-Ahabish, and *Zanj* ed-Damadam—The Horn of Africa between the Ninth and Fifteenth Centuries." *History in Africa* 46 (2019): 57–104.

Aydin, Cemil. *The Idea of the Muslim World: A Global Intellectual History.* Cambridge, Mass.: Harvard University Press, 2017.

Aydinlū, Sajjād. "Muqadamahyi bar naqqālī dar Iran." *Pazhūhish nāmah'i zabān va adab-i fārsī* 12, no. 4 (2010): 35–64.

Ayoub, Mahmoud M. *Redemptive Suffering in Islam.* The Hague: Mouton, 1978.

Āzhand, Ya'qūb. *Namāyishnāmah'nivīsī dar Īrān.* Tehran: Nashr-i Ney, 1994.

Azoulay, Ariella Aïsha. *Potential History: Unlearning Imperialism.* London: Verso, 2019.

Babaie, Sussan, Kathryn Babayan, Ina Baghdiantz-MacCabe, and Massumeh Farhad. *Slaves of the Shah: New Elites of Safavid Iran.* London: I. B. Tauris, 2004.

Babès, Leïla. "Folie douce, vent des ancêtres: La transe au Maghreb." *Social Compass* 42, no. 4 (1995): 461–76.

Badiou, Alain. *Rhapsody for the Theatre,* edited by Bruno Bosteels and Martin Puchner. London: Verso, 2013.

Baghoolizadeh, Beeta. "From Religious Eulogy to War Anthem: Kurdizadeh's 'Layla Bigufta' and Blackness in Late Twentieth-Century Iran." *Comparative Studies of South Asia, Africa and the Middle East* (2021): 441–54.

Baghoolizadeh, Beeta. "The Myths of Haji Firuz: The Racist Contours of the Iranian Minstrel." *Lateral* 10, no. 1 (2021).

Bahār, Mihrdād. *Pazhūhishī dar asāṭīr-i Īrān: pārah-'i nakhust va pārah-'i duyyum.* Edited by Katāyūn Mazdāpūr. Tehran: Nashr-i Āgah, 2002.

Baird, Robert D. "Interpretative Categories and the History of Religions." *History and Theory* 8 (1968): 17–30.

Baker, Houston A. Jr. *Black Studies, Rap, and the Academy.* Chicago: University of Chicago Press, 1993.

Baker, Houston A. Jr., Manthia Diawara, and Ruth H. Lindeborg. *Black British Cultural Studies: A Reader.* Chicago: University of Chicago Press, 1996.

Baker, Houston A., and Merinda Simmons, eds. *The Trouble with Post-Blackness.* New York: Columbia University Press, 2015.

Balanzategui, Jessica. *The Uncanny Child in Transnational Cinema:*

Ghosts of Futurity at the Turn of the Twenty-First Century. Amsterdam: Amsterdam University Press, 2018.

Balibar, Étienne. "Is There a Neo-Racism?" In Étienne Balibar and Immanuel Wallerstein, *Race, Nation, Class: Ambiguous Identities,* 17–28. London: Verso, 1991.

Ballantyne, Tony. *Orientalism and Race: Aryanism in the British Empire.* Houndmills: Palgrave, 2002.

Bannani, Safa. "Un movement contre 'l'invisibilité' des femmes noires en Tunisie est né." *Middle East Eye,* February 12, 2020. https://www.middleeasteye.net/fr/en-bref/un-mouvement-contre-linvisibilite-des-femmes-noires-en-tunisie-est-ne.

Barrett, Ross, ed. *Oil Culture.* Minneapolis: University of Minnesota Press, 2014.

Barrett, Lindon. *Blackness and Value: Seeing Double.* Cambridge: Cambridge University Press, 1999.

Barrett, Lindon. *Racial Blackness and the Discontinuity of Western Modernity,* edited by Justin A. Joyce, Dwight A. McBride, and John Carlos Rowe. Urbana: University of Illinois Press, 2014.

Barth, Fredrik. *Sohar, Culture and Society in an Omani Town.* Baltimore: Johns Hopkins University Press, 1983.

Barthes, Roland. "Ecoute." In *L'obvie et l'obtus: Essais critiques III.* Paris: Seuil, 1982.

Bashiri, Iraj. "Muslims or Shamans: Blacks of the Persian Gulf." *Angelfire* (1983). http://www.angelfire.com/rnb/bashiri/gulf/gulf.html (accessed 4 November 2022).

Bassiri, Kaveh. "Masculinity in Iranian Cinema." In *Global Encyclopedia of Lesbian, Gay, Bisexual, Transgender, and Queer (LGBTQ) History,* edited by Howard Chiang, et al., vol. 2, 1018–23. Farmington Hills, Mich.: Charles Scribner's Sons, 2019.

Basu, Helene. *Journeys and Dwellings: Indian Ocean Themes in South Asia.* Hyderabad: Orient Longman, 2008.

Battain, Tiziana. "Osservazioni sul rito zār di possessione degli spiriti in Yemen." *Quaderni di Studi Arabi* (1995): 117–30.

Baumbach, Nico. *Cinema/Politics/Philosophy.* New York: Columbia University Press, 2019.

Baudelaire, Charles. *De L'essence du Rire.* Paris: Herne, 1868.

Bazin, André. *What Is Cinema? Vol 1.* Translated by Hugh Gray. Berkeley: University of California Press, 1967.

Bazin, André. *What Is Cinema? Vol 2.* Translated by Hugh Gray. Berkeley: University of California Press, 1971.

Beaumont, Daniel E. *Slave of Desire: Sex, Love, and Death in* The 1001 Nights. Madison, Wisc.: Fairleigh Dickinson University Press, 2002.

Becker, Cynthia J. *Blackness in Morocco: Gnawa Identity through Music and Visual Culture.* Minneapolis: University of Minnesota Press, 2020.

Becker, Judith. *Deep Listeners: Music, Emotion, and Trancing.* Bloomington: Indiana University Press, 2004.

Beckerleg, Susan. "African Bedouin in Palestine." *African and Asian Studies* 6 (2007): 289–303.

Beeman, William O. "Understanding the Zār: An African-Iranian Healing Dance Ritual." *Anthropology of the Middle East* 13, no. 1 (2018): 69–81.

Beeman, William O. "Why Do They Laugh?: An Interactional Approach to Humor in Traditional Iranian Improvisatory Theater: Performance and Its Effects." *Journal of American Folklore* 94, no. 374 (1981): 506–26.

Beller, Jonathan. *The Cinematic Mode of Production: Attention Economy and the Society of the Spectacle.* Hanover, N.H.: Dartmouth College Press, 2006.

Bellour, Raymond. "The Cinematic Spectator: A Special Memory." In *Screen Dynamics: Mapping the Borders of Cinema,* edited by Gertrud Koch, Volker Pantenburg, and Simon Rothöhler. Vienna: Österreichisches Film Museum, 2012.

Bellour, Raymond. *Raymond Bellour: Between-the-Images.* Translated by Allyn Hardyck. Zurich: JRP/Ringier, 2012.

Benjamin, Walter. *Illuminations: Essays and Reflections.* Translated by Harry Zohn. New York: Houghton Mifflin Harcourt, 2019.

Berardi, Franco. *And: Phenomenology of the End: Sensibility and Connective Mutation.* South Pasadena, Calif.: Semiotext(e), 2015.

Berg, Lodewijk Willem Christiaan. *Le Ḥadhramout et les colonies arabes dans l'Archipel indien.* Batavia: Imprimerie du gouvernement, 1886.

Bergson, Henri. *Laughter: An Essay on the Meaning of the Comic.* Translated by Cloudesley Brereton and Fred Rothwell. New York: Macmillan, 1914.

Bergstrom, Janet. "Alternation, Segmentation, Hypnosis: Interview with Raymond Bellour." *Camera Obscura* 1–2, no. 3–1 (1979): 70–103.

Berlant, Lauren, and Sianne Ngai. "Comedy Has Issues." *Critical Inquiry* 43, no. 2 (2017): 233–49.

Bernasconi, Robert. "Crossed Lines in the Racialization Process: Race as a Border Concept." *Research in Phenomenology* 42, no. 2 (2012): 206–28.

Bernstein, Robin. *Racial Innocence: Performing American Childhood from Slavery to Civil Rights.* New York: New York University Press, 2011.

Best, Stephen. *None Like Us: Blackness, Belonging, Aesthetic Life.* Durham, N.C.: Duke University Press, 2018.

Bhacker, Redha. "The Cultural Unity of the Gulf and the Indian Ocean: A Longue Durée Historical Perspective." In *The Persian Gulf in History,* edited by Lawrence Potter. New York: Palgrave, 2009.

Bilkhair Khalifa, Aisha. "Spirit Possession and Its Practices in Dubai (UAE)." *Musike* 1, no. 2 (2006): 43–64.

Bilkhair Khalifa, Aisha. "African Influence on Culture and Music in Dubai." *International Social Science Journal* 188 (2006): 227–35.

Bīrūnī, Muḥammad ibn Aḥmad, and Eduard Sachau. *The Chronology of Ancient Nations: An English Version of the Arabic Text of the Athâr-Ul-Bâkiya of Albîrûnî, or "Vestiges of the Past."* Frankfurt am Main: Institute for the History of Arabic-Islamic Science at the Johann Wolfgang Goethe University, 1998.

Bissonnette, Sylvie. "Committed Theatricality." In *Stages of Reality: Theatricality in Cinema,* edited by André Loiselle and Jeremy Maron. Toronto: University of Toronto Press, 2012.

Biswas, S.K. *Autochthon of India and the Aryan Invasion.* New Delhi: Genuine Publications, 1995.

Bleeker, Maaike. *Visuality in the Theatre: The Locus of Looking.* Basingstoke, UK: Palgrave Macmillan, 2008.

Blench, Roger. "Using Diverse Sources of Evidence for Reconstructing the Past History of Musical Exchanges in the Indian Ocean." *African Archaeological Review* 31 (2014): 675–703.

Bodel, John. *On Human Bondage: After Slavery and Social Death.* Chichester, UK: Wiley-Blackwell, 2016.

Bogle, Donald. *Toms, Coons, Mulattoes, Mammies & Bucks: An Interpretive History of Blacks in American Films.* New York: Continuum, 1994.

Bordwell, David. *Narration in the Fiction Film.* Madison: University of Wisconsin Press, 1985.

Borges, Jorge Luis. "Partial Magic in the Quixote." In *Labyrinths: Selected Stories and Other Writings,* edited by Donald A. Yates and James East Irby. New York: New Directions, 2007.

Bosworth, C. E. " 'Ajam," *Encyclopædia Iranica,* I/7, 700–701. http://www.iranicaonline.org/articles/ajam.

Bouanga, Ayda. "Gold, Slaves, and Trading Routes in Southern Blue Nile (Abbay) Societies, Ethiopia, 13th–16th Centuries." *Northeast African Studies* 17, no. 2 (2017): 31–60.

Bouhdiba, Abdelwahab. *Sexuality in Islam.* London: Routledge, 2008.

Bowen, Richard LeBaron Jr. "The Pearl Fisheries of the Persian Gulf." *Middle East Journal* 5, no. 2 (1951): 161–80.

Boyce, Mary. *Textual Sources for the Study of Zoroastrianism.* Chicago: University of Chicago Press, 1990.

Brand, Dionne. *A Map to the Door of No Return: Notes on Belonging.* Toronto: Vintage Canada, 2011.

Breckenridge, Carol A., and Peter van der Veer. *Orientalism and the Postcolonial Predicament: Perspectives on South Asia.* Philadelphia: University of Pennsylvania Press, 1993.

Bresson, Robert. *Notes on the Cinematograph.* Translated by Jonathan Griffin. New York: Penguin, 2016.

Breyley, G. J. "From the 'Sultan' to the Persian Side: Jazz in Iran and Iranian Jazz since the 1920s." In *Jazz and Totalitarianism,* edited by Bruce Johnson. New York: Routledge, 2017.

Brock, André. *Distributed Blackness: African American Cybercultures.* New York: New York University Press, 2020.

Bronfen, Elizabeth. "Death, The Navel of the Image." In *The Point of Theory: Practices of Cultural Analysis,* edited by Mieke Bal and Inge Boer. London: Bloomsbury, 2002.

Brooks, Peter. *The Melodramatic Imagination: Balzac, Henry James, Melodrama, and the Mode of Excess.* New Haven, Conn.: Yale University Press, 1976.

Brookshaw, Dominic Parviz, and Nasrin Rahimieh, eds. *Forugh Farrokhzad, Poet of Modern Iran: Iconic Woman and Feminine Pioneer of New Persian Poetry.* London: I. B. Tauris, 2010.

Brower, Benjamin Claude. *A Desert Named Peace: The Violence of France's Empire in the Algerian Sahara, 1844–1902.* New York: Columbia University Press, 2009.

Brower, Benjamin Claude. "Rethinking Abolition in Algeria. Slavery and the 'Indigenous Question.'" *Cahiers d'Études Africaines* 49, no. 195 (2009): 805–27.

Brown, Cecil. *Dude, Where's My Black Studies Department? The Disappearance of Black Americans from Our Universities.* Berkeley: North Atlantic Books, 2007.

Brown, Kimberly Juanita. *The Repeating Body: Slavery's Visual Resonance in the Contemporary.* Durham, N.C.: Duke University Press, 2015.

Brown, Scot. *Fighting for US: Maulana Karenga, the US organization, and Black Cultural Nationalism.* New York: New York University Press, 2003.

Browne, Simone. *Dark Matters: On the Surveillance of Blackness.* Durham, N.C.: Duke University Press, 2015.

Brownlee, Billie Jeanne. *New Media and Revolution: Resistance and Dissent in Pre-Uprising Syria.* Montreal: McGill-Queen's University Press, 2020.

Buell, Denise Kimber. *Why This New Race: Ethnic Reasoning in Early Christianity.* New York: Columbia University Press, 2005.

Bulūkbāshī, ʿAlī. *Qahvahkhānah'hā-yi Īrān.* Tehran: Daftar-i Pazhūhishhā-yi Farhangī, 1996.

Butler, Judith. *The Psychic Life of Power: Theories in Subjection.* Stanford, Calif.: Stanford University Press, 1997.

Byrd, Dustin J., and Seyed Javad Miri. *Ali Shariati and the Future of Social Theory: Religion: Revolution, and the Role of the Intellectual.* Leiden: Brill, 2017.

Callebert, Ralph. "African Mobility and Labor in Global History." *History Compass* 14, no. 3 (2016): 116–27.

Campbell, Gwyn, ed. *Abolition and Its Aftermath in Indian Ocean Africa and Asia*. London: Routledge, 2005.

Campbell, Gwyn. "Chapter Three. The African-Asian Diaspora: Myth Or Reality?" In *Uncovering the History of Africans in Asia*, 37–56. Leiden: Brill, 2008.

Campbell, Gwyn. "Female Bondage and Agency in the Indian Ocean World." In *African Communities in Asia and the Mediterranean: Identities between Integration and Conflict*, edited by Ehud Toledano. Trenton, N.J.: Africa World Press, 2012.

Campbell, Gwyn. *The Structure of Slavery in Indian Ocean Africa and Asia*. London: Frank Cass, 2004.

Campbell, Gwyn, and Elizabeth Elbourne, eds. *Sex, Power, and Slavery*. Athens: Ohio University Press, 2014.

Campbell, Scott M. *The Early Heidegger's Philosophy of Life: Facticity, Being, and Language*. New York: Fordham University Press, 2012.

Canudo, Ricciotto. "The Triumph of the Cinema." In *Early Film Theories in Italy: 1896–1922*, edited by Francesco Casetti, Silvio Alovisio and Luca Mazzei. Amsterdam: Amsterdam University Press, 2017.

Carter, Jay Kameron. *Race: A Theological Account*. Oxford: Oxford University Press, 2008.

Carter, Robert A. *Sea of Pearls: Seven Thousand Years of the Industry That Shaped the Gulf*. London: Arabian Publishing Limited, 2012.

Caswell, Fuad Matthew. *The Slave Girls of Baghdad: The Qiyān in the Early Abbasid Era*. London: I. B. Tauris, 2011.

Catlin-Jairazbhoy, Amy, and Edward A. Alpers, eds. *Sidis and Scholars: Essays on African Indians*. Trenton, N.J.: Rainbow, 2004.

Cavell, Stanley. *The World Viewed: Reflections on the Ontology of Film*. Cambridge, Mass.: Harvard University Press, 1979.

Chahārmahalī, Muḥamad. *Malakūt: nuqtiyi atf-i rī'ālism-i jādūyī-i dar Īrān*. Tehran: Adabīyāt-i Pārsī-yi Mu'aṣir, 2015.

Chaiklin, Martha, Philip Gooding, and Gwyn Campbell. *Animal Trade Histories in the Indian Ocean World*. Cham, Switzerland: Springer International, 2020.

Chakrabarty, Dipesh. *Provincializing Europe: Postcolonial Thought and Historical Difference*. Princeton, N.J.: Princeton University Press, 2008.

Chakravarty, Surajit. "Discontents of Modernity: Space, Consumption and Loss in Hong Kong New Wave and Bombay Parallel Cinema." In *Hong Kong and Bollywood: Global Cinema*, edited by Joseph Tse-Hei Lee and Satish Kolluri, 193–216. New York: Palgrave Macmillan, 2016.

Chandler, Nahum Dmitri. *X—The Problem of the Negro as a Problem for Thought*. New York: Fordham University Press, 2014.

Chatterjee, Indrani, and Richard M. Eaton, eds. *Slavery and South Asian History*. Bloomington: Indiana University Press, 2006.

Chaudhuri, K. N. *Asia Before Europe: Economy and Civilisation of the*

Indian Ocean from the Rise of Islam to 1750. Cambridge: Cambridge University Press, 1990.

Chion, Michel. *The Voice in Cinema.* Edited by Claudia Gorbman. New York: Columbia University Press, 1999.

Chittick, Neville "The 'Shirazi' Colonization of East Africa." *Journal of African History* 6, no. 3 (1965): 275–94.

Chubin, Shahram, and Charles Tripp. *Iran and Iraq at War.* New York: Routledge, 2019.

Cixous, Hélène, Keit Cohen, and Paula Cohen. "The Laugh of the Medusa." *Signs: Journal of Women in Culture and Society* 1, no. 4 (1976): 875–93.

Clarence-Smith, William Gervase. *The Economics of the Indian Ocean Slave Trade in the Nineteenth Century.* London: F. Cass, 1989.

Clarence-Smith, William Gervase. *Islam and the Abolition of Slavery.* Oxford: Oxford University Press, 2006.

Clifford, James. "On Ethnographic Surrealism." In *The Predicament of Culture: Twentieth Century Ethnography, Literature, and Art.* Cambridge, Mass.: Harvard University Press, 1988.

Cockrell, Dale. *Demons of Disorder: Early Blackface Minstrels and Their World.* Cambridge: Cambridge University Press, 1997.

Colebrook, Claire. "What Is It Like to Be a Human?" *Transgender Studies Quarterly* 2, no. 2 (2015): 227–43.

Constantinides, Pamela. "The History of Zar in the Sudan: Theories of Origin, Recorded Observation and Oral Tradition." In *Women's Medicine: The Zar-Bori Cult in Africa and Beyond,* edited by I. M. Lewis, 83–99. Edinburgh: Edinburgh University Press, 1991.

Cooke, Miriam. *Tribal Modern: Branding New Nations in the Arab Gulf.* Berkeley: University of California Press, 2014.

Cooley, Claire. "Soundscape of a National Cinema Industry: *Filmfarsi* and Its Sonic Connections with Egyptian and Indian Cinemas, 1940s–1960s." *Film History* 32, no. 3 (2020): 43–74.

Cooper, Frederick. *Plantation Slavery on the East Coast of Africa.* New Haven, Conn.: Yale University Press, 1977.

Cooper, Frederick. *From Slaves to Squatters: Plantation Labor and Agriculture in Zanzibar and Coastal Kenya, 1890–1925.* New Haven, Conn.: Yale University Press, 1980.

Couldry, Nick, and Ulises A. Mejias. *The Costs of Connection: How Data Is Colonizing Human Life and Appropriating It for Capitalism.* Stanford, Calif.: Stanford University Press, 2019.

Cowie, Peter. *Revolution! The Explosion of World Cinema in the Sixties.* New York: Faber and Faber, 2004.

Cramer, Lauren McLeod. "'A Very Black Project': A Method for Digital Visual Culture." In *Writing about Screen Media,* edited by Lisa Patti, 122–25. London: Routledge, 2020.

Crawford, Margo Natalie. *Black Post-Blackness: The Black Arts Movement and Twenty-First-Century Aesthetics*. Urbana: University of Illinois Press, 2017.

Crawley, Ashon T. *Blackpentecostal Breath: The Aesthetics of Possibility*. New York: Fordham University Press, 2017.

Crary, Jonathan. *Techniques of the Observer: On Vision and Modernity in the Nineteenth Century*. Cambridge, Mass.: MIT Press, 1992.

Crone, Patricia. *Slaves on Horses. The Evolution of the Islamic Polity*. Cambridge: Cambridge University Press, 1980.

Cronin, Stephanie. *Soldiers, Shahs and Subalterns in Iran: Opposition, Protest and Revolt, 1921–1941*. Basingstoke: Palgrave Macmillan, 2010.

Cronin, Stephanie. *Tribal Politics in Iran: Rural Conflict and the New State, 1921–1941*. New York: Routledge, 2007.

Crouzet, Guillemette. "A Golden Harvest: Exploitation et mondialisation des perles du golfe Arabo-Persique (vers 1870–vers 1910)." *Revue historique* 313, no. 2 (2022): 327–56.

Cruz, Jon. *Culture on the Margins: The Black Spiritual and the Rise of American Cultural Interpretation*. Princeton, N.J.: Princeton University Press, 1999.

Cubitt, Sean. *Anecdotal Evidence: Ecocritique from Hollywood to the Mass Image*. Oxford: Oxford University Press, 2020.

Curtin, Philip D. *Cross-Cultural Trade in World History*. Cambridge: Cambridge University Press, 1984.

Curtis, Edward E. *The Call of Bilal: Islam in the African Diaspora*. Chapel Hill: University of North Carolina Press, 2014.

Dabashi, Hamid. "The Poetics of Politics: Commitment in Modern Persian Literature." *Iranian Studies* 18, no. 2–4 (1985): 147–88.

Dabashi, Hamid. *Masters and Masterpieces of Iranian Cinema*. Washington, D.C.: Mage, 2007.

Dabashi, Hamid. *The Shahnamah: The Persian Epic as World Literature*. New York: Columbia University Press, 2019.

Dabashi, Hamid. *Theology of Discontent: The Ideological Foundation of the Islamic Revolution in Iran*. London: Routledge, 2017.

Dabashi, Hamid. *Shi'ism: A Religion of Protest*. Cambridge, Mass.: Belknap Press of Harvard University Press, 2011.

Dadi, Iftikhar. *Lahore Cinema: Between Realism and Fable*. Seattle: University of Washington Press, 2022.

Dalmuji, Mona. "The Oil City in Focus: The Cinematic Spaces of Abadan in the Anglo-Iranian Oil Company's Persian Story." *Comparative Studies of South Asia, Africa and the Middle East* 33, no. 2 (2013): 135–36.

Dalmuji, Mona. "The Image World of Middle Eastern Oil," in *Subterranean Estates: Life Worlds of Oil and Gas*, edited by Hannah Appel, Arthur Mason, and Michael Watts, 147–64. Ithaca, N.Y.: Cornell University Press, 2015.

Da Silva, Denise Ferreira. *Toward a Global Idea of Race.* Minneapolis: University of Minnesota Press, 2007.

Davari, Arash. "A Return to Which Self? Ali Shari'ati and Frantz Fanon on the Political Ethics of Insurrectionary Violence." *Comparative Studies of South Asia, Africa and the Middle East* 34, no. 1 (2014): 86–105.

Dayan, Daniel. "The Tutor-Code of Classical Cinema." *Film Quarterly* 28, no. 1 (1974): 22–31.

Debray, Regis. *Media Manifestos: On the Technological Transmission of Cultural Forms.* London: Verso, 1996.

Deeb, Lara. "Living Ashura in Lebanon: Mourning Transformed to Sacrifice." *Comparative Studies of South Asia, Africa and the Middle East* 25, no. 1 (2005): 122–37.

Deerr, Noel. *The History of Sugar,* vol. 1. London: Chapman and Hall, 1949.

De la Puente González, Cristina. "Free Fathers, Slave Mothers and Their Children: A Contribution to the Study of Family Structures in Al-Andalus." *Imago temporis. Medium Aevum* 7 (2013): 27–44.

Deleuze, Gilles. *Cinema I: The Movement-Image.* Minneapolis: University of Minnesota Press, 1986.

Deleuze, Gilles. *Cinema II: The Time-Image.* Minneapolis: University of Minnesota Press, 1986.

Deleuze, Gilles. *Difference and Repetition.* New York: Columbia University Press, 1994.

Deleuze, Gilles. *Negotiations: 1972–1990.* Translated by Martin Joughlin. New York: Columbia University Press, 1995.

De Moraes Farias, Paulo Fernando. "Models of the World and Categorical Models: The 'Enslavable Barbarian' as a Mobile Classificatory Label." In *Slaves and Slavery in Muslim Africa: Vol. 2: The Servile Estate,* edited by John Ralph Willis. London: Routledge, 1985.

Dennison, Stephanie and Song Hwee Lim, *Remapping World Cinema: Identity, Culture and Politics in Film.* New York: Wallflower, 2006.

Deren, Maya. "Creative Cutting." *Movie Maker* (1947): 190–206.

Derrida, Jacques. "Resistances." In *Resistances of Psychoanalysis.* Translated by Peggy Kamuf, Pascale-Anne Brault, and Michael Naas. Stanford, Calif.: Stanford University Press, 1998.

Derrida, Jacques. "Signature Event Context." In *Limited Inc.* Evanston, Ill.: Northwestern University Press, 1988.

Derrida, Jacques. *Writing and Difference.* Translated by Alan Bass. Chicago: University of Chicago Press, 1978.

Devic, Louis Marcel. *Le pays des Zandjs ou la côte orientale d'Afrique au Moyen Age d'après les écrivains arabes.* Paris: Hachette, 1883.

Diamant-Berger, Henri. "Le Filmage." In *Le Cinéma,* 145–68. Paris: La Renaissance du livre, 1919.

Dienstag, Joshua Foa. *Cinema Pessimism: A Political Theory of Representation and Reciprocity.* New York: Oxford University Press, 2019.

Doane, Mary Ann. *The Emergence of Cinematic Time: Modernity, Contingency, the Archive.* Cambridge, Mass.: Harvard University Press, 2002.

Doane, Mary Ann. *Femmes Fatales: Feminism, Film Theory, Psychoanalysis.* New York: Routledge, 1991.

Donald, Stephanie, Emma Wilson, and Sarah Wright, eds. *Childhood and Nation in Contemporary World Cinema: Borders and Encounters.* New York: Bloomsbury Academic, 2018.

Doyle, Laura, and Laura A. Winkiel, eds. *Geomodernisms: Race, Modernism, Modernity.* Bloomington: Indiana University Press, 2005.

Du Bois, W. E. B. *The World and Africa: An Inquiry into the Part Which Africa Has Played in World History.* New York: International, 1955.

Du Bois, W. E. B., Isabel Eaton, and Elijah Anderson. *The Philadelphia Negro: A Social Study.* Philadelphia: University of Pennsylvania Press, 1996.

During, Jean. "African Winds and Muslim Djinns. Trance, Healing, and Devotion in Baluchistan." *Yearbook for Traditional Music* 29 (1997): 39–56.

Echard, Nicole. "The Hausa *Bori* Possession Cult in the Ader Region of Niger: Its Origins and Present-Day Function." In *Women's Medicine: The Zar-Bori Cult in Africa and Beyond,* edited by I. M. Lewis, Ahmed Al-Safi, and Sayyid Hurreiz. Edinburgh: Edinburgh University Press, 1991.

Eikelboom, Alexandria. *Rhythm: A Theological Category.* Oxford: Oxford University Press, 2018.

Eleftheriotis, Dimitris. *Cinematic Journeys: Film and Movement.* Edinburgh: Edinburgh University Press, 2010.

Elling, Rasmus Christian. *Minorities in Iran: Nationalism and Ethnicity after Khomeini.* New York: Palgrave Macmillan, 2013.

Elling, Rasmus Christian. "War of Clubs: Struggle for Space in Abadan and the 1945 Oil Strike." In *Violence and the City in the Modern Middle East.* Stanford, Calif.: Stanford University Press, 2016.

Ende, Werner. "The Flagellations of Muḥarram and the Shiʿite 'Ulamā." *Der Islam* 55, no. 1 (1978): 19–36.

Eng, David L., and David Kazanjian, eds. *Loss: The Politics of Mourning.* Berkeley: University of California Press, 2003.

Ennaji, Mohammed. *Slavery, the State, and Islam.* Translated by Teresa Lavender Fagan. New York: Cambridge University Press, 2013.

Epstein, Rebecca, Jamilia Blake, and Thalia Gonzalez. "Girlhood Interrupted: The Erasure of Black Girls' Childhood." *SSRN Electronic Journal* (2017). http://dx.doi.org/10.2139/ssrn.3000695 (accessed 5 November 2022).

Epstein, Steven. *Purity Lost: Transgressing Boundaries in the Eastern Mediterranean, 1000–1400.* Baltimore: Johns Hopkins University Press, 2007.

Erdem, Y. Hakan. *Slavery in the Ottoman Empire and Its Demise, 1800–1909.* New York: St. Martin's, 1996.

Erfani, Farhang. "Committed Perception: Merleau-Ponty, Carroll, and Iranian Cinema." *Philosophy Today* 51, no. 3 (2007): 320–29.

Everett, Anna. *Returning the Gaze, A Genealogy of Black Film Criticism, 1909–1949.* Durham, N.C.: Duke University Press, 2001.

Fakouhi, Nasser "Making and Remaking an Academic Tradition: Towards an Indigenous Anthropology in Iran." In *Conceptualizing Iranian Anthropology: Past and Present Perspectives,* edited by Shahnaz R. Nadjmabadi. New York: Berghahn Books, 2009.

Fanon, Frantz. *Black Skin, White Masks.* New York: Grove Press, 2008.

Fanon, Frantz. *The Wretched of the Earth.* Translated by Richard Philcox. New York: Grove Press, 2021.

Fathalī Baygī, Davūd. "Barkhī istilāhāt-i takht-i hawzī," In *Dar bārah-'i ta'zīyah va ti'ātr dar Īrān,* edited by Lālah Taqiyān. Tehran: Nashr-i Markaz, 1995.

Fattah, Hala Mundhir. *The Politics of Regional Trade in Iraq, Arabia, and the Gulf: 1745–1900.* New York: State University of New York Press, 1997.

Fava, Antonio. *The Comic Mask in the Commedia dell'Arte: Actor Training, Improvisation, and the Poetics of Survival.* Edited by Jenny Gherpelli, translated by Thomas Simpson. Evanston, Ill.: Northwestern University Press, 2007.

Fay, Mary Ann. *Unveiling the Harem: Elite Women and the Paradox of Seclusion in Eighteenth-Century Cairo.* Syracuse, N.Y.: Syracuse University Press, 2012.

Fay, Mary Ann. *Slavery in the Islamic World: Its Characteristics and Commonality.* New York: Palgrave Macmillan, 2019.

Fazaeli, Sudabeh. "Fīrūz-i muqadas: bahsī dar namād shināsī-yi ḥājī fīrūz talāyī dar nowrūz va bahār." *Ulūm Ijtimā'ī,* 64 (2009): 6–9.

Fazeli, Nematollah. *Politics of Culture in Iran: Anthropology, Politics, and Society in the Twentieth Century.* New York: Routledge, 2006.

Fellezs, Kevin. *Birds of Fire: Jazz, Rock, Funk, and the Creation of Fusion.* Durham, N.C.: Duke University Press, 2011.

Fenves, Peter. "What 'Progresses' Has Race-Theory Made Since the Times of Leibniz and Wolff?" In *The German Invention of Race,* edited by Sara Eigen and Mark Larrimore. New York: SUNY Press, 2006.

Fetviet, Arild. "Death, Beauty, and Iconoclastic Nostalgia: Precarious Aesthetics and Lana Del Rey." *European Network for Cinema and Media Studies* 4, no. 2 (2015): 187–207.

Finley, Moses I. *Ancient Slavery and Modern Ideology.* Edited by Brent D. Shaw. New York: Viking Press, 1980.

Fisher, Humphrey J. *Slavery in the History of Muslim Black Africa.* New York: New York University Press, 2001.

Fleetwood, Nicole R. *Troubling Vision: Performance, Visuality, and Blackness.* Chicago: University of Chicago Press, 2011.

Floor, Willem. "Bushehr: Southern Gateway to Iran." In *The Persian Gulf in Modern Times: People, Ports, and History,* edited by Lawrence G. Potter. New York: Palgrave Macmillan, 2014.

Floor, Willem M. *The History of Theater in Iran.* Washington, D.C.: Mage, 2005.

Fogel, Robert William. *The Slavery Debates: 1952–1990: A Retrospective.* Baton Rouge: Louisiana State University Press, 2003.

Foley, Kathy, "Commedia Counterparts: Middle Eastern and Asian Connections." In *The Routledge Companion to Commedia dell'Arte,* edited by Judith Chaffee and Olly Crick. New York: Routledge, 2014.

Forster, Peter G., Michael Hitchcock, and Francis F. Lyimo. *Race and Ethnicity in East Africa.* Houndmills, UK: Macmillan, 2000.

Förster-Nietzsche, Elisabeth. "Introduction: How Zarathustra Came into Being." In Friedrich Nietzsche, *Thus Spake Zarathustra,* translated by Thomas Common. New York: Boni and Liveright, 1921.

Foucault, Michel. *Introduction to Kant's Anthropology.* Los Angeles: Semiotext(e), 2008.

Foucault, Michel. *The Order of Things.* New York: Routledge, 1994.

Fox, Craig, and Britt Harrison, eds. *Philosophy of Film Without Theory.* Cham, Switzerland: Palgrave Macmillan, 2022.

Frampton, Daniel. *Filmosophy.* London: Wallflower, 2006.

Frawley, David. *The Myth of the Aryan Invasion of India.* New Delhi: Voices of India, 1994.

Fretwell, Erica. *Sensory Experiments: Psychophysics, Race, and the Aesthetics of Feeling.* Durham, N.C.: Duke University Press, 2020.

Frosh, Paul. *The Image Factory: Consumer Culture, Photography and the Visual Content Industry.* Oxford: Berg, 2003.

Fuccaro, Nelida. *Histories of City and State in the Persian Gulf: Manama Since 1800.* Cambridge: Cambridge University Press, 2009.

Gadassik, Alla. "A National Filmmaker without a Home: Home and Displacement in the Films of Amir Naderi." *Comparative Studies of South Asia, Africa and the Middle East* 31, no. 2 (2011): 474–86.

Galloway, Alexander R. *The Interface Effect.* Cambridge: Polity, 2012.

Galloway, Alexander R. "Does the Whatever Speak?" In *Race After the Internet,* edited by Lisa Nakamura and Peter A. Chow-White, 111–27. New York: Routledge, 2013.

Galloway, J. H. "The Mediterranean Sugar Industry." *Geographical Review* 67, no. 2 (1977).

Garba, Tapji Paul, and Sara-Maria Sorentino. "Blackness Before Race and Race as Reoccupation: Reading Sylvia Wynter with Hans Blumenberg." *Political Theology* (2022): 1–22.

Gates, Henry Louis Jr. *Figures in Black: Words, Signs, and the "Racial" Self.* New York: Oxford University Press, 1987.

Gerhardt, Mia Irene. *The Art of Story-telling: A Literary Study of the Thousand and One Nights.* Leiden: Brill, 1963.

Ghafārī, Farukh. "Interview with Akbar Etemad." *Iran Oral History Project.* Paris: Foundation for Iranian Studies, 25 November 1983 and 4 July 1984.

Gharībpūr, Bihrūz. *Ti'ātr dar Īrān.* Tehran: Daftar-i Pizhūhishhā-yi Farhangī, 2005.

Gheorghe, Cezar. "Bazin Meets Deleuze: The Fact-Image and Pure Optical Situations in Italian Neo-Realism." *Ekphrasis: Images, Cinema, Theory, Media* 9, no. 1 (2013): 93–99.

Gholipoor, Ali. "Photographic Documentation of Ta'zieh and Taqlid." In *Untold Stories: The Socio-Cultural Life of Images in Qajar Iran,* edited by Pedram Khosronejad. Berlin: Lit Verlag, 2015.

Gibb, Hamilton. *Studies on the Civilization of Islam.* Boston: Beacon, 1962.

Gide, André. *Journals: 1889–1913.* Vol. 1. Urbana: University of Illinois Press, 2000.

Gikandi, Simon. "Africa and the Epiphany of Modernism." In *Geomodernisms: Race, Modernism, Modernity,* edited by Laura Doyle and Laura Winkiel. Bloomington: Indiana University Press, 2005.

Gilroy, Paul. *Against Race: Imagining Political Culture Beyond the Color Line.* Cambridge, Mass.: Belknap Press, 2000.

Giovacchini, Saverio, and Robert Sklar, *Global Neorealism: The Transnational History of a Film Style.* Jackson: University Press of Mississippi, 2012.

Glassman, Jonathon. *Feasts and Riot: Revelry, Rebellion, and Popular Consciousness on the Swahili Coast, 1856–1888.* Portsmouth, N.H.: Heinemann, 1995.

Gledhill, Christine, and Linda Williams, eds. *Melodrama Unbound: Across History, Media, and National Cultures.* New York: Columbia University Press, 2018.

Glissant, Édouard. *Caribbean Discourse: Selected Essays.* Translated by J. Michael Dash. Charlottesville: University Press of Virginia, 1999.

Goings, Kenneth. *Mammy and Uncle Mose: Black Collectibles and American Stereotyping.* Bloomington: Indiana University Press, 1994.

Gooding, Philip. "The Ivory Trade and Political Power in Nineteenth-Century East Africa." In *Animal Trade Histories in the Indian Ocean World,* edited by Martha Chaiklin, Philip Gooding, and Gwyn Campbell, 247–75. Cham, Switzerland: Palgrave Macmillan, 2020.

Gopalan, Lalitha. *Cinema of Interruptions: Action Genres in Contemporary Indian Cinema.* Oxford: Oxford University Press, 2003.

Gordon, Lewis. "Race, Sex, and Matrices of Desire in an Antiblack World: An Essay in Phenomenology and Social Role." In *Her Majesty's Other*

Children: Sketches of Racism from a Neocolonial Age, 73–88. Lanham, Md.: Rowman & Littlefield, 1997.

Gordon, Matthew. "Unhappy Offspring? Concubines and Their Sons in Early Abbasid Society." *International Journal of Middle East Studies* 49, no. 1 (2017): 153–7.

Gordon, Matthew, and Kathryn A. Hain, eds. *Concubines and Courtesans: Women and Slavery in Islamic History.* New York: Oxford University Press, 2017.

Green, Nile. "Rethinking the 'Middle East' After the Oceanic Turn." *Comparative Studies of South Asia, Africa and the Middle East* 34, no. 3 (2014): 556–64.

Greer, Margaret Rich, Walter Mignolo, and Maureen Quilligan, eds. *Rereading the Black Legend: The Discourses of Religious and Racial Difference in the Renaissance Empires.* Chicago: University of Chicago Press, 2008.

Grigor, Talinn. *Building Iran: Modernism, Architecture, and National Heritage under the Pahlavi Monarchs.* New York: Periscope, 2009.

Grusin, Richard, and Jocelyn Szczepaniak-Gillece. *Ends of Cinema.* Minneapolis: University of Minnesota Press, 2020.

Gubar, Susan. *Racechanges: White Skin, Black Face in American Culture.* New York: Oxford University Press, 2000.

Guerrero, Ed. *Framing Blackness: The African-American Image in Film.* Philadelphia: Temple University Press, 1993.

Guha, Ranajit. *History at the Limit of World History.* New York: Columbia University Press, 2002.

Gulistān, Shāhrukh. *Fānūs-i khiyāl: Sarguẕasht-i sīnimā-yi Īrān az āghāz tā pīrūzī-i inqilāb-i islāmī, bih ravāyat-i bī. bī. si.* Tehran: Intishārāt-i Kavīr, 1995.

Guneratne, Anthony R., and Wimal Dissanayake. *Rethinking Third Cinema.* New York: Routledge, 2003.

Hacking, Ian. *Historical Ontology.* Cambridge, Mass.: Harvard University Press, 2004.

Hadidi, Hager El. *Zar: Spirit Possession, Music, and Healing Rituals in Egypt.* Cairo: American University in Cairo Press, 2016.

Ḥadīdī, Hājir. *Zar: Spirit Possession Music and Healing Rituals in Egypt.* Cairo: American University in Cairo Press, 2016.

Haery, Mahmoud M. "Ru-howzi: The Iranian Traditional Improvisatory Theatre." Phd diss., New York University, 1982.

Hahonou, Eric. "Blackness, Slavery and Anti-Racism Activism in Contemporary North Africa." *Racial Formations in Africa and the Middle East: A Transregional Approach* (2021): 41.

Hain, Kathryn A. "Epilogue: Avenues to Social Mobility Available to Courtesans and Concubines." In *Concubines and Courtesans: Women and Slavery in Islamic History,* edited by Matthew Gordon and Kathryn A. Hain. New York: Oxford University Press, 2017.

Hall, Bruce S. *A History of Race in Muslim West Africa, 1600–1960.* Vol. 115. Cambridge: Cambridge University Press, 2011.

Hall, Stuart. "What Is This 'Black' in Black Popular Culture?." *Social Justice* 20, no. 1–2 (1993): 104–14.

Hall, Stuart. *The Fateful Triangle: Race, Ethnicity, Nation.* Edited by Kobena Mercer. Cambridge, Mass.: Harvard University Press, 2017.

Hall, Ute. "Trance Techniques, Cinema, and Cybernetics." In *Trance Mediums and New Media: Spirit Possession in the Age of Technical Reproduction,* edited by Heike Behrend, Anja Dreschke, and Martin Zillinger. New York: Fordham University Press, 2015.

Hall, Ute. *Cinema, Trance, and Cybernetics.* Translated by Daniel Hendrickson. Amsterdam: Amsterdam University Press, 2017.

Hambly, Gavin, "A Note on the Trade in Eunuchs in Mughal Bengal." *Journal of the American Oriental Society* 94, no. 1 (1974): 125–30.

Hamdani, Hakim Sameer. *Shi'ism in Kashmir: A History of Sunni-Shi'i Rivalry and Reconciliation.* London: I. B. Tauris, 2023.

Hamel, Chouki El. *Black Morocco: A History of Slavery, Race, and Islam.* Cambridge: Cambridge University Press, 2013.

Hamel, Chouki El. "Race, Slavery and Islam in Maghribi Mediterranean Thought: The Question of the *Haratin* in Morocco." *Journal of North African Studies* 7, no. 3 (2002).

Hanna, Sami A., and George H. Gardner. *Arab Socialism: A Documentary Survey.* Leiden: Brill, 1969.

Hansen, Miriam. *Cinema and Experience: Siegfried Kracauer, Walter Benjamin, and Theodor W. Adorno.* Berkeley: University of California Press, 2012.

Harban, Jasim. *L'Fjeri: Silsilat al-fann al-sha'bi fi al-Bahrayn.* Manama, Bahrain: al-Mu'assasah al-Arabiyah, 1996.

Harding, Vincent. "Beyond Chaos: Black History and the Search for the New Land." In *Amistad 1,* edited by John A. Williams and Charles F. Harris. New York: Random House, 1970.

Harms, Robert W., David W. Blight, and Bernard K. Freamon, eds. *Indian Ocean Slavery in the Age of Abolition.* New Haven, Conn.: Yale University Press, 2013.

Harney, Stefano. *Nationalism and Identity: Culture and the Imagination in a Caribbean Diaspora.* Kingston, Jamaica: University Press of the West Indies, 2006.

Harpham, Geoffrey Galt. "Roots, Races, and the Return to Philology." *Representations* 106, no. 1 (2009): 34–62.

Harris, Fredrick C. "The Next Civil Rights Movement?" *Dissent* 62, no. 3 (2015): 34–40.

Harris, Joseph E. "The Sea Voyage, Slave Marts, and Dispersian in Asia." In *The African Presence in Asia: Consequences of the East African Slave Trade.* Evanston, Ill.: Northwestern University Press, 1971.

Harris, Joseph E. "Africans in Asian History." In *Global Dimensions of the African Diaspora,* edited by Joseph E. Harris. 2nd ed. Washington, D.C.: Howard University Press, 1993.

Hartman, Saidiya V. "Venus in Two Acts." *Small Axe: A Caribbean Journal of Criticism* 12, no. 2 (2008): 1–14.

Hartman, Saidiya V. "The Belly of the World: A Note on Black Women's Labors." *Souls* 18, no. 1 (2016): 166–73.

Hartman, Saidiya V. *Lose Your Mother: A Journey along the Atlantic Slave Route.* New York: Farrar, Straus & Giroux, 2007.

Hartman, Saidiya V. *Scenes of Subjection: Terror, Slavery, and Self-Making in Nineteenth-Century America.* Oxford: Oxford University Press, 1997.

Hathaway, Jane. *The Chief Eunuch of the Ottoman Harem: From African Slave to Power-Broker.* Cambridge: Cambridge University Press, 2018.

Ḥaydarī, Ghulām, ed. *Muʻarrifī va shinākht-i Nāṣir Taqvāʻi.* Tehran: Nashr-i Qatrah, 2002.

Ḥaydarī, Ghulām. *Trāzhidī-i sīnamā-yi kumidī-i Īrān.* Tehran: Fīlm-khānah-'i Millī-i Īrān, 1991.

Ḥaydarī, Ghulām. *Muʻarrifī va naqd-i āṣāʾr-i Nāṣir Taqvāʻī.* Tehran: Bih Nigār, 1990.

Hayes, Edmund. "The Death of Kings: Group Identity and the Tragedy of Nezhād in Ferdowsi's Shahnameh." *Iranian Studies* 48, no. 3 (2015): 369–93.

Heard-Bey, Frauke. *From Trucial States to United Arab Emirates: A Society in Transition* New ed. London: Longman, 1982.

Heidegger, Martin. *Ontology—The Hermeneutics of Facticity.* Translated by John van Buren. Bloomington: Indiana University Press, 2010.

Heller-Roazen, Daniel. "Glossolalia: From the Unity of the Word to Plurality of Tongues." In *Dictionary of Untranslatables: A Philosophical Lexicon,* edited by Barbara Cassin et al. Princeton, N.J.: Princeton University Press, 2014.

Hendelman-Baavur, Liora. *Creating the Modern Iranian Woman: Popular Culture between Two Revolutions.* Cambridge: Cambridge University Press, 2019.

Heng, Geraldine. *The Invention of Race in the European Middle Ages.* Cambridge: Cambridge University Press, 2018.

Heng, Geraldine. "Reinventing Race, Colonization, and Globalisms across Deep Time: Lessons from the *Longue Durée.*" *PMLA* 130, no. 2 (2015): 358–66.

Hesse, Barnor. "Racialized Modernity: An Analytics of White Mythologies." *Ethnic and Racial Studies* 30, no. 4 (2007): 643–63.

Hidāyat, Ṣādiq. "Fuklur yā farhang-i tūdeh." In *Farhang-i āmīyānah-yi mardum-i Īran.* Tehran: Nashr-i Chishmah, 1999.

Hidayatullah, Aysha. "Māriyya the Copt: Gender, Sex and Heritage in the

Legacy of Muhammad's umm walad." *Islam and Christian–Muslim Relations* 21, no. 3 (2010): 221–43.

Hillier, Jim. *Cahiers du Cinéma: The 1950s, Neo-Realism, Hollywood, New Wave.* Cambridge, Mass.: Harvard University Press, 1985.

hooks, bell. *Ain't I A Woman: Black Women and Feminism.* London: Routledge, 2014.

Hopper, Matthew S. "The African Presence in Eastern Arabia." In *The Persian Gulf in Modern Times,* edited by Lawrence G. Potter. New York: Palgrave Macmillan, 2014.

Hopper, Matthew. "Slavery, Family Life, and the African Diaspora in the Arabian Gulf, 1880–1940." In *Sex, Power, and Slavery,* edited by Gwyn Campbell and Elizabeth Elbourne. Athens: Ohio University Press, 2014.

Hopper, Matthew. *Slaves of One Master: Globalization and Slavery in Arabia in the Age of Empire.* New Haven, Conn.: Yale University Press, 2015.

Hornback, Robert. *Racism and Early Blackface Comic Traditions: From the Old World to the New.* New York: Palgrave Macmillan, 2018.

Horta, Paulo Lemos. *Marvelous Thieves: Secret Authors of the Arabian Nights.* Cambridge, Mass.: Harvard University Press, 2017.

Horta, Paulo Lemos, ed., and Yasmine Seale, trans. *The Annotated Arabian Nights: Tales from 1001 Nights.* New York: Liveright, 2021.

Hourani, George Fadlo, and J. Carswell. *Arab Seafaring in the Indian Ocean in Ancient and Early Medieval Times.* Princeton, N.J.: Princeton University Press, 1995.

Howard, Philip N., and Muzammil M. Hussain. *Democracy's Fourth Wave? Digital Media and the Arab Spring.* Oxford: Oxford University Press, 2013.

Hudūd al-'Ālam: 'The Regions of the World,' A Persian Geography 37 A.H.–982 A.D. Translated by V. Minorsky and edited by C. E. Bosworth. London: Luzac, 1937.

Hunwick, John. "Islamic Law and Polemics over Race and Slavery in North and West Africa (16th–19th Century)." In *Slavery in the Islamic Middle East,* edited by Shaun E. Marmon. Princeton, N.J.: Markus Wiener, 2014.

Hunwick, John O. "Back to West African Zanj Again: A Document of Sale from Timbuktu." *Sudanic Africa* 7 (1996): 53–60.

Hunwick, John O. "A Region of the Mind: Medieval Arab Views of African Geography and Ethnography and Their Legacy." *Sudanic Africa* 16 (2005): 103–36.

Hunwick, John and Eve Trout Powell. *The African Diaspora in the Mediterraean Lands of Islam.* Princeton, N.J.: Markus Wiener, 2002.

Hurgronje, Christian Snouck. *Mekka in the Latter Part of the Nineteenth Century.* Translated by J. H. Monahan. Leiden: Brill, 1979.

Bibliography

Husaynī Tabatabāyi, Mustafā. *Bardigi az dīd-gah-i Islām,* Tehran: Bunyādi Dāyiratolmaārif-i Islāmi, 1993.

Hussain, Ali J. "The Mourning of History and the History of Mourning: The Evolution of Ritual Commemoration of the Battle of Karbala." *Comparative Studies of South Asia, Africa and the Middle East* 25, no. 1 (2005): 78–88.

Ibn Iskandar, Kaykāvūs, 'Unṣur al-Ma'ālī, and Sa'īd Nafīsī. *Kitāb-i Naṣīḥatnāmah: Ma'rūf bih Qābūsnāmah.* Tehran: Furūghī, 1963.

Imāmī, Humayūn. *Sīnimā-yi mardum shinakhtī-i Īran.* Tehran: Nashr-i Afkār, 2006.

Imāmī, Humayūn. "Ta'mmulī dar tajali-i maẕhab dar sīnamā-yi mustanad-i Īrān." *Hunar* 40 (1999): 205–11.

Inayat, Hamid. *Modern Islamic Political Thought: The Response of the Shi'i and Sunni Muslims to the Twentieth Century.* London: I. B. Tauris, 2004.

Inès, Mrad Dali. "Les mobilisations des 'Noirs tunisiens' au lendemain de la révolte de 2011: entre affirmation d'une identité historique et défense d'une 'cause noire.'" *Politique africaine* 4 (2015): 61–81.

Irwin, Robert. *The Arabian Nights: A Companion.* London: Penguin Press, 1993.

Issari, Mohammad A. *Cinema in Iran: 1900–1979.* Metuchen, N.J.: Scarecrow, 1989.

Issawi, Charles Philip. *The Economic History of Iran, 1800–1914.* Chicago: University of Chicago Press, 1971.

Istakari, Ibrahim inb Muhammad al-. *Masālik va mamālik,* edited by Īraj Afshār. Tehran: Bungāh-i Tarjumah va Nashr-i Kitāb, 1961.

Jackson, Zakiyyah Iman. *Becoming Human: Matter and Meaning in an Antiblack World.* New York: New York University Press, 2020.

Jacques-Meunié, D. "Hiérarchiee sociale au Maroc présaharien." *Hespéris* 65 (1958).

Jaffe-Berg Erith. *Commedia dell'Arte and the Mediterranean: Charting Journeys and Mapping 'Others'.* London: Taylor and Francis, 2015.

Jahid, Parviz. *Directory of World Cinema: Iran.* Bristol: Intellect Ltd., 2012.

Jalālī, Ghulām Riza. "Buḥrān-i m'arifatī dar sīnamāyi millī-i Īrān." *Hunar va M'imārī* 205, no 8 (2005): 218–35.

Jalālī, Vandād. "Az *Bād-i Jin* tā nārinjī pūsh yā arzyābī-i intiqādī-i khat mūsīqī dar sīnamā-yi Īrān." *Hunar va mi'imari,* no 6 (2011): 139–55.

Jāmī, Mehdī. *Mā va Mudirnīyat: Guft ū gū ba Daryūsh Āshūrī.* Tehran: Tavana, 2016.

Jamieson, Ross W. "Material Culture and Social Death: African-American Burial Practices." *Historical Archaeology* 29, no. 4 (1995): 39–58.

Jankowsky, Richard C. *Stambeli: Music, Trance, and Alterity in Tunisia.* Chicago: University of Chicago Press, 2010.

JanMohamed, Abdul R. *The Death-Bound-Subject: Richard Wright's Archaeology of Death.* Durham, N.C.: Duke University Press, 2005.

Jayasuriya, Shihan de Silva. "Identifying Africans in Asia: What's in a Name?" *African and Asian Studies* 5, no. 3–4 (2006).

Jāhed, Parvīz. *Nivishtan bā dūrbīn: rū dar rū bā Ibrāhīm Gulistān.* Tehran: Nashr'i Akhtaran, 2006.

Jayasuriya, Shihan de Silva. *Sounds of Identity: The Music of Afro-Asians.* Rome: Semar, 2006.

Jennings, Ronald C. "Black Slaves in Ottoman Cyprus, 1590–1640." *Journal of the Economic and Social History of the Orient* 30, no. 3 (1987): 286–302.

Judy, R. A. *Sentient Flesh: Thinking in Disorder, Poiēsis in Black.* Durham, N.C.: Duke University Press, 2020.

Judy, R. A. *(Dis)Forming the American Canon: African-Arabic Slave Narratives and the Vernacular.* Minneapolis: University of Minnesota Press, 1993.

Judy, R. A. "Beside the Two Camps: Paul Gilroy and the Critique of Raciology." *Boundary 2* 28, no. 3 (2001): 207–16.

Julien, Isaac, and Kobena Mercer. "De Margin and de Centre." *Screen* 29, no. 4 (1988).

Junne, George H. *The Black Eunuchs of the Ottoman Empire: Networks of Power in the Court of the Sultan.* London: I. B. Tauris, 2016.

Juodele, Mykolas. "In Search of Junub, the Hippie Spirit of Iran's South." *The Guardian,* March 16, 2020.

Kahana, Yael. "The Zar Spirits, a Category of Magic in the System of Mental Health Care in Ethiopia." *International Journal of Social Psychiatry* 31, no. 2 (1985): 125–43.

Kane, Ross. *Syncretism and Christian Tradition: Race and Revelation in the Study of Religious Mixture.* New York: Oxford University Press, 2020.

Kanna, Ahmed, Amélie Le Renard, and Neha Vora. *Beyond Exception: New Interpretations of the Arabian Peninsula.* Ithaca, N.Y.: Cornell University Press, 2020.

Kapchan, Deborah. *Traveling Spirit Masters: Moroccan Gnawa Trance and Music in the Global Marketplace.* Middletown, Conn.: Wesleyan University Press, 2007.

Karatani, Kojin. "The Discovery of the Child." In *Origins of Modern Japanese Literature.* Durham, N.C.: Duke University Press, 1993.

Karimi, Pamela. *Domesticity and Consumer Culture in Iran: Interior Revolutions of the Modern Era.* New York: Garland, 2017.

Kashani-Sabet, Firoozeh. "The Anti-Aryan Moment: Decolonization, Diplomacy, and Race in Late Pahlavi Iran." *International Journal of Middle East Studies* 53, no. 4 (2021).

Kashani-Sabet, Firoozeh. *Conceiving Citizens: Women and the Politics of Motherhood in Iran.* New York: Oxford University Press, 2011.

Kasravī, Ahmad. *Sūfīgarī.* Tehran: Intishārāt-i Bungāh-Matbūʿātī-yi Gūtinbirg, 1960.

Katouzian, Homa, ed. *Sadeq Hedayat: His Work and His Wondrous World.* London: Routledge, 2008.

Keeling, Kara. "'In the Interval': Frantz Fanon and the 'Problems' of Visual Representation." *Qui Parle* 13, no. 2 (2003): 91–117.

Kelly, J. B. *Britain and the Persian Gulf: 1795–1880.* Oxford: Clarendon Press, 1968.

Keller, Sarah. *Anxious Cinephilia: Pleasure and Peril at the Movies.* New York: Columbia University Press, 2020.

Kennedy, John. "Nubian Zar Ceremonies as Psychotherapy." *Human Organization* 26, no. 4 (1967): 185–94.

Kenyon, Susan M. *Spirits and Slaves in Central Sudan: The Red Wind of Sennar.* New York: Palgrave Macmillan, 2012.

Khader, Khatija. "Mobile Communities of the Indian Ocean: A Brief Study of Siddi and Hadrami Diaspora in Hyderabad City, India." In *Global Africans: Race, Ethnicity and Shifting Identities,* edited by Tony Falola and Cacee Hoyer. London: Routledge, 2017.

Khan, Aisha. *Callaloo Nation: Metaphors of Race and Religious Identity among South Asians in Trinidad.* Durham, N.C.: Duke University Press, 2004.

Khan, Aisha. "Journey to the Center of the Earth: The Caribbean as Master Symbol." *Cultural Anthropology* 16, no. 3 (2001): 271–302.

Khan, Aisha. "Sacred Subversions? Syncretic Creoles, the Indo-Caribbean, and 'Culture's In-Between.'" *Radical History Review* 89 (2004): 165–84.

Khan, Aisha. *The Deepest Dye: Obeah, Hosay, and Race in the Atlantic World.* Cambridge, Mass.: Harvard University Press, 2021.

Khosronejad, Pedram, ed. *Women's Rituals and Ceremonies in Shiite Iran and Muslim Communities.* Münster, Germany: LIT, 2015.

Kia, Mana. *Persianate Selves: Memories of Place and Origin before Nationalism.* Stanford, Calif.: Stanford University Press, 2020.

Kia, Mana. "Moral Refinement and Manhood in Persian." In *Civilizing Emotions: Concepts in Nineteenth Century Asia and Europe,* edited by Margrit Pernau et al. Oxford: Oxford University Press, 2015.

King, Homay. *Lost in Translation: Orientalism, Cinema, and the Enigmatic Signifier.* Durham, N.C.: Duke University Press, 2010.

King, Stephen J. "Black Arabs and African Migrants: Between Slavery and Racism in North Africa." *Journal of North African Studies* 26, no. 1 (2021): 8–50.

King, Stephen J. "Democracy and Progress towards Racial Equality in Tunisia: Interview with Zied Rouine." Arab Reform Initiative,

March 26, 2021. https://www.arab-reform.net/publication/democracy-and-progress-towards-racial-equality-in-tunisia-interview-with-zied-rouine/.

Kirby, Lynne. *Parallel Tracks: The Railroad and Silent Cinema*. Durham, N.C.: Duke University Press, 1997.

Kirkwood, Jeffrey West. *Endless Intervals: Cinema, Psychology, and Semiotechnics around 1900*. Minneapolis: University of Minnesota Press, 2022.

Kittler, Friedrich A. *Gramophone, Film, Typewriter*. Translated by Geoffrey Winthrop-Young and Michael Wutz. Stanford, Calif.: Stanford University Press, 1999.

Kittler, Friedrich A. *The Truth of the Technological World: Essays on the Genealogy of Presence*. Stanford, Calif.: Stanford University Press, 2014.

Kivy, Peter. *The Fine Art of Repetition: Essays in the Philosophy of Music*. Cambridge: Cambridge University Press, 1993.

Klein, Martin A. *Breaking the Chains: Slavery, Bondage, and Emancipation in Modern Africa and Asia*. Madison: University of Wisconsin Press, 1993.

Kohn, Guizot. "Afghani on Empire, Islam, and Civilization." *Political Theory* 37 (2009): 398–422.

Kolker, Robert Phillip. *The Altering Eye: Contemporary International Cinema*. Oxford: Oxford University Press, 1983.

Kooria, Mahmood. *Narrating Africa in South Asia*. Oxon: Routledge, 2023.

Korom, Frank J. *Hosay Trinidad: Muḥarram Performances in an Indo-Caribbean Diaspora*. Philadelphia: University of Pennsylvania Press, 2003.

Korom, Frank J. "The Transformation of Language to Rhythm: The Hosay Drums of Trinidad." *World of Music* 36, no. 3 (1994).

Korom, Frank J. "Memory, Innovation, and Emergent Ethnicity: The Creolization of an Indo-Trinidadian Performance." *Diaspora: A Journal of Transnational Studies* 3, no. 2 (1994): 135–55.

Kovács, András Bálint. *Screening Modernism: European Art Cinema, 1950–1980*. Chicago: University of Chicago Press, 2007.

Kracauer, Siegfried. *Theory of Film: The Redemption of Physical Reality*. Princeton, N.J.: Princeton University Press, 1997.

Kraidy, Marwan M. *The Naked Blogger of Cairo: Creative Insurgency in the Arab World*. Cambridge, Mass.: Harvard University Press, 2016.

Kramer, Fritz W., *The Red Fez: Art and Spirit Possession in Africa*. Translated by Malcolm Green. London: Verso, 1993.

Kristeva, Julia. *Desire in Language: A Semiotic Approach to Literature and Art*. New York: Columbia University Press, 1980.

Kristeva, Julia. *Revolution in Poetic Language*. New York: Columbia University Press, 1984.

Ksiksi, Khawla. "Faire face au racisme en Tunisie : Entretien avec Khawla Ksiksi." *Arab Reform Initiative*, June 8, 2020. https://www.arab-reform

.net/fr/publication/faire-face-au-racisme-en-tunisie-entretien-avec
-khawla-ksiksi/.

Lacan, Jacques. *Seminar II: The Ego in Freud's Theory and in the Technique of Psychoanalysis 1954–1955.* Translated by Sylvana Tamaselli. New York: Norton, 1991.

Lacan, Jacques, and Miller, Jacques-Alain. *The Psychoses: The Seminar of Jacques Lacan Book III 1955–1956.* London: Routledge, 2000.

Lad, Jateen. "Panoptic Bodies: Black Eunuchs as Guardians of the Topkapi Harem." In *Living in the Ottoman Realm: Empire and Identity 13th to 20th Centuries,* edited by Christine Isom-Verhaaren and Kent F. Schull. Bloomington: Indiana University Press, 2016.

Laffin, John. *The Arabs as Master Slavers.* Englewood, N.J.: SBS, 1982.

La'l Bakhsh, Pidrām. "Barrisī tatbīqī rīshah'hā, darūnmāyah'hā va kar kard'hā'ī sīyāh bazi Irānī va Amrikayi." *Adabiyat-i tatbiqi no 13* (2016): 41–78.

Langford, Michelle. "Iranian Cinema and Social Media." *Social Media in Iran: Politics and Society after 2009* (2015): 251–69.

Larson, Pier. "Reconsidering Trauma, Identity, and the African Diaspora: Enslavement and Historical Memory in Nineteenth-Century Highland Madagascar." *William and Mary Quarterly* 56, no. 2 (1999), 335–62.

La Rue, George Michael. "'My Ninth Master was a European': Enslaved Blacks in European Households in Egypt, 1798–1848." In *Race and Slavery in the Middle East: Histories of Trans-Saharan Africans in Nineteenth-Century Egypt, Sudan, and the Ottoman Mediterranean,* edited by Terence Walz and Kenneth M. Cuno. Cairo: American University in Cairo Press, 2010.

Lavers, John E. "Trans-Saharan Trade before 1800: Towards Quantification." *Paideuma* 40 (1994).

Lawler, Andrew. "The Pearl Trade." *Archaeology* 65, no. 2 (2012): 46–51.

Lebeau, Vicky. *Childhood and Cinema.* London: Reaktion, 2008.

Lebeau, Vicky. *Psychoanalysis and Cinema: The Play of Shadows.* New York: Wallflower Press, 2001.

Lefebvre, Henri. *Rhythmanalysis: Space Time and Everyday Life.* London: Bloomsbury, 2013.

Le Goff, Jacques. *History and Memory.* New York: Columbia University Press, 1992.

Le Goff, Jacques, ed. *Faire de l'histoire.* Paris: Galimard, 1974.

Lehmann, Ann-Sophie. "Hidden Practice: Artists' Working Spaces, Tools, and Materials in the Digital Domain." In *Digital Material: Tracing New Media in Everyday Life and Technology,* edited by Marianna van den Boomen, Sybille Lammes, Ann-Sophie Lehmann, Joost Raessens, and Mirko Tobias Schäfer, 267–82. Amsterdam University Press, 2009.

LeMenager, Stephanie. *Living Oil: Petroleum Culture in the American Century.* Oxford: Oxford University Press, 2014.

Leopold, Anita M., and Jeppe Sinding Jensen, eds. *Syncretism in Religion: A Reader.* New York: Routledge, 2004.

Leslau, Wolf. "An Ethiopian Argot of People Possessed by a Spirit." *Africa* 19, no. 3 (1949): 204–12.

Levinthal, David, and Manthia Diawara. "The Blackface Stereotype." In *Blackface.* Santa Fe: Arena Editions, 1999.

Lewis, Martin W. "Dividing the Ocean Sea." *Geographical Review* 89, no. 2 (1999): 188–214.

Lewis, Bernard. *Race and Color in Islam.* New York: Harper & Row, 1971.

Lewis, I. M., Ahmed El Safi, and Sayed Hamid A. Hurreiz, eds. *Women's Medicine: The Zar-Bori Cult in Africa and Beyond.* Edinburgh: Edinburgh University Press for the International African Institute, 1991.

Lhamon, W. T. *Raising Cain: Blackface Performance from Jim Crow to Hip Hop.* Cambridge, Mass.: Harvard University Press, 1998.

Lienau, Annette Damayanti. "Reframing Vernacular Culture on Arabic Fault Lines: Bamba, Senghor, and Sembene's Translingual Legacies in French West Africa." *PMLA* 130, no. 2 (2015): 419–29.

Lienhardt, Peter. *Shaikhdoms of Eastern Arabia.* New York: Macmillan, 2001.

Lindström, Jan. *Muted Memories: Heritage-Making, Bagamoyo, and the East African Caravan Trade.* New York: Berghahn Books, 2019.

Litvak, Meir, ed. *Constructing Nationalism in Iran: from the Qajars to the Islamic Republic.* Abingdon: Routledge, 2017.

Lloyd, David. *Under Representation, Under Representation: The Racial Regime of Aesthetics.* New York: Fordham University Press, 2018.

Loiselle, André, and Jeremy Maron, eds. *Stages of Reality: Theatricality in Cinema.* Toronto: University of Toronto Press, 2012.

Lombard, Maurice. *The Golden Age of Islam.* Princeton, N.J.: Markus Wiener, 2004.

Loomba, Ania. "Race and the Possibilities of Comparative Critique." *New Literary History* 40, no. 3 (2009): 501–22.

Lott, Eric. *Love and Theft: Blackface Minstrelsy and the American Working Class.* New York: Oxford University Press, 2013.

Lovejoy, Paul E. *Transformations in Slavery: A History of Slavery in Africa.* 2nd ed. Cambridge: Cambridge University Press, 2000.

Lovink, Geert. *Sad by Design: On Platform Nihilism.* London: Pluto Press, 2019.

Löwith, Karl. *Meaning in History: The Theological Implications of the Philosophy of History.* Chicago: University of Chicago Press, 2011.

Lubiano, Wahneema. *Representing Blackness; Issues in Film and Video.* New Brunswick, N.J.: Rutgers University Press, 1997.

Lury, Karen. *The Child in Film: Tears, Fears, and Fairytales.* New Brunswick, N.J.: Rutgers University Press, 2010.

Lury, Karen. "Children in an Open World: Mobility as Ontology in New Iranian and Turkish Cinema." *Feminist Theory* 11, no. 3 (2010): 283–94.

Lyotard, Jean-François. *The Inhuman: Reflections on Time.* Stanford, Calif.: Stanford University Press, 1991.

Lyotard, Jean-François. "Re-Writing Modernity." *SubStance* 16, no. 3 (1987): 3–9.

Macdonald, Duncan B. "Emotional Religion in Islam as Affected by Music and Singing. Being a Translation of a Book of the Ihyā 'Ulūm ad-Dīn of al-Ghazzālī with Analysis, Annotation, and Appendices." *Journal of the Royal Asiatic Society* (April 1901): 195–252.

MacDougall, David. "Beyond Observational Cinema." In *Principles of Visual Anthropology,* edited by Paul Stockings. Berlin: Mouton de Gruyter, 2003.

Machado, Pedro, ed. *Indian Ocean Histories: The Many Worlds of Michael Naylor Pearson.* London: Routledge, 2019.

Machado, Pedro, Steve Mullins, and Joseph Christensen, eds. *Pearls, People, and Power: Pearling and Indian Ocean Worlds.* Athens: Ohio University Press, 2019.

Mackey, Nathaniel. *Splay Anthem.* New York: New Directions, 2006.

Madelung Wilferd. *The Succession to Muḥammad: A Study of the Early Caliphate.* Cambridge: Cambridge University Press, 1998.

Maghbouleh, Neda. *The Limits of Whiteness: Iranian Americans and the Everyday Politics of Race.* Stanford, Calif.: Stanford University Press, 2017.

Mahani, Mahnia Nematollahi. *The Holy Drama: Persian Passion Play in Modern Iran.* Leiden: Leiden University Press, 2013.

Major, Andrea. *Slavery, Abolitionism, and Empire in India, 1772–1843.* Liverpool: Liverpool University Press, 2014.

Mallat, Chibli. *The Renewal of Islamic Law: Muhammad Baqer as-Sadr, Najaf and the Shi'i International.* Cambridge: Cambridge University Press, 2003.

Malti-Douglas, Fedwa. *Woman's Body, Woman's Word: Gender and Discourse in Arabo-Islamic Writing.* Princeton, N.J.: Princeton University Press, 1991.

Manigault-Bryant, LeRhonda S. *Talking to the Dead: Religion, Music, and Lived Memory Among Gullah/Geechee Women.* Durham, N.C.: Duke University Press, 2014.

Mann, Kristin. *Slavery and the Birth of an African City: Lagos, 1760–1900.* Bloomington: Indiana University Press, 2007.

Manring M. M. *Slave in a Box: The Strange Career of Aunt Jemima.* Charlottesville: University Press of Virginia, 1998.

Maʿqūlī, Nādia. "Taḥlīl-i jāmiʾih shinākhtī-i mafhūm-i marg dar mūj-i naw." *Jāmiʾih shināsīyi hunar va adabīyāt* 10, no. 90 (2011): 125–42.

Maqsūdī, Manīzhih. "Bādhā-yi kāfir va duhul-i sih sar dar khalīj-i Fārs: marāsim-i āyīnī-i darmānī-i zār." *Pazhūhishhayih insān shināsī-i Īrān* 2, no. 3 (2012): 117–40.

Marashi, Afshin. *Nationalizing Iran: Culture Power and the State 1870–1940.* Seattle: University of Washington Press, 2008.

Marcus, George E. "Contemporary Problems of Ethnography in the Modern World System." In *Writing Culture: The Poetics and Politics of Ethnography,* edited by James Clifford and George E. Marcus, 165–93. Berkeley: University of California Press, 2011.

Markovits, Claude, Jacques Pouchepadass, and Sanjay Subrahmanyam. *Society and Circulation: Mobile People and Itinerant Cultures in South Asia, 1750–1950.* Delhi: Longman, 2003.

Marks, Laura U. *Hanan al-cinema: Affections for the Moving Image.* Cambridge, Mass.: MIT Press, 2015.

Marks, Laura U. *Touch: Sensuous Theory and Multisensory Media.* Minneapolis: University of Minnesota Press, 2002.

Marmon, Shaun Elizabeth. *Eunuchs and Sacred Boundaries in Islamic Society.* Oxford: Oxford University Press on Demand, 1995.

Marriott, David. *Haunted Life: Visual Culture and Black Modernity.* New Brunswick, N.J.: Rutgers University Press, 2007.

Marriott, David. "Response to Race and the Poetic Avant-Garde." *Boston Review* 10 (2015).

Marriott, David. "Waiting to Fall." *CR: The New Centennial Review* 13, no. 3 (2013): 163–240.

Marriott, David. *Whither Fanon? Studies in the Blackness of Being.* Stanford, Calif.: Stanford University Press, 2018.

Marzolph, Ulrich. *The Arabian Nights in Transnational Perspective.* Detroit, Mich.: Wayne State University Press, 2007.

Marzolph, Ulrich, and Richard van Leeuwen. *The Arabian Nights Encyclopedia.* Santa Barbara, Calif.: ABC-CLIO, 2004.

Matin-Asgari, Afshin. *Both Eastern and Western: An Intellectual History of Iranian Modernity.* Cambridge: Cambridge University Press, 2018.

Matthee, Rudi. "Boom and Bust: The Port of Basra in the Sixteenth and Seventeenth Centuries." In *The Persian Gulf in History,* edited by Lawrence G. Potter. New York: Palgrave Macmillan, 2009.

Maurice, Alice. "The Essence of Motion: Figure, Frame, and the Racial Body in Early Silent Cinema." *The Moving Image: The Journal of the Association of Moving Image Archivists* 1, no. 2 (2001): 124–45.

Mavani, Hamid. *Religious Authority and Political Thought in Twelver Shi'ism.* London: Routledge, 2013.

Mbembe, Achille. *On the Postcolony.* Berkeley: University of California Press, 2001.

Mbembe, Achille. "The Power of the Archive and Its Limits." In *Refiguring the Archive,* edited by Carolyn Hamilton. Cape Town: David Philip, 2002.

McCarthy, Anna. "Visual Pleasure and GIFs." *Compact Cinematics: The Moving Image in the Age of Bit-Sized Media* (2017): 113–22.

McGowan, Todd. *Out of Time: Desire in Atemporal Cinema.* Minneapolis: University of Minnesota Press, 2011.

McGowan, Todd. *Universality and Identity Politics.* New York: Columbia University Press, 2020.

McKee, Sally. "Inherited Status and Slavery in Late Medieval Italy and Venetian Crete." *Past and Present* 182 (2004): 31–53.

McKittrick, Katherine. *Demonic Grounds: Black Women and the Cartographies of Struggle.* Minneapolis: University of Minnesota Press, 2006.

McLuhan, Marshall. *Understanding Media: The Extensions of Man.* London: Routledge and Kegan Paul, 1964.

McNulty Tracy. *Wrestling with the Angel: Experiments in Symbolic Life.* New York: Columbia University Press, 2014.

Meftahi, Ida. *Gender and Dance in Modern Iran: Biopolitics on Stage.* New York: Routledge, 2016.

Mehran, Golnar. "Social Implications of Literacy in Iran." *Comparative Education Review* 36, no. 2 (1992): 194–211.

Meier, Sandy Prita. *Swahili Port Cities: The Architecture of Elsewhere.* Bloomington: Indiana University Press, 2016.

Meillassoux, Claude. "Female Slavery." In *Women and Slavery in Africa,* edited by Claire C. Robertson and Martin A. Klein. Portsmouth, N.H.: Heinemann, 1997.

Meisami, Julie Scott. "Allegorical Gardens in the Persian Poetic Tradition: Nezami, Rumi, Hafez." *International Journal of Middle East Studies* 17, no. 2 (1985): 229–60.

Meloy John Lash. *Imperial Power and Maritime Trade: Mecca and Cairo in the Later Middle Ages.* Chicago: Middle East Documentation Center, 2010.

Menashri, David. "Iran: Doctrine and Reality." In *The Iran-Iraq War: Impact and Implications,* edited by Efraim Karsh. Houndmills, UK: Macmillan, 1989.

Menin, Laura. "'Dans la Peau d'un Noir': Senegalese Students and Young Professionals in Rabat, Morocco." *Antropologia* 7, no. 1 NS (2020): 165–88.

Mernissi, Fatima. *Women's Rebellion and Islamic Memory.* Atlantic Highlands: Zed Books, 1996.

Mernissi, Fatima. *Scheherazade Goes West: Different Cultures, Different Harems.* New York: Washington Square Press, 2001.

Merriam, Alan P. *The Anthropology of Music.* Evanston, Ill.: Northwestern University Press, 1964.

Metz, Christian. "Ponctuations et démarcations dans le film de diègese." In *Essais sur la signification au cinéma, II.* Paris: Klincksieck, 1968.

Mianji, Fahimeh, and Yousef Semnani. "Zār Spirit Possession in Iran and African Countries: Group Distress, Culture-Bound Syndrome or Cultural Concept of Distress?" *Iranian Journal of Psychiatry* 10, no. 4 (2015): 225–32.

Miers, Suzanne. *Britain and the Ending of the Slave Trade.* New York: Africana Pub. Corp, 1974.

Miers, Suzanne, and Igor Kopytoff. *Slavery in Africa: Historical and Anthropological Perspectives.* Madison: University of Wisconsin Press, 1977.

Mihrābī, Mas'ud. *Tārīkh-i Sīnamāyi Īrān as Āghāz tā 1357.* Tehran: Nashr-i Naẓar, 2015.

Miller, Joseph C. *The Problem of Slavery as History: A Global Approach.* New Haven, Conn.: Yale University Press, 2011.

Mintz, Sidney W. *Sweetness and Power: The Place of Sugar in Modern History.* New York: Penguin, 1986.

Miranda, Ana. "Al-Dalfa and the Political Role of the Umm Al-Walad in the Late Umayyad Caliphate of Al-Andalus." In *A Companion to Global Queenship,* edited by Elena Woodacre. Leeds, UK: Arc Humanities Press, 2018.

Mirsepassi, Ali. *Political Islam, Iran, and the Enlightenment: Philosophies of Hope and Despair.* Cambridge: Cambridge University Press, 2011.

Mirsepassi, Ali, and Mehdi Faraji. "Iranian Cinema's 'Quiet Revolution,' 1960–1978." *Middle East Critique* 26, no. 4 (2017): 397–415.

Mirsepassi, Ali. *Transnationalism in Iranian Political Thought: The Life and Times of Ahmad Fardid.* Cambridge: Cambridge University Press, 2017.

Mirza, Younis Y. "Remembering the Umm al-walad: Ibn Kathir's Treatise on the Sale of the Concubine." In *Concubines and Courtesans: Women and Slavery in Islamic History,* edited by Matthew Gordon and Kathryn A. Hain. New York: Oxford University Press, 2017.

Mirzai, Behnaz A. *A History of Slavery and Emancipation in Iran, 1800–1929.* Austin: University of Texas Press, 2017.

Miura, Tōru, and John Edward Philips, eds. *Slave Elites in the Middle East and Africa: A Comparative Study.* London: Kegan Paul International, 2000.

Moallem, Minoo. "Aestheticizing Religion." In *Sensational Religion: Sensory Cultures in Material Practice,* edited by Sally M. Promey. New Haven, Conn.: Yale University Press, 2014.

Moallem, Minoo. *Between Warrior Brother and Veiled Sister: Islamic Fundamentalism and the Politics of Patriarchy in Iran.* Berkeley: University of California Press, 2005.

Modarressi, Taghi. "The Zar Cult in South Iran." In *Trance and Possession*

States: Proceedings, edited by Raymond Prince. Montreal: R. M. Bucke Memorial Society, 1968.

Moghaddam, Maria Sabaye. "Zâr Beliefs and Practices in Bandar Abbâs and Qeshm Island in Iran." *Anthropology of the Middle East* 7, no. 2 (2012): 19–38.

Moghaddam, Maria Sabaye. *Zār dar Īran va kishvarhā-yi dīgar.* Tehran: Naghmah-'i zindigi, 2010.

Mohaghegh Jason Bahbak. *Insurgent, Poet, Mystic, Sectarian: The Four Masks of an Eastern Postmodernism.* Albany: State University of New York Press, 2015.

Mohamed, Hassan Mohamed. "Africanists and Africans of the Maghrib: Casualties of Analogy." *Journal of North African Studies* 15, no. 3 (2010): 349–74.

Mohsenpour, Bahram. "Philosophy of Education in Postrevolutionary Iran." *Comparative Education Review* 32, no. 1 (1988): 76–86.

Montana, Ismael M. "Enslavable Infidels: Sudan-Tunis as a Classificatory Categorization for a New Wave of Enslaved Africans in the Regency of Tunis." *Maghreb Review* 29, no. 1–4 (2004).

Montana, Ismael M. "Bori Practice among Enslaved West Africans of Ottoman Tunis: Unbelief (*Kufr*) or another Dimension of the African Diaspora?." *History of the Family* 16 (2011): 152–59.

Montazeri, Fateme. "A Predestined Break from the Past: Shi'r-i Naw, History, and Hermeneutics." In *Persian Literature and Modernity: Production and Reception,* edited by Hamid Rezaei Yazdi and Arshavez Mozafari, 141–61. London: Routledge, 2018.

Montigny, Anie, Françoise Le Guennec-Coppens, and Sophie Mery. "L'Afrique oubliée des noirs du Qatar." *Journal des africanistes* 72, no. 2 (2002): 213–25.

Moorthy, Shanti, and Ashraf Jamal. *Indian Ocean Studies: Cultural Social and Political Perspectives.* New York: Routledge, 2010.

Morgan, Jennifer L. "Partus sequitur ventrem: Law, Race, and Reproduction in Colonial Slavery." *Small Axe: A Caribbean Journal of Criticism* 22, no. 1 (2018): 1–17.

Moten, Fred. *Black and Blur.* Vol. 1. Durham, N.C.: Duke University Press, 2017.

Moten, Fred. "Blackness and Nothingness: Mysticism in the Flesh," *South Atlantic Quarterly* 112, no. 4 (2013): 737–80.

Moten, Fred. "The Case of Blackness." *Criticism* 50, no. 2 (2008): 177–218.

Moten, Fred. *In the Break: The Aesthetics of the Black Radical Tradition.* Minneapolis: University of Minnesota Press, 2003.

Motlagh, Amy. *Burying the Beloved: Marriage Realism and Reform in Modern Iran.* Stanford, Calif.: Stanford University Press, 2012.

Motta, Marco. "L'écho de la voix." *A contrario* 1 (2019): 97–111.

Mottahedeh, Negar. "Crude Extractions: The Voice in Iranian Cinema."

In *Locating the Voice in Film: Critical Approaches and Global Practices,* edited by Tom Whittaker and Sarah Wright. New York: Oxford University Press, 2017.

Mottahedeh, Negar. *Displaced Allegories: Post-Revolutionary Iranian Cinema.* Durham, N.C.: Duke University Press, 2008.

Mottahedeh, Negar. "Where Are Kiarostami's Women?" In *Subtitles: On the Foreignness of Film,* edited by Ian Balfour and Atom Egoyan. Cambridge, Mass.: MIT Press, 2004.

Mottahedeh, Roy. "The Shu'ubiyah Controversy and the Social History of Early Islamic Iran." *International Journal of Middle East Studies* 7, no. 2 (1976): 161–82.

Mourlet, Michel. *Sur un art ignoré: La mise en scène comme langage.* Paris: Ramsay, 2008.

Mowitt, John. 2002. *Percussion: Drumming Beating Striking.* Durham, N.C.: Duke University Press.

Mu'azzizīniyā, Husayn. *Fīlmfārsī chīst?* Tehran: Nashr-i Sāqī, 1999.

Mudibme, Valentin Y. *The Idea of Africa.* Bloomington: Indiana University Press, 1994.

Muṭaharī, Murtizā. *Ihyā-yi tafākur-i Islāmiī.* Tehran: Intishārat-i ṣadrā, 2001.

Myers, Garth. "Sticks and Stones: Colonialism and Zanzibari Housing." *Africa* 67, no. 2 (1997).

Nadeau, Maurice. *The History of Surrealism.* Translated by Richard Howard. New York: Collier, 1967.

Naficy, Hamid. *An Accented Cinema: Exilic and Diasporic Filmmaking.* Princeton, N.J.: Princeton University Press, 2001.

Naficy, Hamid. *Fīlm-i mustanad, vol. 2, tarīkh-i sīnamā-yi mustanad.* Tehran: Intishārat-i Dānishgah-i Āzād-i Iran, 1978.

Naficy, Hamid. "Iranian Cinema." In *Companion Encyclopedia of Middle Eastern and North African Film,* edited by Oliver Leaman. London: Routledge, 2001.

Naficy, Hamid. *Making of Exilic Culture: Iranian Television in Los Angeles.* Minneapolis: University of Minnesota Press, 1993.

Naficy, Hamid. *A Social History of Iranian Cinema, Volume 2: The Industrializing Years, 1941–1978.* Durham, N.C.: Duke University Press, 2011.

Naficy, Hamid. *A Social History of Iranian Cinema, Volume 4: The Globalizing Era, 1984–2010.* Durham, N.C.: Duke University Press, 2012.

Nagib, Lúcia. *World Cinema and the Ethics of Realism.* New York: Continuum, 2011.

Najmabadi, Afsaneh. "Reading 'Wiles of Women' Stories as Fictions of Masculinity." In *Imagined Masculinities: Male Identity and Culture in the Modern Middle East,* edited by M. Ghaṣṣūb and E. Sinclair Webb. London: Saqi, 2000.

Najmabadi, Afsaneh. *Women with Mustaches and Men without Beards:*

Gender and Sexual Anxieties of Iranian Modernity. Berkeley: University of California Press, 2005.

Nakash, Yitzhak. "An Attempt to Trace the Origin of the Rituals of 'Āshurā.'" *Die Welt des Islams* 33, no. 2 (1993): 161–81.

Nashat, Guity. "Women in Pre-Islamic and Early Islamic Iran." In *Women in Iran: From the Rise of Islam to 1800,* edited by Guity Nashat and Lois Beck. Champaign: University of Illinois Press, 2003.

Nasīrīyān, Ali. *Bungāh-i ti'ātrāl.* Tehran: Nashr-i Andishah, 1978.

Nasr, Vali. *The Shia Revival: How Conflicts within Islam Will Shape the Future.* New York: W. W. Norton, 2006.

Natvig, Richard. "Oromos, Slaves, and the Zar Spirits: A Contribution to the History of the Zar Cult." *International Journal of African Historical Studies* 20, no. 4 (1987).

Nelson, Eric Sean. "Questioning Practice: Heidegger, Historicity, and the Hermeneutics of Facticity." *Philosophy Today* 44, Supplement (2000): 150–59.

Nichanian, Marc. *The Historiographic Perversion.* Translated by Gil Anidjar. New York: Columbia University Press, 2009.

Nicolini, Beatrice. "The Makran-Baluch-African Network in Zanzibar and East Africa during the XIXth Century." *African and Asian Studies* 5, no. 3 (2006): 347–70.

Nikiforuk, Andrew. *Tar Sands: Dirty Oil and the Future of a Continent.* Rev. and updated. Vancouver: Greystone Books, 2010.

Nochlin, Linda. "The Imaginary Orient." In *The Politics of Vision: Essays on Nineteenth-Century Art and Society,* 33–59. New York: Harper and Row, 1989.

Nouvet, Claire. "The Inarticulate Affect: Lyotard and Psychoanalytic Testimony." *Discourse* 25, no. 1 (2003): 231–47.

Nowell-Smith, Geoffrey. *Making Waves: New Cinemas of the 1960s.* New York: Continuum, 2008.

Nūrāyī, Jahānbakhsh. "Parvāz bih Nākujā Ābād." In *Mu 'arrifī va naqd-i filmhāyi Amir Naderi,* by Ghulām Haydarī. Tehran: Suhayl, 1991.

Nūrī, Sa'īd. "Khānah dar filmhāyi Nāsir Taqvāʿī." *Āzmā* 120 (2016): 52–55.

Odabaei, Milad. "Sickness of the Revolution: Loss, Fetishism, and the Impossibility of Politics." In *Critical Times: Interventions in Global Critical Theory,* forthcoming.

Oksiloff, Assenka. *Picturing the Primitive: Visual Culture, Ethnography, and Early German Cinema.* New York: Palgrave, 2001.

Olender, Maurice. *The Languages of Paradise: Race, Religion, and Philology in the Nineteenth Century.* Cambridge, Mass.: Harvard University Press, 1992.

Olender, Maurice. *Race and Erudition.* Cambridge, Mass.: Harvard University Press, 2009.

Olpak, Mustafa. *Biographie d'une famille d'esclaves: Kenya, Crete, Istanbul.* Paris: Librarie Özgül, 2006.

Omi, Michael, and Howard Winant. *Racial Formation in the United States.* New York: Routledge, 2015.

Oruc, Firat. "Petrocolonial Circulations and Cinema's Arrival in the Gulf." *Film History* 32, no. 3 (2020): 10–42.

Oruc, Firat. "Space and Agency in the Petrocolonial Genealogies of Cinema in the Gulf." In *Global Literary Studies: Key Concepts,* edited by Diana Roig-Sanz and Neuz Rotger. Berlin: de Gruyter, 2022.

Osborne, Peter, and Stella Sandford, eds. *Philosophies of Race and Ethnicity.* London: Continuum, 2003.

Osborne, Thomas. "The Ordinariness of the Archive." *History of the Human Sciences* 12, no. 2 (1999): 51–64.

Pak-Shiraz, Nacim. *Shi'i Islam in Iranian Cinema: Religion and Spirituality in Film.* London: I. B. Tauris, 2011.

Painter, Nell Irvin. *The History of White People.* New York: W. W. Norton, 2010.

Palmié, Stephen. "Against Syncretism." In *Counterworks: Managing the Diversity of Knowledge,* edited by Richard Fardon. New York: Routledge, 1995.

Palmié, Stephen. *The Cooking of History: How Not to Study Afro-Cuban Religion.* Chicago: University of Chicago Press, 2013.

Palmié, Stephen. *Wizards and Scientists: Explorations in Afro-Cuban Modernity and Tradition.* Durham, N.C.: Duke University Press, 2002.

Panagia, Davide. *Impressions of Hume: Cinematic Thinking and the Politics of Discontinuity.* Lanham, Md.: Rowman & Littlefield, 2013.

Pankhurst, Richard. "Across the Red Sea and Gulf of Aden: Ethiopia's Ties with Yaman." *Africa* 57, no. 3 (2002): 393–419.

Pardo, Eldad J. "Iranian Cinema, 1968–1978: Female Characters and Social Dilemmas on the Eve of the Revolution." *Middle Eastern Studies* 40, no. 3 (2004): 29–54.

Partovi, Pedram. *Popular Iranian Cinema before the Revolution: Family and Nation in Fīlmfārsī.* Abingdon, UK: Routledge.

Pasolini, Pier Paolo. "Observations on the Long Take." Translated by Norman MacAfee and Craig Owens. *October* 13 (1980): 3–6.

Patterson, Orlando. *Slavery and Social Death: A Comparative Study.* Cambridge, Mass.: Harvard University Press, 1982.

Pearce, Francis Barrow. *Zanzibar: The Island Metropolis of Eastern Africa.* New York: E. P. Dutton and Company, 1920.

Pearson, Michael. *Port Cities and Intruders: The Swahili Coast, India, and Portugal in the Early Modern Era.* Baltimore: Johns Hopkins University Press, 1998.

Peppis, Paul. *Sciences of Modernism: Ethnography, Sexology, and Psychology.* New York: Cambridge University Press, 2014.

Peretz, Eyal. *The Off-Screen: An Investigation of the Cinematic Frame.* Stanford, Calif.: Stanford University Press, 2017.

Perez, Gilberto. *The Material Ghost: Films and Their Medium.* Baltimore: Johns Hopkins University Press, 2006.

Philip, M. Nourbese. *A Genealogy of Resistance and Other Essays.* Toronto: Mercury Press, 1997.

Phillips, William D. Jr. *Slavery from Roman Times to the Early Transatlantic Trade.* Minneapolis: University of Minnesota Press, 1985.

Phillips, William D. Jr. "Sugar in Iberia." In *Tropical Babylons: Sugar and the Making of the Atlantic World, 1450–1680,* edited by Stuart B. Schwartz. Chapel Hill: University of North Carolina Press, 2004.

Pierre, Jemima. "Slavery, Anthropological Knowledge, and the Racialization of Africans." *Current Anthropology* 61 (2020).

Pinault, David. *Horse of Karbala: Muslim Devotional Life in India.* New York: Palgrave, 2001.

Pinault, David. "Lamentation Rituals: Shiite Justifications for Matam (Acts of Mourning and Self-Mortification)." In *The Shiites: Ritual and Popular Piety in a Muslim Community.* New York: St. Martin's, 1993.

Pippin, Robert B. *Filmed Thought: Cinema as Reflective Form.* Chicago: University of Chicago Press, 2020.

Pīrniyā, Hasan. *Īrān-i bāstān, ya tarīkh-i mufaṣal Īrān-i qadīm.* Tehran: Chāpkhānah-i Majlis, 1952.

Plato. *The Republic.* In *The Collected Dialogues of Plato, Including the Letters.* Edited by Edith Hamilton and Huntington Cairns. Princeton, N.J.: Princeton University Press, 1963.

Plato. *Symposium.* Translated by Robin Waterfield. Oxford: Oxford University Press, 2009.

Pomerance, Murray, and R. Barton Palmer, eds. *Thinking in the Dark: Cinema, Theory, Practice.* New Brunswick, N.J.: Rutgers University Press, 2016.

Popenoe, Paul, and Henry Field. *The Date Palm.* Coconut Grove, Fla.: Field Research Projects, 1973.

Popović, Alexandre. *The Revolt of African Slaves in Iraq in the 3rd/9th Century.* Princeton, N.J.: Markus Wiener, 1999.

Potter, Lawrence G., ed. *The Persian Gulf in Modern Times: People, Ports, and History.* New York: Palgrave, 2014.

Pourshariati, Parvaneh. "Local Historiography in Early Medieval Iran and the Tārīkh-i Bayhaq." *Iranian Studies* 33, no. 1/2 (2000): 166–64.

Pouwels, Randall L. "Eastern Africa and the Indian Ocean to 1800: Reviewing Relations in Historical Perspective." *The International Journal of African Historical Studies* 35, no. 2/3 (2002): 385–425.

Prah, Kwesi Kwaa. *Reflections on Arab-Led Slavery of Africans.* Cape Town: Centre for the Advanced Studies of African Society, 2005.

Prince, Raymond, ed. *Trance and Possession States.* Montreal: R. M. Bucke Memorial Society, 1968.

Prochazka, Stephan, and Bahram Gharedaghi-Kloucheh. "The Zār Cult in the Shatt al-'Arab/Arvand Region." *Les cahiers du Crasc* 30, no. 9 (2014): 101–10.

Quinn, Eithne. *Nuthin' but a "G" Thang: The Culture and Commerce of Gangsta Rap.* New York: Columbia University Press, 2004.

Qūkāsiyān, Zāvan. *Guft u gū bā Bahrām Bayzāyī.* Tehran: Mu'assisah-yi Intishārāt-i Agāh, 1992.

Rabbani, Darian Soheil Rahnamaye, and Julio Groppa Aquino. "A infância no cinema de abbas kiarostami." *Childhood and Philosophy* 15 (2019): 1–28.

Raengo, Alessandra, and Laurel Ahnert. "Blackness at the Heart: Extruding Sovereignty in Nancy's and Denis's *The Intruder.*" In *Deep Meditations: Thinking Space in Cinema and Digital Cultures,* edited by Karen Redrobe and Jeff Sheible. Minneapolis: University of Minnesota Press, 2020.

Raffoul, François, and Eric Sean Nelson, eds. *Rethinking Facticity.* Albany: State University of New York Press, 2008.

Rāhgānī, Rūhangīz. *Tārīkh-i mūsīqī-yi Īrān.* Tehran: Pïshraw, 1998.

Rahimi, Babak, ed. *Performing Iran: Culture, Performance, Theatre.* London: I. B. Taurus, 2021.

Rahimi, Babak. *Theater State and the Formation of Early Modern Public Sphere in Iran: Studies on Safavid Muharram Rituals, 1590–1641.* Leiden: Brill, 2012.

Rahimieh, Nasrin. "Marking Gender and Difference in the Myth of the Nation." In *The New Iranian Cinema,* edited by Richard Tapper. London: I. B. Tauris, 2002.

Rahnamā Feraydūn, and Faridah Rahnamāh. *Vāqi'iyat girāyī-i fīlm.* Tehran: Mu'assesah-'i Farhangi Honarī-i Norūz Honar, 2003.

Rasheed, Madawi Al-. ed., *Transnational Connections and the Arab Gulf.* New York: Routledge, 2005.

Rashidirostami, Mahroo. "Performance Traditions of Kurdistan: Towards a More Comprehensive Theatre History." *Iranian Studies* 51, no. 2 (2018): 269–87.

Rastegar, Kamran. "The Changing Value of *Alf Laylah wa Laylah* for Nineteenth-Century Arabic, Persian, and English Readerships." *Journal of Arabic Literature* 36, no. 3 (2005): 269–87.

Rastegar, Kamran. *Surviving Images: Cinema, War, and Cultural Memory in the Middle East.* New York: Oxford University Press, 2015.

Ray, Himanshu Prabha, and Edward A. Alpers. *Cross Currents and Community Networks: The History of the Indian Ocean World.* Delhi: Oxford University Press, 2007.

Raychaudhuri, Tapan. *Europe Reconsidered: Perceptions of the West in Nineteenth Century Bengal.* Delhi: Oxford University Press, 2002.

Razī, Hāshim. *Jashnhā-yi Āb: nawrūz savābiq-i tarikhī ta imrūz jashnhā-yi tīrgān va āb-pāshān.* Tehran: Intishārāt-i Bihjat, 1979.

Redrobe, Karen, and Jeff Scheible. *Deep Mediations: Thinking Space in Cinema and Digital Cultures.* Minneapolis: University of Minnesota Press, 2020.

Rehin, George F. "Harlequin Jim Crow: Continuity and Convergence in Blackface Clowning." *Journal of Popular Culture* 9, no. 3 (1975): 682–701.

Reilly, Benjamin. "Revisiting Consanguineous Marriage in the Greater Middle East: Milk, Blood, and Bedouins." *American Anthropologist* 115, no. 3 (2013): 374–87.

Reilly, Benjamin. *Slavery, Agriculture, and Malaria in the Arabian Peninsula.* Athens: Ohio University Press, 2015.

Rekabtalaei, Golbarg. *Iranian Cosmopolitanism: A Cinematic History.* Cambridge: Cambridge University Press, 2019.

Renner, Karen J. "Evil Children in Film and Literature." In *The 'Evil Child' in Literature, Film and Popular Culture.* London: Routledge, 2013.

Reyes, Angelita D. "Performativity and Representation in Transnational Blackface: Mammy (USA), Zwarte Piet (Netherlands), and Haji Firuz (Iran)." *Atlantic Studies* 16, no. 4 (2019): 521–50.

Richardson, Riché. "E-Raced: #Touré, Twitter, and Trayvon." In *The Trouble with Post-Blackness,* edited by Houston A. Baker Jr. and K. Merinda Simmons. New York: Columbia University Press, 2015.

Ricks, Thomas M. "Persian Gulf Seafaring and East Africa: Ninth–Twelfth Centuries." *African Historical Studies* (1970): 339–57.

Ricks, Thomas M. "Slaves and Slave Trading in Shi'i Iran AD 1500–1900." *Journal of Asian and African Studies* 36 no. 4 (2001).

Ridgeon, Lloyd V. J. *Sufi Castigator: Ahmad Kasravi and the Iranian Mystical Tradition.* London: Routledge, 2006.

Ringrose, Kathryn M. *The Perfect Servant: Eunuchs and the Social Construction of Gender in Byzantium.* Chicago: University of Chicago Press, 2007.

Robb, Peter. *The Concept of Race in South Asia.* New York: University of Oxford Press, 1995.

Roberts, Diane. *The Myth of Aunt Jemima: Representations of Race and Region.* London: Routledge, 1994.

Robinson, Cedric J. *Forgeries of Memory and Meaning: Blacks and the Regimes of Race in American Theater and Film before World War II.* Chapel Hill: University of North Carolina Press, 2007.

Robinson, Cedric. *Black Marxism: The Making of the Black Radical Tradition.* Chapel Hill: University of North Carolina Press, 2000.

Rodowick, D. N. *What Philosophy Wants from Images*. Chicago: University of Chicago Press, 2017.

Rollo, Toby. "The Color of Childhood: The Role of the Child/Human Binary in the Production of Anti-black Racism." *Journal of Black Studies* 49, no. 4 (2018): 307–29.

Rony, Fatimah Tobing. *The Third Eye: Race, Cinema, and Ethnographic Spectacle*. Durham, N.C.: Duke University Press, 1996.

Rose, Tricia. *Black Noise: Rap Music and Black Culture in Contemporary America*. Middletown, Conn.: Wesleyan University Press, 1994.

Rosen, Philip, ed. *Narrative, Apparatus, Ideology: A Film Theory Reader*. New York: Columbia University Press, 1986.

Rostam-Kolayi, Jasamin. "Expanding Agendas for the 'New' Iranian Woman: Family, Law, Work, and Unveiling." In *The Making of Modern Iran: State and Society under Riza Shah: 1921–1941,* edited by Stephanie Cronin. New York: Routledge Curzon, 2003.

Rouch, Jean. *Ciné-Ethnography*. Translated by Steven Feld. Minneapolis: University of Minnesota Press, 2003.

Ruberto, Laura E., and Kristi M. Wilson. *Italian Neorealism and Global Cinema*. Detroit: Wayne State University Press, 2007.

Ruffle, Karen G. *Gender, Sainthood, and Everyday Practice in South Asian Shi'Ism*. Chapel Hill: University of North Carolina Press, 2011.

Russell, Catherine. *Experimental Ethnography: The Work of Film in the Age of Video*. Durham, N.C.: Duke University Press, 1999.

Russell-Wood, A. J. *The Portuguese Empire, 1415–1808: A World on the Move*. Baltimore: Johns Hopkins University Press, 1998.

Sāʿidī, Ghulām Ḥusayn. *Fear and Trembling*. Translated by Minoo Southgate, Washington, D.C.: Three Continents, 1984.

Sāʿidī, Ghulām Ḥusayn. *Ahl-i Havā*. Tehran: Chāpkhānah-ʿi Dānishgāh, 1966.

Sāʿidī, Ghulām Ḥusayn. "An Autobiographical Sketch." *Iranian Studies* 18, no. 2–4 (1985).

Sabri-Tabrizi, G. R. "Gholam-Hoseyn Saʿedi: A Voice for the Poor." *Index on Censorship* 15, no. 4 (1986): 11–13.

Sadr, Hamid Reza. "Children in Iranian Post-Revolutionary Cinema," in *The New Iranian Cinema,* edited by Richard Tapper. London: I. B. Tauris, 2002.

Sadr, Hamid Reza. *Iranian Cinema: A Political History*. London, I. B. Tauris, 2006.

Safa, Kaveh. "Reading Saedi's Ahl-e Hava: Pattern and Significance in Spirit Possession Beliefs on the Southern Coasts of Iran." *Culture, Medicine and Psychiatry* 12, no. 1 (1988): 85–111.

Saffari, Siavash. *Beyond Shariati: Modernity, Cosmopolitanism, and Islam in Iranian Political Thought*. Cambridge: Cambridge University Press, 2017.

Said, Edward. *Orientalism*. New York: Vintage Books, 1979.

Ṣāliḥī, Muhamad Riẓā Māzandarānī, and Nasrīn Gabanchī. "Naqd-i ravānkāvaneh-'i bāvarhā va kunishhāyi 'āmīyanih dar majmu'i-'ih dāstān-i azādārān-i bayal-i Ghulām Husayn Sā'idī." *Adabīyāt-i Pārsī-i mu'āṣir* 17, no 1 (2016): 25–50.

Saljoughi, Sara. "Political Cinema, Revolution, and Failure: The Iranian New Wave, 1962–79." In *1968 and Global Cinema,* edited by Christina Gerhardt and Sara Saljoughi. Detroit: Wayne State University Press, 2018.

Sandler, Rivanne. "Literary Developments in Iran in the 1960s and the 1970s Prior to the 1978 Revolution." *World Literature Today* 60, no. 2 (1986): 246–51.

Santner, Eric L. *Stranded Objects: Mourning, Memory, and Film in Postwar Germany.* Ithaca, N.Y.: Cornell University Press, 1990.

Saramifar, Younes. "Circling Around the Really Real in Iran: Ethnography of Muharram Laments among Shi'i Volunteer Militants in the Middle East." *Focaal* 2020, no. 88 (2020): 76–88.

Saucier, P. Khalil, and Tryon P. Woods, *Conceptual Aphasia in Black: Displacing Racial Formation.* Lanham, Md.: Lexington Books, 2016.

Sayf, Muḥsin. "Āhistah va amīgh birān." *Naqd-i Sīnamā* 16 (1999): 49–51.

Scahill, Andrew. *The Revolting Child in Horror Cinema: Youth Rebellion and Queer Spectatorship.* New York: Palgrave Macmillan, 2015.

Schacht, Joseph. *The Origins of Muhammadan Jurisprudence.* Oxford: Clarendon Press, 1950.

Schayegh, Cyrus. *Who Is Knowledgeable, Is Strong: Science, Class, and the Formation of Modern Iranian Society, 1900–1950.* Berkeley: University of California Press, 2009.

Schine, Rachel. "Race and Blackness in Premodern Arabic Literature." In *Oxford Research Encyclopedia of Literature.* 2021. https://oxfordre .com/literature/view/10.1093/acrefore/9780190201098.001.0001/ acrefore-9780190201098-e-1298 (accessed 5 November 2022).

Schneider, Arnd, and Caterina Pasqualino. *Experimental Film and Anthropology.* New York: Routledge, 2014.

Schnepel, Burkhard, and Julia Verne, eds. *Cargoes in Motion: Materiality and Connectivity Across the Indian Ocean.* Athens: Ohio University Press, 2022.

Scholz, Piotr O. *Eunuchs and Castrati: A Cultural History.* Princeton, N.J.: Markus Wiener, 2001.

Schoonover, Karl. "Sinkholes." *JCMS: Journal of Cinema and Media Studies* 58, no. 2 (2019): 169–74.

Schwartz, Stuart B., ed. *Tropical Babylons: Sugar and the Making of the Atlantic World, 1450–1680.* Chapel Hill: University of North Carolina Press, 2004.

Sebiane, Maho. "Entre l'Afrique et l'Arabie: les esprits de possession sawahili et leurs frontières." *Journal des africanistes* 84-2 (2014): 48–79.

Segal, Ronald. *Islam's Black Slaves: The Other Black Diaspora.* New York: Farrar, Straus and Giroux, 2001.

Sellier, Geneviève. *La Nouvelle Vague: Un Cinéma Au Masculin Singulier.* Paris: CNRS, 2005.

Serrano, Shea. *The Rap Yearbook: The Most Important Rap Song from Every Year since 1979, Discussed, Debated, and Deconstructed.* New York: Abrams, 2015.

Sexton, Jared. "The Social Life of Social Death: On Afro-Pessimism and Black Optimism." *InTensions* (2011) 5.

Sexton, Jared Yates. *Amalgamation Schemes: Antiblackness and the Critique of Multiracialism.* Minneapolis: University of Minnesota Press, 2008.

Shahbāzī, Rāmtīn. "Jūnūbī: murūrī bar zindigī va āsār-i Nāsir Taqvāʾī." *Naqd-i sīnamā* 32 (2002).

Shamlan, Saif Marzooq al-. *Pearling in the Arabian Gulf: A Kuwaiti Memoir.* Translated by Peter Clark. London: London Center for Arabic Studies, 2000.

Shamma, Tarek. "Women and Slaves: Gender Politics in *The Arabian Nights*." *Marvels and Tales* 31, no. 2 (2017): 239–60.

Sharabi, Hisham. *Nationalism and Revolution in the Arab World (the Middle East and North Africa).* Princeton, N.J.: Van Nostrand, 1966.

Sharīfīyān, Muḥsin. *Ahl-i mātam: āvāʾhā va āyīn-i sūgvārī dar Būshihr.* Tehran: Dīrīn, 2004.

Sharīfīyān, Muḥsin. *Mūsīqi-i Būshihr.* Būshihr: Dānishnāmah-ʾi Ustān-i Būshihr, 2010.

Sharīfīyān, Muḥsin. *Mardūm shināsī va mūsīqī-i navār-i -sāḥilī-i Shībkūh.* Tehran: Nashr-i Nigāh, 2018.

Sharifi-Yazdi, Farzad Cyrus. *Arab-Iranian Rivalry in the Persian Gulf.* New York: I.B. Taurus, 2015.

Sharpe, Christina. *In the Wake: On Blackness and Being.* Durham, N.C.: Duke University Press, 2016.

Sharpe, Christina. *Monstrous Intimacies: Making Post-slavery Subjects.* Durham, N.C.: Duke University Press, 2010.

Shaviro, Steven. "Supa Dupa Fly: Black Women as Cyborgs in Hiphop Videos." *Quarterly Review of Film and Video* 22, no. 2 (2005): 169–79.

Shaw, Rosalind, and Charles Stewart. "Introduction: Problematizing Syncretism." In *Syncretism/Anti-Syncretism: The Politics of Religious Synthesis.* London: Routledge, 1994.

Shay, Anthony. *The Dangerous Lives of Public Performers: Dancing, Sex, and Entertainment in the Islamic World.* New York: Palgrave Macmillan, 2014.

Shay, Anthony, and Barbara Sellers-Young. *Belly Dance: Orientalism Transnationalism and Harem Fantasy.* Costa Mesa, Calif.: Mazda, 2005.

Sheibani, Khatereh. *The Poetics of Iranian Cinema: Aesthetics, Modernity and Film after the Revolution.* New York: I. B. Tauris, 2011.

Sheil, Mary Leonora. *Glimpses of Life and Manners in Persia.* London: John Murray, 1856.

Sheriff, Abdul. *Afro-Arab Interaction in the Indian Ocean: Social Consequences of the Dhow Trade.* Cape Town: Centre for Advanced Studies of African Society, 2001.

Sheriff, Abdul. *Dhow Cultures of the Indian Ocean: Cosmopolitanism, Commerce and Islam.* London: Hurst, 2010.

Sheriff, Abdul. "The Persian Gulf and the Swahili Coast: A History of Acculturation Over the Longue Durée," in *The Persian Gulf in History,* edited by Lawrence G. Potter, 173–88. New York: Palgrave Macmillan, 2009.

Sheriff, Abdul. *Slaves, Spices, and Ivory in Zanzibar: Integration of an East African Commercial Empire into the World Economy, 1770–1873.* Athens: Ohio University Press, 1987.

Sheriff, Abdul. "The Slave Trade and Slavery in the Western Indian Ocean: Significant Contrasts." In *Facing Up to the Past: Perspectives on the Commemoration of Slavery from Africa, the Americas and Europe,* edited by Gert Oostindie. Kingston, Jamaica: Ian Randle, 2001.

Sheriff, Abdul, and Engseng Ho, eds. *The Indian Ocean: Oceanic Connections and the Creation of New Societies.* London: Hurst, 2014.

Shirazi, Maziar. "A Review of Tarabnameh, or, Why Are Iranian-Americans Laughing at Blackface in 2016?." *Ajam Media Collective* 7 (2016). https://ajammc.com/2016/12/07/why-are-iranian-americans -laughing-at-blackface-in-2016/ (accessed 5 November 2022).

Shujāʾīnasab, Bahman. "Naqsh-i iqtisādī-i Bandar Lingih dar hawẓih-ʿi -ʿi khalīj-i Fārs." *Faṣlnāmah-ʿi takhaṣṣusī-i muṭālʾātī-i khalīj-i Fārs* 2, no. 6 (2016): 25–34.

Silverman, Kaja. *Male Subjectivity at the Margins.* New York: Routledge, 1992.

Simpson, Edward, and Kai Kresse, eds. *Struggling with History: Islam and Cosmopolitanism in the Western Indian Ocean.* New York: Columbia University Press, 2008.

Singer, Ben. *Melodrama and Modernity: Early Sensational Cinema and Its Contexts.* New York: Columbia University Press, 2001.

Sinnerbrink, Robert. "Hugo Münsterberg, Film, and Philosophy." In *Film as Philosophy,* edited by Bernd Herzogenrath, 23–44. Minneapolis: University of Minnesota Press, 2017.

Sīstānī, Īraj Afshār. *Khūzistān va tamaddun-i dīrīnī-i ān, vol. 1.* Tehran: Sāzmān-i Chāp va Intishārāt-i Vizārat-i Farhang va Irshād-i Islāmī, 1994.

Smith, Valerie, ed. *Representing Blackness: Issues in Film and Video.* New Brunswick, N.J.: Rutgers University Press, 1997.

Snead, James. *White Screens/Black Images: Hollywood from the Dark Side.* New York: Routledge, 1994.

Snorton, C. Riley. *Black on Both Sides: A Racial History of Trans Identity.* Minneapolis: University of Minnesota Press, 2017.

Sohoni, Pushkar, and Torsten Tschacher, eds. *Non-Shia Practices of Muharram in South Asia and the Diaspora*. Abingdon, UK: Routledge, 2022.

Solow, Barbara L. "Capitalism and Slavery in the Exceedingly Long Run." *Journal of Interdisciplinary History* 17, no. 4 (1987): 711–37.

Somer, Eli, and Meir Saadon. "Stambali: Dissociative Possession and Trance in a Tunisian Healing Dance." *Transcultural Psychiatry* 37, no. 4 (2000): 580–600.

Southgate, Minoo. "The Negative Images of Blacks in Some Medieval Iranian Writings." *Iranian Studies* 17, no. 1 (1984): 3–36.

Spillers, Hortense. "Mama's Baby, Papa's Maybe: An American Grammar Book." *Diacritics* 17, no. 2 (1987): 64–81.

Spillers, Hortense. *Black, White, and in Color: Essays on American Literature and Culture*. Chicago: University of Chicago Press, 2003.

Spivak, Gayatri Chakravorty. "Nationalism and the Imagination." *Lectora: revista de dones i textualitat* (2009): 75–98.

Spyropoulos, Yannis. "Beys, Sheikhs, Kolbaşıs, and Godiyas: Some Notes on the Leading Figures of the Ottoman-African Diaspora." *Turcica* 48 (2017): 187–218.

Stam, Robert, and Toby Miller. *Film and Theory: An Anthology*. Malden, Mass.: Blackwell, 2000.

Stanziani, Alessandro. *Sailors, Slaves, and Immigrants: Bondage in the Indian Ocean World, 1750–1914*. New York: Palgrave Macmillan, 2014.

Stewart, Charles. "Syncretism and Its Synonyms: Reflections on Cultural Mixture." *Diacritics* 29, no. 3 (1999).

Stewart, Charles, and Rosalind Shaw, eds. *Syncretism/Anti-Syncretism: The Politics of Religious Synthesis*. New York: Routledge, 2003.

Stewart, Garrett. *Between Film and Screen: Modernism's Photo Synthesis*. Chicago: University of Chicago Press, 2000.

Stewart, Garrett. *Framed Time: Toward a Postfilmic Cinema*. Chicago: University of Chicago Press, 2007.

Stiegler, Bernard. *Technics and Time, Vol. II: Disorientation*. Translated by Stephen Barker. Stanford, Calif.: Stanford University Press, 2009.

Stiegler, Bernard, and Stephen Francis Barker. *Technics and Time 3: Cinematic Time and the Question of Malaise*. Stanford, Calif.: Stanford University Press, 2011.

Stocking, George W. Jr. "Afterword: A View from the Center." *Ethnos* 47 (1982): 172–86.

Stoler, Ann Laura. "Colonial Archives and the Arts of Governance." *Archival Science* 2, no. 1–2 (2002): 87–109.

Stuckey, Sterling. *Slave Culture: Nationalist Theory and the Foundations of Black America*. New York: Oxford University Press, 1987.

Suhr, Christian, and Rane Willerslev, eds. *Transcultural Montage*. New York: Berghahn Books, 2013.

Suleiman, Yasir. *Arabic in the Fray: Language Ideology and Cultural Politics.* Edinburgh: Edinburgh University Press, 2013.

Suleiman, Yasir. *The Arabic Language and National Identity: A Study in Ideology.* Edinburgh: Edinburgh University Press, 2003.

Sulṭānmuhammadi, Husayn. "Ruydād." *Hunar va Mi'mārī* 14 (1992).

Sunya, Samhita. *Sirens of Modernity: World Cinema via Bombay.* Oakland: University of California Press, 2022.

Sweet, James. "The Iberian Roots of American Racist Thought." *William and Mary Quarterly* 54, no. 1 (1997): 143–66.

Szakolczai, Árpád. *Comedy and the Public Sphere: The Rebirth of Theatre as Comedy and the Genealogy of the Modern Public Arena.* New York: Routledge, 2015.

Tabarraee, Babak. "Iranian Cult Cinema." In *The Routledge Companion to Cult Cinema,* edited by Ernest Mathijs and Jamie Sexton, 98–104. London: Routledge, 2019.

Taee, Nasser Al-. "'Enough, Enough, Oh Ocean': Music of the Pearl Divers in the Arabian Gulf." *Middle East Studies Association Bulletin* 39, no. 1 (2005): 19–30.

Tahāmī-nijād, Muhammad. "Insān shināsī baṣarī dar sīnamāyi mustanad-i Īran, 'amil-i shinākht yā mawzū'-i shinākht." *Kitāb-i māh-i hunar* 73 (2004): 34–42.

Talib, Y. "The African Diaspora in Asia." In *General History of Africa,* vol. 3: *Africa from the Seventh to the Eleventh Century,* edited by M. El Fasi. London: UNESCO, 1988.

Tavakoli-Targhi, Mohamad. "Narrative Identity in the Works of Hedayat and His Contemporaries." In *Sadeq Hedayat: His Work and his Wondrous World,* edited by Homayun Katouzian. New York: Routledge, 2008.

Tavakoli-Targhi, Mohamad. "Refashioning Iran: Language and Culture during the Constitutional Revolution." *Iranian Studies* 23, no. 1–4 (1990): 77–101.

Tavakoli-Targhi, Mohamad. *Refashioning Iran: Orientalism, Occidentalism, and Historiography.* New York: Palgrave, 2001.

Tatchell, Jo. *A Diamond in the Desert: Behind the Scenes in Abu Dhabi, the World's Richest City.* New York: Black Cat, 2009.

Terkourafi, Marina, ed. *The Languages of Global Hip Hop.* London: A & C Black, 2010.

Teshome, Tezeru, and K. Wayne Yang. "Not Child but Meager: Sexualization and Negation of Black Childhood." *Small Axe: A Caribbean Journal of Criticism* 22, no. 3 (2018): 160–70.

Thomas, Sarah. *Inhabiting the In-Between: Childhood and Cinema in Spain's Long Transition.* Toronto: University of Toronto Press, 2019.

Thorn, Jennifer. "The Work of Writing Race: Galland, Burton, and the Arabian Nights." In *Monstrous Dreams of Reason: Body, Self, and Other in the Enlightenment,* edited by Laura J. Rosenthal and Mita Choudhury, 151–69. Lewisburg, Penn.: Bucknell University Press, 2002.

Tikku, Girdhari L., and Alireza Anushiravani. *A Conversation with Modern Persian Poets.* Costa Mesa, Calif.: Mazda, 2004.

Tillery, Alvin B. Jr. "What Kind of Movement Is Black Lives Matter? The View from Twitter." *Journal of Race, Ethnicity, and Politics* 4, no. 2 (2019): 297–323.

Toledano, Ehud R. *As If Silent and Absent: Bonds of Enslavement in the Islamic Middle East.* New Haven, Conn.: Yale University Press, 2007.

Toledano, Ehud R. "The Imperial Eunuchs of Istanbul: From Africa to the Heart of Islam." *Middle Eastern Studies* 20, no. 3 (1984): 379–90.

Toledano, Ehud R. *Slavery and Abolition in the Ottoman Middle East.* Seattle: University of Washington Press, 1998.

Torlasco, Domietta. *The Rhythm of Images: Cinema beyond Measure.* Minneapolis: University of Minnesota Press, 2021.

Totaro, Donato. "Time, Bergson, and the Cinematographical Mechanism." *Offscreen* 5, no. 1 (2001): 10.

Trouillot, Michel-Rolph. *Silencing the Past: Power and the Production of History.* Boston: Beacon Press, 1995.

Trautmann, Thomas R. *Aryans and British India.* Berkeley: University of California Press, 1997.

Tucker, Judith E. *Women in Nineteenth-Century Egypt.* Cambridge: Cambridge University Press, 1985.

Tufekci, Zeynep. *Twitter and Tear Gas: The Power and Fragility of Networked Protest.* New Haven, Conn.: Yale University Press, 2017.

Ture, Kwame, and Charles V. Hamilton. *Black Power: The Politics of Liberation in America.* New York: Vintage Books, 1992.

Turner, Tamara. "The 'Right' Kind of *Ḥāl*: Feeling and Foregrounding Atmospheric Identity in an Algerian Music Ritual." In *Music as Atmosphere: Collective Feelings and Affective Sounds.* New York: Routledge, 2020.

Turner, Tamara. "Music and Trance as Methods for Engaging with Suffering." *Ethnos* 48, no. 1 (2020): 74–92.

Turner, James. *Philology: The Forgotten Origins of the Modern Humanities.* Princeton, N.J.: Princeton University Press, 2014.

Tweedie, James. *The Age of New Waves: Art Cinema and the Staging of Globalization.* New York: Oxford University Press, 2013.

Ty, M. "The Riot of the Literal." *Oxford Literary Review* 42, no. 1 (2020): 76–108.

Uhlin, Graig. "Playing in the Gif(t) Economy." *Games and Culture* 9, no. 6 (2014): 517–27.

Umīd, Jamāl. *Tārīkh-i sīnamā-yi Īrān: 1279–1357.* Tehran: Intishārāt-i Rawzanah, 1998.

Urkevich, Lisa. "Incoming Arts: African and Persian." In *Music and Tra-*

ditions of the Arabian Peninsula: Saudi Arabia, Kuwait, Bahrain, and Qatar. New York: Routledge, 2015.

Uskū'i, Mustafā. *Sayrī dar tarīkh-i ti'ātr-i Īran.* Tehran: Anahita Oskooie, 1999.

Vähäkangas, Mika, and Patrik Fridlund. *Philosophical and Theological Responses to Syncretism: Beyond the Mirage of Pure Religion.* Leiden: Brill, 2017.

Vargas, João H. Costa. *The Denial of Antiblackness: Multiracial Redemption and Black Suffering.* Minneapolis: University of Minnesota Press, 2018.

Vaziri, Parisa. "Antiblack Joy: Transmedial Sīyāh Bāzī and Global Public Spheres." *TDR* 66, no. 1 (2022): 62–79.

Vaziri, Parisa. "False Differends: Racial Slavery and the Genocidal Example." *Philosophy Today* 66, no. 2 (2022): 237–59.

Vaziri, Parisa. "No One's Memory: Blackness at the Limits of Comparative Slavery." *Racial Formations in Africa and the Middle East: A Transregional Approach* (2021): 14. https://pomeps.org/no-ones-memory-blackness-at-the-limits-of-comparative-slavery.

Vaziri, Parisa. "On 'Saidiya': Indian Ocean Slavery and Blackness Beyond Horizon." *Qui Parle* 28, no. 2 (2019): 241–80.

Vaziri, Parisa. "Slavery and the Virtual Archive: On Iran's Dāsh Ākul." In *The Cambridge Companion to Global Literature and Slavery,* edited by Laura T. Murphy. Cambridge: Cambridge University Press, 2023.

Vaziri, Parisa. "Thaumaturgic, Cartoon Blackface." *Lateral: Journal of the Cultural Studies Association* 10, no. 1 (2021), https://csalateral.org/forum/cultural-constructions-race-racism-middle-east-north-africa-southwest-asia-mena-swana/thaumaturgic-cartoon-blackface-vaziri/#fnref-7767-15.

Vaziri, Parisa. "Ultimate Slaves in the Dead Zone." In *Reorienting with the Gulf: Film and Digital Media between the Middle East and South Asia,* edited by Dale Hudson and Alia Yunis. Bloomington: Indiana University Press, forthcoming.

Vejdani, Farzin. "The Place of Islam in Interwar Nationalist Historiography." In *Rethinking Iranian Nationalism and Modernity,* edited by Kamran Scot Aghaie and Afshin Marashi. Austin: University of Texas Press, 2014.

Vernallis, Carol. *Unruly Media: YouTube, Music Video, and the New Digital Cinema.* New York: Oxford University Press, 2013.

Villiers, Alan. *The Indian Ocean.* London: Museum Press, 1952.

Vink, Marcus. "'The World's Oldest Trade': Dutch Slavery and Slave Trade in the Indian Ocean in the Seventeenth Century." *Journal of World History* 14, no. 2 (2003): 131–77.

Visser, Reidar. *Basra, the Failed Gulf State: Separatism and Nationalism in Southern Iraq.* Münster: Lit, 2005.

Walz, Terence, and Kenneth M. Cuno, eds. *Race and Slavery in the Middle*

East: Histories of Trans-Saharan Africans in Nineteenth-Century Egypt, Sudan, and the Ottoman Mediterranean. Cairo: American University in Cairo Press, 2010.

Ware, Rudolph T. III. *The Walking Qur'an: Islamic Education, Embodied Knowledge, and History in West Africa.* Chapel Hill: University of North Carolina Press, 2014.

Warren, Calvin. "Improper Bodies: A Nihilistic Meditation on Sexuality, the Black Belly, and Sexual Difference." *Palimpsest* 8, no. 2 (2019): 35–51.

Warren, Charles. *Writ on Water: The Sources and Reach of Film Imagination.* Albany: State University Press of New York, 2022.

Watson, Andrew M. *Agricultural Innovation in the Early Islamic World: The Diffusion of Crops and Farming Techniques, 700–1100.* Cambridge: Cambridge University Press, 1983.

Watson, James L. *Asian and African Systems of Slavery.* Berkeley: University of California Press, 1980.

Wayne, Mike. *Political Film: The Dialectics of Third Cinema.* London: Pluto, 2001.

Weber, Samuel. *The Legend of Freud.* Stanford, Calif.: Stanford University Press, 2000.

Weber, Samuel. *Theatricality as Medium.* New York: Fordham University Press, 2004.

Weheliye, Alexander G. *Habeas Viscus: Racializing Assemblages, Biopolitics, and Black Feminist Theories of the Human.* Durham, N.C.: Duke University Press, 2014.

Weinbaum, Alys Eve. *Wayward Reproductions: Genealogies of Race and Nation in Transatlantic Modern Thought.* Durham, N.C.: Duke University Press, 2004.

Westrup, Laurel, and David Laderman. "Into the Remix: The Culture of Sampling." *Sampling Media* (2014): 1–10.

Wheeler, Deborah L. *Digital Resistance in the Middle East: New Media Activism in Everyday Life.* Edinburgh: Edinburgh University Press, 2017.

Whittaker, Tom, and Sarah Wright, eds. *Locating the Voice in Film: Critical Approaches and Global Practices.* New York: Oxford University Press, 2017.

Wick, Alexis. *The Red Sea: In Search of Lost Space.* Oakland: University of California Press, 2016.

Wilderson, Frank B. III. *Afropessimism.* New York: Liveright, 2020.

Wilderson, Frank B. III. *Red, White & Black: Cinema and the Structure of U.S. Antagonisms.* Durham, N.C.: Duke University Press, 2010.

Willis, John Ralph, ed. *Slaves and Slavery in Muslim Africa: Vol. 2: The Servile Estate.* London: Routledge, 1985.

Wingham, Zavier. "Blackness on the Iranian Periphery: Ethnicity, Language, and Nation in *Bashu, the Little Stranger.*" *Ajam Media Collective*

(2015). https://ajammc.com/2015/09/23/blackness-on-the-iranian
-periphery/ (accessed 5 November 2022).

Wolf, Richard K. "Embodiment and Ambivalence: Emotion in South
Asian Muharram Drumming." *Yearbook for Traditional Music* 32
(2000): 81–116.

Wolf, Richard K. *The Voice in the Drum: Music, Language, and Emotion in
Islamicate South Asia.* Urbana: University of Illinois Press, 2014.

Wood, Donald. *Trinidad in Transition: The Years After Slavery.* London:
Oxford University Press, 1968.

Wortham, Simon Morgan. "Resistances—after Derrida after Freud."
Mosaic: A Journal for the Interdisciplinary Study of Literature 44, no. 4
(2011): 51–61.

Wright, John. *The Trans-Saharan Slave Trade.* London: Routledge, 2007.

Wynter, Sylvia. "1492: A New World." In *Race, Discourse, and the Origin of
the Americas: A New World View,* edited by Vera Lawrence Hyatt and
Rex Nettleford. Washington, D.C.: Smithsonian Institution Press, 1995.

Wynter, Sylvia. "On How We Mistook the Map for the Territory, and
Re-Imprisoned Ourselves in Our Unbearable Wrongness of Being, of
Desêtre: Black Studies toward the Human Project." *A Companion to
African-American Studies* (2006): 107–18.

Wynter, Sylvia. "Unsettling the Coloniality of Being/Power/Truth/
Freedom: Towards the Human, After Man, Its Overrepresentation—An Argument." *New Centennial Review* 3, no. 3 (2003): 257–337.

Yacavone, David. *Film Worlds: A Philosophical Aesthetics of Cinema.* New
York: Columbia University Press, 2015.

Yamamoto, Kumiko. *The Oral Background of Persian Epics: Storytelling
and Poetry.* Leiden: Brill, 2003.

Yimene, Ababu Minda. *An African Indian Community in Hyderabad:
Siddi Identity, Its Maintenance and Change.* Göttingen: Cuvillier, 2004.

Yusoff, Kathryn. *A Billion Black Anthropocenes or None.* Minneapolis:
University of Minnesota Press, 2018.

Zahedi, Farshad. "The Myth of Bastoor and the Children of Iranian Independent Cinema." *Film International* 12, no. 3 (2014): 21–30.

Zahiri, Abdollah. "Frantz Fanon in Iran: Darling of the Right and the Left
in the 1960s and 1970s." *Interventions: International Journal of Postcolonial Studies* 23, no. 4 (2021): 506–25.

Zarrīnkūb, 'Abdulhusayn. *Daw Qarn Sukūt: sarguzasht-i ḥavādis va
awzā'-i tarīkhī-i Īrān dar daw qarn-i avval-i Islām az ḥamlah-'i 'arāb
ta zuhūr-i dawlat-i ṭahīrīyān.* Tehran: chāp-i yik, 2012.

Zdanowski, Jerzy. "Contesting Enslavement: Voices of the Female Slaves
from the Persian Gulf in the 1930s." *Die Welt des Islams* 55, no. 1 (2015):
62–82.

Zdanowski, Jerzy. *Slavery and Manumission: British Policy in the Red Sea and the Persian Gulf in the First Half of the 20th Century.* Reading, UK: Ithaca Press, 2013.

Zeydabadi-Nejad, Saeed. "Iranian Intellectuals and Contact with the West: The Case of Iranian Cinema." *British Journal of Middle Eastern Studies* 34, no. 3 (2007): 375–98.

Zia-Ebrahimi, Reza. *The Emergence of Iranian Nationalism: Race and the Politics of Dislocation.* New York: Columbia University Press, 2016.

Zia-Ebrahimi, Reza. "Self-Orientalization and Dislocation: The Uses and Abuses of the 'Aryan' Discourse in Iran." *Iranian Studies* 44, no. 4 (2011).

Ziegler, Joseph. "Physiognomy, Science, and Proto-Racism 1200–1500." In *The Origins of Racism in the West,* edited by Miriam Eliav-Feldon, Benjamin Isaac, and Joseph Ziegler, 181–99. Cambridge: Cambridge University Press, 2009.

Zilfi, Madeline C. *Women and Slavery in the Late Ottoman Empire: The Design of Difference.* New York: Cambridge University Press, 2010.

Zillinger, Martin. "Absence and the Mediation of the Audiovisual Unconscious." In *Trance Mediums and New Media: Spirit Possession in the Age of Technical Reproduction,* edited by Heike Behrend, Anja Dreschke, and Martin Zillinger. New York: Fordham University Press, 2015.

Index

Abadan, 83, 135, 196, 199, 288n142
Abadan Oil Refinery, 239n48
Abbas, King, 241n67
Abbasid period, 152, 181
abstraction, 6, 11, 16, 74, 77, 83, 82, 86, 88, 94, 99, 102, 105, 107, 108, 111, 116, 124, 193, 194, 198, 199
Abyssinians, 142
Achaemenid period, 40, 126
activism, 150, 212, 226, 277n132
adab, 149; *akhlāq* and, 276n126
adabīyāt-i mutahid, 114
aesthetics, 11, 27, 75, 82, 95, 97, 99, 103, 122, 127, 136, 146, 150, 214, 216, 217, 218, 225, 229; digital, 28; modernity, 76–77
Afro-Iranians, 26, 124, 143, 193, 213, 227, 291n9; translation for, 139. *See also* Black Iranians
Afro-Trinidadians, 158, 159
ahl-i havā (people of the wind), 78, 81, 82, 84, 88, 93–94, 93 (fig.), 106, 256n2
Ahmad, Jalāl al-i, 21, 265n131
Ahvaz, 136, 155
'ajam, 150–53, 278n143
alternative cinema (*sīnamā-yi dīgar*), 7, 10, 11, 26
American Reconstruction period, 62, 67, 219
Amharic, 17, 193
anachronisms, 55, 181, 182, 183; racial, 21–25

Anglo-Iranian Oil Company, 135, 199, 239n49
anthropology, 82, 84, 85, 125, 127, 157, 257n13; institutionalized, 75; mythology and, 151; visual, 257–58n13
anti-Arabness, 122, 164, 278
antiblackness, 49, 114, 194, 208, 226, 251n65, 277n132, 280n165, 292n9, 293n40
anticolonialism, 11, 13, 15, 19–21, 75, 115, 116
anti-imperialism, 115, 135
anxiety, 2, 6, 7, 12, 19, 21, 26, 27, 32, 49, 67, 71, 74, 77, 103–4, 107, 109, 115, 116, 117, 124, 134, 138, 157–58, 159, 164, 184, 188; New Wave, 108
Arabian Peninsula, 66, 132, 185
arbāb (master), 25, 36, 44
arba'īn, 119–22, 124–32, 137, 142, 146, 149, 150, 266n7, 272n72; Būshihrī, 120, 121, 127, 134, 153, 156, 158. *See also* chest striking
Arba'īn (Taqvā'i), 27, 107, 119, 120, 122, 123, 124, 125, 129 (fig.), 130, 131 (fig.), 132, 134, 136, 137–38, 139 (fig.), 144 (fig.), 145, 147, 148 (fig.), 154, 160
Aryans, 39, 122, 203, 206, 207; Semites and, 123, 149
'āshūrā, 121, 127, 137, 146, 147
assimilation, 4, 11, 27–28, 148, 172, 179, 184, 185, 208, 212

authenticity, 221, 243n89, 294n48
authoritarianism, 11, 43, 164, 222
automatism, 51, 109, 231

bābā zārs, 94, 139, 208
badawa, 164
bahā-'i khurmā, 89, 91, 92
Bahār, Mihrdād, 41, 221, 222
Bakhshū, 121, 128, 130, 137, 266n4; blackness of, 138; elegy of, 153
Bandar Abbas, 101, 139, 210
Bandar Lingih, 73, 77, 80, 84, 85, 102, 264n110; destruction of, 98, 117
Bandar Qishm, 106
Baraka, Amiri, 125, 268n17
Barrett, Lindon, 200, 216
Bashu, 162–63, 164, 165–66, 166 (fig.), 167, 167 (fig.), 173 (fig.), 176, 177–78, 186–87, 188, 190, 193, 194, 196, 202, 203, 205, 208; ancestry of, 191; Arabness of, 204; blackness of, 27, 163, 172, 195; as cinematic child, 168–75; literacy and, 195, 207; mother of, 187, 189 (fig.), 191 (fig.); multiculturalism and, 184; *zār* and, 169
Bashu, the Little Stranger (Beyzai), 27, 76, 161, 162–68, 166 (fig.), 170, 172–73, 173 (fig.), 174 (fig.), 177 (fig.), 189 (fig.), 194, 196, 198, 200, 203; background of, 164; black maternal and, 188, 192, 208; blackness in, 207; conclusion of, 190; counternarrative of, 201–2; maternal figures and, 176; story of, 162–68
Basra, 51, 66, 231
Bazin, André, 188, 237n31, 237n38, 258n23, 269n28
Beyzai, Bahram, 27, 56, 67, 103, 161–62, 163, 164, 167, 168, 169, 170, 172, 175, 176, 187, 188, 189,

198, 200, 201–2, 203, 204, 210; improvisatory theater and, 248n25; *zār* and, 166, 192–93
Bilad-al Sudan, 141
Biruni, Abu Rayhan al-, 214
Black Arts movement, 219
Black Consciousness, 217, 220
blackface, 52, 60; female, 65–72, 66 (fig.); *filmfārsī* and, 65; *siyāh bāzī* and, 65, 69
blackface minstrelsy, 21, 25, 32, 36, 38, 39, 40, 43, 44, 47, 50, 51, 62, 99, 221, 222, 223; origins of, 70; political iterations of, 41; racist, 68
Black feminism, 178
Black Iranians, 23, 135, 144, 210–11, 212, 226, 227, 291n9, 292n9; Black Americans and, 219; vignettes of, 218. *See also* Afro-Iranians
Black liberation, 218
Black Lives Matter, 212, 223, 224
Black Moroccans, 226
blackness, 3, 27–28, 32, 44, 49, 51, 61, 64, 67, 70, 77, 84, 101, 109–17, 121, 123, 138, 139, 142, 144, 159, 165, 172, 196, 204, 207, 208, 215, 218, 219–22, 224; decontextualization of, 213; *desêtre* and, 220; globalized, 23, 122; nonracial, 93, 185; racial, 1–2, 8, 21–25, 33, 40, 92, 93, 184, 185, 213, 214, 220–21, 225, 286n97. *See also siyāh*
black play. *See siyāh bāzī*
black studies, 1, 20, 21, 227, 283n38
Black Tunisians, 226
bori, 17, 83, 259n37
Brand, Dionne, 72
bur, 19, 131 (fig.), 132
Būshihr, 2, 23, 27, 128, 134, 136, 140, 143, 154, 156, 157

Index

« 347 »

Caribbean, 155, 157, 159, 160, 219

castration, 54, 55, 60, 61, 99, 168, 252n85, 253n91, 254n105

censorship, 36, 65, 111, 176

Center for the Intellectual Development of Children and Young Adolescents, 169–70

chest striking (*sīnah-zanī*), 120, 121, 128, 129–30, 132, 159, 272n66. See also *arba'īn*

childhood, 77, 168, 171, 172, 175, 180, 183–84, 202, 209, 284n66

cinema, 11, 12, 16, 21, 27, 79, 171, 202; alternative, 95; art, 7, 105; commercial, 9, 34; oil, 13

civilization, 91, 123, 134, 158, 205, 243n89, 267n11; barbarism and, 149, 153; East African, 142; Islamic, 143, 173; Persian, 146, 163–64

Collective for Black Iranians, 28, 209, 210, 211 (fig.), 212, 213, 214, 215, 218, 220, 221, 224, 227, 228, 228 (fig.), 229–30, 279n157, 291n9, 295n68; art of, 29, 216, 217, 231

commedia dell'arte, 39, 40, 42, 43, 70, 252n79, 253n94

conjunction, 6, 85, 88, 122; cinematic form and, 7–15; connection and, 237n37

consciousness, 8, 10, 17, 20, 21, 38, 41, 74, 102, 103, 134, 146, 166, 171, 194; Black, 217, 220; loss of, 15, 26, 79, 115; popular, 136, 254n102

consumerism, 14, 51, 95, 100, 110–11, 113

cosmopolitanism, 92, 156, 158

courtyard theater (*rūḥawẓī*), 43

Cow (*Gav*, Sā'idī), 95, 259n33

creolization, 127, 145–50, 157, 158

culture, 51, 86, 97, 125, 145, 155, 158, 171, 185, 205, 208, 249n48;

aesthetic, 123, 127, 156, 157; Būshihrī mourning, 127–28; Caribbean, 160; coastal, 168; creolization of, 157; national, 96, 122; Persian, 209, 222; Swahili, 143; term, 111–12

Curse, The (*Nifrīn,* Taqvā'i), 99, 101, 101 (fig.), 102

cymbals (*sinj*), 126, 159

damām (drums), 120, 121, 126, 127, 128, 130, 131, 150

dancing belly, 34 (fig.), 35, 61

Danishvar, Simin, 146

D'Arcy, William Knox, 135

Darvish, Baba, 106

Dasein, 235n20

Dash Akol (Kimiyā'ī), 259n33

daw ragih, 212–13

Dear Uncle Napoleon (Taqvā'i), 107

decontextualization, 2, 6, 24, 39, 184, 225, 231, 294n40

Deleuze, Gilles, 170, 236n25

dhows, 2, 80, 102, 106, 132, 140, 144 (fig.), 199

diaspora, 28, 205; African, 120, 234n10; black, 23, 185; European, 223

Dingomaro, 26, 83

dirge singing (*nūhah-khūnī*), 121, 128, 129, 130, 136, 154, 157. *See also* music

dīwān, 16, 193

documentary films, 13, 26, 74–77, 93

Du Bois, W. E. B., 14, 90, 91, 113, 174, 219, 220, 294n41

duhul, 83, 84, 87, 106, 109, 159, 260n39

East Africa, 1, 140, 143, 155, 226; Persian influence in, 17

Elamites, 22, 206, 207

« 348 »   Index

enslavement, 20, 51, 54, 55, 61, 141, 158, 172–73, 179; African, 14, 69, 70, 89–94, 126, 173, 220; pearling and, 132, 136; racial blackness and, 1; taxonomies of, 178

epistemology, 15, 82, 88, 140, 147, 213

ethnicity, 40, 162, 204, 205; blackness and, 227; culture and, 163

ethnography, 81, 107, 108, 113, 123, 145, 151; salvage, 76–77

ethnomusicology, 125, 126

eunuchs, 51, 52, 60, 69, 248n31; demand for, 54; genealogical isolation of, 253n92; sexuality/slavery and, 55

facticity, 24, 108, 109, 235n20; incapacity for, 16; turmoil of, 83

facts: cinema and, 8; destitution of, 3–6

Fajr film festival, 103, 154

Fanon, Frantz, 19, 60, 219, 262n72

Farukhzād, Furūgh, 75, 257n5

Fear and Trembling (*Tars va Larz*, Sāʾidī), 103, 104, 114

fīlmfārsī, 7, 8, 9, 10, 11, 12, 25, 33, 34, 35, 36, 37, 42, 43, 52, 55, 56, 57, 61, 64, 66, 67, 69, 71, 74, 79, 80, 95, 97, 99, 100, 102, 105, 110–11, 113, 115, 150, 169, 202; dance segments and, 45, 46; dream-weaving by, 111; female body and, 47, 49; *siyāh bāzī* and, 26, 45, 47, 49–50, 54, 65. *See also* melodrama

filmmaking, 7, 58, 94, 107, 112; documentary, 13, 26, 80, 81; ethnographic, 26, 75, 76, 79, 169

film noir, 99, 100

film studies, 170, 210

film theory, 8, 62, 79, 128, 170

Fīrūz, Hājī, 40, 44, 67, 221, 222, 223, 224, 248n31

folklore, Persian, 111

Forced Vacation (*Murakhaṣī-ʾi Ijbārī*, Karīmī), 33–34, 65, 66, 66 (fig.); blackface and, 67, 68, 69

Freud, Sigmund: Irma and, 246n2, 256n133

Frobenius, Leo, 17

Gāhnāmah hunar va adabīyāt-i jūnūb, 112

Galland, Antoine, 48

gender, 23, 97; difference, 47, 48, 54, 176, 254n110

genocide, 20, 224, 242n80

Ghafārī, Farukh, 31, 33, 34, 35, 36, 43, 51, 53, 57, 58, 59, 60, 61, 101, 136, 254n98, 254n102

Ghaysar (Kimiyāʾī), 100

Ghazzālī, al-, 17, 18

Gīlakī, 177, 178, 203, 204

Gīlān, 163, 184, 190, 203

Glissant, Eduoard, 218

globalization, 9, 157, 227

Global South, 11, 27, 75, 169

glossolalia, 193, 194

Grass (film), 257n9

Gulistān, Ebrāhīm, 35, 136, 256n127, 275n112

Gulistān Film Workshop, 135–36

gwati, 94

Hābashī, 24, 142

haft sīn, 209, 218

Hanifeh, Mama, 106

Haratin, 23, 245n105, 290n171

Harlequin, 43, 51, 249n36, 252n79

Heidegger, Martin, 235n20

Hidāyat, Sādiq, 111, 112, 259n33

historiography, 5, 121, 130, 133, 158, 182, 230, 231; Indian Ocean, 8–9; Iranian, 267n9; model of, 17; nationalist, 205, 267n9, 269n38; philology and, 290n168

Hollywood, 68, 69

horns (*būq*), 126, 137

Hosay, 127, 153, 156, 158, 159, 160;
Caribbean, 154–55; preservation
of, 279n155
Hurmuz, 1, 99, 134, 210, 241n67,
266n7
Husayn ibn Ali, 76, 119, 120, 130,
134, 135, 137, 146, 147, 148, 148
(fig.), 150, 153, 159, 266n2,
266n4, 268n24, 276n127
hybridity, 156, 157, 212, 227, 267n14;
syncretism and, 3, 27, 127, 144,
194; as tautology, 139–45

Ibn Khaldūn, 164, 276n126
Indian Ocean, 1, 2, 13, 22, 121,
125–26, 132, 133, 140, 180,
269–70n38
Indo-European, 38, 124, 204, 205,
206, 207, 223
invisibility, 185; hypervisibility and,
188
Iranian Revolution (1979), 13, 21,
28, 76, 95, 164, 169, 170, 202,
203, 223
Iran–Iraq War, 153, 164, 170, 171,
190, 196, 200, 201, 202, 204
Islam, 91, 149, 158; African, 134,
271n50; civilizational image of,
150; denigration of, 148; essence
of, 134; revalorization of, 223;
spread of, 151
Islamic Republic of Iran, 149, 196,
202, 278n147, 289n155
Istakhri, Ibrahim ibn Muhammad
al-, 132, 240n55

Jamālzādih, Muhammad Alī, 111,
112
James, C. L. R., 174
javānmard, 56, 57
jazz, 46, 250n51, 268n17

Karbala, 75, 119, 130, 137, 149–50,
159, 266n4, 276n127; martyrdom

at, 120; origin of, 147; popularization of, 149
Kāvūsī, Amīr Hūshang, 9, 58,
238n41; *filmfārsī* and, 36,
247n12
Khāchikiyān, Sāmū'il, 33, 61, 64,
68, 263n102
khaymah bāzī (puppet play), 50–51
Khūzistān, 14, 83, 99, 136, 161, 162,
173, 190, 197, 206
Kiarostami, Abbas, 12, 169, 170, 171,
282n30
Kīmīyā'ī, Mas'ūd, 100, 259n33
Kīmīyāvi, Parvīz, 82, 135, 275n112
kinship, 55, 172, 178, 188, 189–90,
207, 269n31
Kish, 1, 140, 241n67
Kiswahili, 141

latam, 120, 129, 130, 131
literacy, 115, 162, 176, 195, 196, 200,
202, 207, 289n155
Lor Girl, The (Dukhtar-i Lur,
Īrānī), 45
lūtīgarī, 56, 57

maddah, 138, 150, 279n148
Mahmūd, Ahmad, 85–86
māmā zār, 168, 193, 208
marsiyahs, 159, 280n168
masculinity, 56, 190, 195, 283n34;
black, 60; warrior, 57
Masūdi, al-, 248n31
maternal, 46, 169, 179; black, 175,
176, 186–92, 194, 208
Maybe Some Other Time (Shāyad
Vaghtī Dīgar, Taslimi), 188–89
melodrama, 7, 52, 95, 111, 249n40,
253n94; cultural myth and, 56;
Egyptian, 35, 246n11. See also
filmfārsī
Middle Passage, 1, 4, 54, 168, 175
Midnight Terror, The (Faryād-i
Nīm-i Shab, Khāchikiyān), 33,

61, 64 (fig.), 65, 68; narrative of, 63–64

Mihrjūyi, Dāryūsh, 95, 259n33

Ministry of Culture and Arts, 76, 102, 257n10

misogyny, 49, 181, 251n67

Modarressi, Taghi, 16, 83, 84, 241n67

modernism, 80, 104, 112, 123, 146, 229, 257n13; cinematic, 11, 26, 103; New Wave and, 111; Persian, 12, 111, 117; slavery and, 14, 20, 90

modernity, 2, 6, 9, 10, 11, 12, 13, 19, 21–22, 24, 74, 75, 76, 77, 78, 83, 86, 91–92, 95, 98–99, 100, 102, 103, 105, 107, 111, 112, 113, 116, 122, 133, 149, 156, 164, 171, 172, 200, 231; anticolonial critique of, 115; slavery and, 20

Mosaddeq, Prime Minister, 11, 135

mourning, 27, 40, 83, 105, 120, 127–28, 146, 158, 222; feminine, 121, 130; public, 268n24

Muhammad, 60, 119, 130, 182; biographies of, 181

Muharram, 27, 119, 120, 129–30, 134, 135, 147, 148, 153, 154–55, 156, 158; blackness in, 160; political agency and, 150; religious reform of, 150; rituals of, 21, 121, 127, 128, 146, 149, 154; Shi'i, 159

Mūj-i naw, 74, 94

multiculturalism, 157, 184, 226, 227

music, 125, 127, 215, 272n67; Black, 126, 216, 218, 268n17; *jūnūbī*, 128; Persian, 37, 268n19. *See also* dirge singing

Nādirī, Amīr, 162, 197, 198, 199, 200, 201, 202, 259n33, 288n142

Naficy, Hamid, 76, 177, 195, 263n102, 272n72, 280n3

naqqālī, 11, 133, 134

National Iranian Oil Consortium, 136

National Iranian Radio and Television, 76, 113, 169, 257n10, 264n110

nationalism, 122, 155, 163, 169, 206, 226, 257n11; Arab, 278n141; cultural, 27, 164, 198; Iranian, 22, 38–39, 76, 200, 210, 280n165; Pahlavi, 111, 223, 247n19, 267n9; Persian, 123, 149, 158, 202, 207; racial, 2, 247n19

neorealism, 74, 237n30, 237n31, 239n47, 258n23

New Wave, 7, 9, 10, 12, 26, 35, 36, 74, 75, 79, 80, 81, 94–105, 107, 111, 113, 115; blackness and, 115; documentary films and, 13; *fīlmfārsī* and, 21; Iranian, 97, 100, 109, 116; realism, 109, 128, 136; *zār* and, 117

Night of the Hunchback (Ghāfarī), 31, 32, 33, 36, 37, 44, 46, 48, 50–51, 59, 61, 65, 66, 68, 70; *siyāh bāzī* scene from, 34 (fig.), 35, 43, 47, 56, 69

North Africa, 1, 213, 225; activism in, 226; blackness in, 184

Nowruz, 209–10, 215, 216, 218, 221, 222; repressions of, 223; Zoroastrian, 214

oil, 13, 15, 89, 136, 239n47, 239n49, 240n52

One Thousand and One Nights, The (The Arabian Nights) (*Hizār va Yak Shab*), 31, 33, 36, 37, 48–49, 50, 52, 63, 64, 70, 247n14; Ghafarī and, 35, 48; mise en abyme of, 71; translations of, 251n65

Orientalism, 21, 55, 86, 224

Ottoman Empire, 54, 55, 228, 229

Pahlavi, 38, 45, 95, 203, 223; domestic modernization and, 257n3; language, 203; racial nationalism and, 111, 223, 247n19, 267n9. *See also* Reza Shah Pahlavi, Muhammad

Pan-Africanism, 217, 218

partus sequitur ventrem (1662), rejection of, 179–80

Pasolini, Pier Paulo: montage and, 136–37

patriarchy, 49, 97, 178

Patterson, Orlando, 178, 179

pearling, 132–39; enslavement and, 132, 136

People of the Wind (*Ahl-i Havā*, Sā'idī), 82, 83, 99, 114, 117

Persian Gulf, 1, 13, 66, 81, 94, 106, 113, 119, 121, 137, 139, 142, 143; African presence in, 89, 92; export economies of, 14, 89–90; Indian Ocean and, 132; pearling industry and, 133, 134, 136; slave trade in, 140, 235n16

Persian language, 92, 203, 204, 219; alphabet, 198, 199, 200

Persian New Year, 40, 67, 120, 209–10, 214, 221

philology, 22, 122, 205, 290n168

pīshpardah, 43, 67

platform capitalism, 212, 231; digital politics and, 217

poetry, 1, 11, 50, 91, 100, 108, 112, 150, 164, 276n131, 277n131

politics, 10, 12, 21, 24, 75, 96, 97, 114, 149, 183, 211, 217, 239n48, 277n132; identity, 213, 214, 292n9

postcolonialism, 20, 155, 243n89

race, 22, 139, 162, 176, 204, 206, 211, 214, 223; blackness and, 184; concept of, 21, 290n166; ideology of, 185; Indo-Iranian, 111; language and, 205; literacy/humanity and, 196; modernity and, 24; religion and, 268n16, 289n166

racialization, 22, 23–24, 116–17, 123, 139, 204, 220, 281n5

raqāṣ, 44, 47, 66, 99

Rashid, Harun al-, 37, 181

rawzah, 154

Rayshahr, 158

Razī, Hāshim, 248n31

realism, 9, 104, 105, 109–17, 130, 150, 192, 239n47; modernist, 85, 99; New Wave, 109, 136; poetic, 75, 136

Red Sea, 1, 90, 168

religion, 277n132; art and, 269n37; race and, 289n166; tradition and, 267n10

repetition, 32, 109, 115, 135, 216, 221, 225

Reza Shah Pahlavi, Muhammad, 10–11, 37, 44, 49, 76, 135, 202, 247n19, 249n38, 288n138, 289n155. *See also* Pahlavi

rhythm, 125, 129, 130, 131, 132, 135, 137, 159, 167, 196

Rig Vedas, 206

rituals, 21, 78, 120, 122, 127, 128, 146, 247n19; healing, 15–19; mourning, 27; spirit, 19, 210

Rivalry in the City (*Riqābat dar Shahr*, Ghafārī), 52 (fig.), 56–57, 58 (fig.), 59, 60 (fig.), 61, 64, 65, 66, 68, 101; *siyāh bāzī* scene from, 33, 46 (fig.), 51, 55, 69

rotana, 193

Rouch, Jean, 82

rūḥawzī, 40, 43

Runner, The (*Nādirī*), 162, 164, 196–208, 197 (fig.), 201 (fig.); literacy/humanity/race and, 196

Rūz-i tabīyat (Nature Day), 222

« 352 »   Index

Sacred Defense, 170, 201
Sadiq the Kurd (Sadiq Kurdih, Taqvāʾi), 99, 102
Safavid period, 40, 134, 145, 248n31
safhat, 133, 270n48
Said, Edward, 21, 265n131, 276n119
Sāʾidī, Ghulām Husayn, 77, 82, 83, 95, 96–97, 98, 99, 102, 103, 104, 106, 112, 114, 115, 117, 259n33, 265n132
Samad film series, 37
Sasanians, 40, 139, 152, 180, 273n79
Sayād, Parvīz, 37
Semites, 122, 153, 280n165; Aryans and, 123, 149
sexuality, 23, 32, 49, 97, 233n3; female, 251n67; slavery and, 55
Shāhnāmah (Book of Kings, Firdawsī), 56, 57, 146, 147, 271n55
Shāmlū, Ahmad, 73, 77, 80, 81, 84, 86, 91–92, 93, 107, 115, 117, 135; blackness and, 92; poetry of, 112; zār and, 88
Shariʿati, Ali, 21
Sharīfīyān, Muḥsin, 158, 266n7
Sheriff, Abdul, 185
Shiʿism, 57, 119, 120, 128, 130, 145, 147–48, 149, 154, 155, 156, 164, 159, 180, 222, 223; mourning ritual of, 27; nation-state and, 275n111; politicized, 123, 124
Shirazi, 231; self-identification, 226; Swahili kinship with, 142; thesis of, 143
shirk (sin of idolatry), 147, 222
shuʿūbiyah, 152, 278n141
Siddis, 186, 281n12
sinj ū damām, 120, 121, 127–28, 129, 131, 150
Sitārih Sīnamā, 98
siyāh (black), 25, 34, 36, 38, 44, 50, 51, 52, 53 (fig.), 54, 59, 62,

70, 91, 92–93; filmfārsī and, 47, 55; mythologization of, 42; slave genealogy of, 26. See also blackness
siyāh bāzī (black play), 3, 25, 32, 33, 35–44, 47, 51, 55, 56, 58, 60, 61, 62, 64, 65, 66, 68, 70, 71, 72, 210, 222, 223; comedy of, 69; filmfārsī and, 26, 45, 49–50, 54
Siyāvashūn (Danishvar), 146, 222
slave trade, 14, 91, 94, 140, 185, 220; ivory and, 90; qualitative data and, 4; trans-oceanic, 235n14. See also slavery; transatlantic slavery; trans-Saharan slavery
slavery, 2, 3–4, 24, 27, 28, 32, 40, 42, 48, 74, 83, 88, 89–94, 107, 113, 138, 160, 168, 173, 178, 180, 183–84, 185, 225–32; abolition of, 183, 224, 226; African, 220, 224; domestic, 3, 14, 54; global economy and, 89; historiography of, 228, 229–30; modernism and, 14, 20, 90, 91, 136; oil and, 13, 136; racial, 22, 244n105. See also slave trade; transatlantic slavery; trans-Saharan slavery
social mobility, 181, 185; economic rhetoric of, 182
South Asia, 1, 154, 155, 186
South of the City (Ghafārī), 36, 51, 56, 57, 59
Southwest Asia, 2, 3, 13, 33, 47, 90, 159, 168, 172, 184, 185, 213, 225, 226
sovereignty, 26, 217, 218, 275n116
Spillers, Hortense J., 54, 168, 178
spirit healing, 19, 78, 81, 82, 103, 192–93, 229
spiritualism, 17, 102, 111, 194
stambeli, 16, 153, 231, 260n50
sūdanī, 141, 142

Index « 353 »

sugar cultivation, 14, 90, 173, 174, 240n55
Sumerians, 40, 222
Swahili, 18, 142, 143, 200
symbolism, 25–26, 32, 46, 81, 111, 151
syncretism, 122, 123, 124–25, 129, 130, 134, 138, 139, 146, 149, 156, 157, 158, 160, 193; hybridity and, 3, 27, 127, 144, 194; musical, 125; religious, 148

tadjahs, 154, 160
Tāhirīdūst, Ghulām Husayn, 82
takht-i hawẓī, 40, 67
taqlīd, 69, 71, 248n25
Taqvā'i, Nasir, 12, 73, 74, 77, 80, 86, 87, 94, 96, 97, 98, 103, 104, 106, 107, 110, 116, 124, 128, 130, 131, 134–35, 138, 144, 148, 154, 156; documentary films of, 27, 112, 113, 114, 119, 121, 264n110; work of, 82, 83, 88, 95, 99, 101, 102, 109, 121, 122, 136, 137, 146; *zār* and, 79, 81, 113
Tarabnāmah (Beyzai), 67
t'āruf, 92
Taslimi, Susan, 163, 177, 178, 188–89; *Bashu* and, 284n52; close up of, 177 (fig.)
Ta'zīyah theaters, 37, 120, 146, 187, 266n2; ban on, 247n9; construction of, 154
technology, 6, 10, 43, 116, 126; indigenous, 145
Tehran, 32, 45, 46, 56, 57, 59, 67, 112, 221, 227
television, 25, 101, 102, 107, 113, 280n1; Iranian economy and, 253n96
Telfilm, 264n110
temporality, 11, 37, 55, 70, 80, 91, 163
theater halls (*tamāshawkhānah*), 43
Tranquility in the Presence of

Others (*Aramish dar Huzur-i Digaran,* Taqvā'i), 12, 81, 95, 96 (fig.), 97, 98–99, 100, 102, 103, 104, 105, 107, 108, 110 (fig.), 264n110
transatlantic slavery, 1, 3, 92, 174, 180, 181; barbarities of, 175, 178; consumerism and, 91; European capitalism and, 89; Indian Ocean slavery and, 4, 14–15, 19–20, 90, 150. *See also* slavery; trans-Saharan slavery
transnationalism, 218, 239n47
transracial, 3, 190, 210, 234n6
trans-Saharan slavery, 14, 15, 78, 230. *See also* slavery; transatlantic slavery
Trinidad, 155, 156, 158, 279n155
tunbak, 150

uganga, 194
ulamas, 148, 149, 150, 154
Umayyads, 152, 220

vatan (homeland), 100, 165, 169, 202, 281n17

Wahhabism, 134
wārgliyya, 23
Westoxification (*Gharbzadegi,* al-i Ahmad), 21, 265n131
whiteness, 25, 39, 122, 124, 224
White Revolution, 11
Wind of Jin (*Bād-i Jin,* Taqvā'i), 73, 74, 77, 82, 85, 86, 87 (fig.), 91, 93–94, 95, 97, 98, 99, 102, 104, 107, 108, 116–17, 116 (fig.), 119, 132; ethnographic subjects of, 105; facticity in, 115–16; *zār* ceremony and, 79, 80–81, 84, 101, 103, 106, 135
World and Africa, The (Du Bois), 14, 90

« 354 » Index

Wretched of the Earth, The
   (Fanon), 19
Wynter, Sylvia, 24, 152, 219, 227,
   293n40

Zang, 24, 139–45, 153, 204
zanni (servant characters), 42, 51,
   252n79
Zanzibar, 22, 139–45, 194; slaves
   from, 206
zār, 3, 80–81, 83, 84, 88, 93, 94,
99, 101, 103, 105, 106, 107, 108,
109, 114, 115, 135, 159, 161, 166,
168–69, 192–96; ethnographic
accounts of, 18, 113, 193; films
about, 15–16; healing ritual of,
15–19; linguistic dispossession
and, 18; long take and, 78–89;
slavery and, 15, 16, 18, 20, 26, 82,
116; spirit, 73, 79
Zarathustra, 214
Zoroaster, 214–15

Parisa Vaziri is assistant professor of comparative literature and Near Eastern studies at Cornell University.

Printed in the USA
CPSIA information can be obtained
at www.ICGtesting.com
LVHW050818211223
766345LV00002B/2

9 781517 914745